The Wines and Vineyards of Portugal

Richard Mayson

MITCHELL BEAZLEY

To Katrina

The Wines and Vineyards of Portugal
by Richard Mayson

Published in Great Britain in 2003 by Mitchell Beazley, an
imprint of Octopus Publishing Group Limited, 2–4 Heron Quays, London E14 4JP.

A CIP catalogue record for this book is available from the British Library.

ISBN: 1 84000 733 8

The author and publishers will be grateful for any information
which will assist them in keeping future editions up-to-date.
Although all reasonable care has been taken in the preparation
of this book, neither the publishers nor the author can accept any
liability for any consequences arising from the use thereof, or the
information contained therein.

Phototypeset in Berkeley Book by Intype London Ltd

Printed and bound in the UK

Contents

Acknowledgements vii

List of Illustrations and Maps ix

Preface xi

1 The Wines of Portugal in History 1

2 Vines, Vineyards and Vintages 50
  i Red grape varieties 60
  ii White grape varieties 89
  iii Vintages 111

3 Atlantic Wines 121
  i Vinho Verde 125
  ii Minho 144
  iii Lafões 145
  iv Bairrada 146
  v Buçaco 156
  vi Beiras 159
  vii Estremadura 160
  viii Bucelas 172
  ix Colares 175
  x Carcavelos and "Lisbon" 180

4 Mountain Wines 183
  i Port 186
  ii Moscatel de Favaios 200
  iii Douro 201
  iv Trás-os-Montes 221

v Tavora/Varosa 224
vi Dão 224
vii Beira Interior 235
viii Beiras 237

5 Wines of the Plains 238
  i Ribatejo 242
  ii The Setúbal Peninsula 253
  iii Alentejo 263
  iv Algarve 281

6 Wines of the Islands 285
  i Madeira and Porto Santo 285
  ii The Azores 296

7 The Rosé Wines of Portugal 298

8 The Sparkling Wines of Portugal 305

9 Cork 312

Postscript 317

Glossary of Portuguese terms 320

Glossary of technical terms 324

Appendix I: List of officially approved grape varieties and their synonyms 325

Appendix II: Acronyms 335

Bibliography 337

Index 340

Acknowledgements

So many individuals and organizations have helped me over the twenty-year period during which I have been associated with Portuguese wines that it is impossible to list them all here. I would, however, like to acknowledge the cooperation and friendship of a number of people without whom this book would never have taken shape. At the outset I particularly want to acknowledge the support of the late Jorge Maria Cabral Ferreira who, back in 1980, soon after I had left school, first encouraged me to take an interest in wine. Since then the Bergqvist family of Quinta de la Rosa, Adrian Bridge and David Guimaraens of Taylor and Fonseca, Dirk Niepoort, Jim Reader of Cockburn, Alistair and Gillyane Robertson of Taylor and Fonseca, Jorge Rosas of Ramos Pinto, Jorge and "Tita" Roquette of Quinta do Crasto, and Paul and Jane Symington have all provided wonderful hospitality and sound guidance in the Douro. My sincere thanks are due to all of them. Elsewhere in Portugal I would like to thank David Baverstock and Luís Duarte of Herdade do Esporão, the Blandy family in Madeira, John Cossart of Henriques & Henriques, Alberto and Luís Costa of Caves São João, Luís Pato and António and Domingos Soares Franco of José Maria da Fonseca for the time and information that they have given me over many years. In the preparation of this book I make specific mention of the help given by Eng João Carvalho Ghira of the *Comissão Interprofessional dos Vinhos da Estremadura* (CIVE), Eng Pedro Castro Rego and Carlos Santos of the *Comissão Vitivinicola Regional Ribatejana* (CVRR) and Dr Manuel Pinheiro of the *Comissão de Viticultura da Região dos Vinhos Verdes* (CVRR). They are excellent ambassadors for their respective regions.

In the United Kingdom I am grateful to ICEP, the Portuguese Trade and Tourism Office in London, for its support over many years, and to

Julian Jeffs who, while patiently editing my work, always comes up with some fascinating and amusing anecdotes. I am indebted to him. Leo Duff, whose work I have admired and collected over a number of years, has provided some witty and evocative illustrations of local peculiarities that could never be captured in the same way on film. Finally, I would like to thank my parents, my wife Katrina, family and friends for being on hand as this book was being researched and written. In a world where techniques, fashions and opinions change, no book is ever entirely complete. On the other hand this is my fifth book, and any factual inaccuracies are, as always, my own responsibility.

Richard Mayson, London, 2003

List of Illustrations and Maps

Guimarães: the birthplace of modern Portugal 2
A traditional still in the Ribatejo 34
The Junta Nacional do Vinho, Torres Vedras 39
Vineyard anarchy: Vinho Verde 52
Wine vessels 89
The *garrafeira* (wine cellar) at Buçaco 111
Vinho Verde: *espigueros* (granaries) and cabbages 126
Casa de Sezim 141
Mosaic façade on the Convent of Buçaco 157
Estremadura: *balões* or "mamas" for bulk wine storage 166
Colares: pines, vines and sand 177
Lazy "z" bends in the mountains of northern Portugal 185
Terraces at Quinta do Bomfim overlooking the Douro 201
Trásmontano house 221
The granite cathedral of Viseu 226
Storks' nests at Quinta Fonte Bela near Cartaxo 246
The plains of the Alentejo 264
Madeira: *poios* (terraces) overlooking the Atlantic 287
Madeira: two baskets of grapes 290
The Palace of Mateus near Vila Real 299
Denuded cork trees in southern Portugal 313

DOC / IPR 56
Regional wines 58
Northern Portugal 122
Southern Portugal 239
Madeira 284

Preface

This book is not just about wine; it is about Portugal. It stems from my visits to the country as a child in the early 1970s, long before I was able to appreciate a glass of wine. I recall in those days being overcome by the heady aromas which seemed to emanate from every doorway. Charcoal-grilled fish, the pungent, almost rancid smell of *bacalhau* (dried salt cod), a peculiarly waxy floor polish, baking bread, fresh coriander, piri-piri, spicy *chouriço* sausage and the occasional whiff of something that I eventually recognized as fermenting grape must. It was this that tied me to Portugal.

Much has changed over the past thirty years. In the early 1970s Portugal was an introverted nation still clinging onto an empire in Africa. A turbulent revolution in 1974–5 suddenly brought Portugal back into the real world, and since the late 1980s the transformation has been hastened by membership of the European Union. It was during this period of transition that I began my first job, in a bar and restaurant near Lagos in south-west Portugal. The establishment was called Godots because, like the character in Samuel Beckett's play who never arrived, the owners thought it would never be completed. By now aged eighteen and fresh from school in England, I was put in charge of the restaurant wine list. It involved restocking a limited range of exclusively Portuguese wines with then unfamiliar names like Topázio, BSE, Lancers, Terras Altas and Frei João. This sent me in search of books on Portuguese wine, but at the historic Livraria Bertrand in Lisbon's fashionable Chiado I found that at the time there was remarkably little in print. Eventually I bought two books: *Vinhos do Nosso País*, published by the rather menacingly-named Junta Nacional do Vinho, and Wyndham Fletcher's delightful book on *Port*. I read them on the beach during my afternoons off.

Wine must have left an indelible mark for, travelling around Portugal during the winter of 1979–80, I began visiting vineyards. I was particularly taken by the Douro – those terraces which look like hanging gardens – and back in England, reading geography at university, I made a study of the microclimate within Port vineyards. A sojourn at Ferreira's Quinta do Seixo during the summer of 1982 finally sealed my destiny, and on leaving university a year later, I joined the wine trade and worked for the Wine Society in England. I shall always be grateful to them for my thorough education in wine, and at the end of five years tasting and drinking, I felt sufficiently confident to separate good wine from bad, no matter where it came from. Although I am now fortunate enough to visit, taste in and write about wine regions all over the world, Portugal has engraved itself on my soul. This small, diverse, receptive nation gets under the skin. It has been favoured by the English as a habitat almost since it took shape as a country, and despite my relatively shallow roots I am proud to call Portugal my second home.

It is against this background that *The Wines and Vineyards of Portugal* has been written. The development of the wine trade is inescapably intertwined with the history of the nation, and the story of Port, Madeira and Portugal's wines is told in Chapter 1. The book goes on to explore Portugal's vineyards and the grape varieties, many of them unique, that go some way to explaining the character and flavour of Portuguese wines. As the vines untangle themselves from the haphazard cultivation practised in the past, there is an ever greater understanding of Portuguese grapes. Over 120 different varieties are profiled, many for the first time. Grapes with suggestive and sometimes sensuous names like lady's finger, cockerel's heart, tail-of-the-cat, dog strangler, fly droppings and love-don't-leave-me all have a place in Portugal's vineyard lexicon.

In an effort to explain and simplify the profusion of different wine regions, the main body of the book divides Portugal into four broad geographical zones. Wines from the Atlantic littoral, the mountains of the interior, the southern plains and the offshore islands have common roots often extending beyond climate and geology. Although there is no Portuguese translation of the word, it is encouraging to find growers and winemakers talking in terms of *terroir*, that holistic term which encompasses the site-specific environment in which different wines are produced. Portugal's rosé and sparkling wines are covered in separate sections towards the end of the book, followed by a chapter on cork, a Portuguese product which is intimately linked to wine. The book concludes with a short postscript which speculates on the future of Port, Madeira and Portuguese wines.

The Wines and Vineyards of Portugal is intended for interested consumers, tourists and wine trade students alike. Individual sections may therefore be used for reference, but together they form part of a complete narrative which is intended to paint a picture of Portugal's wines and vineyards at the start of the twenty-first century. In my endeavour to make this book a "good read" I have purposely kept technical information to a minimum. Where a Portuguese expression or technical term requires further explanation, it may be found in the glossary at the end of the book. Above all, I hope that my enthusiasm for Portugal is contagious and that this book will encourage wine drinkers present and future to explore the wines and vineyards of Portugal.

Richard Mayson, London, 2003

1

The Wines of Portugal in History

THE BIRTH OF A NATION

Aqui Nasceu Portugal: three words written in white on a granite wall in the centre of Guimarães mark the birthplace of modern Portugal. It was here in the heart of the modern-day *Vinho Verde* region that Afonso Henriques became the first king of Portugal in 1139. The country over which Afonso I reigned initially was but a small shard of Iberia stretching from the River Minho in the north to the River Mondego 160 kilometres (99 miles) further south. The territory below the Mondego and beyond the Tagus was in the thrall of the Moors, by then annexed to the declining empire of the Almoravids. In 1147 Afonso Henriques was able to capture the cities of Santarém and Lisbon from the Moors and took Portugal's frontiers south of the Tagus. The new kingdom received papal recognition in 1179 and seventy years later, under Afonso III, the Portuguese finally captured Faro in the Algarve. Thus Portugal took shape: a long, rectangular slice of Iberia approximately 600 kilometres (373 miles) long and 200 kilometres (124 miles) wide, dissected by three great rivers, the Douro, Mondego and Tagus (Tejo) (see maps on pages 122 and 239). Bounded by the Atlantic on two sides and the frequently hostile kingdoms of Spain on the other, Portugal's frontiers have survived almost intact for over seven centuries, making them the oldest on the continent of Europe.

THE ROOTS OF WINE

Records of human habitation on the Atlantic seaboard of the Iberian peninsula date back to the Paleolithic period, toward the end of the last glaciation. The sheet of ice that covered Great Britain and northern

Europe did not reach Portugal, and the discovery in 1992 of a series of remarkable engravings in the schist of the Coa valley confirms that the north of Portugal was inhabited by nomadic hunting people at least 26,000 years ago. As the climate became warmer, the population moved toward a more maritime existence, and during the Mesolithic period the people of western Iberia lived around the estuaries of the great rivers that flow into the Atlantic, especially the lower reaches of the Tagus.

Guimarães: the birthplace of modern Portugal

The peoples of the Iberian peninsula seem to have remained in total isolation until the Neolithic (3,000–5,000 years ago), by which time the civilizations of Mesopotamia and Egypt (known to be wine producers) were already well developed. It is at this stage that a distinct north–south cultural divide seems to emerge in western Iberia. During the first millennium before Christ, the north (extending from Galicia to the Mondego) became populated by Celts, who were engaged in iron founding and shepherding as well as the cultivation of the valleys. Defensive settlements called *castros* were built on the hilltops, and the names live on in towns like Castro Daire, Castro de Avelãs and Castro Laboreiro. South of the River Mondego the inhabitants of the peninsula looked toward the Mediterranean. As early as 800 BC the Phoenicians established a trading post on the Atlantic promontory occupied today by Cadiz. They moved west into the southern part of Portugal, but hardly ventured north of present-day Estremadura. The Algarve was certainly well colonized and the city of Ossonobra near modern-day Faro is thought to be of Phoenician origin.

Although vines may have been introduced to the Iberian peninsula by the Tartesians as early as 2000 BC, the Phoenicians almost certainly introduced winemaking to Portugal. It is therefore likely that the earliest commercial vineyards were established in the south of the country, possibly stretching as far north as the Rivers Sado and Tagus. The Romans reached Portugal around the turn of the second century BC. They considerably refined the tradition of winemaking, taking the vine further north as they fought off the tribal Celts and imposed their own civilization on central Portugal – the land they called Lusitania. Populations began to stabilize and by the first century BC there is evidence that viticulture was being practised as far north as Conimbriga (the Roman settlement just south of modern-day Coimbra) and Trás-os-Montes (which includes the Douro). For a time in the first century AD the River Lima formed the northern frontier of Roman Lusitania. According to legend, a horde of Celts had traversed the river and never returned. Junius Brutus thought that the Lima was the "river of forgetfulness" and his troops refused to cross. Eventually the Romans ventured north, over the River Minho, and founded Callaecia (Galicia). By this time viticulture was implanted both in the Douro and Alentejo. The Romans brought *amphorae*, and the clay *talhas* and *anforas* still occasionally used for winemaking in the Alentejo are their descendants. A sarcophagus dated to between the first and third centuries AD found near Reguengos de Monsaraz in the Alentejo (now in the Soares dos Reis Museum, Oporto) shows two young men dancing while treading grapes. Nearby Ebora (Évora) became an important Roman administrative centre.

Christianity reached Portugal during the second century AD, and a number of cities began to emerge as centres of religious as well as political and economic significance. By the fourth century there were bishoprics in Ossonobra (Faro), Ebora, Olissipo (Lisbon), Aquea Flavia (Chaves) and Bracara (Braga). Wine was a vital part of the Christian rite and vineyards would have been planted in the countryside surrounding these cities, which in the main corresponded to the old Roman *municipia*.

With the decline and fall of the Roman Empire, the Iberian peninsula was overrun by successive tribes of Suevi, Visigoths and Moors. The Suevi and Visigoths who occupied the north of modern-day Portugal continued to defend the Christian faith, establishing new dioceses at Pax (Beja), Conimbriga (Coimbra), Veseo (Viseu), Lamecum (Lamego), Tude (near the River Lima) and Portucale (Oporto). Trás-os-Montes and the mountains of the Beiras are punctured by small troughs dating from this period, carved from the granite bedrock and known as *pias* or *laragetas*. It is likely that they were used for making both olive oil and wine.

 In 711 Iberia was invaded by Muslims from the south and within five years most of the peninsula had been conquered by Islam. Viticulture clearly suffered under Islamic rule, although during the early part of the occupation winemaking was tacitly permitted by the Emir of Cordoba, who governed Lusitania. Later rulers, such as the Almoravids, took a much more orthodox line and prohibited the production and trade of wine.

PORTUCALE AND THE RECONQUEST

The seeds of Christian reconquest were sown in Galicia and the Minho only a few years after the Moorish occupation. The Moors fought hard to retain their territory and for a century or more the countryside between the Rivers Minho and Douro was an insecure no man's land fought over by Christians and Muslims. From the middle of the ninth century, as the Christians gained the upper hand, the area was gradually reorganized and recolonized. The towns of Portucale and Chaves became centres of Christian administration within the Kingdom of Asturias (subsequently León). Later in the century the land between the Rivers Lima and Douro (the major part of today's Vinho Verde region) was sufficiently densely populated to warrant its own governor. The seat of government was Portucale, which lent its name to the surrounding territory, known in the local parlance as *Portugal*.

The frontier between Christian and Muslim territory continued to move back and forth until the latter part of the eleventh century, when the bishopric at Coimbra, just north of the River Mondego, was finally reinstated in 1088. This newly conquered territory formed a separate province (Coimbra), but unlike Portucale, where ducal courts had been established at Portucale itself, Vimaranis (Guimarães) and Braga, in the Coimbra province there was no hereditary system of government. The entire territory still remained part of the Kingdom of León, but with its own court, Portucale established a degree of autonomy.

In the meantime, Afonso VI of León seemed intent on restoring the old Visigothic empire. He suffered a reversal of fortune when he was soundly defeated by the Moors near Badajoz. Afonso had taken a Burgundian wife, so he naturally called on the French for support in preventing an invasion of León. The queen's nephew Henry (a cousin of the Duke of Burgundy) arrived in Iberia in 1094 and married Afonso's illegitimate daughter Teresa. The provinces of Portucale and Coimbra became Teresa's dowry and, known by the names of Count of Portugal and Count of Coimbra, Henry established his court at Guimarães. He is reputed to have brought the Pinot Noir grape to Portugal, a name that lives on in the guise of a variety called Tinta Francisca, but the embattled Henry otherwise made little impact on his adopted territory. He died in 1112 leaving his powerful wife and a young son (then no more than five years old) named Afonso Henriques.

For a time the nascent Portugal was governed by the boy's mother, the scheming Countess Teresa, who favoured her new Galician husband over and above her son. However, the Portuguese barons took sides and backed the young Afonso Henriques against his mother, thereby consolidating the court at Guimarães and extending his authority as far east as Bragança. In 1128 Teresa's forces were defeated. She was exiled to Galicia and Afonso Henriques became the ruler of the country of Portugal. He immediately graduated from being *Portugalensium princepus* to become the self-styled *Alphonsus glorioissimus princepus et Dei gratia Portugalensium rex*.

In the meantime, the greater part of the country south of the Mondego continued under Muslim domination. The country west of the River Guadiana was known as al-Garb al-Andalus (west of Andalus) and, having consolidated his rule in the north, Afonso Henriques embarked on a series of campaigns to expel the Moors from their territory. He was greatly aided by English, German and Flemish crusaders, who already knew something of the coast of western Iberia from the time of the First Crusade. In 1140, a fleet of seventy ships carrying English and Norman crusaders bound for Palestine sailed into the Douro and agreed to join the

Portuguese in a combined attack on the Moors. They were induced to stay in Portugal with the promise of wine aplenty and a share in the spoils of war that lay ahead.

As the Moors were driven southwards, their lands were immediately colonized by the Christian Portuguese. In 1137 Afonso Henriques authorized the planting of vines in the Bairrada region below the highway "from Vilarinium to monte Buzaco" (Vilarinho to Buçaco) in return for a levy amounting to a quarter of the total production. Fifteen years later, as his forces drove south, he granted the Cistercians a huge agricultural estate at Alcobaça, north of Lisbon, which would certainly have included vineyards. Even in the Alentejo, where vineyards had been all but eradicated by the Moors, vines were interplanted with olive trees as the population resettled the area. The Christian expeditionary force was so successful that by 1168 only the southern coastal strip of the al-Garb (Algarve) remained in possession of the Moors. This succumbed to Portuguese forces in 1249, a good two centuries before the Moors were finally driven out of neighbouring Andalusia.

FROM WAR TO TRADE

By the middle of the thirteenth century a good understanding had developed between the Portuguese and English monarchs. A number of unsuccessful attempts were made to formalize this relationship by marriage, but against a background of relative peace, trade between the two nations began to flourish. English merchants manufactured cloth in exchange for primary produce: olive oil, fruit and wine. Mercantile communities were established by the English in Viana, Oporto and Lisbon and a series of commercial treaties were signed, beginning in 1294 and concluding in 1353, when merchants in Lisbon and Oporto, led by Afonso Martins Alho ("garlic"), negotiated a treaty that guaranteed the safety of both nations, allowing free access to each other's markets.

It took an invasion of Portugal by neighbouring Castile to formalize this trading relationship. In 1373 an alliance was sealed between John of Gaunt, Duke of Lancaster, and Fernando I of Portugal with the intention of defeating King Enrique de Trástamara of Castile. But when Fernando I died in 1383, leaving his only daughter married to Juan I of Castile, the Castilians laid claim to Portugal. With the help of five hundred English archers, the Castilians were soundly defeated in 1385 at the Battle of Aljubarota in Portuguese Estremadura. Portugal's ambassadors remained behind in England and concluded an all-embracing treaty at St George's Chapel, Windsor on May 9, 1386. The Treaty of Windsor, as it became known, promised "to ensure the public good and the tranquillity both of the Kings and the subjects of either Kingdom . . . and their heirs and successors, and between subjects of both Kingdoms, a solid, perpetual and real league, amity, confederacy and union". True to its word, the treaty marked the beginning of the world's oldest alliance between two nation states. It was invoked in the twentieth century by Winston Churchill during the darkest days of the Second World War and again in 1982 during the Falklands campaign. On both occasions the British forces requested (and were granted) use of the Lajes air base in the Azores.

The Treaty of Windsor was sealed by the marriage of João I, Mestre de Aviz, to John of Gaunt's daughter, Philippa of Lancaster, in 1387. Their union was an unqualified success. Philippa gave birth to eight children, the most significant of whom was their third-born son, named after his English uncle, later Henry IV. Born in Oporto in 1394, the Infante Dom Henrique has become better known worldwide as Prince Henry "the navigator". Henry was encouraged in his studies by Philippa and established a maritime observatory at Sagres, near Cape St Vincent. From here he instigated Portugal's golden age of discovery with courageous voyages down the west coast of Africa. He also owned a property near Silgueiros in the Dão region where wine was a source of income. Henry's mantle was inherited in the fifteenth and sixteenth centuries by a long line of Portuguese explorers, among them João Goncalves Zarco (who discovered Madeira and Porto Santo), Gil Eanes, Bartolomeu Dias, Vasco da Gama, Fernão Magalhães (Ferdinand Magellan), Tristão de Cunha and Pedro Alves Cabral, who discovered Brazil for Portugal in 1500.

CODFISH AND WINE

During the reign of Manuel I "the fortunate" (1494–1521) Portugal reached the zenith of its overseas influence, with the blue and white Portuguese flag planted on four continents. The Cantino map of 1502 shows that Portugal even laid claim to the barren wastes of Greenland, Newfoundland and Labrador, all three having been reached by Gaspar

Corte Real in 1500–01. Portuguese ships ventured ever further into the cold waters of the North Atlantic in search of that most precious of Portuguese commodities: cod.

Cod (*bacalhau*) had become – and remains – a staple of everyday life in Portugal. From the reign of Edward III (1327–77), codfish from the waters around the British Isles (dried and salted to preserve it on the voyage home) was particularly highly prized in Portugal, and wine from the vineyards of the Minho in the north of the country became the principal currency in this trade. These northern wines were never particularly well regarded by the English, whose taste was for bigger, full-bodied wines from southern climes, like the Spanish "Lepe" – famous, according to Chaucer, for its "fumositee". In fact, Chaucer's French contemporary Froissart records that the wines from north-west Iberia were so "ardent" that the English could scarcely drink them. In his scholarly book *The Story of Wine*, Hugh Johnson recounts how the archers sent to Portugal by John of Gaunt came across the wines of "Ribadavia" but attributes them to Galicia. The modern-day Ribadave is an industrial zone corresponding to the valley of the River Ave between Vila do Conde and Guimarães. It therefore seems probable that some of the earliest Portuguese wines to reach England's shores in any volume were similar in style to the thin, rasping, red Vinhos Verdes that are produced along the Ave valley today (see page 131).

This lucrative trade – *bacalhau* for wine – was further enhanced by the English Reformation, which began in 1536. With the majority of English now eschewing fish on Fridays and saint's days, earning themselves the Portuguese nickname of *rosbifes* ("roast beefs") in the process, Portugal became the principal market for British fish. English and Scottish merchants or "factors" settled in the northern port of Viana do Castelo at the mouth of the River Lima and began sourcing and shipping wine from the country between Monção (called "Monson" by the English), Melgaço and Ponte de Lima. Known as "Red Portugal", these thin red wines must have been inherently unstable and spoiled long before they reached British shores.

But the early trade in wine was not confined entirely to the north of the country. Lisbon, a growing centre of trade, almost certainly exported its own wine. In his largely historical book *The Wines of Portugal*, H Warner Allen describes a metrical romance from the early fourteenth century entitled *The Squire of Low Degree*. This tells of the wonderful, rich wines with which the King of Hungary proposes to regale his daughter, one of which is "Algarde" (probably Algarve) and another "Osey". Warner Allen suggests that Osey (variously spelt "Oseye" and "Osaye") was a sweet wine from the Setúbal region in the south of Portugal, possibly made by concentrating the grape must to a thick, treacle-like syrup. It was almost certainly fortified, as it was classed at the time as one of the "Sacks" from Portugal. By the fifteenth century it was an established drink in England, being listed by Sir John Fortescue in his *Comodytes of England* as among the imports "out of Portugal and Algarbe". Osey commanded a relatively high price. In 1504 Archbishop Warham's accounts show that a butt of highly esteemed Malmsey from Crete cost £4, whereas a pipe (cask) of Osey fetched a price of £3. It is impossible to be certain about the origin of Osey, which may have been an English corruption of the Portuguese place name Azóia. There are a number of localities called Azóia near Lisbon, the closest of which are Santa Iria de Azóia and Portela de Azóia overlooking the Tagus on the way to Bucelas. Given the poor communications in Portugal at the time and that wine was a port-based commodity, it seems highly likely that this was the source of Osey.

Another Portuguese wine to reach England toward the end of the sixteenth century was Charneco. As with Osey, there is a great deal of uncertainty as to the origin of this wine, but it seems likely that it came from the Lisbon region and is the precursor of the fortified wines that were merely known by the name of "Lisbon" in the eighteenth and nineteenth centuries. The word *charneca* means heath, and there is an area known as Charneca between Lisbon airport and Odivelas that was once planted with vines. Another locality called Charneca is within the present-day Bucelas DOC some ten kilometres distant. Charneco is mentioned in Act II of Shakespeare's *Henry VI, Part II*, where it is drunk by Horner along with a cup of Sack and a pot of beer. It is referred to again in the early seventeenth century, but by 1660 both Osey and Charneco seem to have fallen from favour.

Wine was produced in other parts of Portugal but, estranged from the great seaports, these wines seem to have been made purely for domestic consumption. Évora in the Alentejo was surrounded by 3,000 hectares of vineyard, the best known of which was Peramanca, a property on the outskirts of the city belonging to the Convento de Espinheiro (see page 272).

The significance of wine in this region is apparent from the *Parodia Bacchia*, written by students from the University of Évora in 1590, which appears in Canto I of the *Lusiadas* by Luís de Camões.

PORT: WINE OF THE ENGLISH

By the middle of the sixteenth century, Portugal's rapid overseas expansion had drained her economy. With the country's resources stretched to the limit, fields at home were left untended and Portugal was forced to import even the most basic produce to survive. Vineyards all over the country were abandoned as the agricultural labour force migrated to Lisbon or journeyed overseas, and wines had to be imported from Castille, Catalonia and even France. The crisis point was reached in 1578, when King Sebastião ("the regretted") was killed in a battle with the Moors at Alcazar-Quivir in North Africa. He died without an heir to the throne and after a brief interregnum Philip II of Spain marched into Portugal and annexed the country by force. To a proud and independent nation it was a humiliating end to a brief but brilliant golden age. A succession of three Spanish Philips reigned over Portugal for sixty years.

Possibly owing to the silting up of the Lima estuary at Viana, and lured by the security of the larger city, the majority of English and Scottish factors moved south to Oporto during the Spanish occupation. Portugal's second city already had its own English *feitoria* or "factory" of merchants engaged in selling cloth and *bacalhau* to the Portuguese, mainly in exchange for oil and fruit. Following the overthrow of the Spanish governor and the restoration of the Portuguese monarchy in 1640, the status of these merchants was considerably enhanced in 1654 by a one-sided treaty between João IV and Oliver Cromwell. In return for supporting the Portuguese in their wars with the Spanish and the Dutch, Cromwell extracted huge privileges for the English and Scottish factors, which put them in a more powerful position than the Portuguese themselves. Their special status was further reinforced in 1662 when Charles II married Afonso VI's sister, Catherine of Bragança. In a treaty concluded a year earlier, the English agreed to defend Portugal "as if it were England itself".

By this time, exports of Portuguese wine were almost non-existent. In the 1660s so little Portuguese wine reached England's shores that it did not even warrant a listing in the customs books. However, Portugal's fortunes changed decisively in 1667 when, as a result of England's deteriorating relations with France, Louis XIV and his minister Colbert initiated a tariff war which closed the French market to English cloth. Charles II swiftly retaliated by prohibiting the importation of French goods into England, including wine. This must have raised the prospect of considerable hardship to the well-heeled English who had become accustomed to drinking the refined wines of Bordeaux. Recorded annual shipments of wines from Portugal rose from just 120 tuns (about 120,000 litres) in the mid-1670s to 6,880 tuns (6.81 million litres) a decade later, although much of this was probably French masquerading as Portuguese.

When war broke out between England and France in 1689, the supply of French wine dried up completely. The Dutch (who were already at war with the French) had turned to Portugal for their wines, and the English followed suit. The thin, lean wines from the northern Atlantic *litoral* were no match for the refinement of Claret and, in search of a more acceptable substitute, the merchants journeyed inland along the deeply incised valley of the River Douro. Here, as in the Vinho Verde region today, grapes were just one of a multitude of different crops cultivated largely for subsistence. In order to make maximum use of the available space in this difficult terrain, vines were planted in small holes (*pilheiros*) punctured in the vertical terrace walls, leaving the flat surfaces for the cultivation of cereals. The wines from the Douro were the opposite of those down on the coast. Overripe grapes, combined with fast and furious fermentation in the most unhygienic conditions, produced impenetrable, inky red wines that earned the derogatory name of "black-strap". They were fermented dry and, in a brazen attempt to ensure that the wine reached its destination in passable condition, a measure of brandy was added to bolster the level of alcohol and stabilize the wine before shipment in cask. In spite of these precautions, by all accounts the wines reached London in an abysmal condition.

Port Wine (wine shipped from Oporto) was a rude awakening for those weaned on wines from Bordeaux. Richard Ames scoured London in search of Claret in the early 1690s and penned a series of ditties like these written in 1693:

"Some Claret boy!" – *"Indeed sir, we have none.*
Claret, sir! Lord there's not a drop in town.

> But we have the best Red Port" – "What's that you call
> Red Port?" – "A wine, sir, comes from Portugal:
> I'll fetch a pint, sir."

But Ames was not a happy customer:

> Mark how it smells, me thinks a real pain
> Is by the odour thrown upon my brain.
> I've tasted it – 'tis spiritless and flat,
> And has as many tastes as can be found in compound
> pastes . . .
> But fetch us a pint of any sort,
> Navarre, Galicia, anything but Port.

However, at the end of the eighteenth century England's drinking habits were shaped less by personal whim than by political loyalty. After the expulsion of James II in 1688, the Jacobites would toast "the king over the water" in Claret, whereas the loyal Whigs raised their tankards of Port to King William and the Glorious Revolution! Thus the Scots who remained loyal to the exiled Stuart king had a sad ditty of their own:

> Firm and erect the Highland chieftain stood,
> Sweet was his mutton and his claret good,
> "Thou shalt drink Port" the English statesman cried;
> He drank the poison, and his spirit died.

But so dire was the wine that, south of the border, even the English Tories needed some persuasion from a patriotic Jonathan Swift:

> Be sometimes to your country true,
> Have once the public good in view;
> Bravely despise champagne at court
> And choose to dine at home with Port.

A number of well-known Port shipping firms date back to this time. The Newmans, a family based at Dartmouth in Devon, are among the first recorded. They began trading *bacalhau* in the fifteenth century but by the 1670s they were also shipping wine. Their company went on to become Hunt Roope (now owned by Port shippers Ferreira), although the Newman family still owns Quinta de Eira Velha, a prominent vineyard near Pinhão in the Douro. Other English families followed. Warre & Co was founded in 1670, followed by Phayre & Bradley (forerunner of Croft) in 1678, Quarles Harris in 1680 and Bearsley (forerunner of Taylor) in 1692. The oldest of all the surviving Port shippers is Kopke & Co, which was established in 1638 as a general trader but only began specializing in wine a century later.

Portugal's favoured status as a source of wine was sealed by the Methuen Treaty in 1703. This succeeded in securing preferential treatment for the sale of English textiles in Portugal in return for duties on Portuguese wines amounting to less than half those levied on wines from France. By 1698, during the reign of William III, the duty on French wine had reached £51 2s 0d a tun (1,000 litres), whereas Portuguese wines were taxed at £21 2s 5d. The influx of English cloth practically destroyed the Portuguese textile industry based inland at Portalegre and Covilhã, but the preferential rate of duty on wines was hugely beneficial for the wine trade based around the seaports of Lisbon and Oporto. It lasted for over 150 years until it was finally dropped by Gladstone's budget in 1860.

The Minho continued to export wine to England even after the Methuen Treaty was signed. With the Douro unable to satisfy demand, so-called "Port" was no doubt stretched with lighter wine from coastal vineyards. In 1704 English coopers were sent to the Minho to improve the local cooperage. Thomas Woodmas, son of a Kettering wine merchant, who served his apprenticeship at Viana before moving onto Oporto, describes the English coopers as "a drunken lot, but ye natives now know how to make casks". John Croft, writing over eighty years later in his *Treatise on the Wines of Portugal*, recalls "a thin sort of wine; the red not unlike what is called or termed in Portugal Palhete – straw-coloured – or Methuen Wine, from one Paul Methuen[1] who was the first that mixed red and white grapes together". He continues to recount that when the demand for Port outstripped supply, the English merchants from Viana and Oporto would teach the Portuguese to cultivate the vineyards on the heights or mountains bordering the Douro. These vineyards continue to be the source of illegal Port grapes apprehended in the Douro during the vintage of 2000. *Plus ça change.*

Lisbon wines also had their place on the English market. Shipped in

---

[1] Paul Methuen was the son of John Methuen, Ambassador to Portugal, who signed the Methuen Treaty on May 16, 1703.

much smaller quantities than Port, at the time they were almost certainly of a higher quality. In 1710 red and white Oporto (described as "deep, bright, fresh and neat") was on sale at five shillings a gallon (4.5 litres) and Red Barrabar Lisbon ("very strong, extraordinarily good and neat") was priced at sixpence a gallon more. Three years later Oporto was being sold for between £24 10s 0d and £27 10s 0d a pipe (550 litres), against £32 10s 0d for Lisbon.

When Queen Anne's ministers overturned the monopoly enjoyed by the Distillers Company in England and passed a Bill "for encouraging the consumption of malted corn and the better preventing the running of French and Foreign Brandy", the country embarked on a drunken orgy. The production of spirits rose from two million gallons (90,000 hectolitres) in 1714 to twenty million gallons (900,000 hectolitres) in 1742, in a country populated by just six million people. The light, stretched wines of northern Portugal can have had little appeal in Hogarth's Gin Lane, so the shippers responded by raising the alcohol level.

POMBAL'S WINES

The trading advantage enjoyed by Port in England led directly to unprincipled over-production. Vineyards were planted all over the north of Portugal, often on fertile land that was better suited to growing cereals. Genuine Port wines from the Douro were eked out increasingly with pale, thin wines from the Minho and Bairrada and then mixed with ever-growing amounts of brandy. An early winemaking manual, *A Agricultura das Vinhas*, recommends the addition of three gallons (13.6 litres) of brandy to each pipe (550 litres) of wine, although the amount continued to rise to between 8 and 10.6 gallons (36 and 48 litres) per pipe during the eighteenth century. In order to compensate for the lack of colour in the wines, elderberry (*baga*) was used as a dye. Sugar and sometimes pepper were added to embellish the flavour. With Spanish wine (the colour of "bullock's blood"), raisin wines and cheap English spirit also used as admixtures, Port must have been a curious concoction.

Prices fell dramatically. A pipe of Port worth sixty escudos at the turn of the eighteenth century fell to forty-eight in 1731 and just 6.4 escudos after 1750. The shippers and growers accused each other of malpractice, but with supply now outstripping demand neither had a market for their wines. The Douro farmers, desperate at the loss of their livelihoods, took their complaint to the Portuguese prime minister, Sebastião José de Carvalho, later known as Marquês de Pombal. Pombal had a reputation for decisiveness and the ineffectual king, José I (1750–77), awarded his prime minister dictatorial powers. He acted swiftly to quell the problems in the Douro and in 1756 with the backing of a large number of growers he created the *Real Companhia das Vinhas do Alto Douro*.

The *Companhia*, as it became known, had monopoly powers and provoked a storm of protest from the factory of British shippers, who felt unfairly excluded. Riots erupted in Oporto, which Pombal was quick to blame on the British, and, had it not been for Britain's involvement in the Seven Years War with France and Spain, the carefully nurtured Anglo-Portuguese alliance might have come to an abrupt end. In the event, Britain's prime minister, William Pitt, was so anxious to remain on good terms with Portugal that he turned a deaf ear to the Port shipper's complaints.

Pombal accompanied the establishment of the *Companhia* with a series of far-reaching measures to protect the authenticity of Port. A commission was set up to delimit the Alto Douro wine region, restricting the production of Port to vineyards within the demarcation. The region was staked out with sturdy granite posts (over a hundred of which still remain) that separated two zones, one for inexpensive wines for home consumption (*vinho do ramo*) and the other for the production of high-quality wines destined for export (*vinho da feitoria*). In a determined effort to stamp out the blatant adulteration of previous years, Pombal ruled that all elderberry trees were to be uprooted and that every vineyard should be registered. Production quotas were issued to stabilize prices and the *Companhia* was handed the exclusive right to supply the spirit used in fortifying Port wine. Any infringement of these rules would be met with severe punishment, the ultimate threat being deportation to one of the African colonies.

Pombal's strict demarcation of the Douro should not be seen out of context, for it was part of a more wide-ranging policy to boost the production of food in continental Portugal, which now had a rising population. The amount of land given over to cereals had been contracting, due to the priority given to wine, and nearly twenty per cent of all grain had to be imported from abroad. A charter dated October 26, 1765 ordered the uprooting of all vines "on the banks and fields of the Rivers Mondego and Vouga and in all the lands that are *paúl* [water meadow or fen] and *leziria* [flood plain], and in their place be grown what is for bread, as they are unable to produce good wine". Four months later this order was extended to cover all low-lying vineyards in Torres Vedras (Estremadura), Anadia, Mogofores, Arcos, Avelãs de Caminha and Fermentelos (all in Bairrada). The economy of the Bairrada region was severely damaged as a result, but by restricting vineyards to higher slopes, the overall quality of the wine improved and more land was made available for other crops. However, it is known that the *Companhia* took advantage of the better quality wine and continued to buy red and white wines from Bairrada to blend with Port.

Pombal's measures also extended to Lisbon, where adulteration and fraud must have also been taking place, albeit on a smaller scale. He banned consignments of "inferior and sour wines" from Anadia and Aveiro (Bairrada) from entering the capital, as well as wines from as far afield as Monção, the Algarve and the Portuguese islands of Madeira and the Azores. Pombal's brand of protectionism and absolutism did not however extend as far as his own vineyards at Oeiras, between Lisbon and Carcavelos (Calcavella), where he continued to sell his wines for blending with Port. In order to protect and further his own interests, he ordered that vineyards from Sacavém (on the outskirts of Lisbon) to Golegã in the Ribatejo sixty miles or so upriver be uprooted, ostensibly to make way for cereals.

Pombal's regime, loathed by vine growers outside the Douro, was undoubtedly corrupt, but it succeeded in reviving the reputation of Port and Portuguese wines in general (he was rather less successful in feeding the nation). Wine exports recovered and although a number of shippers failed, the majority of Port producers found themselves in a stronger position at the end of his regime than at the beginning. His draconian measures were as far-sighted as they were far-reaching, and were replicated in part by the authoritarian Salazar regime when it too embarked on a programme to feed the nation nearly two hundred years later.

MADEIRA: WINE OF THE AMERICAS

Discovered by João Gonçalves Zarco (a disciple of Prince Henry the Navigator) in 1418, Madeira was swiftly colonized by the Portuguese nobility in the fifteenth century. The steeply inclined, heavily wooded terrain (Madeira means "wood") on the south side of the island was initially planted with subsistence crops including cereals and vines. As early as 1461, the first of a complex series of irrigation channels known as *levadas* was constructed, channelling spring water from the uninhabited mountains in the centre of the island to the growing population on the coast. As the Portuguese explorers extended their forays down the west coast of Africa, Madeira gained strategic importance. Sugar cane flourished on the fertile soils, and by the late 1460s it had become the island's principal crop, exported to northern Europe and the Mediterranean. Columbus travelled to Madeira in 1478 and later married the daughter of Bartolomeu Perestrelo, the captain of the neighbouring island of Porto Santo.

It is more than likely that the first vines to be planted on the island came from the Portuguese mainland. Indeed, Sercial is the same variety as Esgana Cão in Bucelas, near Lisbon, and Verdelho is similar to (if not the same as) Gouveio in the Douro. Malvasia was reputedly introduced to the island by Prince Henry the Navigator, who brought the vines from Candia (Crete), although the variety may have already been planted in Portugal. Nowadays there are a number of different grapes known as Malvasia (see Chapter 2) but one is still identified by the sobriquet *Candida*.

By the end of the fifteenth century Madeira was already home to a thriving colony of foreign traders, especially Italians. Among the early names were those of Lomelino and Acciaioli, whose descendants became established as significant wine shippers. Sugar declined in significance when Brazil (discovered by the Portuguese in 1500) became a cheaper alternative source. Wine took its place and became the island's main export, finding a new market in the Americas and West Indies. By the 1580s Madeira was producing around 1,700 pipes (9,350 hectolitres) of wine, nearly all of which must have been exported.

With the strengthening of trading relations between England and Portugal in the mid-seventeenth century, a number of British families settled on the island. An English factory was established in 1658, accompanied by the appointment of a consul in Funchal. The trading position of the British was considerably reinforced in 1663 by the Staple Act, which exempted Madeira and the Azores from the provisions of an Act three years earlier prohibiting the export of goods to the English colonies other than from English ports. The merchants in Funchal were thereby handed a virtual monopoly in the shipment of wine between the West Indies and the Americas, and a lucrative triangular trade opened up between Madeira, the American colonies and England. In his book *Madeira: The Island Vineyard*, Noel Cossart records that by 1680 there were thirty shippers on Madeira (this compares with the six shippers that remain today). At the end of the century annual sales of Madeira were in the order of 6,000–8,000 pipes (33,000–44,000 hectolitres).

There is no evidence to suggest that the Madeira shipped overseas up to this time was anything other than young wine from the previous vintage. However, in the late seventeenth century it was discovered, almost certainly by accident, that Madeira wine was much improved after pitching and rolling across the tropics. A fashion consequently developed both in Britain and America for *vinho da roda*: wine that had benefited from a round voyage. There are also references at this time to a Madeira wine known as "tent". This, in all probability, was red wine or "*tinto*" (although the grape variety from which it was made is unknown). Sir Hans Sloane, who visited the island in 1687, described white wine mixed with a little *tinto* "expos'd to the Sun-beams and heat . . . instead of putting it in a cool Cellar". He adds, "it seems to those unaccustomed to it to have a very unpleasant Tast [sic], though something like sherry", suggesting that the wine was probably fortified. John Ovington, who visited the island a few years later, describes wine "meliorated by the heat of the sun" and "expos'd to the air". As a result of such treatment these wines were obviously oxidized – "maderized" – and able to withstand the heat of the American plantations, the West Indies and the English colonies in the East Indies.

At the turn of the eighteenth century, England was still a small market for Madeira wines, so the impact of the Methuen Treaty (page 13) was considerably less in Funchal than in Oporto. Nevertheless, from the middle of the century a number of British families whose names are still associated with Madeira wine began trading on the island, among them Thomas Gordon, John Leacock and Francis Newton. With American independence in 1776 and the return of the colonial forces, the market opened up in Britain. Wine shipments grew steadily until demand had outstripped supply, leading to fraud and adulteration similar to that on the Portuguese mainland. Like Port, Madeira wines were becoming increasingly fortified. Poor quality wines from the cooler north side of the island were blended with those from the south and genuine Madeiras were stretched with wines from other sources (the Azores and Canaries), sometimes dyed with black cherries (aka elderberry on the mainland). In 1768 the governor of Madeira initiated a series of measures to regulate the trade, and a demarcation was made to separate the different qualities of wine from various locations on the island. In an edict similar to that issued in the Douro, black cherry trees were either to be uprooted or regrafted with red cherries.

It was at the end of the eighteenth century that another highly controversial practice began: *estufagem*. The word *estufa* means both "oven" and "greenhouse" in Portuguese, and the artificial heating of Madeira in a hothouse warmed by a stove or boiler quickly became the logical means of accelerating the maturation of the wine, simulating both the effect of the sun and the tropical sea voyages that had proved to be so beneficial. There was, however, much abuse of the *estufa* system, with excessively high temperatures merely serving to cook the wines. Genuine *vinho da roda* continued to command a high price in Britain where, in the late eighteenth century, it was one of the most fashionable of all wines. John Leacock, on the other hand, clearly thought that *estufagem* might help to improve the quality of the cheaper wines from the island, and this is a view that persists among the majority of shippers today (see Chapter 6).

AFTER POMBAL

One of Pombal's last and most draconian acts was to prohibit the export of the wines of Monção, Viana and Bairrada from any port in the kingdom. His regime, however, did not survive the death of King José I in 1777. Pombal was dismissed from office and returned to his palace and vineyards at Oeiras. However, he clearly continued to profit from wine for, according to John Croft writing in 1788, between 4,000 and 5,000 tuns (40,000 and 50,000 hectolitres) of wine were being shipped from Lisbon "all promiscuously called Carcavelos". Carcavelos was no doubt more highly prized than the ordinary wines from the Lisbon region, although these too must have had a considerable following judging by some of the Hester Bateman silver decanter neck labels made at the time simply bearing the name "Lisbon".

Under the more proactive but relatively benign reign of Queen Maria I, the *Companhia* lost much of its monopoly, and wines from northern Portugal could once again be freely exported. This led to a steady increase in the production of *vinhos da feitoria* and in 1788 Dona Maria authorized the enlargement of the demarcated region of the Alto Douro. The rapids on the River Douro at Valeira were still a major barrier to the eastward expansion of the region and, in 1780, the *Companhia* undertook the considerable task of clearing the river, financed by a levy on the transportation of wine. As the work progressed, more vineyards were planted and the British preference for bigger, bolder wines was reflected in a significant increase in the production of Port from the hotter slopes upstream around Pinhão and Tua.

The rapid expansion in the wine trade in the late eighteenth century had much to do with the science of the bottle. The earliest glass bottles had been used merely to convey a wine from cask to the table. They were short and squat in shape, and therefore totally impractical for laying down and maturing wine. But, as the century wore on, a more elongated bottle evolved, which by 1770 could be cellared on its side without much difficulty. This led to an entirely new approach to wine in general and to Port in particular. Instead of the Port being advertised as "new", it was now possible to age it in bottle. The cylindrical bottle was available for the great 1775 vintage, so, claims H Warner Allen in *The Wines of Portugal*, "it seems a fair guess that the best Douro wine of 1775 profited by it to become the first great Vintage Port in history" – although the first vintage to be quoted in Christie's catalogue is 1765, which was auctioned in 1773. By the beginning of the nineteenth century the Douro could lay claim to a series of fine vintages: 1765, 1775, 1790 and 1797. A bottle of the latter was shared by the Duke of Wellington and George Sandeman at Torres Vedras in 1809. Sandeman declared at the time that he believed it to be the finest Port year within his experience.

WINE AND WAR

At the end of the eighteenth century France was racked by revolutionary fervour and the royal houses in both Spain and Portugal did their utmost to prevent the spread of radical propaganda over the Pyrenees into the Iberian peninsula. Possessed by the idea that she was damned, Dona Maria became increasingly prone to nightmares and fits of melancholy.

She was treated by the same doctor who ministered to the mad King George of England, but to no avail, and she ceased to reign in 1792, replaced by her second son, Dom João, who became regent. Threatened for a time by a Spanish invasion, the beleaguered Portuguese regent was torn between a policy of appeasing Napoleon or adhering to the terms of the Anglo-Portuguese alliance. His mind was made up in the summer of 1807, when the French demanded that all Portuguese ports should be closed to British shipping, adding that "no people [and] no government has more reason to complain of England than Portugal". This strengthened into an ultimatum that all Englishmen in Portugal should be arrested and their property seized. The Portuguese prince regent was unable to accept this, and in October 1807 a treaty was concluded between France and Spain which provided for the partition of Portugal into three. A month later, French troops under the command of Marshal Junot invaded Portugal. The Portuguese royal family fled the country for Brazil, Junot declared that the house of Bragança had ceased to rule, and the French tricolour was raised over the Castelo de São Jorge above the centre of Lisbon.

This was the first in a series of three French invasions of Portugal that were eventually repelled by British and Portuguese troops under the command of Sir Arthur Wellesley. Wellesley, later the Duke of Wellington, landed initially near the mouth of the River Mondego in August 1808, and for the duration of the Peninsular campaign he and his officers spent the greater part of their time in the country around Torres Vedras, Leiria and Óbidos (Estremadura). Although Oporto was recaptured for the Portuguese in May 1809, the Peninsular War continued to rage in the hill country north of Lisbon for another three years. The prince regent appointed an Englishman, William Carr Beresford, to reorganize the Portuguese army, granting him the rank of marshal and commander-in-chief. One of the most decisive battles of the campaign took place at Buçaco in September 1810, when Wellington defeated Massena on what he called "a damned long hill". An obelisk above the famous Palace Hotel at Buçaco marks the site of the battle, the anniversary of which is still commemorated by the Portuguese army.

Wellington and his officers were clearly well supplied with Port by the grateful British shippers, but they also took to drinking the local wines from the Lisbon region. Lisbon, Carcavelos and Bucelas enjoyed a period of vogue in Britain immediately following the return of Wellington's heroic troops, when French wines were once again virtually out of bounds. All three wines are celebrated in the decorative decanter labels of the early nineteenth century, as well as a wine called "Arinto". This was almost certainly a dry white wine from the Lisbon region, similar in style to Bucelas, which is made mainly from the Arinto grape – although one authority compares it to a Manzanilla, which suggests that it was fortified. "Bucellas", as it used to be written, clearly became a readily available, inexpensive wine, for it is listed as one of the three wines responsible for the merriment at Mrs Tibb's boarding house in Dickens's *Sketches by Boz*, written in 1836. Like so many popular wines at the time it was also heavily adulterated, as is evident from a little rhyme coined by Thomas Hood at a mayoral banquet, where he described:

Bucelas made handy
By Cape and bad brandy.

Wellington's fortifications (an extension of the famous Lines of Torres Vedras) can still be seen above the vineyards of Quinta da Romeira in Bucelas. His legacy can also be found nearby in the Ribatejo, where a pack of foxhounds, the Equipagem de Santo Humberto, originally established by Wellington's officers, still hunts the country just south of the Tagus.

Madeira was subject to an unpopular invasion in the early years of the nineteenth century, this time by the British. In order to protect the islands from being taken by the French, the British occupied Madeira on two occasions between 1801 and 1814. The troops went on a drunken rampage, even desecrating churches, and the islanders suspected that the British wanted to colonize the island. The Peninsular War, however, further helped to popularize the Madeira wine, and one British soldier who returned to Madeira was John Blandy who, in 1811, set himself up as a merchant in Funchal. With Spanish and French ports closed to trade, annual shipments of Madeira rose to 18,000 pipes (99,000 hectolitres).

In the aftermath of the Peninsular Wars, Portugal found itself in a political vacuum. Maria I died in 1816, tormented by twenty-four years of insanity, and Dom João, the prince regent residing in Brazil, was crowned João VI. He and his family were reluctant to return to Portugal, which was itself now racked by Jacobinism inspired by the Masonic lodges. In May 1817 General Gomes Freire, who had commanded the Portuguese army when Junot invaded and was now grand master of the Portuguese Masons, was sentenced to death for conspiracy. Beresford, still in command of the Portuguese army, was popularly blamed for the severity of the sentence, which further aggravated the unrest. By 1819 the council for the regency was insolvent and Beresford was unable to pay his men. He left for Rio de Janeiro in the hope of persuading Dom João to return to Portugal.

In 1820 attention shifted to Oporto, where both the army and populace rose in revolt to demand the dismissal of Beresford and the return of the King. This was accompanied by a demand for an assembly or *cortes* and a liberal constitution, which were reluctantly granted. In 1821 Dom João grudgingly returned to Portugal, leaving his eldest son Pedro to govern Brazil. He became constitutional emperor and was eventually granted full sovereignty, securing Brazil its independence from Portugal in 1825. Following the death of João VI a year later and Pedro's accession to the Portuguese throne, Portugal was pitched into renewed turmoil by the king's younger brother Miguel, who led the absolutists in revolt. Oporto naturally supported Pedro and the constitutionalist cause against his usurper brother, and in 1832 the north of Portugal erupted into barbarous civil war. Pedro's troops held the centre of Oporto while the Miguelites bombarded the city from the heights above the Port lodges in Vila Nova de Gaia. In the meantime the citizens starved.

It was little better outside the city, with gangs of armed militia terrorizing the towns and villages of northern Portugal. As the constitutionalists gained the upper hand, properties belonging to the clergy and absolutist nobility were seized and auctioned off. Much as in France some forty years earlier, the whole structure of Portuguese agriculture changed. Many vineyards in the south of the country were simply abandoned. As late as 1877, Henry Vizetelly *en route* to Bucelas is "struck by the number of dismantled mansions and dilapidated houses – momentoes of the disastrous civil war of 1826–33". In the north of Portugal medium-sized landowners and bourgeois merchants divided up properties expropriated from religious orders, and a number of families like the Ferreiras from Régua built up substantial private vineyard holdings in the Douro.

TO FORTIFY OR NOT TO FORTIFY?

Caught in the midst of the fighting, the British Port shippers who lived in Oporto naturally tended to side with the constitutionalists, although they flew Union Flags over their lodges in an effort to exempt themselves from attack. One newcomer to the city, however, remained curiously aloof from the fray. Joseph James Forrester was born in Hull, Yorkshire, in 1809 and arrived in Oporto to work for his uncle's Port shipping firm, Offley Forrester, in 1831, immediately before the civil war. Forrester quickly mastered the Portuguese language – something that eluded most British Port shippers at the time – and became *persona grata* with the leaders of both factions in the civil war. (Some years later he managed to entertain opposing generals at his house on the same day but in separate rooms.)

At a time when most shippers clearly preferred the relative comfort of Oporto to the appalling privations of rural Portugal, Forrester travelled extensively and came to know every twist and turn of the Douro. He put his intimate knowledge to good use, mapping and illustrating the region, as well as (from the late 1840s onwards) photographing the river and surrounding countryside. But Forrester never endeared himself to his English compatriots, largely because of his forthright views on Port. In a pamphlet entitled *A Word or Two about Port Wine* he accused the shippers of adulteration and fraud, adding that his purpose was "to enable the consumer to discriminate between *pure* and *impure* wine", presupposing that "he will prefer what is genuine". Forrester is an early advocate of *terroir*, for in the opening paragraphs he defines a pure wine as one made "naturally according to the kind of grape, the soil, the height, and aspect of the vineyard where it is grown", as well as one which reflects the season, "good or bad". But he continues: "The practice of wine-merchants has been to disregard all the circumstances just mentioned, and try to produce in all seasons, wet or dry, hot or cold, from grapes in every variety of situation, and of all qualities, wines of one and the same kind only; viz. – what is called by some 'full, high coloured, and fruity' but by others, more properly, 'black, strong and sweet'."

Forrester dates the fashion for full, sweet Port wines as originating with the extraordinarily fine 1820 vintage, and states that merchants, witnessing their popularity, wanted to have such wines each and every year.

He goes on to say how the merchants, encouraged by "petty inn-keepers, retail dealers, and others", are wont to mix Port "with Benecarlo[2], or other harsh inferior red wine" as well as elderberry. The pamphlet lists other complaints that were no doubt equally valid: namely, the lack of any means to control the quality of the wine from the farmer, and the absence of a legal starting date for the vintage, which meant that grapes were being harvested unripe and the wines were then bolstered by adding jeropiga[3].

Much less valid, however, were Forrester's complaints about the use of águardente or "brandy" in Port. Although águardente was no doubt abused on occasion, Forrester's assertion that Port should be a dry, unfortified wine was clearly wide of the mark and the prevailing consumer taste. By the 1840s it was not uncommon to add twenty-six gallons (118 litres) of spirit per 550-litre pipe, similar to the quantity used to fortify Port today. This did not correspond with Forrester's notion of a *pure* wine, for he states that "the custom of stopping the fermentation is now common, but a *real* wine of any kind, cannot be formed by those who have adopted it, still less Port-wine". His opposition to the rich, sweet style of Port wine that we appreciate today is plain, for he wrote that the Port shippers "state as an axiom, that 'the richest wine requires the greatest quantity of brandy' – a statement very far from being correct. In fact rich wine requires little or no brandy, except for the purpose of preserving it from the ill effects of the agitation on board ship during the voyage to England, and the change of climate; and an admixture of a large quantity of brandy with such wine is highly injurious, many years being necessary for the complete incorporation of the spirit with it, so that the real vinous qualities may again appear."

[2] The small Mediterranean port of Benicarlo, located between Tarragona and Valencia, once shipped powerful wines from the hinterland for blending with lighter wines from France and Portugal. It no longer has any connection with wine.

[3] Forrester offers the following "receipt" or recipe for *jeropiga*: "To fifty-six pounds of dried elderberry, and sixty pounds of coarse brown sugar, or treacle, add seventy-eight gallons of unfermented grape juice, and thirty-nine gallons of the strongest brandy. Mix all thoroughly together." The term *jeropiga* is still in use today, meaning fresh grape must prevented from fermenting by the addition of spirit (*águardente*). This rich admixture is commonly used to correct the sweetness in a Port which has fermented for too long and has therefore become too dry.

Earlier in the pamphlet Forrester discusses the main grape varieties planted in the Douro. Once again, his opinions seem rather wide of the mark. Assessing the Bastardo variety, he writes that "it produces a rich, delicate wine, with delicious flavour and bouquet, and *with little colour*. The Bastardo wine, *properly made* and judiciously treated will in Portugal keep for any length of time *without brandy*" (his own italics). Likewise, on Alvarilhão (today spelt Alvarelhão), Forrester writes: "It is a very durable wine; and if perfectly made, may be kept in Portugal altogether without brandy." Few growers or Port shippers would agree with these assertions today, for the Bastardo grape is something of a *bastardo* by nature, producing light, insubstantial, sugary wines. It also has an alarming tendency to rot on the vine (see Chapter 2). Alvarelhão, still planted in significant quantities on the higher margins of the Douro region, produces even lighter, paler wines, and a significant amount used to end up in Mateus Rosé!

In the furore that followed the publication of the pamphlet, Forrester claimed that his opinions were backed by most of the *freguesias* or parishes in the Douro. He had also elicited the support of a number of leading opinion formers, including the Church. However, few of Forrester's backers can have been in any way conversant with the British market and the growing demand for a sweet, fortified style of Port. Oswald Crawfurd, the British Consul in Oporto, summed up the debate with the benefit of hindsight in *Portugal Old and New*, published in 1880, describing "unfortified Port wine" as "an unmarketable product . . . every Oporto wine merchant has tried the experiment . . . it is a pity they cannot sell it for they would quickly make their fortunes; but the plain truth is that it is an abominable drink".

Indeed, anyone who has experienced the rough and ready unfortified wines that were made in the Douro before the advent of temperature-controlled fermentation in stainless steel would be in agreement. Forrester himself was drowned in an accident when his boat foundered at Cachão de Valeira on the Douro in 1861, and his forthright opinions died with him. The unfortified wines of the Douro received little or no attention until the 1950s, when Fernando Nicolau de Almeida began making Barca Velha. The story is taken up in the section on Douro wines in Chapter 4.

PORTUGUESE WINES IN THE MID-NINETEENTH CENTURY

The middle decades of the nineteenth century proved to be something of a golden age for Portuguese wines. Port shipments reached 43,000 pipes (236,500 hectolitres) in 1849 and exceeded 50,000 pipes (275,000 hectolitres) in the 1870s, with Britain and Brazil the main markets. Lisbon, Carcavelos and Bucelas continued to be exported to Britain in large volumes. The wine shipping firm of Sandeman, which was established in both Oporto and Jerez in 1790, owned substantial cellars at Cabo Ruivo on the Tagus just outside Lisbon. During the course of the century it was joined by other shippers including José Domingos Barreiros (producers of "Special Lisbon Wine"), Wynn & Custance, Abel Perreira da Fonseca at both Lisbon and Torres Vedras, and on the south side of the river at Arealva (Almada) the Sociedade Vinicola Sul de Portugal Lda (subsequently J Serra) and José Maria da Fonseca at Azeitão near Setúbal. No doubt greatly helped by the construction of the first stretch of railway in Portugal, from Lisbon to Carregado in 1856, the wine trade became a flourishing port-based industry, with vineyards planted in the hinterland on the rolling hills around the city. There were vineyards well within the city limits at Olivais and Sacavém, as well as just outside at Frielas, Unhos and Tojal. These wines were commonly sold as "Câmarate", a locality now close to the end of the runway at Lisbon airport and which lent its name to a red wine described at the time as being "not dissimilar to the unfortified wines of the Douro". Câmarate was the scene of a mysterious plane crash in 1980 which killed Francisco Sá Carneio, the Portuguese prime minister, and lives on as the name of a grape variety that is still widely planted in the country north of Lisbon.

Henry Vizetelly gives an idea of the range of wines produced in the Lisbon region when he describes a visit to the cellars of Wynn and Custance, shippers of wine to Russia, the Baltic and to a lesser extent Brazil and England. "Here", he writes, "were deep-tinted Sacavém red wines, some of them dry and clean tasting, and others extremely sweet; a rich and potent Arinto from the same vineyards, the soil of which is darker and richer than in the Bucellas district; red Lisbons and white Lisbons – the former principally designed for the Brazilian market, while dry and rich varieties of the latter are shipped to England, the more luscious qualities – soft, sweet ladies' wines – going chiefly to Russia and the

Baltic." The wines of Carcavelos, fortified in the manner of a Sherry or Madeira, are described as "agreeable, with a pleasant nutty aroma; a much older wine had great body and a pronounced almondy flavour; while an even more ancient sample . . . powerful and concentrated had developed the characteristics of a fine old Madeira."

There were a number of sweet fortified wines produced on the south bank of the Tagus where Moscatel was planted around Azeitão and Palmela near Setúbal and the Bastardo grape grew at Lavradio, near Barreiro. The latter vines have now been completely extinguished by concrete, but in the 1870s Vizetelly describes vineyards that "extend almost from the shore for some half-a-dozen miles [9.6 kilometres] inland, occupying all the low sandy slopes and occasionally the plains". Known by the affectionate diminutive Bastardinho ("little bastard"), the last grapes from Lavradio and the nearby Costa da Caparica were harvested in 1963. Lisbon wines, apparently widely drunk in England during the early part of the nineteenth century "by city men at lunch", declined from fashion. "Rich" and "Dry Lisbon" were still listed by Hedges & Butler at 42 shillings a dozen in 1893.

The fashion for Bucelas continued through most of the nineteeth century, and by the 1870s there was no longer any need to fortify the wine before shipment. Vizetelly tasted "Bucellas wines in endless variety", some of which were pale and fresh, others more pronounced and even slightly pungent in taste, and yet more wines "mellowed and developed by great age". Indeed, Vizetelly's visit took place three years after the foundation of the International Exhibition Cooperative Wine Society at the Albert Hall, London. Now known simply as "The Wine Society", this – one of the most long standing and respected of all British retail wine merchants – was established when "a committee of gentlemen", led by Major General Henry Scott (architect of the Albert Hall), decided to sell themselves a number of pipes of Bucelas at the end of the International Exhibition of 1874. The Society continued to sell "Bucellas" at 19 shillings a dozen until it was finally delisted in 1886.

The pamphlet entitled *Breve Noticia da Viticultura Portugueza* that accompanied the International Exhibition provides a revealing contemporary snapshot of the Portuguese wine trade. Total production amounted to 3.7 million hectolitres, of which around 400,000 hectolitres were exported. The structure of the country's land holdings was much as it is today, with the majority of producers making between two and six hectolitres a year, the wines being purchased by private merchants or negociates in the ports of Lisbon, Figueira de Foz and Oporto. The wines of the Douro were still classified in much the same way as they had been in Pombal's era, and the categorization of wines into first, second, third and sometimes fourth class extended into other regions of the country.

The phenomenal growth in sales that Madeira had experienced during the Napoleonic wars proved to be short lived. The *estufas* on the island continued to be abused and wine masquerading as Madeira was shipped from the Azores, Tenerife, Sicily and even from as far as the Cape of Good Hope. Exports to the United States of America fell dramatically in the 1820s and were wiped out completely in 1861 with the outbreak of the American Civil War. The merchants, heavily taxed by the authorities, ceased to buy from the growers and the greater proportion of the 100,000 islanders (reliant on wine for their living) suffered dire poverty. In the mid-nineteenth century Madeira experienced almost total destruction when two virulent diseases ravaged Europe's vineyards. The island's wine trade and that of many other regions of Portugal never fully recovered.

DISEASE, DISASTER AND OPPORTUNITY

Oidium tuckeri, better known as powdery mildew, was first identified in the United States in 1834. It reached Europe in 1845, when it was detected in Mr Tucker's garden at Margate in Kent. The disease attacks the leaves of a vine, causing a fine, powdery white growth to form around the spot where the fungus first penetrates. It then goes on to infect the stems, and the leaves eventually wither and fall to the ground. Oidium was first noticed in Portugal near Régua in 1848, imparting "a strange bitter flavour" to the wines. It spread rapidly, reaching Bairrada in 1851 and Madeira the following year. There was no known cure and within four years vineyard yields in certain parts of the country fell to almost nothing. Some grape varieties were more susceptible than others, the American variety Isabella, for example, being almost completely resistant whereas most traditional *vitis vinifera* varieties invariably succumbed. Growers in the Bairrada region opted for the Baga grape, which resisted oidium, and enjoyed a brief flicker of prosperity while the economy collapsed around them. The Alentejo, Carcavelos and parts of the Dão region were almost completely wiped out. Oidium is at its most virulent in a warm, humid environment and Madeira's subtropical climate proved to be the perfect place for its propagation. The island's monocrop economy was quickly ruined and nearly half the population left. The men that remained were employed in building the new road, the Estrada Monumental, that links Funchal with Câmara de Lobos, and more than a thousand women were engaged in embroidery. Many farmers abandoned viticulture for sugar cane. A remedy was discovered in 1854 by the same Mr Tucker who had identified oidium at the outset. Vines were dusted with sulphur, which brought the disease under control. Vineyards were replanted, often with a greater proportion of disease-resistant varieties such as Isabella, which understandably proved popular with growers even if they did nothing to benefit the quality of Portuguese wines over the longer term.

The advent of the steamship and a growing interest in the plants and botany of other continents meant that hitherto unknown pests and diseases took hold in Europe. By far the most devastating from a viticultural point of view was phylloxera. This tiny yellow aphid was discovered in a greenhouse at Hammersmith, London, in 1863, and within ten years it had spread throughout Europe feeding on the roots of European vines. Phylloxera reached the north of Portugal in 1868, its dispersal accelerated by the construction of the railways. The impact was not as immediate as that of oidium, but over two or three seasons yields began to fall and the vines eventually withered and died. Phylloxera was noticed on Madeira in 1873, and Henry Vizetelly, visiting the island four years later, at the height of the epidemic, describes the extraordinary lengths that some growers went to in an effort to save their vineyards. He found Thomas Leacock, who owned a vineyard at São João behind Funchal, painting the roots of his vines with "a kind of varnish". On the mainland the Baron Roeda of Quinta da Roeda in the Douro had tried "phosphate of lime, coal tar, sulphate of potash, natural magnesia, and sulphate of carbon, all being applied to the roots of the vines but with little effect". An unnamed British wine merchant visiting the Douro in 1874 compared the effects of the plague "to the nature of that which destroyed potatoes in Ireland". Reliant on just one crop, the populace appealed for divine intercession just to enable them to survive.

Phylloxera took longer to reach central and southern Portugal, where in the interim growers prospered greatly from the misfortune of others. They were helped unwittingly by the minister of agriculture, Joaquim António de Aguiar, who in 1865 had greatly liberalized the trade in wine, overturning many of Pombal's measures from a century earlier. Phylloxera only found its way to Dão in 1881 and Bairrada in 1883, by which time both regions were selling their wines to France through the port of Figueira da Foz at hugely inflated prices. The Dão region also made large quantities of *jeropiga* to supplement the catastrophic shortfall in the Douro. As a consequence Port shipments were not even dented by phylloxera and exports continued to increase throughout the 1870s, reaching 60,000 pipes (330,000 hectolitres) in 1880 as the supply of wine from other countries dried up.

In central-southern Portugal, producers in Colares and Estremadura seem to have shipped large quantities of wine to France, no doubt to augment the miserable volumes of Bordeaux and Burgundy being produced at the time. Vizetelly, seemingly no fan of the French, records a visit to a grower in Colares whose wines had risen in price from £10 to £16 a pipe (550 litres) in just nine months. He adds that "it would surely be better for us to import them direct, instead of receiving them through France, after they have been emasculated by mixture with the undrinkable *vins verts* of our enterprising French neighbours". Before phylloxera, France had barely registered as a market for Portuguese wine, but by the late 1880s was buying up nearly a million hectolitres a year.

RESTOCKING AND REPLANTING

With its vineyards deeply rooted below the sand, Colares remained blissfully immune from the effects of phylloxera (see page 175), and by the time the plague had worked its way to southern Portugal a solution had been found. The American vines that had, in all probability, carried the phylloxera aphid to Europe in the first place were found to be largely resistant to the pest. The grapes from these species are not suited for winemaking in their own right, as they produce wines with off-putting musky or wild strawberry-like aromas and flavours. However, it was established that by grafting the European *Vitis vinifera* onto rootstock from *Vitis aestivalis, rupestris* or *riparia* from the east coast of North America, native grape varieties could be enabled to survive and indeed flourish.

The restocking and replanting of Portuguese vineyards proved to be painfully slow and erratic. The Visconde de Chanceleiros, who owned a property near Alenquer in Estremadura, is credited with introducing the first American rootstock to Portugal at the end of the 1870s. But the Portuguese government prohibited the importation of American vines for a time, still believing them to be the cause of oidium rather than a cure for phylloxera. In their haste to replant, many growers merely restocked their vineyards with high-yielding *vinifera* varieties. Planted on their own rootstocks, they immediately succumbed once more to phylloxera. Some clandestine replanting on American rootstock undoubtedly took place, for example at Quinta da Boa Vista, which in 1880 became the first grafted vineyard in the Douro. Following pressure from both growers and shippers, the ban on American rootstocks was lifted in 1883 and replanting began in earnest. Nurseries were established throughout the country to propagate and distribute American rootstock. But even as late as 1896, in a detailed manual on viticulture in the Douro and the north of Portugal, Visconde Vilarinho de São Romão still recommends flooding the vineyards as a means of controlling phylloxera.

In much of the country, smaller growers took the shortest route back to normal production. Isabella (*Vitis labrusca*), Jacquet and Cunningham (both of which are *aestivalis* and *vinifera* hybrids) were found to resist disease and produce large quantities of grapes. Whole tracts of land were replanted with so-called direct producers and/or hybrids, most growers happy that high yields more than made up for the poor quality of the wine. In local *tascas* or taverns throughout the land, people became accustomed to drinking *americano*, sometimes known as *morangueiro* because of its sickly resemblance to wild strawberries. Besides being uniquely unpleasant to drink, wines made from these American hybrids contain a substance known as *malvina* (anthocyanin diglucoside). Rumours circulated that it was carcinogenic, and it is still held, somewhat jokingly, that *malvina* is the cause of mental deficiency in remote Portuguese villages, although this has never been proved. As a result of these scares the European Union has banned the bottling of wines made from American hybrids and direct producers. Both the Port Wine Institute (IVP) and the Madeira Wine Institute (IVM) regularly test wines in their laboratories to ensure that *vinho americano* does not enter the final blend. But despite government incentives to replant, a significant amount of vineyard on the north side of Madeira is still peppered with direct producers and hybrids. When one visits a farmer both on Madeira and in the north of Portugal, it is still far from uncommon to be presented with a glass of local *morangueiro* or *vinho americano*.

UNREST AND UPHEAVAL

The slow but steady return to pre-phylloxera levels of production in the rest of Europe led to a sharp decline in demand for Portuguese wines. Visconde Vilarinho de São Romão remarked ruefully that "the Bairrada region, which a short time ago was so prosperous thanks to its puissant vineyards, is today completely devastated". For growers in the Dão who had come to rely totally on wine, the collapse in the market brought severe hardship. At a crisis meeting in Viseu on January 10, 1901 a leading grower announced that "we are penniless. Soon we shall have to pay our tithes to the State in wine, not money." Likewise in the 1890s, wines from the Lisbon region fell from fashion, Brazil being the only international market of any great worth. The crisis in the vineyards was depicted graphically in a series of devastating cartoons by Rafael Bordalo Pinheiro spanning the period from 1879 to 1901. One dated 1882 depicts Portugal as a vine sucked into debt by phylloxera in the person of Henry Burnay, a leading banker and industrialist at the time. Another dating from January 1901 shows vineyard owners expiring from hunger whereas those who have planted cereals are wealthy.

The hardship in the north of the country was aggravated by a production imbalance in the south. In the wake of phylloxera, Estremadura and the Ribatejo were replanted with productive *vinifera* grapes, especially white varieties like Seara Nova, Vital, Jampal and Fernão Pires, to make wine for distillation. Every major quinta in central-southern Portugal was equipped with its own still for making *águardente*, which found a ready market with Port producers in the Douro. At the same time genuine Port was also being undermined by wines masquerading as "Port" from other sources including Tarragona (Spain), California, Australia and southern Portugal. In the spring of 1901 the Portuguese government announced that it intended to subsidize wines from the *Companhia Vinicola do Sul de Portugal*, a measure which received short shrift from hard-pressed growers all over the north and was eventually dropped. In the same year

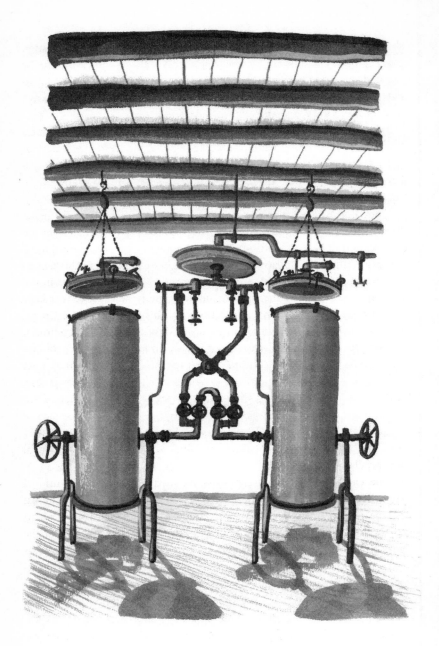

A traditional still in the Ribatejo

shipments of both Port and Madeira were further hit by the Russian government's decision to double the rate of duty, which eventually reached the equivalent of £60 a pipe (550 litres). As the production of Portuguese wines rose to seven million hectolitres in 1908, the opportunity for fraud increased and exports fell.

In a somewhat belated attempt to protect the authenticity of wines from Portugal's historic wine-producing regions, the short-lived dictatorial government of João Franco (1907–8) followed the example set by Pombal and proposed the demarcation of Carcavelos, Colares, Dão, Setúbal and Vinho Verde. The boundaries of the Douro region were also redefined, and it was established that any wine with the right to the name "Port" had to be shipped either across the bar of the Douro or from the new seaport of Leixões north of Oporto. But these measures proved to be the swansong of an increasingly unstable regime and much of the legislation was delayed or, in the case of the proposed regions of Borba in the Alentejo and Fuzeta in the Algarve, never properly enacted. A year later King Carlos I was assassinated together with his eldest son, the Crown Prince Luís Filipe, as they rode into the Terreiro do Paço in the centre of Lisbon. It was the one and only regicide in eight centuries of the Portuguese monarchy. The throne passed to Carlos's second son Manuel ("the unfortunate"), who at the age of eighteen was in no position to cope with the political infighting. The unpopular João Franco was forced from office but it was too late to save the Portuguese throne. In the face of a mutiny by the navy in 1910, Manuel II abdicated and left quietly from the beach at Ericeira bound for London. On October 5, Portugal was proclaimed a republic.

The early republican governments pursued a radical constitutional and social agenda but continued to follow the previous monarchist regime in demarcating wine regions. Bucelas and Madeira were added to the list of regions in 1911 and 1913 respectively, and a year later the government of Bernadino Machado set up a credit fund to help growers establish local cooperatives (see below). These well-intentioned liberal gestures were, however, quickly overwhelmed by political chaos. In a country used to *personalismo*, the new democratic republic lacked a strong leader and Portugal became impossible to govern. As strikes and riots broke out in Oporto, the anti-clericalism which took hold among Lisbon's liberal élite merely served to alienate the deeply Catholic rural populace of northern Portugal. One government followed another. The regional commissions established by João Franco to oversee the wine trade in the new demarcated regions were powerless, and legislation introduced to protect growers was impossible to enforce in the unstable political climate.

The situation was further undermined by the outbreak of the First World War. Fearing that the African colonies would become mere bargaining pawns among the combatants, Portugal joined the war on the side of the Allies in 1916. This caused a little local difficulty in Funchal, where the Germans had become the main customers for Madeira wine and had established a number of successful businesses on the island. When Portugal entered the war, all German assets were seized. However, with submarines prowling the Atlantic, wine exports collapsed. Despite these hazards and the loss of what remained of the Russian market in 1917, Port enjoyed a minor boom. The tax on spirits was raised in Britain to the extent that many people gave up whisky or gin for a glass of Port. A drink called "Port and Lemon" (a shot of Ruby made into a long drink by the addition of fizzy lemonade) became the everyday drink in pubs throughout the land. Shipments to the UK alone reached 70,000 pipes.

On the other hand, the effect of the war on Portugal's fragile economy was catastrophic. The escudo, valued at 4 shillings in 1917, fell to 2s 10d a year later. As prices rose there were repeated strikes. In 1919 the railwaymen went on strike for two months, followed by metalworkers, civil servants, tramwaymen, seamen, printers and electrical workers. The Port shippers were hit by successive rises in the price of fortifying spirit, which increased from 300 escudos a pipe (550 litres) in 1918 to 1,600 escudos in 1922. In the meantime the boatmen on the Douro, the lodgemen and the coopers walked out on strike demanding a fifty per cent pay rise. In spite of a succession of wage increases, by 1920 prices had increased by a multiple of twelve on 1910, whereas over the same period the wage index rose by just four-and-a-half. The situation was especially acute in the armed forces and in 1925 they rose in rebellion on three occasions. When the conspirators defended their action in court with a bitter attack on the conduct of the civilian politicians, they were acquitted. On May 28, 1926 General Gomes da Costa led a march on Lisbon from Braga in the north and the so-called First Republic collapsed. In the sixteen years since the fall of the monarchy there had been no fewer than forty-nine different administrations and sixty-nine ministers of agriculture.

WINE AND SALAZAR

For a time under the military, the economic and political instability continued as before. Republican budgets were creative in the extreme and the 1925–6 deficit, thought to be 63,000 contos, turned out to be over five times greater (one conto equalled a thousand escudos). Portugal had amassed a huge war debt in the UK which, despite intense negotiations with Winston Churchill, could not be paid. A revolt broke out in Oporto in February 1927, during which the local correspondent of the London-based *Wine Trade Review* reported on a bombardment "as good as any I've heard on the Western Front". Amid the turmoil it is surprising that the government found time to draw up the boundaries of a bonded *entreposto* (entrepôt) in Vila Nova de Gaia through which all Port wine destined for export had to be shipped.

Such was the despair at the seemingly irreparable condition of the economy that no one took much notice when the demure son of a Dão smallholder, Dr António de Oliveira Salazar, was appointed minister of finance in 1928. He had briefly been elected as a deputy for the city of Guimarães in 1921, but having no great respect for the banter of democratic politics, he returned to an academic post at Coimbra University, where one of his theses covered the production of wheat. Salazar accepted the post of finance minister on condition that he had complete control of the purse strings. On being sworn in, he declared ominously, "I know quite well what I want and where I am going . . . when the time comes to give orders I shall expect it [the country] to obey." By pruning expenditure and raising new taxes, Salazar managed to transform the nation's finances, turning the massive deficit into a budgetary surplus in his first year. As a result of these measures Portugal survived the 1929–31 depression virtually unscathed and, in recognition of his growing power, Salazar was appointed president of the council (prime minister) in 1932. Although the prime minister could technically be dismissed by the president of the republic, Salazar wielded so much power that he ruled as virtual dictator for thirty-six years.

Salazar was not interested in party political games and his new constitution, the *Estado Novo* (new state), created a unitary corporate regime with a one-party National Assembly and tiers of bureaucratic *federações* (federations) and *grémios* (guilds). Seeking a remedy for Portugal's external trade deficit, Salazar began to reform Portuguese agriculture with a series of campaigns to increase the production of wheat from 1929 onwards. The Alentejo region was, according to the *Estado Novo* slogan, to be "the granary of Portugal". Vines were uprooted and cereals took their place.

In 1933, the same year as the *Estado Novo* came into being, the government embarked upon a new regulatory regime for the wine industry. A series of *Federações dos Vinicultores* (Federations of Wine Producers) were established to oversee winemaking in Portugal. They were given a wide-ranging brief that included taxation and regulation of the market and the creation of cooperative wineries. The same decree established the *Grémio do Comércio de Exportação de Vinho* (Wine Exporters' Guild), whose task was to create new markets for Portuguese wines abroad. Many wine producers were in dire need of new markets, having lost Brazil (one of the most lucrative) after the revolution in 1930 when the new leader, Getúlio Vargas, issued an embargo on all wine imports. Colares, a popular wine in Brazil at the time, was badly affected.

The Port trade became subject to its own corporate institutions. Based in Oporto, the *Instituto do Vinho do Porto* (Port Wine Institute, or IVP) became the senior body, with responsibility for the overall supervision of the industry and a particular interest in the day-to-day business of the Gaia *entreposto*. The *Casa do Douro* was set up as a secondary though immensely powerful body, with overall regulatory responsibility for the 30,000 growers within the demarcated region. In order to balance the equation, all Port shippers had to belong to the *Grémio dos Exportadores do Vinho do Porto* (Port Wine Exporters' Guild), to which the IVP granted the Certificates of Origin that accompanied shipments overseas.

In 1937 Salazar's regulatory regime was further reinforced by the creation of the *Junta Nacional do Vinho* (JNV). Based in Lisbon, this all-powerful institution took precedence over all the previously created federations except for those in Vinho Verde, Dão and the Douro, which retained their quasi-independent status. The entire Portuguese wine industry became subject to a series of bureaucratic *selos de garantia* (seals

The Junta Nacional do Vinho, Torres Vedras

of guarantee), which were awarded to wines that met the standards required by their respective federations or the JNV. Apart from one or two politically inspired alterations to the nomenclature, all these institutions remain largely intact in the post-Salazar era.

THE MARCH OF THE COOPERATIVES

The need to coordinate certain aspects of Portuguese viniculture was first recognized in the crisis that followed in the wake of phylloxera. In 1895 the first *Adega Social* (winery association) was established in Viana do Alentejo. The need for such associations was even greater in the north of the country, where the fragmentation of holdings was more acute, and in the late 1890s a number of leading landowners in the Dão region established agricultural syndicates at Nelas and Tazem. Other associations followed, including the *Adega Regional de Coimbra* and the *Associação Vinicola de Bairrada*, which were amalgamated in 1905 to form the *Real Companhia Central Vinicola de Portugal*. However, in spite of numerous appeals for government support, these remained stand-alone organizations throughout the financial crises and political instability of the early twentieth century.

With the advent of the *Estado Novo* in the 1930s, the state began to take a more proactive role. The first *Adega Cooperativa* (cooperative winery) was founded at Colares in 1931, followed by another at Muge in the Ribatejo in 1935, but initially the programme was slow to make an impact. In 1947 the JNV calculated that ninety per cent of Portugal's 330 thousand wine producers were still turning out fewer than ten pipes (5,500 litres) of wine apiece. The cooperative movement only gained momentum after the Second World War, when the minister of finance, Ulisses Cortes, gave the go-ahead for a far reaching plan for a network of over a hundred cooperative wineries with a total production capacity of two million hectolitres of wine. Taxes were levied on wine to help support the programme.

During the 1950s and 1960s cooperatives were built all over Portugal, but mainly in the countryside north of the Tagus dominated by small-holdings. The cooperatives were mostly built to a similar, state-approved plan and were furnished with the most modern equipment available at the time. The cooperativization of Portuguese wines was not accepted unconditionally. As early as 1950 the *Federação dos Viticultores do Dão* warned of the danger of creating cooperatives in areas where the quality of wines was inconsistent, adding that by standardizing the wines they would be "neither good nor bad, but mediocre". In the event the majority of cooperatives produced wines that were at best mediocre and in many cases completely undrinkable. In Dão and Colares, then two of Portugal's leading wine regions, laws were passed to protect the cooperatives from private competition, effectively handing them a monopoly on winemaking in their respective regions. The cooperatives had a captive market, not just in mainland Portugal, which under Salazar shunned nearly all imported goods, but also in the African colonies, particularly Angola and Mozambique, which became important outlets for Portuguese wine.

Consequently there was little incentive to produce quality wine, and by the end of the 1960s Portugal's introspective cooperatives were already looking outdated. Divorced from the winemaking process, farmers lost the incentive to grow quality grapes and small wine producers closed their cellar doors. As wines became increasingly standardized, even the *négociant* firms based around Lisbon and Oporto were driven to buy large quantities from the cooperatives. Although the co-ops may have brought about an improvement in the quality of wine at the most basic level, the overall standard of Portuguese wine undoubtedly deteriorated.

WAR AND ROSÉ

On the outbreak of war in 1939, the *Estado Novo* was at its zenith. Having isolated the country from the earlier civil conflict in Spain, Salazar declared neutrality and avoided being sucked into the vortex of world war. Madeira was the only part of Portuguese territory threatened by German invasion, and gun placements were built around the coast at Praia Formosa and Doca do Caracas near Funchal and at Ribeira da Janela. Compared to the remainder of Europe, the Portuguese enjoyed a quiet but by no means uneventful war. Lisbon became a hotbed of espionage and Portugal supplied wolfram to the Germans from mines near Quinta do Vesúvio in the Douro Superior. In 1943 the British briefly toyed with the idea of invading the Azores but, in the spirit of the Treaty of Windsor and sensing an Allied victory, Salazar granted the use of the islands for a naval base.

With Port shipments at their lowest level ever recorded (just 11,000 pipes/60,500 hectolitres in 1942), the country was awash with wine. Sensing an opportunity that was too good to miss, Fernando Van Zeller Guedes decided along with a group of friends to establish a new company to export wine to Brazil. Inspired by the spritzy Vinho Verde that was already well known in the ex-Portuguese colony, Guedes dreamed up a new wine with the same slight sparkle but pink and medium-sweet in style. Commercial production began in a rented winery on the northern margins of the Douro, near the baroque palace of Mateus. The wine was by no means an instant success, but in the years that followed the war, Mateus Rosé and a number of lookalikes captured the imagination of a new generation of wine drinkers. The wine came to be sourced from a number of different regions: the Douro, Estremadura and latterly Bairrada, bringing a certain amount of prosperity to hard-pressed growers in these regions. Sogrape, the company formed in the darkest days of the Second World War, is still controlled by the Guedes family and is now Portugal's largest wine producer. The story of Mateus and its sibling Lancers is taken up in Chapter 7.

Immediately after the war, the Port shippers fully expected a rapid recovery similar to that which followed the First World War. They were sorely disappointed when even a duo of outstanding vintages – 1945 and 1947 – failed to rekindle the interest of the traditional British market. With the fashion turning against fortified wines, Madeira was similarly blighted and exports never recovered their pre-war levels. Scandinavia was the most important market for quality Madeira, but France began to take increasing volumes of bargain-basement wine in bulk for cooking. As grapes lost their appeal, farmers in some of the best locations on the south side of the island uprooted their vines and planted bananas.

The post-war slump in Port sales meant that many shippers fell on hard times. They were not helped by the sudden imposition of the so-called *Lei do Terço* (Law of a Third) in 1960, which obliged all Port shippers to maintain a three-to-one stock ratio. Shippers fell over each other in the rush to acquire the necessary stock, some being forced to sell treasured quintas whereas others decided to merge in order to survive. During the course of the 1960s the structure of the Port trade began to change shape, with multinational-owned firms (Cockburn, Croft, Delaforce and Sandeman) competing alongside ever larger family-owned groups (Taylor-Fonseca, Barros Almeida and the Symington family's houses of Dow, Graham and Warre).

SALAZAR'S DEMISE

In 1961 the Portuguese enclave of Goa on the Indian sub-continent was invaded by Indian troops. It was a bitter blow to Salazar, who viewed the *ultramar* (overseas possessions) with both personal and national pride. This was followed by rebel insurgency in Angola, Mozambique and Guinea-Bissau, which during the 1960s developed into a full-scale colonial war. At home in Portugal, the rural economy began to suffer a breakdown as the young and able-bodied left to fight in the colonies or emigrated overseas to avoid military service. Between 1961 and 1974 1.5 million Portuguese found employment abroad. The north was especially badly hit and, facing an acute shortage of manpower, many wine producers were forced to abandon the time-honoured method of foot-treading grapes in stone *lagares* (see page 191). The exceptional, universally declared 1963 vintage was almost certainly the last to have been entirely foot-trodden. For many shippers it was commercially the most successful vintage since the war, and for some since the great post-phylloxera year of 1896. It marked the start of a slow but sustained revival in the Port trade.

In Lisbon, the 1960s became the era of grand projects but few political gestures. In May 1961 President Americo Tomás opened Portugal's first short stretch of motorway connecting the capital with Vila Franca de Xira (following the same route as the first railway a century earlier). But because the economy was being bled by the colonial wars, the motorway network went little further for another twenty-five years. In 1966 a bridge was built across the Tagus connecting Lisbon with the south side of the river. Originally named the Ponte Salazar in honour of the septuagenarian dictator, it led to the rapid urbanization of the country around Almada and Barreiro that had once supported vineyards. Likewise, the remaining vineyards around Carcavelos were swallowed up as Lisbon expanded westwards along the so-called *marginal* toward Estoril. In the Douro a project was drawn up to build a series of monumental dams, the first of which was completed at Carrapatelo, upstream from Oporto, in 1971.

Salazar himself became incapacitated in 1968, supposedly when his deckchair collapsed beneath him, but the regime dragged on. He was replaced by another economist, Professor Marcelo Caetano, but for the remaining twenty months of his life Salazar continued to receive ministers fully believing that he was still in office. Caetano began to liberalize the regime, but his reforms were insufficient to satisfy the younger officers in the armed forces, who believed increasingly in a negotiated political rather than military solution to the long-running colonial wars. On the morning of April 25, 1974 there was little resistance and much jubilation in the streets of Lisbon when the Armed Forces Movement (MFA) took over the capital and both Tomás and Caetano were bundled off Madeira en route to exile in Brazil. The *Estado Novo* collapsed amid much jubilation.

REVOLUTION

The military coup itself was a typically Portuguese affair, good-natured with little bloodletting. Red carnations were placed in the barrels of guns and, apart from the lifting of political censorship, in the immediate aftermath of the coup life continued much as it had before. At first it seemed as though the new military junta would do no more than tinker with the existing institutions. Salazar's cherished *grémios* were abolished and a commission was set up to liquidate the *Casa do Douro*, which was viewed as a political instrument of the old regime. But apart from a few new faces in key positions as a result of the post-revolutionary *saneamento* (purge), business continued unabated through the summer following the coup.

However, the 1974 vintage took place amid political chaos, when President António Spinola, the charismatic, monocled general who had taken office just five months before, resigned, warning the Portuguese people of a "new slavery". During the winter of 1974 and throughout most of 1975 left-wing officers in the armed forces, many of whom had learned their politics from the African liberation movements, sought to turn Portugal into a Marxist state. This culminated in the so-called *Verão Quente* ("Hot Summer"), when the ostensibly democratic revolution ran completely out of control.

The country divided along socio-religious lines. The rural north, populated by deeply conservative and Catholic smallholders, grew increasingly at odds with the largely atheist, revolutionary south. Much of the economy fell into state ownership when the banks and insurance companies were nationalized in March 1975. Although only one wine-producing company, Borges & Irmão, was directly affected, the huge private estates in the Alentejo became collective farms and firms throughout the country were occupied as their workers marched in and took control. Foreign assets were largely untouched, but there were well-founded rumours in August 1975 that the entire Port trade was on the brink of being nationalized.

The backlash that began in the north of the country in the autumn of 1975 briefly threatened to precipitate a civil war, with the Ribatejo town of Rio Maior, astride the main Lisbon–Oporto road, setting itself up on the front line. Another confused bid for power by the extreme left on November 25, 1975 was used by the political mainstream as an excuse to reassert authority. It paved the way for the country's first genuinely free elections, won by the moderate, pro-European Socialist Party. But the political bickering had reduced the economy to tatters. Many Portuguese wine producers lost their most important market overnight when the

African colonies gained their independence and descended into civil war. Cooperatives in Estremadura were reduced to selling wine in bulk to the Soviet Union for a fraction of an escudo a litre. Interest rates were high and foreign investment was lacking, leaving little scope for growers or winemakers to improve their lot.

WINE AND EUROPE

Portugal's economic saviour came in the form of the European Union (EU). In spite of much well-intentioned plain speaking after the revolution, little had been done to reform Portugal's sclerotic institutions, which still bore Salazar's hallmark. The long overdue demarcation of Bairrada and the politically inspired promotion of the Algarve to *Região Demarcada* status in 1979 were the only gestures proffered to the wine industry by the new regime. A succession of governments expended most of their energy on self-preservation.

On joining what was then the European Community in 1986, the Portuguese government was forced to embark on a series of measures to liberalize domestic trade. The *Junta Nacional do Vinho* immediately mutated into the *Instituto da Vinha e do Vinho* (IVV), a similarly bureaucratic body but with a rather more user-friendly name. Monopolies in Dão and Colares that had been established by the *Estado Novo* in the interests of promoting the cooperative ideal were overturned, and growers in the Douro won back the right to export Port wine without having to ship their product through the bonded *entreposto* (entrepôt) in Vila Nova de Gaia.

Portugal's wine legislation was thoroughly reformed, bringing it into line with that of other European countries. Between 1989 and 2000 a string of decrees brought the somewhat sporadic network of *Regiões Demarcadas* (Demarcated Regions) into a new four-tier system matching that of France, Spain and Italy. Initially the system was the source of much confusion, with VQPRDs, RDs, DOCs and IPRs satisfying Portugal's love for acronyms. There were also some silly irregularities, such as the boundaries between regions running through the middle of vineyards and the case of Torres (Vedras), which briefly challenged the legitimacy of the much more famous Torres (family), well-established wine producers in Spain. Putting aside doubts about the geographical integrity of some of the new regions, the system has settled down and *Denominação de Origem Controlada* (DOC), *Indicação de Proveniência Regulamentada* (IPR), *Vinho Regional* and *Vinho de Mesa* are now an established part of the Portuguese lexicon. The relative status and significance of each of these categories is covered in more detail in Chapter 2.

More significant than any of these reforms has been the huge amount of investment lavished on Portugal's infrastructure since the country became part of the EU. At first the funding seemed somewhat slow in coming, and at the end of the 1980s Portugal's pot-holed roads and ailing telephone system were worse than they had been two decades earlier. But by the mid-1990s Portugal was receiving more in EU grants and loans per capita than any other member state. The impact on the landscape has been dramatic. Dual carriageways carve their way across mountains where once there were only cart tracks, and electricity pylons march alongside. Whereas it used to be quicker to send a letter than to make a telephone call, Portugal now has a telecommunications system that functions more efficiently than most. Isolated villages, charming but anachronistic, have been plucked from the Dark Ages and admitted into the twenty-first century. As immigrant families returned to the villages they abandoned in the 1960s, anomalous little houses have sprung up all over northern Portugal whose architectural styles derive from France, Germany and Switzerland, where many of their occupants spent the intervening years. The effect of all this investment has been to bring rural Portugal in touch with the towns and cities on the coast. Journey times have been slashed by more than half, and vineyard regions like the Douro, Dão and Alentejo are now effectively a day's commute from Oporto or Lisbon rather than an overnight stopover. In spite of this, however, rural depopulation has continued and the cities on the coastal *litoral* have mushroomed at a frightening pace.

European funds have served to transform the wine industry. From one vintage to the next, dingy concrete wineries have been replaced by shiny stainless steel accompanied by temperature control, and cooperatives whose only outlet was sale in bulk have been furnished with bottling lines. Between 1994 and 1999 a total of 109 million contos (approximately £40 million, or €64 million) was spent on modernizing wineries, of which roughly half came in the form of European grants. Less has been spent in the vineyards, where the transformation has necessarily been slower. Just short of 29 million contos (£12 million, or €20 million) was shared between 16,000 hectares over the five years between 1994 and 1999, mainly in Trás-os-Montes, Ribatejo and Estremadura. Growers have spent a decade and a half rediscovering grape varieties that were effectively lost in the haphazard approach to planting in times past. Clonal selection, canopy management and mechanization are still in their infancy, but at least they have entered the lexicon of a new generation of academics and growers, whose awareness is more international and far less isolationist than that of their parents or grandparents. Although the former colonies of Angola, Mozambique, Guinea-Bissau and even Brazil still weigh heavily on the Portuguese conscience, over a twenty-year period Portugal has turned her hand from running an overseas empire to playing an active role in Brussels and Europe.

FROM SINGLE QUINTA TO CULT WINE

Perhaps the most promising trend to accompany Portugal's entry into Europe has been the rise of the single estate or quinta. Spurred on by the relaxation of state bureaucracy and the ready availability of capital, growing numbers of enterprising growers are cutting their ties with the local cooperative in order to make and market wines in their own right. Although many still lack know-how and direction, the advance of the single quinta has reintroduced diversity into a sector that had become all too depressingly standardized during the second half of the twentieth century. Small has thankfully become beautiful once more.

But the triumph of the single quinta reflects a more profound socio-economic transformation in modern-day Portugal. Until as recently as the 1980s Portugal was almost without an urban middle class. With the influx of Euro-funds and the steady migration of rural dwellers to the towns, the Portuguese middle class has grown at a phenomenal rate. In the space of just over ten years the traditional *tasca* or tavern selling wine in five-litre *garafões* has largely been replaced by a large out-of-town supermarket. Where a ruddy-faced peasant once marched home with a *garafão* of wine balanced on his or (more likely) her head, today's Portuguese family is more likely to fill the trolley with wine and drive home at breakneck speed in the latest "hot hatch". In the suburbs of Lisbon and Oporto, wine is seen as one of the new aspirational trappings of middle-class life. Each of the main supermarket chains runs an annual *feira do vinho*, with glossy brochures to educate their customers about wine. Portugal's only dedicated wine magazine, *Revista de Vinhos*, has proved to be a huge success, with a circulation matching that of international titles. But in one respect Portugal's insularity remains undiluted. There is almost no demand for wine produced outside Portugal. French, Italian, Australian, even Spanish wines are noticeably absent from the shelves of Portuguese shops and supermarkets. This puts huge pressure on Portugal's leading wine producers, whose wines often fetch unrealistically high prices. Wines like Barca Velha, Quinta do Côtto Grande Escolha, Niepoort's Batuta, Quinta do Vale Meão and Pera Manca have acquired cult status in Portugal, even though they are relatively unknown elsewhere. While British wine drinkers flock to continental Europe on the so-called "booze cruise", it is by no means unknown for their Portuguese counterparts to travel in the opposite direction to find Portugal's leading wines on sale in London at a lower price than in Lisbon.

THE WINES OF PORTUGAL IN THE TWENTY-FIRST CENTURY

At the outset of the twenty-first century, Portugal lays claim to a total of 238,000 hectares of vineyard split among 300,000 growers. Between 1995 and 2001 Portugal produced an average of seven million hectolitres of wine a year, with yields fluctuating wildly from 9.7 million hectolitres in 1996 down to just 3.7 million hectolitres in 1998. Including Port and Madeira, this makes Portugal the tenth largest wine producer in the world and the sixth largest in the EU.

Of Portugal's total wine production fifty-eight per cent is red or rosé and forty-two per cent is white. Around forty-eight per cent of Portuguese wine is produced by thirty-two delimited VQPRD regions (the DOCs and IPRs shown on Map 1, page 56). Twenty per cent qualifies as *Vinho Regional* (Regional Wine; see Map 2, page 58) and the remaining thirty-two per cent of production is declassified as *Vinho de Mesa* or Table Wine. Twenty-two per cent of Portugal's wine production is fortified. In spite of the rise of the single estate or quinta, forty-five per cent of Portugal's wine is still produced by around one hundred cooperative wineries. Over half the country's *Vinho de Mesa* is produced by the cooperative sector.

Between 1995 and 2001 wine exports averaged 1.8 million hectolitres per annum (just under a third of Portugal's total production). In terms of volume, the principal export markets in order of importance are Angola, France, the United Kingdom, Germany and the USA. Of these, the United Kingdom is the most important in terms of value. Worldwide sales of Port reached around ten million cases (900,000 hectolitres) in the late 1990s, with France, Holland, Belgium-Luxembourg, the United Kingdom and Germany as the top five markets in volume terms. Exports of Madeira remain static at around 330,000 cases (30,000 hectolitres), with France still by far the largest market. Germany, the United Kingdom, Japan and the USA complete the top five.

As regards wine consumption, Portugal has always been a thirsty nation, consuming around fifty-two litres per capita per annum. This puts the Portuguese in fourth place on the world league table just behind Luxembourg, France and Italy. They used to vie for first place but, as is the case with other wine-producing nations, per capita consumption in Portugal has halved since 1965. "Drink less but better" seems to be the promising Portuguese maxim at the start of the twenty-first century.

2

Vines, Vineyards and Vintages

Body parts and animals, facial expressions and romance are common themes in Portugal's vineyards. "Lady's finger", "cockerel's heart", "tail of the cat", "dog strangler", "fly droppings" and "love-don't-leave-me" are all either officially recognized names or synonyms for different Portuguese grape varieties. No wonder that in the foreword to my earlier book, *Portugal's Wines and Wine Makers*, Hugh Johnson chose to describe Portugal as "a Site of Special Scientific and Sensuous Interest".

Geography and history have conspired together to cause Portuguese vineyards to develop in almost total isolation from the rest of the world. With the Atlantic to one side and an often adversarial neighbour to the other, Portugal has evolved as a viticultural island on the edge of Europe. Few grapes have made the journey across Iberia, and apart from the recent and perhaps inevitable incursion of a handful of global varieties (Cabernet Sauvignon, Merlot and Chardonnay spring quickly to mind), the Portuguese have proudly tended their vineyards with a disposition akin to secrecy.

Within the country itself, little pockets of vineyard have developed seemingly in complete isolation from each other. Although neighbouring parishes often cultivated the same or similar grape varieties, they christened them with different names. A number of quixotic and sometimes mystical synonyms often lead you to the same variety, causing any amount of confusion in the quest to identify individual grapes. Rabo de Ovelha ("tail of the ewe"), Rabo de Carneiro ("tail of the sheep") and Rabigato ("tail of the cat") are thus names given to the same grape planted in different parts of the country. The wry amusement brought on by these names quickly gives way to intense frustration when you come to study

Portuguese wine, for Portugal's vines, grapes and vineyards are not only unknown to outsiders, but in many cases are still *terra incognita* to the growers themselves.

ANARCHY IN THE VINEYARD

For as long as anyone can recall, Portuguese vineyards have been set out in a haphazard fashion, with numerous different grape varieties cohabiting on the same small plot. For growers eking a living from these tiny parcels of vineyard, the interplanting of numerous different grape varieties must have seemed like a good insurance policy after the double whammy of oidium and phylloxera (see pages 29–31). A variety susceptible to, say, uneven flowering could be offset by another, more resistant grape that might however be prone to rot. In this way, even in Portugal's unpredictable climate, growers could assure themselves of a reasonable crop of grapes in all but the direst of years. As early as 1531, a writer named Ruy Fernandes observed that "if some varieties fail to yield well in a particular year the others would compensate".

Although a number of authorities like Ruy Fernandes and Rebello da Fonseca have commented on individual Portuguese varieties, it wasn't until the mid-nineteenth century that the first of many attempts was made to list and categorize the principal Portuguese grapes. With Port having been an important export commodity since the seventeenth century, it is not surprising that much of the research focused on the Douro. In 1853, Baron Forrester complained that "an infinite number of different wines could be produced in the Douro if only there could be a separation of grape varieties". The situation was shortly compounded by the phylloxera epidemic, during which a number of the more troublesome European *vinifera* varieties were probably driven to extinction. Writing in 1876, when phylloxera was at its height, the Visconde de Vila Maior lists a total of twenty-eight grapes commonly planted in the Douro at the time, including Pé-agudo ("pointed foot") and Entreverde ("green-between"), both of which have long since left the local lexicon. Others, like the Tinta Castelloa (probably Castelão), Tinto Cão, Mureto (Moreto), Touriga and Tinta Amarella (Trincadeira) are still widely planted either in the Douro or elsewhere in Portugal, but Vila Maior adds a proviso which is still valid today: "It must be borne in mind that the same kinds [of

Vineyard anarchy: Vinho Verde

grapes] are known in different places by different names; and what still more thwarts the study of ampelography, is that the same name is often used in different places to denote very dissimilar kinds. To avoid any confusion and mistakes that might arise from this species of anarchy, the best plan would be to verify their synonymes [*sic*], by giving a complete description of all the kinds cultivated – an investigation quite indispensable in making a methodical classification; – yet we are still far from seeing this undertaking realized."

   This daunting undertaking was almost realized at the very end of the nineteenth century by Professor Bernardino Cincinnato da Costa (1866–1930). His thorough survey of Portugal's vineyards was written up in both Portuguese and French and published in a heavy, handsome tome entitled *O Portugal Vinicola* (*Le Portugal Vinicole*) for the Paris Exhibition in 1900. The book is illustrated with a series of detailed botanical watercolours by Alfredo Roque Gameiro depicting the principal grape varieties of the day. These include Arinto, Moscatel de Setúbal, Roupeiro, João de Santarém, Sousão, Ramisco, Tinto Cão and Touriga Nacional, all of which are still significant to a greater or lesser extent a century later.

Cincinnato da Costa's authoritative work has never really been equalled, but he was followed by Pedro Bravo and Duarte d'Oliveira, who travelled the country and in a manual entitled *Viticultura Moderna* (1916) listed the names of 900 grape varieties growing in Portuguese vineyards. Bravo and Oliveira readily admit that many of these are the same varieties with different names and complain, like Forrester over half a century before, about the lack of research to date. On Madeira and throughout much of mainland Portugal, the picture was further complicated post-phylloxera by the widespread use of direct producers and hybrids intended for use as rootstock. These were planted in their own right among various vines of the European *Vitis vinifera* genus, and Portugal descended into a state of viticultural anarchy.

REGAINING CONTROL

Portugal's turbulent early twentieth-century politics meant that little was undertaken in the vineyards until the Salazar regime gained a grip on the country in the 1930s. Isolated attempts at varietal research were pursued by Port shippers in the Douro, but it was not until the *Junta Nacional do Vinho* (JNV) was formed in 1937 that a coordinated approach became apparent. In the dark days of the Second World War, against a background of falling prices and over-production, the JNV began drawing up a *cadastro* (register) of Portuguese vineyards. The introduction to the two lengthy preparatory volumes published in 1942 rather sums up the spirit of the age. Representing the Federation of Wine Producers in the Centre and South of Portugal, Albano Castro Homem de Melo triumphantly declares: "We trust . . . that our determination will not slow the rhythm of our march ahead. At the end there is victory."

If there was a victory it was Pyrrhic in the extreme. Although the *cadastro* was eventually completed, it did little either to advance or clarify the situation in Portuguese vineyards. In fact the postwar march toward cooperativization proved to be a huge step in reverse. Putting quantity before quality, in the 1960s and early 1970s Professor José Leão Ferreira de Almeida of the *Estação de Agronomia Nacional* at Oeiras near Lisbon developed a series of hybrid grapes with less than promising names like Vaca Leiteira ("milk cow") and Carrega Burros ("load-the-donkeys"). These varieties were widely distributed throughout Estremadura, the Ribatejo and Dão, where growers delivering consignments of grapes to the new generation of cooperative wineries were paid by weight rather than quality. Without any varietal separation, high-yielding hybrids were simply mixed with traditional varieties and the quality of wines from the Dão region in particular took a significant turn for the worse.

The revolution of 1974–5 brought the cooperative programme to a halt and when democracy was restored in 1976 Portugal's much weakened economy was in no position to finance improvements either in the winery or the vineyard. However, the first coordinated attempt at varietal research was undertaken privately in the Douro during the 1970s. After five years of intensive investigation led by José Rosas and João Nicolau de Almeida of Port shippers Ramos Pinto, five red varieties were selected in 1981 and promoted as the leading grapes in the region. Touriga Nacional, Touriga Francesa, Tinta Barroca, Tinta Roriz and Tinto Cão became known as the *top cinco* and 2,500 hectares of these varieties (mostly Touriga Francesa and Tinta Roriz) were subsequently batch planted in single varietal plots under the so-called PDRTIM or World Bank Scheme of the 1980s.

The rest of the country had to await the arrival of the EU. Immediately prior to Portugal's accession in 1986, the Ministry of Agriculture drew up a list of "authorized" and "recommended" grapes for each and every demarcated region. This included some strange anomalies but it represented a significant step toward regaining control of Portugal's chaotic vineyards. At much the same time, Professor P Truel of the Viticultural Research Station at Montpellier in France undertook the first thorough research into Portuguese grape varieties and their synonyms since Cincinnato da Costa's *obra mestre* almost a century earlier. Once the funds began to flow in from Brussels, priority was given to weeding out the direct producers and hybrids and replacing them with approved European stock. Madeira faced the greatest challenge. At the end of the

1980s over half the island's output originated from direct producers. Most of the wine was still masquerading as Sercial, Verdelho, Bual and Malvasia, yet these noble grapes made up just six per cent of total production. Although this situation has improved considerably, Madeira is still hampered by the lack of an accurate or up-to-date *cadastro* (register) of the island's vineyards.

On the mainland, the varietal planting that took place in the Douro in the 1980s has been gradually emulated elsewhere. A few growers in central and southern Portugal have flirted with international varieties like Cabernet and Chardonnay, but, apart from in the Ribatejo, where there is something of an historical precedent for these grapes, they have made few inroads. Although the Portuguese retain a considerable amount of pride in their own grapes, this does not stem exclusively from xenophobia. The varietal experiments conducted in the 1970s and 1980s have revealed some high-quality grape varieties that have been adopted just as enthusiastically by foreign growers as the Portuguese themselves. During the 1990s a sufficient area of vineyard was replanted for winemakers to consider making varietal wines from indigenous grapes. When the Portuguese Trade Office (ICEP) in London proposed to organize the first ever tasting of Portuguese varietal wines in 1997, this was met with a certain amount of resistance and misunderstanding. However, varietal fever is highly contagious and so many producers have subsequently jumped onto the varietal bandwagon that in the Douro and Dão in particular it has begun to be detrimental to some of the time-honoured regional blends. On the other hand, the move toward varietal labelling has recreated an awareness of Portugal's unique indigenous grapes. For anyone suffering from a condition termed ABC ("Anything But Chardonnay"– interchangeable with "Anything But Cabernet"), Portugal is a useful country to turn to.

DOC, IPR, VINHO REGIONAL AND VINHO DE MESA

It has taken nearly 250 years for Portugal to establish a workable matrix of wine regions. Pombal started the process when he drew a boundary around the Douro in 1755, and it has continued in fits and starts ever since. Ten regions were demarcated between 1908 and 1979, but most Portuguese wines continued to be sold without any regional identity. The

Key to numbers
DOC / IPR ⃰

1 Vinho Verde
2 Chaves⃰
3 Valpaços⃰
4 Planalto Mirandês⃰
5 Porto/Douro
6 Távora-Varosa
7 Lafões
8 Bairrada
9 Dão
10 Beira Interior
11 Encostas de Aire⃰
12 Alcobaça⃰
13 Lourinhã
14 Óbidos
15 Alenquer
16 Arruda
17 Torres Vedras
18 Bucelas
19 Carcavelos
20 Colares
21 Ribatejo
22 Setúbal
23 Palmela
24 Alentejo
25 Lagos
26 Portimão
27 Lagoa
28 Tavira

DOC/IPR

merchant firms who scoured the country for wine blended and bottled their finest as *garrafeiras*, a category that put their own private brand names before either grape variety or provenance. Only when the Portuguese joined the ranks of the EU in 1986 were they given notice to change their ways, and over the following decade an entirely new pyramid of wine regions emerged.

At the apex of the pyramid is DOC (*Denominação de Origem Controlada*). Roughly equivalent in status to the French AOC, this is a category of delimited wine regions with prescribed maximum yields, grape varieties, minimum alcohol levels and (sometimes) ageing requirements. In order to qualify, every region must have its own Regional Commission drawn from among the wine producers and growers. The list of DOCs continues to lengthen, but it includes all the former *Regiões Demarcadas* (Demarcated Regions) as well as a growing number that have been promoted from the tier of IPRs immediately below. The acronym IPR stands for *Indicação de Proveniência Regulamentada*, an intermediate category of wine regions which parallels the French VDQS. The rules and regulations are just as prescriptive as for DOC, but those IPRs that remain are left out in the cold because they still lack a Regional Commission. Often they are simply too small to justify a bureaucracy of their own and some of the regions that were awarded IPR status in the early 1990s have either merged or faded away. Reflecting Portugal's love of acronyms, the DOCs and IPRs are collectively known in bureaucratic terms as VQPRDs (*Vinho de Qualidade Produzido em Região Determinada*). See map on facing page. For a map of Madeira, see page 284.

Beneath IPR in the hierarchy is an important category entitled *Vinho Regional*. This is equivalent in status to the French *Vin de Pays* but is accorded rather more significance, particularly by producers in the south of the country, as it gives them considerably more leeway than either DOC or IPR. Apart from a remote corner of northern Portugal, the entire country is divided into eight large provincial regions (see map overleaf). Winemakers are permitted to blend wines from anywhere within these regions and from just about any grape. Whereas the DOCs tend to limit themselves to native local varieties in an attempt to protect much-vaunted *tipicidade* (typicity), the *Vinhos Regionais* permit all manner of grapes, including a large number of international varieties. Finally, underpinning the entire pyramid is a category common to every EU

Key to numbers
Vinho Regional
(Regional Wines)

1 Minho
2 Trás-os-Montes
3 Beiras
4 Ribatejano
5 Estremadura
6 Alentejano
7 Terras do Sado
8 Algarve

Regional wines

country: Table Wine or *Vinho de Mesa*. In Portugal, which is no different from anywhere else, the date of vintage, grape variety or geographic provenance is not permitted on the label of *Vinho de Mesa*, which, apart from the name of the bottler, is merely an anonymous blend.

The control of Portugal's wine sector (with the exception of Port and Madeira) is the remit of the *Instituto da Vinha e do Vinho* (IVV). Based in Lisbon, but with offices throughout the country, the IVV is, in its own words, responsible for "wine policy making, managing the domestic wine heritage and seeing to the application of the instruments required to increase the competitiveness of Portuguese wines". It is also responsible for maintaining and updating the national vineyard register, ensuring compliance with legislation, "vine planning and improvement", regulation of the market, control and certification of the DOCs, IPRs and Vinhos Regionais, professional training, promotion of wine on both the domestic and international market and the representation of the wine sector within the EU. Yes, the all-embracing IVV is just as bureaucratic as it sounds. The *Instituto do Vinho do Porto* (IVP) and *Instituto do Vinho da Madeira* (IVM) operate under similar remits. A list of the generic bodies responsible for controlling and promoting Portuguese wines can be found in Appendix II.

One area where the IVV has made useful progress is in the naming of individual grape varieties. In accordance with the International Code of Botanical Nomenclature and the International Code of Cultivated Plants, it has drawn up a list of permitted grapes, the names of which can appear on the labels of VQPRD and *Vinhos Regionais*. There are 341 varieties in total (including table grapes), the vast majority of which are indigenous to Portugal. The IVV's list goes a long way toward sorting out the age-old problem of regional synonyms. It identifies a principal name for each variety along with an officially recognized synonym where appropriate. In a few cases, for the sake of ensuring a gradual transition to the approved nomenclature, a second recognized synonym may be included. Other local synonyms are also listed, and although they continue to be used in the day-to-day lexicon, these names are no longer authorized for use on labels. One or two principal names have been altered. Touriga Francesa is now to be known officially as Touriga Franca and Castelão Francês (formerly known also as João de Santarém and Periquita) is now simply registered as Castelão.

The following directory of Portuguese grapes is based on the IVV's list. It is by no means exhaustive but includes all those varieties that are likely to be seen on labels or back labels as well some which winemakers would rather ignore but are still planted in large quantities in some parts of the country. Where a locally recognized synonym is still in use, this is cross-referenced with its officially approved name. The complete IVV list of approved grape varieties and their synonyms can be found in Appendix I.

Based on my experience of talking to growers and winemakers and tasting varietal wines over a period of nearly twenty years, I have drawn up a quality assessment as follows:

***** a grape variety with potential international status, outstanding in its own right or of major significance in a blend.
**** a grape capable of making very good wines both on its own or in a blend with other varieties.
*** a grape that is sometimes capable of making good wines in its own right but which is usually improved by blending with other varieties.
** a grape that has its uses in blends but is not particularly good as a varietal.
* an unexciting variety that may be capable of better.
no stars: beyond the pale.

International varieties are awarded stars according to their performance to date in Portugal rather than in their global context. Where possible I have included a recommended varietal wine for the benefit of anyone seeking a good example of a particular grape variety.

I. Red grape varieties

ÁGUA SANTA*

"Holy water" is a relatively new hybrid of Preto Mortágua and Castelão. It has proved to be useful in the Beiras (especially Bairrada and Beira Litoral), where the Água Santa's loose bunches resist rot. It also resists oidium, ripens early, yields well and is capable of high levels of alcohol, but I have never had an opportunity to sample a varietal wine.

ALFROCHEIRO ****

One of the most promising grapes in the Dão region (where it was also known colloquially as Pé do Rato or "mouse paw"), Alfrocheiro is found as far afield as the Alentejo, Ribatejo and Bairrada. It was introduced to the region after phylloxera, but this vigorous variety with a high susceptibility to disease (especially oidium and grey rot) is therefore not as popular with growers as the quality of the wine might suggest. However, it yields reasonably well, ripens early and produces grapes with good sugar and acid balance. Wines made from Alfrocheiro tend to be deep in colour with dense, fine-grained tannins and lively blackberry aromas and flavours if not overoaked. It is often referred to as Alfrocheiro Preto ("black Alfrocheiro").
Recommended varietal wines: Quinta dos Roques, Alfrocheiro Preto (Dão); Herdade do Peso, Alfrocheiro (Vinho Regional Alentejano)

ALICANTE BOUSCHET **/***

There used to be a swathe of Alicante Bouschet in southern France, but along with the much less inspiring Aramon much of it was uprooted in the 1980s and replaced by the so-called *cépages améliorateurs*. In Portugal there have long been significant pockets of Alicante in the Alentejo, particularly in the old vineyards around Borba and Portalegre, where it was often interplanted with Grand Noir (qv). When Portalegre became an IPR in 1989, it came as something of a surprise to find that both Alicante Bouschet and Grand Noir were actually listed as "recommended" varieties, *tipicidade* (typicity) being the byword used by the authorities at the time. However, during the 1990s Alicante Bouschet began to prove its worth. Perhaps the clearest demonstration of this is the dramatic change in the style of Quinta do Carmo (see page 273), which became emasculated once Alicante had been excluded from the blend. Although no one would ever credit Alicante Bouschet with finesse, this red-fleshed variety does contribute both structure and colour. The wines start out inky-black and remain that way for years to come, developing a powerful rustic character which is the hallmark of the best Alentejano reds from old, dry-farmed vineyards. Alicante is also known rather appropriately by the name of Tinta de Escrever ("writing ink"). Now that growers are sensing its worth in a blend (although not really as a varietal), Alicante Bouschet is making a welcome comeback to parts of the Alentejo, whereas in the vineyards of Mouchão (page 279) thankfully it never left.

ALVARELHÃO*

In the mid-nineteenth century Joseph James Forrester lavished praise on Alvarelhão, a variety formerly much planted on the *altos* (high plateau) north of the Douro. It may have been suitable for his brand of unfortified Port wine, but it has certainly fallen from favour today. There were two varieties of Alvarelhão, distinguished by Vila Maior as Pé Roxo ("purple foot") or Pé de Perdiz ("partridge foot") and Pé Branco ("white foot") or Pé Verde ("green foot"). Evidently the Pé Roxo was considered superior. The distinction seems to have been lost, for the Alvarelhão planted around Vila Real and Trás-os-Montes today produces light, pale-red wines which represent something of a transition between Vinho Verde and the Douro. Mateus Rosé, which used to be sourced entirely from this area, contained a high percentage of Alvarelhão. The grape has fallen from favour, although it still exists in old mixed vineyards north of the Douro. Mondavi also have some Alvarelhão in their Woodbridge vineyard in California and use it to make their own Port-style fortified wine. Alvarelhão is thought to be the same as Brancelho, which is sometimes grown for red Vinho Verde.

AMARAL

Officially listed as Amaral, this grape is much better known by the name of Azal Tinto (or merely Azal). One of the principal grape varieties in red Vinho Verde, it is mainly planted around Amarante and Felgueiras, where it ripens with some difficulty to produce purple, acidic, mouth-puckering red wines for early drinking. Cincinnato da Costa equates Azal with Touriga, although he makes no distinction between Touriga Franca and Touriga Nacional (qv). In the Minho it has little chance of matching either.

AMOR-NÃO-ME-DEIXAS

I have never encountered this grape either in the vineyard or a wine, but it appears on the IVV's official list and the name ("love-don't-leave-me") is loaded with promise. On the other hand, maybe it is just a variety susceptible to poor fruit set!

AMOSTRINHA

Another grape that is better known by its synonym, Preto Martinho. Favoured by growers but disliked by winemakers, Preto Martinho is an easy variety to grow, but obstinate when it comes to producing good wine. In the nineteenth century it was widely cultivated in the fertile soils of the Ribatejo and Estremadura, particularly around Cartaxo, Santarém and Alenquer. Preto Martinho is still a recommended variety in Alenquer, Arruda, Cartaxo, Santarém and what is left of Carcavelos, but it has fallen from favour.

ARAGONEZ ****

Rioja's Tempranillo suffers from something of an identity crisis. It grows throughout Iberia under a multitude of different names: Ull de Llebre (Catalonia), Cencibel (La Mancha), Tinto de Toro (Toro) and Tinto del País and Tinto Fino (Ribera del Duero). Downstream in the Portuguese Douro it is known as Tinta Roriz, but in the Alentejo it acknowledges its Spanish heritage with the name Aragonez (although Cincinnato da Costa equates this with Garnacha). Growers in Estremadura recognize its potential as a heavy cropper and call it Abundante, the name now used in the Alentejo for Garnacha.

Although Aragonez/Tinta Roriz has been planted in the Douro since the early nineteenth century (presumably having been planted at Quinta do Roriz), it is not listed by Vila Maior as an important pre-phylloxera variety. Even Cincinnato da Costa identifies it as a grape belonging to the high vineyards of Trás-os-Montes (Alfandega de Fé, Macedo de Cavaleiros, Moncorvo and Vila Flor) rather than the Douro Valley. Helped by the replanting programme in the 1980s, Tinta Roriz is now the second most important grape variety for Port after Touriga Franca (qv), taking up about ten per cent of Douro vineyards.

Aragonez/Tinta Roriz is justifiably popular with growers as, compared to Touriga Nacional, it is a doddle to grow. It sprouts vertically and has a short vegetative cycle, flowering late, which reduces the risk of damage by spring frosts, and ripening early, thereby enabling picking before the onset of the worst autumn rains. Quality, however, can vary alarmingly. It performs best in those years where yields are inherently low, producing wines which combine tight, firm fruit with finesse and length but with a tendency to low levels of acidity. However, one grower in the Douro claims that Tinta Roriz only performs well two years in every ten! The wines resist oxidation and therefore respond well to ageing in new oak. However, as Tinta Roriz in the Douro, it is very sensitive to September rainfall, which rapidly leads to dilution of colour and strength. And in a year of naturally high yields like 1996, Roriz produces dull, weedy wines. It remains to be seen how, as Aragonez, it responds to widespread irrigation in the Alentejo.

Despite having been introduced as recently as the 1980s, Tinta Roriz has already become well established in the Dão region, where it is making wines of elegance and distinction rather than concentration and strength. It is also found under yet another set of names in California and Australia and, as Tempranillo, seems to be gaining ground as an international varietal.

Recommended varietal wines: Quinta do Crasto, Tinta Roriz (Douro); Esporão, Aragonez (Alentejo); Quinta dos Roques, Tinta Roriz (Dão)

Azal Tinto
see Amaral

BAGA **/****
Ex libris Bairrada, but also planted elsewhere in the Beiras and the northern part of Estremadura and Ribatejo, Baga made a strong comeback after phylloxera ravaged the area in the late nineteenth century. It currently makes up around fifty per cent of the red grape stock in Dão and as much as ninety per cent in Bairrada. Like many Portuguese grapes Baga is found under a number of different local guises: Baga de Louro, Tinta da Baga and Poeirinha ("small and dusty"). It yields a small grape, hence the name most commonly used is Baga ("berry"). Rather like the ubiquitous Castelão grape in the south of Portugal, Baga is capable of producing the best and worst of wines. It is a fairly vigorous variety and lent itself to stand-alone *taça* (gobelet) pruning. This method has gradually been abandoned in favour of training on wires, but owing to the variety's natural vigour there is a clear need for the most rudimentary canopy management techniques to be applied. Although Baga is resistant to oidium, it ripens late and has an alarming tendency to rot in the Atlantic climate of Portugal's western seaboard. In order to perform, Baga needs well-drained, sandy clay or limestone soils, not the heavy clay or shallow granite in which it is often planted. With a high ratio of skin to flesh, wines made exclusively from Baga can taste green and undrinkably astringent, a characteristic that is accentuated if the wine is fermented on the stalks. Some of

these wines are so numbingly astringent and tannic that they never have a chance to soften before the fruit fades away. No wonder "Baga" is sometimes spat out rather like the familiar English swear word with which it resonates! However, well-made Baga wines from a ripe year possess a deep colour with plenty of fresh, lively berry fruit and a leafy, hedgerow character before the tannin cuts in on the finish. A handful of growers in Bairrada are almost the only progenitors of such wines, which, to my way of thinking, do not take well to the fashion for using new wood. The best examples, all from Bairrada (and listed below), seem to last for ever.

Most Baga ends up in a very different style of wine: Mateus Rosé. Sogrape's principal winery is at Anadia in the Bairrada region, and Baga with its colour and natural astringency is ideally suited for making rosé with the minimum of skin contact (thereby overcoming some of the problems associated with rot). Baga occasionally makes some good red sparkling wine or *espumante*.

Recommended varietal wines: Quinta das Bágeiras, Garrafeira (Bairrada); Frei João, Reserva (cork label, Bairrada); Casa de Saima, Garrafeira (Bairrada); Luís Pato Vinha Pan (Vinho Regional Beiras)

BARCA **

This unfashionable grape has been relegated to the hot country of the Douro Superior, where it is usually known as Tinta de Barca. It produces a distinctive, concentrated style of wine and makes up around twenty-five per cent of the *vinha velha* (old vines) at Taylor's Quinta de Vargellas. I have not come across it anywhere else in Portugal although Tinta de Barca is sometimes confused with Touriga Franca.

BASTARDINHO ***

The "little bastard" is almost extinct, having been supplanted by concrete on the south bank of the Tagus around Lavradio and Moita. An unofficial sub-variety of Bastardo (see below), this productive, sugary variety used to be highly prized for making sweet fortified wine. José Maria da Fonseca is attempting to revive the tradition.

Recommended varietal wines: Bastardinho de Azeitão José Maria da Fonseca

BASTARDO TINTO */**

There are two officially recognized grapes with the name Bastardo: Bastardo Tinto and Bastardo Roxo. The latter, one suspects, is probably the Bastardinho ("little bastard"; see above). Bastardo Tinto is a vigorous, early-ripening variety that was favoured by growers in the Douro and Dão prior to phylloxera, where it was often planted alongside Alvarelhão (qv). Forrester singles it out for praise in his controversial pamphlet, *A Word or Two on Port Wine*, published in 1844. Bastardo's virtues must have made it popular with growers. According to Cincinnato da Costa, it ripened as early as June and the intensely sweet grapes were eaten during the popular festival of São João (June 25). Small amounts of Bastardo remain today in old mixed vineyards in the Douro and Dão, where its main characteristics seem to be high levels of sugar and low acidity. It produces wine with a pale red colour that fades to onion skin within two years, making it the ideal grape for inexpensive Tawny Port. However, Bastardo is extremely susceptible to rot in wet weather. It is also grown in tiny quantities on Madeira and Porto Santo, mostly in experimental vineyards. Here, Bastardo remains an officially "recommended" variety but low yields and its susceptibility to disease mean that it has lost favour with growers.

BONVEDRO

see Monvedro

BORRAÇAL

This vigorous variety climbs the trees, trellises and pergolas in north-west Portugal from Monção and Caminha all the way down the coastal belt to the outskirts of Oporto. It is extremely productive and is at best (in the words of Cincinnato da Costa) *uma casta neutra*, a neutral grape for blending with the other red varieties (Vinhão and Amaral) with which it is interplanted. Also known by the following local synonyms: Bogalhal, Cainho Grosso, Olho de Sapo ("toad's eye"), Esfarrapa and Murraçal.

BRANCELHO

Found in parts of the Minho, where it yields pale-coloured wines, Brancelho is thought to be the same as Alvarelhão (see above).

CABERNET SAUVIGNON ****

This global grape has found its way to Portugal, but is by no means as widespread as you might expect. With the notable exception of Palmela on the Setúbal Peninsula, Cabernet Sauvignon is effectively excluded from all of Portugal's DOCs and is still only permitted as Vinho Regional. From north to south, there are small pockets of Cabernet in the Minho and Beiras where, near the coast, it struggles to ripen and tends to produce a wine that is often unpleasantly green and harsh. Cabernet performs better inland and has been grown successfully in Trás-os-Montes and on the south side of the Douro (Terras Durienses). The variety is being grown successfully in Estremadura, where it is sometimes blended with native grape varieties, particularly Castelão. There are commercial quantities of Cabernet Sauvignon in the Ribatejo, particularly on the alluvial soils close to the river, where high yields tend to produce wines that are rather herbaceous in character, despite the southern warmth. Cabernet Sauvignon probably performs at its best on the gentle, north-facing slopes of the Arrabida hills in the Palmela region, where it is capable of producing ripe, minty wines tending toward the New World in style. By the time it reaches the Alentejo (where there are no more than a few isolated pockets), the variety loses definition and becomes jammy with the heat. There can be little doubt that Cabernet Sauvignon could perform well in Portugal provided it is planted on the correct site. But with the exception of Fiuza-Bright in the Ribatejo, it is mostly planted as a curiosity for the domestic market and most growers are reluctant to shun their indigenous grapes.

CALADOC **

A newcomer to Portugal, Caladoc is the result of the crossing of Grenache and Cot (Malbec). It yields well (up to seventy-five hl/ha) and the small berries resist botrytis, hence the interest in Estremadura, where trial vineyards have been planted. As might be expected from its parentage, Caladoc produces a dark, inky wine.

CÂMARATE *

There is a locality called Câmarate close to Lisbon airport that once produced a popular wine of the same name. It lent its name to a grape variety, also known by the synonym Castelão Nacional. Câmarate is now mainly planted on the Atlantic seaboard north of Lisbon, both in Estremadura and the Ribatejo as well as in Beira Litoral (Bairrada). Although this is not a red-fleshed *teinturier* variety, it produces similarly dark, black, aggressively tannic wines with a powerful streak of acidity. Consequently it is rarely (if ever) used to make varietal wines. Vilarinho de São Romão recounts how the grape was planted at Olivais (now a high-rise suburb of Lisbon) where it was known as Baldoeira. Other synonyms include Moreto de Soure and the racist Negro Mouro ("black Moor").

CANIÇA
see Cunningham

CARREGA BURROS
The "load-the-donkeys" grape appears on the IVV's official list of approved varieties with the intriguing synonym of Esgana Raposas ("fox strangler"). It was one of a number of high-yielding grapes developed in the 1960s by the *Estação Agronomica Nacional* at Oeiras and subsequently distributed throughout Estremadura and the Ribatejo. I have never come across anyone who admits to having this grape in their vineyard, but it doesn't sound promising.

CASTELÃO ***/****
Although it is better known to many as Periquita, the authorities have settled on Castelão as the principal name for this grape variety, which has long been planted under a variety of synonyms all over southern Portugal. It used to be known as Castelão Francês ("French" Castelão) and continues to suffer from something of an identity crisis, for it is also known as João de Santarém in the Ribatejo and Trincadeira or Trincadeiro in Estremadura (not to be confused with the Trincadeira Preta growing in the Ribatejo and Alentejo, which is completely different). To complete the picture, it also crops up as the Tinta Merousa in Santa Marta de Penaguião (Douro) and is thought to be the Bastardo Espanhol ("Spanish bastard") on Madeira, but there is no evidence to suggest that this grape is either French or Spanish in origin. A variety named Castelão Nacional is a synonym for Câmarate (qv).

Castelão performs at its best in the dry, sandy soils to the east of the Palmela DOC on the Setúbal Peninsula. It was here that it acquired its nickname when, in the mid-nineteenth century, José Maria da Fonseca planted cuttings of Castelão at Cova de Periquita ("parrot hollow") in the Arrábida foothills above Azeitão. This became the brand name for a wine which was so successful on the home market that the name attached itself to the grape (although Periquita the wine was never actually made exclusively from the "Periquita" grape). In his weighty tome *O Portugal Vinicola*, Cincinnato da Costa equates Periquita with João de Santarém, but lists Castelão Francês as a completely separate variety.

From a well-situated, low-yielding vineyard on the Setúbal Peninsula, Castelão produces firm but rarely powerful or intense red wines with a pronounced raspberry-like aroma, flavour (and astringency) when young. With age in wood and bottle, the wines gain in complexity, taking on a tar-like quality but never really losing their youthful aggression. It is a productive variety and therefore popular with growers. However, planted in damp or fertile land (and there is plenty of both in the Ribatejo and Estremadura) it tends to produce poor, emasculated wines with the character of underripe (and sometimes rotten) raspberries. Castelão is very susceptible to *coulure* and *millerandage*, and cool, wet weather is therefore damaging during flowering. Conversely, Castelão does not take to the hot, dry climate of the Alentejo. Palmela and the Terras do Sado region seem to provide a happy medium.

Recommended varietal wines: Pegos Claros (Palmela); Periquita Classico, José Maria da Fonseca (Terras do Sado)

CASTELÃO NACIONAL
see Câmarate

CINSAUT**
Planted in and among the old mixed vineyards of Portalegre in the northern Alentejo, Cinsaut does not command the respect it probably deserves. There are no varietal wines as yet, but this grape is undoubtedly responsible for the success of some of the wines in this region, which occasionally bear a resemblance to Châteauneuf-du-Pape – of which Cinsaut is frequently an important constituent.

CLINTON

A name more readily associated with a past US president, Clinton is an undistinguished American direct producer that was brought to Madeira following the onset of phylloxera and has now, thankfully, all but disappeared.

COMPLEXA*

Developed at the *Estação Agronomica Nacional* at Oeiras in the 1960s, Complexa earns its name by being a tetrahybrid of Castelão with Tintinha and Tintinha with Moscatel de Hamburgo. It was introduced to Madeira as an experimental alternative to Tinta Negra Mole, where it is classified as a "good" rather than "noble" grape. Complexa produces a darker and slightly less astringent wine than Negra Mole, and is planted mainly on the south side of the island around Calheta and on the north around São Jorge.

CORAÇÃO DO GALO

"Cockerel's heart" sounds like an intriguing grape that seems to have been lost in the old vineyards of Beiras, where it is still permitted for *Vinho Regional*.

CORNIFESTO

Once favoured by growers north of the Douro, this vigorous, productive variety is now found only in old interplanted vineyards throughout Trás-os-Montes, where it produces light, inconsequential red wines. The popularity of Cornifesto in the wake of phylloxera was probably due to its resistance to disease, especially oidium and anthracnose.

CUNNINGHAM

Often known in local parlance as Caniça, this direct producer was brought to Madeira for use as a phylloxera-resistant rootstock, but came to be planted in its own right. It is still grown extensively on Madeira, where its pale red juice was used as the basis for lighter Rainwater-style wines. Now that the EU forbids its use in bottled wines, Cunningham is either being uprooted and replaced by *vinifera* varieties or made into a pale red wine served by the glass in local *tascas* (taverns).

DELICIOSA

A variety officially authorized for Madeira wine, the "delicious" grape exists only in the government's experimental vineyards.

DOÇAL

The name of this grape, once known as Doçar, suggests sweetness. It is an extremely vigorous variety, really only suited to the high culture systems of north-west Portugal. Doçal is no longer planted, and is therefore only found in old mixed vineyards, particularly along the River Lima in the north of the Vinho Verde region – although I have never detected much in the way of sweetness or ripeness in the wines from this region. Doçal is also known as Folhal.

DONZELINHO

There are three officially recognized Donzelinhos: branco (white), roxo (purple) and tinto (pink). Donzelinho Tinto is occasionally found in old mixed vineyards in the Douro, where it resists oidium but produces poor yields and pale, thin wines.

ESPADEIRO*

This productive variety is found occasionally in the Vinho Verde region, but was one of the traditional grapes of the Vale de Sousa. It ripens with difficulty to produce a light, fragrant red wine, verging on rosé. Usually blended with other varieties, on its own Espadeiro makes a wine that has an affinity with underripe Pinot Noir. It has evidently been planted in the Minho for some time, for Vilarinho de São Romão identifies three variants of Espadeiro: Espadeiro do Basto, Espadeiro da Terra and Espadeiro Molle. The latter is now listed by the IVV as a distinct variety. Espadeiro was also planted in Carcavelos under the name of Torneiro. A different variety sometimes referred to as Espadeiro in the Lisbon region is the same as Trincadeira (qv).

FERRAL

No longer officially recognized or authorized, Ferral was planted for wine around Funchal, Seixal and Ponta Delgada on Madeira, where it now seems to have been relegated to the status of a table grape.

GRAND NOIR

This *teinturier* grape is often planted alongside Alicante Bouschet (qv) in old interplanted vineyards in the Alentejo. As a result it is inseparable, but Grand Noir is much the less distinguished of these two red-fleshed varieties, its chief attributes being productivity and resistance to spring frosts. It is hard to justify how this grape variety came to be among those "recommended" in the Alentejo sub-regions of Portalegre, Borba, Reguengos and Évora, other than the fact that it merely enshrines the status quo. In Estremadura, Grand Noir is known as Sousão (qv), but this appears to be the result of some confusion with a separate though similar grape. Grand Noir is also known rather appropriately as Sumo Tinto ("red juice").

HERBREMONT

Thought to have been brought to Madeira from Georgia on the eastern seaboard of America in the eighteenth century, Herbremont is a direct producer making undistinguished red wine.

ISABELLA

A wine known as *morangueiro* is still cherished by those who frequent the spit and sawdust *tascas* (taverns) on Madeira and in the rural north of mainland Portugal. *Morango* means "strawberry" and it aptly describes the penetrating, sickly aroma of wine made predominantly from the Isabella grape. A hybrid of *Vitis labrusca* and vini/era, Isabella was named after one Isabella Gibbs who cultivated the variety in her garden in Brooklyn, New York. It was introduced to Portugal from Africa in the 1840s and earned its keep when oidium reached Madeira a decade later. Despite being resistant to oidium, it is susceptible to rot and prone to attack by phylloxera. Nevertheless, it still survives ungrafted on Madeira and, with a vigorous growth habit and an insatiable thirst for water, it is well suited to the pergolas of north-west Portugal where it produces characteristically pale, acidic wine.

JACQUET

Virtually immune to phylloxera, Jacquet (or Jacquez) was introduced to Madeira in an attempt to boost yields in the 1870s. For a time it overtook all the well-known *vinifera* varieties on the island and became one of

Madeira's most planted grapes. Although its yields are fairly small, Jacquet ripens under the sub-tropical sun to produce rich, sugary musts that are naturally low in acidity. As with the other direct producers and hybrids growing on the island and in mainland Portugal (see Caniça, Clinton, Isabella, Herbremont), under EU legislation wine made from Jacquet can no longer be bottled and much is drunk locally. The *Instituto do Vinho da Madeira* (IVM) routinely tests wines destined for export for the presence of *malvina* (anthocyanin diglucoside), a constituent common to all wines made from American hybrids and direct producers.

JAEN**/***

Although Jaen is encountered in Galicia as Mencia, the Spanish-sounding name of this grape belies the fact that it does not seem to have Spanish origins. It is likely that Jaen originated in the Dão, where it is the second most widely planted grape variety after Baga. Jaen's popularity with growers is due to the fact that it yields well and ripens early, although it is not very resistant to mildew. It seems to perform best in Dão around Gouveia, Mangualde and Nelas, but in the more fertile soils around Silgueiros and Tondela it can produce thin, unattractive wines. Jaen produces wines with plenty of colour but low levels of acidity and generally needs bolstering with other varieties like Touriga Nacional or Alfrocheiro Preto. It does, however, contribute a certain amount of finesse to a blend and has proved its worth in Sogrape's Dão Novo, an early bottled red made like Beaujolais Nouveau by carbonic maceration.

Recommended varietal wines: Quinta dos Roques, Jaen (Dão); Quinta de Saes, Jaen (Dão)

JOÃO DE SANTARÉM
see Castelão

MALVASIA PRETA*
The name Malvasia is attached to so many Portuguese grapes, mostly white, that it is difficult to separate fact from fiction (see pages 101–3). No one ever talks about Malvasia Preta ("black Malvasia"), but it exists in old mixed vineyards in the Douro, where it is still the sixth most planted

variety, representing about four per cent of the total vine stock. In the Dão it is known confusingly as Moreto (qv).

MALVASIA ROXA
The red Malvasia is still on the list of recommended varieties for Madeira, but is now found only in experimental vineyards on the island and therefore for all intents and commercial purposes has ceased to exist.

MARUFO*
A grape with four synonyms: Mourisco Tinto (qv), Moroco, Uva de Rei and Olho de Rei.

MERLOT ***
Immensely fashionable in the United States, Merlot has made its way to southern Portugal where it is planted in commercial quantities in the Ribatejo, Estremadura and Terras do Sado. In hot conditions it produces wines that are jammy and over-alcoholic, but planted in the right place, Merlot is capable of making wines that combine richness and finesse.
Recommended varietal wine: Quinta de Cortezia, Merlot (Vinho Regional Estremadura)

MONVEDRO*
This productive variety is probably the same as Bonvedro, a grape that used to be grown around Lisbon (especially in Azeitão, Torres Vedras and Arruda) but has now fallen from favour. On the IVV's official register of grapes another variety, Tinta Caiada ("fallen red"), also has the synonym Monvedro.
Recommended varietal wine: João Portugal Ramos, Tinta Caiada (Vinho Regional Alentejano)

MORETO */**
This productive variety is still widely planted in the country south of the Tagus, especially in the Alentejo around Redondo and Reguengos, although it was apparently found in the north of Portugal in the late nineteenth century. This may, however, have been due to a confusion with Câmarate (qv), which is occasionally known as Moreto de Soure. Despite

the hot sunshine in southern Portugal, Moreto generally produces dull, emaciated wines and is useful (and even then only grudgingly) for carbonic maceration. But with low yields Moreto is clearly capable of something better. It is a major constituent in the remarkable wines of Granja-Amareleja (see page 269). Both Cincinnato da Costa and Vilarinho de São Romão consider that Moreto is the same as Blauer Portugieser in Germany. Confusingly, Moreto do Dão is a completely different grape (see Malvasia Preta).

MORTÁGUA
There is much confusion over the true identity of this variety, because it seems to be a synonym for a number of different Portuguese grapes. Thought at one time to be Ramisco, Mortágua is the local name for Castelão in Estremadura and for Touriga Nacional in Dão (where there is a town called Mortágua) and the Ribatejo. It is also known as Preto Mortágua ("black Mortágua").

MOSCATEL GALEGO ROXO (MOSCATEL ROXO) ****
Neither red nor white, the purple Moscatel is grown alongside its Muscat cousins in a few isolated pockets north of the Douro and at Azeitão on the Setúbal Peninsula. It was once more widespread, but as Cincinnato da Costa records, it is susceptible to attack by wasps as well as mildew and bunch rot. With a small, round, purple-pink berry it has a low yield of about a kilo per vine. When it comes to making wine, Moscatel Roxo (probably a mutation of Muscat à Petit Grains) is much superior to the Muscat of Alexandria planted throughout Portugal under a variety of different names (see Moscatel Graudo in the section on white grapes).
Recommended varietal wine: José Maria da Fonseca, Moscatel Roxo (Setúbal)

MOSCATEL GALEGO TINTO *
The red Muscat is occasionally found in old mixed vineyards in the Douro, especially around the town of Favaios, which is known locally for its Moscatel wines. Occasionally a hint of Muscat can be detected in a grower's Tawny Port, but in the larger lots put together by shippers any traces are invariably lost in blending.

MOURISCO*

Officially there are two red grapes by the name of Mourisco: Mourisco de Semente and Mourisco de Trevões. Either way, winemakers in the Douro tend to have a love-hate relationship with Mourisco, a variety that came to prominence in the nineteenth century owing to its resistance to phylloxera. The sentiment is mostly hate, for the pale, fat Mourisco resembles a table grape rather than a wine variety. It is difficult to pollinate and is therefore subject to poor fruit set unless it is interplanted in the old-fashioned way with other varieties. There are few instances where Mourisco crops up on its own, but it is found in old vineyards all over the Douro and therefore makes up around five per cent of the total vineyard area, making it the fifth most popular red variety in the region. Cockburn's are one of the few Mourisco fans and have a significant amount in their Vilariça vineyard. Although it produces pale-coloured wine, Mourisco is rich in sugar and therefore provides a good aromatic base for old Tawny Port. It is almost never seen as a varietal, even in the rarefied tasting rooms of Vila Nova de Gaia. Mourisco is also planted throughout Trás-os-Montes, where (along with Alvarelhão) it is the progenitor of semi-sweet rosé for export markets (see also Marufo).

NEGRÃO
see Sousão

NEVOEIRA

Meaning "misty", Nevoeira was a productive variety planted throughout the north of Portugal at the end of the nineteenth century. It also went under the name of Tinta dos Pobres ("red for the poor"), suggesting that quantity was more significant than quality. Cincinnato da Costa suggests that it may be the same grape as Tinta Caiada (see Monvedro).

PARREIRA MATIAS

Cincinnato da Costa devotes an entire page of his book to Parreira Matias, stating that it is "a good red variety, excellent for wine". It was planted throughout Estremadura, where it made a light, perfumed red wine in the style of *Clarete*. In spite of these attributes, Parreira Matias is now little more than a name on the IVV's official register, although it is still permitted for Vinho Regional.

PEDRAL
Sometimes spelt Padral, this grape is confined to the Monção area in the northernmost part of Portugal, where it produces little and suffers from poor fruit set.

PERIQUITA
see Castelão

PINOT NOIR
This fickle, finicky grape is hardly at home in Portugal. It is confined to two very different vineyards: one near Lamego south of the Douro, where it is used for sparkling wine, and another in the Ribatejo (Casa Cadaval), where it makes a ripe but rather lumpy red. Strangely enough, I came across a cask sample of red wine from São João de Pesquera in the Douro with a distinct Pinot Noir character – could this have anything to do with Tinta Francisca (qv)?

POEIRINHA
see Baga

PRETO MARTINHO
see Amostrinha

RABO DE OVELHA TINTO
see Trincadeira Preta

RAMISCO ****
Confined as it is to the shrinking vineyards of Colares, there is so little Ramisco remaining that one has to go back to the glory days of the nineteenth and early twentieth centuries to consider the qualities of this remarkable grape. Cincinnato da Costa lavishes praise on Ramisco, describing it as capable of making wines with "freshness, finesse, perfume, flavour and softness – lacking nothing". With its roots embedded in clay below a thick layer of protective sand, Ramisco resisted phylloxera in the nineteenth century and the few vines that remain are still ungrafted. But this unique grape variety is finding it much harder to resist the advance of Lisbon toward the Atlantic coast and only a handful

of gnarled old vines remain, producing minute quantities of small, thick-skinned grapes. The wines start out being hard and astringent and need time in bottle to reveal Ramisco's floral, blackcurrant fruit. Recent wine-making has sadly been a hindrance rather than a help, and within a few years Ramisco could be consigned to memory.

RUFETE*
This productive, early ripening grape still makes up a significant propor-tion of old mixed vineyards in the Douro, where it represents about one per cent of the total vine stock. Both in the Douro and in Beira Alta and Beira Baixa (where it is known as Tinta Pinheira or occasionally Penamacor), Rufete produces wines which lack colour, structure and vol-ume. Both Rebello de Fonseca and Vila Maior consider that Tinta Pinheira is the same as a French grape then grown in Sillery (Champagne) known as Pinot Aigret or Pinot Dru.

SEIBEL
Once grown widely in France, and in the cooler climates of New Zealand, Canada and England, Seibel is a hybrid which crops up occasionally on Madeira and the Azores.

SOUSÃO **
"The reddest grape cultivated in Portugal" is Cincinnato da Costa's open-ing line on the red-fleshed Sousão. It probably originated in the Minho, where it is known by the name of Vinhão, and spread to the Douro in the early eighteenth century. In 1791 Rebello de Fonseca described a detailed experiment in which he added three almudes (about seventy-six litres) of wine made from Sousão to a nine-pipe vat of pale wine and ended up with a "very lively coloured" blend. Nothing much has changed, for Sousão is still planted in old interplanted vineyards in the Douro, where it compensates for the lack of colour in varieties like Mourisco and Rufete (qv). Judging by its synonyms there would seem to be three variants: Sousão Forte ("strong Sousão"), Sousão de Comer ("eating Sousão") and Sousão Vermelho ("red Sousão"). Sousão would not deserve much in the way of an accolade but for its presence in Quinta do Noval's ungrafted Nacional vineyard, where in the past it made up to twenty-five per cent of the blend. The deep colouring matter that it lends to a wine is said by

some to be unstable, but anyone who has witnessed and tasted Noval's 1963 or 1966 Nacional will know this to be untrue. In the Minho, Vinhão is responsible for much of the rasping, inky-red Vinho Verde, especially in the Basto sub-region (where it was known as Espadeiro de Basto) and adjoining the country around Fafe, Lousada and Amarante. In the area around Monção it is known as Negrão, which at least hints at its depth of colour. It also crept into the Bairrada region, where for a time in the early twentieth century it held court with Baga. The combined tannic astringency of the two grapes must have been little short of unbearable. Sousão is also planted in South Africa and California, where one fortified wine producer described it to me as providing "colour, acid and more acid".

Recommended varietal wine: António Pires da Silva, red Vinho Verde made mostly from Vinhão (Sousão).

SYRAH ****

Australians in Portugal insist on calling it Shiraz, but the officially recognized name for this grape and the one that appears on the label is Syrah. It is a newcomer, even among the international grapes that have been planted in Portugal during the 1980s and 1990s. However, Syrah has quickly shot to stardom in the Ribatejo (where it was first planted at Quinta de Lagoalva) and subsequently in the Alentejo and Estremadura. Syrah in Portugal is something of a chameleon. In the arid soils of the Ribatejo and Alentejo it produces wines that resemble Australian Shiraz: big, burly and verging on brash. In cooler, maritime Estremadura (where so far there is only one small vineyard near Alenquer), it is producing wines with a refined, peppery character akin to the northern Rhône. Either way it seems from the trials that have taken place so far that Syrah has a big future in Portugal for those with the temerity to plant it. Sir Cliff Richard has even planted some on his property in the Algarve (see page 283). It has to be said that the authorities have been less than keen on Syrah, but it is a permitted grape for Vinho Regional wines in the Ribatejo and seems likely to be added to the growing list of grapes in the Alentejo, Estremadura and Algarve as well. A few pockets of Syrah have also been planted outside the law by a handful of adventurous growers in the Douro.

Recommended varietal wines: Incognito, Cortes de Cima (Vinho Regional Alentejano); Quinta de Monte d'Oiro (Vinho Regional Estremadura)

TANNAT**

Small quantities of this grape, which originates from south-west France, are planted on the Setúbal Peninsula. Tannat produces firm, raspberryish reds, similar in style to the native Castelão.

TINTA

There are numerous grapes in Portugal with the suffix Tinta/Tinto ("red"), with no fewer than twenty-two such vines on the IVV's official list. Some are mainstream grapes (see those listed below), but others (such as Tinta Tabuaço and Tinto Pegões) seem to be local varieties that have either been renamed or are extinct. Tinta, however, seems to be the official name for a grape called Tinta da Madeira, a variety that is sometimes confused with Tinta Negra Mole. Although Tinta da Madeira is still an officially recommended variety, there is very little remaining on the island that bears its name. In the past, the name Tinta was often corrupted by the English to "Tent".

TINTA AMARELA
see Trincadeira

TINTA DE BARCA
see Barca

TINTA BARROCA**

The third most planted grape variety in the Douro (after Touriga Franca and Tinta Roriz, qv), Tinta Barroca is favoured by growers for yielding large quantities of grapes with exceptionally high levels of sugar. As one of the "top five" varieties authorized for replanting under the PDRTIM or World Bank Scheme in the 1980s, Barroca is found mainly in the Cima Corgo, often at higher altitudes or on cooler, north-facing slopes where other varieties might face difficulty in ripening. With a thin skin, Barroca is easily damaged by extreme heat, and the berries have a tendency to raisinize or shrivel on the vine. On a south-facing slope – as at Dow's Quinta do Bomfim, where it accounts for a significant portion of the vineyard – Barroca will yield up to 2.5 kilograms (5.5 pounds) per vine at the same time as producing a must with a Baumé reading of up to 15 or 16 degrees. Barroca-based wines are typically deep in colour, supple and well structured, but with a distinctly rustic, earthy overtone. As a result it is almost never bottled as a varietal, and, to date, there is only one instance of Barroca being planted outside the Douro or Trás-os-Montes — at Alenquer in Estremadura. Formerly known by the names Boca da Mina ("mouth of the spring"), Tinta Grossa and Tinta Gorda ("fat red"), Tinta Barroca has made a successful foray into South Africa where it is used primarily for fortified wines.

TINTA CAIADA
see Monvedro

TINTA CARVALHA*
Still one of the most planted grapes in the Douro (ahead of Touriga Nacional), Tinta Carvalha is favoured by growers for its high yields and therefore makes up a significant proportion of older interplanted vineyards. Cincinnato da Costa records that it was much planted in the Cima Corgo between Pinhão and Tua, but as many of these vineyards have been replanted, it has lost ground in favour of Touriga Franca, Tinta Roriz and Tinta Barroca. The wine from Tinta Carvalha apparently has some good aromatic properties, but is generally pale and rather hollow.

TINTA FRANCISCA *
Not to be confused with Touriga Franca (formerly Francesa, qv), Tinta Francisca is thought to have originated in Burgundy as Pinot Noir. There are two stories as to its genesis, neither of which can be verified. One asserts that it came to Portugal in the eleventh century with Henry of Burgundy (see page 5), the other that it was brought from Burgundy by Robert Archibald, founder of Quinta do Roriz. It only survives today in old mixed vineyards in the Douro and Beira Alta and is not particularly highly thought of by growers.

TINTA GROSSA
The "fat red" grape survives in old mixed vineyards in Estremadura where it is permitted for Vinho Regional. There is also a significant quantity in the Baixo Alentejo around Vidigueira (see Tinta Barroca).

TINTA LISBOA
A grape which, somewhat perversely, used to grow around Funchal, capital of Madeira, and now seems to have been relegated to the status of a table grape.

TINTA MERANCÃ
Confined to Trás-os-Montes, this grape variety has been virtually extinguished as a result of the decline of viticulture in the region over the past century.

TINTA MIUDA **/***
This was one of the grapes found in the (now urbanized) vineyards around Lisbon at the turn of the twentieth century. It spread further afield to Torres Vedras, Arruda, Alenquer, Cartaxo, Almeirim, Coruche and Azeitão, but is now mainly found in Estremadura. Also known in the past as Tinta do Padre António, Tinta Miuda ("the small red one") is thought to be the same as Graciano in Spain. It ripens very late, tending to be up to 3 degrees Baumé behind Castelão, which is often planted alongside. As a result of the autumn rains, it is susceptible to rot, particularly in the Atlantic country west of the Serra do Montejunto (see page 163). In spite of this, Tinta Miuda is still valued by winemakers for the colour and acidity (7–9 grams/litre total acidity) that it contributes to a blend. The few varietal reds produced from Tinta Miuda tend to be dark and astringent.
Recommended varietal wine: JP Vinhos, Tinta Miuda (Estremadura)

TINTA NEGREDA
A Trásmontano grape variety cited by Cincinnato da Costa that seems to have been driven to extinction – unless, of course, it is none other than Tinta Negra Mole (see below).

TINTA NEGRA (MOLE) */**
Officially registered as Tinta Negra, this grape is usually referred to by its full name: Tinta Negra Mole (or sometimes merely as Negra Mole). Planted on Madeira and in the Algarve, it is still claimed by some that Tinta Negra Mole is related to Pinot Noir or Grenache. However, this does not seem to stand up to ampelographic scrutiny. Red grapes were being

grown on Madeira as far back as the seventeenth century, but there is no record of when Tinta Negra Mole was first introduced to the island. During the twentieth century it gained popularity both with growers, who appreciated its productivity, and winemakers, who favoured its versatility. Until the legislation changed in 1993 the vast majority of Madeira wine masquerading under the names Sercial, Verdelho, Bual/Boal and Malvasia was in fact made from the ubiquitous Tinta Negra Mole (or the now illegal direct producers). Such is its popularity that this chameleon of a grape now makes ninety per cent of all Madeira, ranging in style from dry through medium sweet to rich.

For many years Tinta Negra Mole was classified merely as a "good" variety, the term "noble" being reserved for the previously mentioned varieties along with Terrantez (see individual entries in the section on white grapes). Now Tinta Negra Mole is officially classified alongside the others as "recommended". Much has been planted in the 1990s to take the place of the so-called direct producers: Isabella, Jacquet, Cunningham and Herbremont (see separate entries). Compared with these, Tinta Negra Mole is a distinct improvement, being a *vinifera* grape which produces pale, pink-red base wines that quickly oxidize to a nut-brown colour during the *estufagem* process (see page 291). The grapes themselves are soft and fleshy (hence the name "Mole") and the musts are never particularly concentrated, registering Baumés of between 8 and 12 degrees depending on where the grapes are grown. Most Tinta Negra Mole is grown on the south side of the island, where the higher sugar readings favour the sweeter, richer styles of wine, but there is also some Tinta Negra Mole in the north at São Vicente.

It is possible that the grape known as Negra Mole in the Algarve is different from that in Madeira. However, it makes similarly pale, washed-out reds, the only distinction being that it achieves higher levels of alcohol.

TINTINHA

A grape apparently as diminutive and undistinguished as its name and still planted in Estremadura and permitted for Vinho Regional. It lives on in a complex hybrid grape planted on Madeira appropriately known as Complexa (qv).

TINTO CÃO ****/*****

"Red dog" is a somewhat demeaning name for one of the Douro's most fascinating grapes. It was apparently one of the grape varieties preferred by the English Port shippers when they began to colonize parts of the Cima Corgo in the mid-eighteenth century. Rebello de Fonseca mentions Francis Bearsley (an early partner in the Port shipping firm that subsequently became Taylor's) as one of the proponents of Tinto Cão, adding that he was prepared to pay an extraordinarily high price for it. The high price was a consequence of very low yields and, following phylloxera, Tinto Cão was almost driven to extinction by growers seeking production above all else. Thankfully, in the late 1970s it became one of the "top five" recommended varieties in the Douro and so began a modest revival, mostly at the behest of larger shippers, who are intrigued by its capacity to make dense, long-lasting wines as well as its ability to resist mildew and rot. Tinto Cão ripens late and needs the correct exposure to achieve the delicate balance of acidity and alcohol for which it is renowned. Apart from being a constituent (albeit a minor one) in the finest Ports, it is also being used for Douro wines, occasionally as a varietal. Small quantities are also planted in Dão, where it seems to perform well on the light granite soils. José Maria da Fonseca have also planted some on the Setúbal Peninsula. A few growers are experimenting with Tinto Cão in Australia and California. Tinto Cão is also known as Padeiro in the Basto sub-region of Vinho Verde and Tinta Mata.

Recommended varietal wine: Quinta da Gaivosa, Tinto Cão (Douro) Quinta dos Roques, Tinto Cão (Dão)

TINTA PINHEIRA
see Rufete

TINTA RORIZ
see Aragonez

TINTO NEGRO
An authorized variety on Madeira (not to be confused with Tinta Negra Mole, qv) that does not appear on the IVV's official list. Tinto Negro is thought to exist only in minute quantities on the island of Porto Santo, where it yields large amounts of sweet grapes.

TOURIGA FRANCA (FRANCESA) ***/****

There is a grape variety which growers outside Portugal identify merely as "Touriga". This is not usually Touriga Nacional, but the grape officially registered since July 2000 as Touriga Franca (but still much better known by its former name, Touriga Francesa). In Portugal Touriga Franca is largely confined to the Douro, where it is the most widely planted of all grape varieties, accounting for twenty per cent of the total vineyard area. The variety has only proliferated during the twentieth century. It was not even mentioned by Cincinnato da Costa, and speculation continues as to whether Touriga Franca is a recent mutation of Touriga Nacional or the result of a crossing with another variety. There are certainly a number of different clones, including the somewhat inferior Tinto Bragão which features in a number of Douro vineyards. Touriga Franca flourishes on warmer, south-facing slopes and is favoured by growers for relatively consistent, moderately high yields (roughly 2.5 kilograms/5.5 pounds per vine). Like many Douro varieties, it suffers from excess vigour and produces grapes with low sugar levels if yields are too high or the local climatic conditions are less than ideal. At high altitudes above the Douro, sugar levels sometimes struggle to reach 11 degrees Baumé. When it reaches the winery, Touriga Franca demands plenty of work to extract both colour and tannin from the relatively thick skins. Although by no means the most highly prized of the Port grapes (that accolade is reserved for Touriga Nacional), it is nevertheless respected by winemakers for its aromatic qualities, which lend a floral (some say "violety") character to the blend. Young Touriga Franca wine is more expressive than Touriga Nacional, but it seems unlikely that Franca can match Nacional for sheer weight, depth and longevity. Despite its name, there is no ampelographic evidence that Touriga Franca (alias Francesa) has any connection with France. Apart from in the tasting room, until the late 1990s Touriga Franca was never seen as a varietal. Early in the twenty-first century, it is slowly being disseminated from the Douro to regions as far flung as Bairrada, Estremadura, the Setúbal Peninsula and the Ribatejo. With the capacity to make good (if not yet great) wine and being relatively easy to grow, Touriga Franca looks set to become one of Portugal's leading red grapes.

TOURIGA NACIONAL *****

If ever Portugal became identified with a single grape in the way that Spain has with Tempranillo or Italy with Nebbiolo, that variety would be Touriga Nacional. If anything, Touriga Nacional has been most closely identified with Port, although it registers a lowly eighth on the list of the Douro's most planted red grape varieties and accounts for a mere two per cent of the region's vine stock. It is something of an affront to growers in the Douro to state that Touriga Nacional is thought to have originated in Dão, where, prior to phylloxera, it dominated the region's vineyards. It is sometimes known here as Preto Mortágua and there is a village in the heart of Dão, between Santa Comba Dão and Tondela, named Tourigo. Mortágua is also a town near by, reinforcing the variety's claim to have originated in the Dão region.

Touriga Nacional's pre-eminence among Portuguese grapes was acknowledged as long ago as the 1870s, when Vila Maior described it the progenitor of some of the best wines in Portugal. It was noted at the time for its inherent astringency and various authorities recommended blending Touriga Nacional with Alvarelhão or Bastardo, both of which produce much paler, lighter styles of wine. Touriga Nacional lost much of its pre-eminence during the twentieth century, not because of its quality, which is indisputable, but because of its inherently low yields. Added to this, a lack of suitably vigorous root stock increased its susceptibility to poor fruit set. As one farmer described it, "Touriga Nacional is a winemaker's grape rather than a grower's grape." Such was its fall from grace that by the 1970s Touriga Nacional barely registered among the vine varieties planted in either the Douro or Dão.

During the dark years of cooperative dominance in the Dão region, Touriga Nacional was kept alive by the Centro dos Estudos Vincolas at Quinta do Cale, Nelas – which made some outstanding red wines from Touriga Nacional – along with Jaen and Alfrocheiro Preto (see page 225). In the Douro it is only since the PDRITM or World Bank project of the 1980s that Touriga Nacional has returned *en masse*, but then only to the Cima Corgo and Douro Superior, where in some prominent Port quintas it now accounts for twenty to thirty per cent of the vineyard.

In the late 1970s, when varietal planting began to take place in the Douro, Touriga Nacional commonly produced a meagre 0.5–0.8 kilograms (1.1–1.8 pounds) per vine. It is hardly surprising that growers were not quick to take it up, preferring the more reliable Touriga Franca. A programme of clonal selection has helped to increase yields to 1–1.5 kilograms (2.2–3.3 pounds) per vine (compared to 2.5 kilograms/5.5 pounds per vine for Touriga Franca), but Touriga Nacional continues to suffer from excess vigour and is extremely susceptible to cool, damp weather during flowering. Yields are consequently very variable. For example, in three successive years a five-hectare plot of Touriga Nacional at Quinta do Crasto in the Douro produced 40 pipes (220 hectolitres), 25 pipes (138 hectolitres) and then just six pipes (33 hectolitres).

Provided the grapes are picked at the right moment – Touriga Nacional easily over-ripens – its small, thick-skinned berries produce the darkest and most concentrated of wines. Capable of high levels of alcohol, Touriga Nacional nevertheless retains its distinctive floral aroma (some say violets, others bergamot) and an air of civility and finesse. Its reputation, aided by improved clones, has helped the variety to migrate south from the Douro and Dão into Bairrada, Estremadura, the Ribatejo, the Setúbal Peninsula and Alentejo. There is even reputed to be a patch in the Algarve. Growers and winemakers all over Portugal still have much to learn about Touriga Nacional and there is a great deal of inconsistency in quality, with too many wines emasculated by new oak. Nonetheless, there can be little doubt that Touriga Nacional is well on the way to international stardom.

Recommended varietal wines: Quinta das Carvalhas, Touriga Nacional (Dão); Herdade do Esporão, Touriga Nacional (Alentejo); Cálem, Quinta da Foz 1996 (an unusual Vintage Port made entirely from Touriga Nacional); Quinta dos Roques, Touriga Nacional (Dão); Quinta de Pellada, Touriga Nacional (Dão); Quinta do Crasto, Touriga Nacional (Douro); Quinta da Leda, Touriga Nacional (Douro); Quinta de Pancas, Special Selection Touriga Nacional (Vinho Regional Estremadura); Quinta do Vale de Raposa, Touriga Nacional (Douro)

TRINCADEIRA PRETA *****

There are two Trincadeiras with confusingly similar names. The red grape is called Trincadeira Preta and the white variety is known as Trincadeira das Pratas. The red variety is much the more significant and is usually emblazoned on labels merely as Trincadeira. It is a grape that may be Tunisian in origin but has become one of the most widely planted varieties in Portugal, cropping up under a variety of guises. In the Douro it is known as Tinta Amarela, but it also travels under the names of Espadeiro (Lisbon region), Crato Preto, Murteira and Rabo de Ovelha Tinto (Vinho Verde). As the latter ("red ewe's tail"), it is found high in the Basto sub-region and was also found under the same name in Pinhel (Beiras) and the Cartaxo area during the nineteenth century. But it is as Trincadeira in the Alentejo (and subsequently parts of the Ribatejo) that this grape has recently earned its stripes. Here in the hot, dry climate of southern Portugal it is capable of making deep-coloured wines, fruity but herbaceous if picked underripe but taking on a broad pepper and spice character in the right conditions.

In the vineyard Trincadeira is a vigorous variety which yields well, making it popular with growers, but its major drawback is an alarming tendency to rot when there is the merest whiff of humidity in the air, a fact that was recognized by Cincinnato da Costa in the late nineteenth century. It is therefore somewhat surprising that, as Tinta Amarela, it comes in fourth place as the most planted grape, behind Touriga Franca, Tinta Roriz and Tinta Barroca. It is potentially better than all three, but failed to be included in the top five recommended grapes because of its susceptibility to rot. However, on well-exposed, arid soils in the Cima Corgo and Douro Superior, Tinta Amarela produces extremely fine, fragrant wines with balance and poise. In all but the best years it is rather less successful in the more humid climate of the Baixo Corgo, where it still forms a significant part of many of the old mixed vineyards.

Recommended varietal wines: Esporão, Trincadeira (Vinho Regional Alentejano) João Portugal Ramos, Trincadeira (Vinho Regional Alentejano) Quinta de Almargem Reserva (Vinho Regional Ribatejano)

TRINCADEIRO

This is a confusing local synonym in Estremadura for the Castelão grape (qv).

TRIUNFO

Planted as an experimental variety on Madeira, Triunfo is not the same as the Chasselas/Concord hybrid developed in America, but a cross between Castelão (qv) and Moscatel de Hamburgo. It produces must with reasonable levels of sugar but low acidity.

VERDELHO TINTO

Although a name more immediately associated with Madeira, there are a number of red Verdelhos in the Minho, especially around Ponte de Lima and Monção. Planted in the nineteenth century alongside Vinhão, Espadeiro and Borraçal, both Verdelho Tinto and Verdelho Feijão were presumably popular because of their resistence to phylloxera. However, like so many grapes in the Vinho Verde region, they succumbed to fungal diseases and have fallen from favour. Verdelho Tinto is all but extinct on Madeira. See also Verdelho in the section on white grapes.

Wine vessels

VINHÃO
see Sousão.

II. White grape varieties

ALBELHAL
A grape variety formerly grown in Trás-os-Montes, particularly around Arcas and Lamalonga near Macedo de Cavaleiros, that is now seemingly extinct.

ALICANTE BRANCO
A poor quality, productive variety with a confused pedigree. The IVV lists contradictory synonyms: Uva Rei, Boal de Alicante, Boal Cachudo (in the Douro) and Branco Conceição. See Boal.

ALVA
see Síria

ALVADURÃO
see Síria

ALVARINHO ★★★★

Known by the name of Albariño in Galicia, Alvarinho is one of the few grapes to have nudged its way across the border from Spain. I emphasize the word "nudged" because Alvarinho is only planted in any quantity along the River Minho, which forms Portugal's northern frontier with Spain. Although it is an ancient variety cited in various eighteenth-century texts, Alvarinho was not even mentioned by Cincinnato da Costa in his comprehensive survey of Portuguese grapes at the beginning of the twentieth century (see also Cainho). Both the Portuguese and the Galicians claim Alvarinho as their own, but to be fair the synonyms Galego and Galeguinho suggest that it belongs to the latter. Alvarinho was certainly planted along the Minho from Vila Nova de Cerveira to Melgaço in the eighteenth and nineteenth centuries, but seems to have been adversely affected by phylloxera and only returned to the region in the 1920s. It regularly produces wine with a higher level of alcohol than the other main Vinho Verde varieties (see Azal, Loureiro, Padernã and Trajadura) and so earned a special dispensation in the 1950s that permitted varietal Alvarinho from the municipalities of Monção and Melgaço. This has proved to be controversial with other Vinho Verde growers (see Chapter 3), but it seems that Alvarinho is particularly well suited to the deep alluvial soils along the Minho, as opposed to the granite and schist that makes up the remainder of the Vinho Verde region. Alvarinho is an unstable variety that after many years mutates to form a red clone. This (together with the soil type) accounts for the variation in the styles of wine from Monção and Melgaço, some of which have a different aromatic profile, along with an occasional pinkish tinge.

Overall, Alvarinho is a low yielding grape with small bunches and a high proportion of pips. One ton of grapes produces less than a pipe (550 litres) of wine, but the Regional Commission still permits yields of up to sixty hl/ha. Alvarinho is also an extremely vigorous variety that benefits from rigorous canopy management to give the correct exposure to the fruit. The cruzeta training system (see page 129) that has been used widely in the Vinho Verde region has proved to be especially prejudicial to even ripening. Alvarinho is, indisputably, an aromatic grape, with a scent that ranges from jasmine, orange blossom to Cox's apple depending on the clone and method of vinification. The introduction of stainless steel in the late 1980s has helped to further this fresh, fruit-driven style, although some producers have already gone a stage further by choosing to ferment Alvarinho in new French oak. This in my opinion is misguided, for the beauty of this, one of Portugal's leading (albeit adopted) grapes, is the purity of its fruit.

In the late 1990s a number of growers began to consider planting Alvarinho in other parts of Portugal than the Minho valley. This necessitated a certain amount of circumventing the law for, although Alvarinho is among the permitted varieties for Vinho Regional Minho, Estremadura and Terras do Sado, it has not yet made its way onto the statute book in other regions. Parts of Estremadura are probably well suited to Alvarinho, which used to be planted on the border with the Ribatejo at Ourém. However, the first tentative steps in growing Alvarinho in Estremadura are somewhat blurred by the fact that it is currently being blended with Chardonnay.

Recommended varietal wines: Aveleda Alvarinho Deu-la-Deu (Adega Co-op de Monção); Soalheiro (António Esteves Ferreira)

ANTÃO VAZ **/***

This is turning out to be one of the better white varieties in the hotter parts of the Alentejo, particularly in Vidigueira, Reguengos, Évora and Moura. It is one of those unusual grape varieties that seems to suit everyone. Antão Vaz is fairly productive, ripens evenly and resists disease. Some growers now choose to pick as early as mid-August, making fresh-driven wines with crisp acidity and 11.5° alcohol. Left on the vine, Antão Vaz will ripen to 13 degrees Baumé, with correspondingly lower levels of acidity. This is compensated for by breadth of flavour, which makes Antão Vaz a useful variety for barrel fermentation and subsequent blending with Roupeiro and/or with the more acidic Arinto (qv). Antão Vaz is also widely planted on the Setúbal Peninsula, where it is permitted as a variety for Vinho Regional Terras do Sado.

Recommended varietal wine: João Portugal Ramos, Antão Vaz

ARINTO **/****

The name Arinto crops up all over Portugal. The Arinto do Dão, however, is emphatically not the same grape as the Arinto that grows in Bucelas, Estremadura and the Ribatejo, where it has the capacity to make some of

Portugal's freshest, most steely dry white wines (see Malvasia Fina). Acidity is Arinto's main hallmark and, as Padernã in the Vinho Verde region, it becomes rather too much of a good thing! In the south of Portugal, however, Arinto has the capacity to retain much-needed acidity even after a run of 30°C summer days. For most of the twentieth century, Arinto was rarely given the opportunity to prove its worth. Although (along with the corrosively acidic Esgana Cão) it formed the basis for Bucelas, the wines were usually tired and oxidized (but still acidic) owing to heavy-handed, primitive winemaking. Prior to this the wines were often fortified, leaving Arinto to provide both sweetness and acidity in equal measure. This may have led a number of authorities (including Cincinnato da Costa) to conjecture a link between Arinto and Riesling which does not stand up to ampelographic scrutiny. Arinto's mentor and possible saviour arrived only in the late 1980s, in the form of stainless steel. Long, slow fermentation at low temperatures is at last helping to coax the true character from this grape, and there are one or two wines showing green, leafy aromas and mouthwatering, minerally freshness. But it seems to me that there is still much to be done, probably in the vineyard, to develop Arinto into one of the leading white varieties in southern Europe. For the moment, however, the emphasis has shifted away from white grapes to red and it may still be some time before Arinto fulfills its potential. As Padernã, the Arinto grape produces steely-minerally Vinhos Verdes with little else in the way of aroma or flavour. It usually forms part of a triumvrate with Loureiro and Trajadura (qv). Other (little-used) synonyms for Arinto and Padernã include Pé de Perdiz Branco, Chapeludo, Azal Espanhol and Azal Galego.

Recommended varietal wines: Quinta Dom Carlos, Arinto (Vinho Regional Estremadura); Prova Regia (Bucelas) Casa do Valle, Arinto (Vinho Verde); Quinta da Lixa, Padernã (Vinho Verde)

ARINTO DO DÃO
see Malvasia Fina

ARNSBURGER
Developed at Geisenheim in Germany for sparkling wine, this crossing of two Riesling clones has mysteriously made its way to Madeira. It

owes its presence to an EU-funded project (with a German consultant) to make unfortified wines on the north side of the island (see page 295). This productive variety resists disease and makes a rather tart dry white wine.

ASSARIO
see Malvasia Fina

AVESSO**
The word avesso means "contrary" in Portuguese, which is a fitting description for this Vinho Verde grape that is quite capable (unlike most of the others) of ripening to register quite high levels of sugar (12–13 degrees Baumé). It is mostly planted around the town of Baião, the warmest and driest part of the Vinho Verde region, adjacent to the Douro, where Avesso has frequently crossed swords with the authorities for producing wines that exceed the official maximum of 11.5 degrees of alcohol. A bucket or two of water is the only way to put things right! Given a free run, Avesso is capable of making a softer, more full-bodied style of wine that might just help to endear Vinho Verde to wine consumers. A well-made Avesso wine possesses a vaguely tropical character reminiscent of underripe peaches and apricots, but, unless it is handled very carefully, has a nasty habit of oxidizing rather rapidly. In the vineyard Avesso is popular with growers. It is a vigorous variety that suits pergola training, resists disease and yields around thirteen pipes per hectare (seventy hl/ha).

AZAL
Planted mainly around Amarante, Penafiel and in the Basto sub-region, this late ripening grape is the last of all the Vinho Verde varieties to be harvested. Azal is also susceptible to rot, which means picking often becomes a race against time as the autumn rains sweep in from the Atlantic. Perhaps owing to the fact that it is often picked too early, Azal produces the most acidic style of Vinho Verde, typically with 12 grams/litre (expressed as tartaric). It also has very little in the way of aroma – all of which means that Azal has very little to recommend it apart from heavy yields.

BARCELO**

Indigenous to the Dão region, Barcelo was grown extensively around Viseu and Gouveia, where small quantities still exist. It was once considered to be the best white grape in the region and until 1953 it was obligatory to have no less than twenty per cent of Barcelo among white varieties growing in a Dão vineyard. Perhaps because of its susceptibility to rot, Barcelo's place has been taken by Encruzado (qv), which by all accounts produces very similar wines.

BATOCA

This secondary Vinho Verde grape is planted around Baião, Cinfães and in the Basto region. It produces a heavy crop which, like Azal (qv), is especially prone to rot in the damp climate of north-west Portugal. The wines have little to distinguish them. Other (little-used) synonyms are Alvaraça, Alvaroça and Sedouro.

BICAL**/****

Planted extensively in Bairrada, Dão and throughout the Beiras, Bical has the potential to be one of Portugal's leading white grape varieties. It had long been used to provide a fresh but rather crude base wine for traditional method sparkling wines, but as a result of the viticultural sort-out in the 1990s it has now become a favoured grape in its own right. Although Bical is very sensitive to oidium early in the growing season, in Bairrada it is capable of producing wonderfully scented, peachy wines with sub-tropical weight in a ripe year. It is also helpfully resistant to rot. Balanced by crisp acidity, a well-made Bical has the capacity to age gracefully, taking on a petroleum character reminiscent of Riesling after about ten years in bottle. In the Dão region Bical is known as Borrado das Moscas ("fly droppings") owing to the speckled appearance of the grape when ripe. To date it seems to have performed better in Bairrada's deeper soils and cool maritime climate, but I am ready to be proved wrong.
Recommended varietal wine: Casa de Saima, Bical (Bairrada)

BOAL ****

As with Malvasia (qv), there are so many grapes in Portugal claiming the name Boal that it is hard to know where to start. Cincinnato da Costa lists sixteen, identifying Boal de Alicante, Boal Branco, Boal Cachudo, Boal

Carrasquenho and Boal Bonifácio (see Vital) as separate varieties. But Boal (or Bual in English) is best known as a style of wine, which until 1993 was no more than a medium sweet Madeira made mainly from the versatile Tinta Negra Mole (qv). The Boal growing on Madeira is thought to be Boal Cachudo, which the IVV identifies as being synonymous with Malvasia Fina (qv). Boal Cachudo is found at low altitudes on the south side of island, where it yields small, tightly packed bunches of small, relatively sweet grapes. In spite of its intrinsic quality, Boal accounts for less than one per cent of the island's crop. Total production amounts to less than 200 tons.

Boal Cachudo (also known as Boal Commum) is also found on the Portuguese mainland, around Leiria in Estremadura, where they used to imitate the wines of Madeira. Boal Carrasquenho was also planted around Leiria and the southern part of Estremadura around Alenquer, Torres Vedras and Bucelas. It was favoured by growers for its late budding, which reduced the risk of frost damage in spring. A productive grape variety named Boal de Alicante (Alicante Branco) is found in the Ribatejo, and the IVV lists four further Boal grapes: Boal Barreiro, Boal Branco, Boal Espinho and Boal Ratinho.

Recommended varietal wine: Henriques & Henriques Fifteen Year Old Boal (Madeira)

BORRADO DAS MOSCAS
see Bical

CACHORRINHO
see Uva Cão

CAINHO **
Described to me by a grower as a "cousin of Alvarinho" (qv), small quantities of Cainho are planted in the country around Ponte de Lima. This description is probably near the truth, as Alvarinho is an unstable variety that mutates readily. Cainho is almost certainly the same variety as Cainho Branco, which Cincinnato da Costa describes as being favoured by growers for its productivity and richness of sugar. He equates it with Alvarinho (which, strangely, does not warrant a separate entry in his book) and remarks on the grapes that he was sent for analysis as being from Quinta de Moreira. The variety is still known locally as Cainho de Moreira.

CARACOL
The "snail" is an authorized grape for Madeira, but seems to be grown mostly as a table grape.

CARÃO DE MOÇA
Although this is an authorized variety for Madeira, I have never knowingly encountered it either in a vineyard or in a wine, but the name still features on the IVV's official list and roughly translates as "frowning girl". It will be a challenge for a future edition of this book to find out how and why it was so christened.

CERCEAL BRANCO (CERCIAL) */**
There is a certain amount of confusion surrounding this grape (or these two grapes) planted throughout northern Portugal. It is worth stating that neither is the same as the Sercial (qv) growing on Madeira, which is also found on the mainland under a number of different synonyms. The IVV lists Cerceal and Cercial as two different grapes, although this productive but late ripening variety seems to be much the same in the Douro, Dão and Bairrada. Although Cerceal generally produces rather dull wines, it is still valued in the Dão region where, on the foothills of the Serra da Estrela around Gouveia, it contributes a certain freshness and liveliness to blends. In Bairrada it is very sensitive to oidium and the thin-skinned grapes are prone to rot. One authority recommends that it should be the first Bairrada grape to be harvested "or at the very least when it begins to rain".

CHARDONNAY ***/****
The grape that has travelled the world from its native Burgundy has made remarkably few inroads into Portugal. There is a smattering of experimental Chardonnay in almost every region, but commercial quantities are found only in the Ribatejo and on the Setúbal Peninsula, the two regions that have been most strongly influenced by the New World. Renowned for its adaptability, Chardonnay produces a full spectrum of aromas and flavours in Portugal reflecting the diversity of *terroir*. In maritime areas like Bairrada and Estremadura it produces wines with a crisp, apple-like character, whereas in the Setúbal Peninsula it produces fat, rich wines of almost Australian proportions. In the Ribatejo, where there is more

Chardonnay than in any other region of Portugal, it seems to be stretched somewhat by consistently high yields and in the Alentejo (where there is still only a tiny amount) the climate appears to be too extreme for the variety to retain much in the way of balance or finesse. To date the best site for Chardonnay in Portugal appears to be the more lofty vineyards above the Douro, where Real Companhia Velha have produced a wine that deservedly wins medals on the international stage. Much is down to skilful winemaking, but I am assured that at an altitude of around 500 metres (1,640 feet) Chardonnay needs little or nothing in the way of acid adjustment (and it shows). Of course DOC Douro cannot be applied to Chardonnay and the wine, like all the others in Portugal, belongs to the Vinho Regional category.

Recommended varietal wines: Quinta do Sidrô, Chardonnay, Real Companhia Velha (Vinho Regional Trás-os-Montes) Cova da Ursa, JP Vinhos (Vinho Regional Terras do Sado)

CODEGA *

The most planted white grape variety in the Douro does not feature on the IVV's official list, not even as a synonym. This may be due to some confusion over its identity, as it is possibly the same as the Síria (qv) grape planted to the south in Beira Alta and in the Alentejo, where it is known as Roupeiro. In the Douro, Codega accounts for around 30 per cent of the white grape varieties planted in the region and large quantities have traditionally been planted in the Douro Superior. It yields well (2–3 kilograms/4.4–6.6 pounds per vine) and produces wine that is soft, flat and low in acidity, providing the basis for dry white Port.

CODO SÍRIA
see Síria

CRATO BRANCO
see Síria

DEDO DA DAMA
These elongated grapes known as "lady's finger" are frequently found on pergolas in the Douro, where they are much appreciated for the table. The berries have the shape of a long but well-manicured fingernail.

DIAGALVES

This dreary white grape variety crops up all over the Alentejo, where it is an (albeit secondary) authorized grape variety throughout the DOC, except in Borba and Moura. Diagalves grapes are good to eat, which may explain why they are so poor for producing wine. Large, productive bunches of overripe grapes produce fat, flabby white wines that form the lowest common denominator in so many Alentejano blends.

DONA BRANCA

An undistinguished, productive grape variety that is still planted widely in Dão and which crops up in the Douro.

DONZELINHO BRANCO

Another localized name for the Gouveio grape.

DOURADINHA

see Tália

ENCRUZADO ***/****

In qualitative terms, Encruzado is the most important white grape variety in the Dão region and could turn out to be one of Portugal's most promising native grapes. Like so many of Portugal's grape varieties, its origins are obscure, but Encruzado was certainly planted in the Dão region in the nineteenth century under the (now extinct) synonym of Salgueirinho. As far as I am aware, it is not yet planted anywhere else, suggesting that it is probably indigenous to the region. It yields well (2.5 kilograms/5.5 pounds per vine) and manages to achieve a remarkable balance of sugar and acidity, which means that Encruzado stands up on its own as a varietal wine. The wines have the capacity to age but nowadays rarely have the chance. Five years in bottle is a good rule of thumb for a well-made, well-balanced Encruzado-based wine. In the 1990s Encruzado has proved suitable for barrel fermentation and subsequent maturation on lees, taking on a Burgundian quality. It is no coincidence that the barrel-fermented Encruzado from Quinta dos Roques has become one of Portugal's leading white wines.

Recommended varietal wines: Quinta dos Roques, Encruzado (Dão) Quinta dos Carvalhais, Encruzado, Sogrape (Dão)

ESGANA CÃO
see Sercial

ESGANOSO
see Sercial

FERNÃO PIRES **/***
Fernão Pires is one of Portugal's most adaptable white grapes, not least in its Christian name, which undergoes a sex change from Fernão (Ferdinand) in the south of Portugal to Maria in the north. As Maria Gomes it is the most planted white grape in Bairrada where, despite the climatic difficulties, it yields well and ripens easily, producing soft, simple, sometimes slightly spicy dry white wines. Its only drawback is the fact that because it buds early, it is prone to attack by spring frosts. In terms of quality, Maria Gomes is, however, outshone by the rather more tetchy Bical (qv), and in the better white Bairradas this grape makes up the greater part of the blend. In the Ribatejo and adjoining parts of Estremadura, Fernão Pires has long been the most planted grape variety, yielding up to 160 hl/ha on the fertile *lezíria* (alluvial flood plain) beside the Tagus. Much Fernão Pires-based wine was either distilled or used to make local brands of vermouth, but since the introduction of stainless steel it has been shown to be capable of better. Although Fernão Pires will never produce complex, long-lasting wine, it has the capacity to make large volumes of simple, honeyed, slighty spicy dry white. It is also well suited to short oak ageing, which sometimes adds a Chardonnayesque dimension. All this makes Fernão Pires into a good deal for prospectors seeking out wine to match a particular price point. For a short time in the late 1980s Fernão Pires rose above this when it produced a deliciously sweet wine from late-picked botrytized grapes grown alongside the Tagus. A considerable amount of Fernão Pires has since been uprooted in the general shift away from white wine toward red.

Recommended varietal wines: Casa de Cadaval, Fernão Pires (Vinho Regional Ribatejano); Segada/Casa do Lago, DFJ Vinhos (Vinho Regional Ribatejano)

FOLGASÃO
see Terrantez

GALEGO DOURADO
The "golden Galician" is one of the white grape varieties recommended for Carcavelos (see page 182). So little vineyard remains within the DOC that it is now impossible to ascertain the characteristics of this, presumably ancient, grape. However, consistently high sugar readings seem to be its main attribute.

GEWÜRZTRAMINER
There are two pockets of Gewürztraminer along the River Douro, in the Vinho Verde region and within the Douro DOC, although it is only permitted in Trás-os-Montes for Vinho Regional. From the samples that I have tasted so far I wonder whether it is really worth the bother.

GOUVEIO **
Planted in the Douro, Gouveio was long thought to be the same as Verdelho (qv), but the IVV now lists it as a separate grape. There are a number of officially registered Gouveios, including Gouveio Estimado, Gouveio Real, Gouveio Roxo (purple) and Gouveio Preto (black), which suggests that it is a fairly unstable variety. It is also known by the synonym Verdelho. Gouveio produces aromatic wines with high levels of acidity. It is therefore favoured by winemakers for dry white Douro wines and white Port, but it is hampered in the vineyard by low yields and only represents about seven per cent of the Douro's white vine stock. Gouveio is mostly found within old, interplanted vineyards and is therefore rarely seen as a varietal. Gouveio Real, which ostensibly has marginally higher acidity, is planted above the Douro in Tavora-Varosa, where it is used to make a base wine for *espumante*.

JAMPAL
A "recommended" variety in Estremadura, Jampal (occasionally called João Paulo) has little to recommend it. Planted alongside Vital (qv), Jampal is supposedly capable of producing fresh, dry white wine, but uninspired vinification methods around Torres Vedras, where most of it is planted, mean that it rarely has the chance. Jampal also overflows into the western hills of the Ribatejo.

LISTRÃO*

Grown on Madeira as a table grape, Listrão makes on the nearby island of Porto Santo a flabby dry white and a fortified wine known as Listrão de Porto Santo. In the semi-desert conditions on the island it reaches sugar levels in excess of 13 degrees Baumé, with a corresponding lack of acidity.
Recommended varietal wine: Listrão de Porto Santo, Artur Barros e Sousa

LOUREIRO **/***

This productive variety has turned into one of the leading grapes for Vinho Verde. It was once known as Dourada ("golden") owing to the yellow hue of its berries and was interplanted with Trajadura and Padernã (qv). Cincinnato da Costa singled out Loureiro as a promising variety at the end of the nineteenth century, commenting that it was reminiscent of Moscatel. This is somewhat over the top, but, when carefully vinified, Loureiro does produce wines with fleeting floral aroma vaguely reminiscent of Riesling. It performs at its best in the centre of the Vinho Verde region between the Rivers Cavado and Lima and is a recommended grape for the Braga and Lima sub-regions (see page 131). In this rain-drenched area Loureiro is easily capable of yielding 100 hl/ha and wines with correspondingly dilute levels of alcohol.
Recommended varietal wines: Quinta do Ameal (Vinho Verde); Quinta do Minho, Loureiro (Vinho Verde); Quinta de Tamariz (Vinho Verde)

MALVASIA BABOSA

There are no fewer than twelve different Malvasias on the IVV's official list, but Malvasia Babosa does not feature among them. It was apparently introduced to Madeira by Simon Acciaioli, a Genoese nobleman, in 1515. Malvasia Babosa exists in São Jorge and in the experimental vineyard belonging to the Madeiran government. It remains an officially authorized variety for Madeira wine.

MALVASIA CANDIDA ****

Of Cretan origin (Candia was the capital of Crete), Malvasia Candida was either brought to Madeira by Venetian traders in the fifteenth century or introduced to the island by the Infante Dom Henrique (Prince Henry the Navigator). Malvasia has always been in short supply. Between 1748 and 1800, Francis Newton wrote frequently to his London partners informing them of the lack of wine. By the mid-twentieth century, however, Malvasia Candida was virtually extinct, the last vintage having been made in 1920. It is especially prone to mildew and requires a well-exposed site at low altitudes on the south side of the island to flourish. The grapes are only picked when they begin to shrivel and raisinize on the vine, thereby concentrating the natural sugars. A tiny quantity of Malvasia Candida is still grown at Jardim do Mar, which is located at sea level between Câmara de Lobos and Ribeira Brava on the south side of the island. There is so little that the Duke of Clarence would have difficulty drowning in it, but this is the source of the greatest of Malmseys.

MALVASIA CORADA
see Vital

MALVASIA FINA *
There seems to be a great deal of confusion over the true identity of this variety, which is an authorized grape on Madeira and the second most widely planted white grape in the Douro. It is almost certainly identical to Arinto do Dão or Assario planted in the Beiras, but not, as the IVV's official list implies, the same as Boal (Branco or Cachudo). The source of this uncertainty may be the fact that Malvasia Fina is a notoriously unstable variety which readily mutates and that the quality of the wine varies greatly from one clone to another. It is very susceptible to oidium and poor fruit set, making yields extremely variable. For this reason there is very little Malvasia Fina left on Madeira. With a soft, fat, vaguely honeyed character, the wine is better than that produced by Codega (the most planted white grape in the Douro), but could hardly be described as "fine". In the past it used to be known as Malvasia de Passa because of its tendency to shrivel and raisinize on the vine.

MALVASIA GROSSA
see Codega

MALVASIA REI
By no means the "king" of the grapes christened Malvasia, Malvasia Rei is the third most planted white grape in the Douro after Malvasia Fina and Codega (qv). It produces huge quantities of bland wine. Other synonyms

include Seminário (in Estremadura), Pérola ("pearl") and Olho de Lebre ("eye of the hare").

MANTEÚDO

A small cut above Diagalves (qv), Manteudo produces large volumes of bland, alcoholic white wine in the Alentejo, especially around Redondo, Reguengos and Vidigueira. This disease-resistant variety is understandably popular with growers, but is much less favoured by the growing band of quality-conscious wine producers in the region. Much has been uprooted in favour of red varieties.

MARIA GOMES**

The synonym in Bairrada for Fernão Pires (qv).

MOSCATEL GRAÚDO***

There are almost as many different names for Moscatel (Muscat) in Portugal as there are for Malvasia. The best-known variant, the Moscatel de Setúbal, is officially registered as Moscatel Graudo ("great Muscat"), but is none other than the Muscat of Alexandria. This is planted all round the Mediterranean basin, where it produces rich, often rather coarse, raisiny dessert wines. Nevertheless, anyone who has had the opportunity to taste José Maria da Fonseca's Setúbal wines dating back to the nineteenth century will vouch for the fact that, in Portugal at least, Muscat of Alexandria is capable of something truly world class.

Recommended varietal wines: Moscatel de Setúbal, Alambre, Twenty Year Old (José Maria da Fonseca); Moscatel de Setúbal (JP Vinhos)

MOSCATEL GALEGO BRANCO ****

A variety of Moscatel is grown in the Douro, where it is used either on its own for Moscatel de Favaios or as a component of white Port. Known officially as Moscatel Galego Branco, this is none other than Muscat à Petit Grains. This is much the best and most refined variety of Muscat (used for Muscat de Beaumes de Venise), but heavy-handed winemaking in the north of Portugal means that it rarely has the chance to shine.

Moscatel is also planted on Madeira, but most is now diverted to the table rather than the winery, and I have no idea which variety of Muscat produced some of the remarkable old wines that one occasionally encounters on the island or at auction. Portugal also has a small quantity of "purple" Muscat; see Moscatel Galego Roxo and Moscatel Galego Tinto in the section on red grapes.

PADERNÃ
This Vinho Verde grape variety is officially known by the name Arinto (qv).

PÉ COMPRIDO
The "big foot" grape features in the IVV's official list, but I have never come across it in the vineyard.

PERRUM
Appreciated by growers but detested by most winemakers, Perrum is really only capable of producing bland, dry white wines. It is planted widely in the Baixo Alentejo and is still a "recommended" variety in the Reguengos, Vidigueira and Évora sub-regions. In spite of the arid climate, Perrum is an extremely vigorous variety that yields reasonably well and resists disease. It is also planted around Huelva in Andalusia, where it is called Zalema and is often confused with the equally bland Palomino. The two may even be related.

PROMISSÃO
Listed by Cincinnato da Costa, Promissão is a high yielding variety that bears enormous bunches of grapes better suited for the table than for wine.

RABIGATO **/***
The "cat's tail" is one of the better white grapes growing in the Douro, where it accounts for around twelve per cent of the white varieties, putting it in fourth place behind Codega, Malvasia Fina and Malvasia Rei. Named after the elongated shape of its bunches, Rabigato yields well (up to 3 kilograms/6.6 pounds per vine) and tends to be planted at higher altitudes, where it is favoured by winemakers for the fresh acidity that it contributes to white Port as well as a smattering of white Douro wines. A grape by the name of Rabigato also grows in the neighbouring Vinho Verde region, but this seems to be a different variety (see under Rabo de Ovelha).

RABO DE OVELHA

The "ewe's tail" is found throughout southern Portugal and in the Vinho Verde region, where the animal concerned becomes a cat and the grape is known confusingly as Rabigato (qv). The IVV also lists Medock as another synonym, but there is no evidence that this variety has any connection with Bordeaux. Rabo de Ovelha is essentially a warm-country grape, planted in the Ribatejo, on the Setúbal Peninsula and throughout the Alentejo, where it is a recommended variety in all the sub-regions except Portalegre. The grapes ripen quickly, turning amber-brown in colour when they are fully ripe. To be of any value in the winery, Rabo de Ovelha needs to be harvested early, before acidity dives to depressingly low levels. Cincinnato da Costa recommends it as a table grape.

RIESLING

Like Gewürztraminer, Riesling has been planted in two vineyards along the Douro, where it is hard to envisage that this predominantly cool-climate grape has much of a future.

RIO GRANDE

Still present on the IVV's official list and as an authorized grape for Madeira, Rio Grande appears to exist only in the Madeiran government's experimental vineyard.

ROUPEIRO

Well known in the Alentejo as one of the region's better white grape varieties, Roupeiro is a recognized synonym for a grape now officially known as Síria (qv).

SAMARRINHO

Found in old mixed vineyards in the Douro, this undistinguished grape variety plays a minor part in white Port.

SAUVIGNON**

There are commercial quantities of Sauvignon in the Ribatejo as well as smaller plots in Trás-os-Montes and on the Setúbal Peninsula, where it is permitted as a constituent of Vinho Regional. In the warm climate of southern Portugal, Sauvignon tends to lose some of its varietal character, taking on asparagus-like overtones. It may yet have a future in the north.

SEARA NOVA

This productive grape is the undistinguished child of Diagalves crossed with Fernão Pires. It is mostly planted in Estremadura, where the grapes ripen very quickly, thereby reducing the risk of a dousing by the autumn rains. Seara Nova is a commodity grape – quality is not a consideration.

SÉMILLON**

A tiny quantity of Sémillon is planted in one old vineyard in the Dão region, although, given its performance in Australia, Sémillon could be well suited to parts of the Ribatejo and Alentejo. The IVV's official list gives the title Boal as a synonym for Sémillon in the Douro, thereby creating even more confusion over the true nature of Boal (qv).

SEMINÁRIO
see Malvasia Rei

SERCIAL **/****

Not to be confused with Cerceal (qv), Sercial, as it is known on Madeira, has the synonym Esgana Cão ("dog strangler") on the Portuguese mainland. This gives more of a clue to its temperament, for almost wherever it is planted, Sercial produces austere, dry wines with ferocious levels of natural acidity. On Madeira, Sercial is found growing at high altitudes (600–700 metres/1,968–2,296 feet) on the south side of the island and at lower levels on the north. Not much is grown, but Jardim da Serra, Estreito de Câmara de Lobos, Porto Moniz and Seixal seem to be favoured habitats although total production has now fallen to below one hundred tons. Resistant to both mildew and oidium, Sercial ripens with difficulty to 11 degrees Baumé but provides some of the finest and most enduring Madeira, kept alive for decades (sometimes centuries) by punishing levels of acidity. Sercial is often a wine for masochists! On the mainland Sercial is planted in the Vinho Verde region, where it is known as Esganoso (plain "strangler"), and as Esgana Cão in Bucelas and neighbouring areas of Estremadura and the Ribatejo. In Bucelas it is much the junior partner to Arinto (qv) and is never seen anywhere as a varietal, in spite of the undoubted temptation for marketeers to develop a wine called "dog strangler". As with Arinto, it is sometimes said that Sercial is related to Riesling, but no connection has ever been proved.

Recommended varietal wine: Henriques & Henriques Ten Year Old Sercial Madeira; Sercial Madeira from an old vintage

SERCIALINHO*

This cross between Vital and Alvarinho (qv) is highly regarded by some growers in Bairrada, although I have never encountered a Sercialinho-based wine worthy of much commendation. It is reputedly capable of making wines with good levels of alcohol balanced by aroma and acidity.

SÍRIA***

This grape variety is planted throughout inland Portugal, where it masquerades under a number of different names. It is almost certainly the same as Codega (qv) in the Douro, and is known as Alvadurão in Dão, Síria or Codo Síria in the Beiras, Alva in Portalegre, Roupeiro throughout the rest of the Alentejo and Crato Branco in the Algarve. It is as Roupeiro that this grape has gained its reputation, having been described by Cincinnato da Costa as "the noble grape of the Alentejo". The competition isn't fierce, but Roupeiro is considerably better than its peers (see Diagalves, Manteudo, Perrum and Trincadeira das Pratas/Tamarêz), producing reasonable yields of ripe, flavoursome grapes. With the exception of the Granja/Amareleja sub-region, Roupeiro represents between twenty-five and forty-five per cent of the white grapes in the Alentejo. Helped by early picking and with the benefit of temperature-controlled fermentation, Roupeiro makes soft, slightly honeyed dry white wines. It is frequently blended with Antão Vaz (qv) and seems to be well suited to barrel fermentation and short ageing in new oak.

VARIETAL RECOMMENDATION:

Esporão, Roupeiro (Vinho Regional Alentejano)

TÁLIA

Italy's seemingly ubiquitous Trebbiano – Ugni Blanc in France – turns up in Portugal as Tália (presumably named after Itália). It is mostly confined to the Ribatejo, where it produces large volumes of flat, neutral white wine but is nonetheless registered as a "recommended" variety in Almeirim, Cartaxo, Chamusca, Coruche, Santarém and Tomar. Other officially recognized synonyms include Douradinha (Vinho Verde), Alfrocheiro Branco and, strangely for a grape with so little acidity, Esgana Rapazes ("boy strangler"). The IVV also records Malvasia Fina (qv) as another synonym.

TAMARÊZ

see Trincadeira das Pratas

TERRANTEZ ***/****

Terrantez is recorded as having been planted on mainland Portugal as early as the sixteenth century, and it still lives on in parts of the Douro under the name of Folgasão. By the eighteenth century Terrantez had found its way to Madeira and it is here that this grape now finds fame, albeit in very limited quantities. Terrantez was almost completely wiped out by phylloxera and by the 1920s it was reported as being almost extinct on Madeira, although a small quantity was still cultivated on the nearby island of Porto Santo. However, Cincinnato da Costa contradicts this notion, writing about a grape called Folgasona (almost certainly the same as Folgosão) that is very resistant to phylloxera but susceptible to mildew, which may have contributed to its demise. Terrantez is now virtually extinct. The last of these grapes from the famed Torrebella estate were harvested in 1988 but a small quantity remains in the government's experimental vineyard.

Terrantez makes wines that are at once sweet and astringent. It used to be so highly prized that a ditty was coined in praise of the grape:

As uvas de Terrantez,
Não coma nem as des,
Para vinho Deus as fez.[1]

Recommended varietal wine: Blandy's Ten Year Old Terrantez

---

[1] "Terrantez grapes; neither eat or give them away for God made them to produce wine." It rhymes in Portuguese.

TRAJADURA */**

This productive grape is favoured by growers throughout the Vinho Verde region, but especially by those in the Lima, Braga and Amarante sub-regions. It ripens rapidly to achieve 13 per cent potential alcohol by volume (well above the permitted maximum for Vinho Verde of 11.5 per cent) and is relatively low in acidity compared to the other permitted Vinho Verde varieties. Consequently Trajadura is often used in conjunction with Loureiro (qv) and Padernã (qv) for filling out blends and is only rarely seen as a varietal.

Recommended varietal wine: Aveleda, Trajadura (Vinho Verde); Casa de Vila Boa, Trajadura (Vinho Verde)

TRINCADEIRA DAS PRATAS

Planted in the Ribatejo, Alentejo and on the Setúbal Peninsula, Trincadeira das Pratas is an early ripening grape that quickly shrivels to a raisin if left for too long on the vine. It is of little use in the winery, producing flat, neutral wines. Nonetheless, it is listed as a "recommended" variety in the Cartaxo, Chamusca, Coruche, Santarém and Tomar sub-regions of the Ribatejo. On the Setúbal Peninsula and in the Alentejo (where it is also "recommended") Trincadeira das Pratas is known by the synonym of Tamarêz.

UVA CÃO**

Portugal's obsession with dogs continues with the Uva Cão ("dog grape"), also known as Cachorrinho ("little puppy dog"). A late flowering grape (which helps it to evade spring frosts), Uva Cão is the fourth most planted white variety in Dão. It has a good reputation (although I have never seen an Uva Cão or Cachorrinho varietal) for combining good levels of sugar with plenty of acidity. However, low yields, late ripening and a tendency to rot on the vine prevent it from being more widely planted. The distribution of Uva Cão tends to be concentrated in the warmer parts of the Dão region around Carregal do Sal, Nelas and Tondela.

VALVEIRINHO

Once planted on Madeira (and still listed as an authorized variety), Valveirinho (sometimes written Valveirinha) is now thought to be extinct.

VERDELHO ***/****

There is still some confusion over the true identity of Verdelho, which (as with Malvasia) is not helped by the rather liberal use of the name. Some consider that Verdelho is the same as Gouveio (qv) in the Douro but it is most closely identified with Madeira, where, until the arrival of phylloxera, it made up two-thirds of the island's vineyards. Verdelho was only promoted to "noble" status (from being merely "good") early in the twentieth century. This coincided with its relegation to a few pockets on the north side of the island, where it seems to be well suited to the relatively cool climate, producing musts with moderate levels of sugar and high acidity. The best Verdelho is said to come from vineyards around the villages of Ponta Delgada and São Vicente.

The Verdelho growing on Madeira is the same as that found growing on the Azores, but it is now thought to be different from Gouveio (qv), which grows on the mainland but is still known by the synonym Verdelho. A variety of Verdelho has also been planted with some success in Victoria and Western Australia. There is also a red Verdelho, Verdelho Tinto (qv), sometimes known as Verdelho Feijão, which is all but extinct on Madeira.

Recommended varietal wine: Henriques & Henriques Ten or Fifteen Year Old Verdelho Madeira

VIOGNIER

Naturalized in the northern Rhône and increasingly planted in southern France and California, Viognier has yet to make an impact in Portugal. It is found in two vineyards, one near the Douro in the Vinho Verde region and the other near Alenquer in Estremadura. There is no reason why this tantalizing grape should not perform well in the warmer parts of Portugal, provided that growers can put up with its capricious nature.

VIOSINHO**

This low yielding Douro variety seems to be capable of producing some high-quality wines but has been largely ignored until recently. Mostly planted in old mixed vineyards, Viosinho performs best at high altitudes, where it produces aromatic wines that retain more natural acidity. Sensitive to both oidium and rot, Viosinho is one of the few white varieties that is currently undergoing a programme of clonal selection.

VITAL

Flattered by the synonyms Boal Bonifácio and Malvasia Corada, this early ripening grape variety produces large quantities of bland white wine in Estremadura and the Ribatejo. Vital is officially recommended, nonetheless, in the DOCs of Alenquer, Arruda, Óbidos and Torres Vedras as well as the Ribatejo sub-regions of Almeirim, Chamusca, Coruche and Santarém.

III. Vintages

Despite views to the contrary, vintages really do matter in Portugal. The climate is unpredictable, especially on the Atlantic seaboard, where rain-bearing westerlies are an ever-present threat. Even inland, cool weather at

The garrafeira *(wine cellar) at Buçaco*

the time of flowering or a late spring frost can have a devastating impact on yield, as the figures below reveal. Again, contrary to the opinion of many so-called wine experts, the finest Portuguese red wines improve greatly with cellaring. Port and Madeira aside, the Douro, Dão and Bairrada are all capable of producing some long-lived wines, the best of which will continue to develop over two decades or more. Further south, where the new generation of wines tends to be softer and more fruit-driven, there are isolated properties with a track record for making wines that will keep for much the same length of time. When they are on form, Mouchão, Quinta do Carmo and Tapada do Chaves in the Alentejo and Pegos Claros on the Setúbal Peninsula spring to mind. The best wines from leading vintages are often designated as *garrafeiras*, a uniquely Portuguese category used to signify the cream of the crop. However, winemaking has changed so much in the last fifteen years that it is increasingly difficult to generalize about Portuguese vintages, and, apart from the Port shippers, producers keep few detailed climatic records. The following guide therefore covers all the harvests from 1990 to 2001 and all the major Port vintages back to 1963. It is no coincidence that the best years for Bairrada, Dão and the Douro usually correspond with declared Port vintages. A compendium of Port vintages back to 1896 can be found in my book *Port and the Douro*, published by Mitchell Beazley.

2002

After one of the driest summers on record, many vineyards in the interior and south of the country were suffering from extreme stress. Barca d'Alva on the Spanish border registered just sixty millimetres (2.5 inches) of rain between the end of the previous harvest and the beginning of September 2002. Fortunately there was none of the excessive heat that sometimes shrivels the berries and in early September (after a little light rain) the grapes were generally in good condition. A fine vintage seemed to be in prospect with yields estimated to be down by about thirty per cent on the previous year. In the Ribatejo, Alentejo and Douro Superior picking began in early September whereas growers in the rest of the country held off until the middle of the month. On Friday 13th an unusually deep depression settled over the Iberian Peninsula and the rain did not let up for five days. Thin-skinned grapes like Trincadeira started to rot on the vine and, throughout the country, the vintage became a race against time.

The unsettled weather continued into October spelling disaster for Bairrada and Vinho Verde where many growers did not even bother to pick. Some excellent Ports were produced in the Douro by those who harvested early and there are small quantities of good wine from the south. But for most producers, 2002 is a vintage they would rather forget.

2001

The winter of 2000–1 was the wettest since records began, with rain falling almost continuously from October to April. There were widespread landslides which blocked roads and railways. The bridge over the Douro at Entre-os-Rios collapsed in February, causing the tragic deaths of over seventy people. Growers in the Ribatejo visited their vineyards by boat. With groundwater supplies thoroughly replenished and warm weather during flowering, the 2001 harvest produced a hefty crop, certainly the largest since 1996. However, in the north of Portugal an unusually cool and variable August led to some uneven ripening. In the Douro the daytime temperature dropped from 40°C to 20°C from one day to the next. However, warm weather in early September saved the day and by the time that the harvest was underway some high sugar readings were being recorded. Torrential September rain in the Alentejo brought Baumés down but, nonetheless, Moreto (usually an insipid grape) was being harvested at 14 degrees Baumé. In the Douro Tinta Barroca was occasionally registering 18 degrees Baumé! In the Dão and Alentejo, as the harvest dragged on into late October, growers and winemakers became somewhat weary. However, with total production at 7.8 million hectolitres, 2001 seems to have matched quantity with quality.

2000

The season began early with mild and dry weather in February and March, but changed dramatically in the spring, which was cool and exceptionally wet. Snow fell on the northern mountains at Easter. Much of the flowering took place under adverse conditions, and by late May it looked as though 2000 would be the third small harvest in a row. However, unlike 1999 and 1998, warm summer weather continued into October, allowing the harvest to take place throughout the country in near-perfect conditions. Bairrada, Dão and the Douro produced some exceptional wines. Although yields were down dramatically in places, overall production was around average at 6.7 million hectolitres. For the Port shippers 2000 was a gift horse; a magic number backed by some truly excellent wines. A universal declaration in the spring and early summer of 2002 revealed some powerful wines, lacking the richness of 1994 but with more poise and harmony than 1997. Fonseca, Graham, Niepoort, Quinta do Noval and the tantalizingly scarce Quinta do Noval Nacional top the bill with impressive wines from Croft, Dow, Smith Woodhouse, Taylor and Warre. Even after the frenzied speculation involving 2000 Bordeaux, prices for the 2000 Vintage Ports remain reasonable.

1999

The winter of 1998–9 was cold and dry throughout Portugal, compensated by wet weather during April and May. This brought yields down, significantly in some places, for the second year in a row. The summer was hot and dry and by mid-September prospects looked good. Then, just as picking began in the north of the country, the weather broke as the remains of Hurricane Floyd blew in from the Atlantic. Conditions were worst in the north along the coast, with Bairrada and much of Dão particularly badly affected, but those inland and to the south who managed to harvest before the rain made some excellent wines. 1999 proved to be a good year for the Castelão grape on the Setúbal Peninsula. In the Douro it looked like a miracle vintage which was destroyed by rain at the last minute. There are, however, some good single-quinta Ports from those who made a careful selection in the vineyard. In the main, the Douro Superior fared better than the Cima or Baixo Corgo, where rot set in at an early stage. Total production was just above average at 7.8 million hectolitres.

1998

Blighted in the north of the country by a poor spring that reduced yields and precipitated an attack of oidium and mildew, 1998 looked set to produce minute quantities of potentially outstanding wines after a period of unrelenting summer heat. However, as soon as picking began in late September, rain swept in from the Atlantic. Grape sugars were diluted and the old, interplanted vineyards of the Douro, Dão, Bairrada and Vinho Verde were devastated by grey rot. The south fared much better and good wines were made, albeit in small quantities, in the Ribatejo, Alentejo and on the Setúbal Peninsula. Total production was miniscule at just 3.7 million hectolitres (half the ten-year average). The Douro produced some sound single-quinta or second-label Ports. Quinta do Bomfim (Dow), Quinta da Cavadinha (Warre), Senhora da Ribeira (Dow), Fonseca Guimaraens, Madelena (Smith Woodhouse), Malvedos (Graham), Quinta do Panascal (Fonseca), Silval and Quinta de Vargellas (Taylor) are among those recommended for drinking in the medium term.

1997

An extraordinarily warm spring gave way to cooler wet weather in June and July. The heat returned in August and by mid-September high Baumés were registered throughout the country. Apart from the occasional thunderstorm in the north, the harvest continued into early October under clear skies. 1997 was declared as a fully fledged vintage by the majority of Port shippers; those in the premier league are Dow, Fonseca, Graham, Niepoort and Noval, with Noval Nacional at its best for three decades. It was an unusual year in Bairrada, where the Baga grape ripened to give wines with abnormally high levels of alcohol and supple tannins. Some excellent *garrafeiras* (the best since 1990) were bottled. Casa de Saima in particular is a massive wine with ripe tannins that disguise the natural acidity. The ageing potential of these wines is enormous. 1997 was less successful in Estremadura and Terras do Sado. However, the Alentejo produced small quantities of high-quality wine; the Castelão grape produced unusually well-balanced red wines. The overall crop was just below average at 6.1 million hectolitres.

1996

After four years of drought, heavy rain fell throughout Portugal during the winter of 1995–6. Flowering took place in perfect conditions, but cool weather during August and September delayed ripening. The crop was huge (nearly ten million hectolitres) and the harvest became a test of skill and stamina, with fermentations continuing into November. Many producers turned out large quantities of thin wine, but there were one or two high spots, notably in the Dão region, where it was the best vintage of the decade. Some remarkable wines with good structure and balance were produced. Quinta dos Roques, Quinta dos Carvalhais and Quinta da Pellada Touriga Nacional are exemplary. Yields were higher in the Douro and many of the red wines are somewhat attenuated, but there are some successful single-quinta Ports, notably Quinta do Noval Nacional, Quinta de la Rosa, Quinta do Vesúvio and Quinta da Água Alta (Churchill).

1995
Severe drought cut yields, especially in the south of the country, but overall quality was good to excellent – even if some of the wines in the Alentejo are a little unbalanced. Both the Douro and Bairrada produced some impressive wines from well-ripened grapes, fruit driven and with good structure. Luís Pato was particularly successful with Vinha Pan and Vinha Barossa, the first time that these two single vineyard wines were bottled separately. Casa de Saima also produced a great *garrafeira*. A number of Port shippers opted for an outright vintage declaration, but in the wake of a universal declaration a year earlier, the majority decided to declare single-quinta or second-label wines. Fonseca Guimaraens, Quinta do Noval, Osborne, Quinta de la Rosa, Quinta de Vargellas Vinha Velha and Quinta do Vesuvio are the pick of the vintage. At this stage the wines from the 1995 vintage appear to be well balanced, but they are not wines to cellar over the long term. Total production amounted to seven million hectolitres.

1994
Yields were depressed by a combination of localized frost and poor flowering, followed in the south of Portugal by acute summer drought. Production was down in some parts of the country by as much as fifty per cent on the average, although the national total of 6.3 million hectolitres was about average. The lack of quantity was compensated by high quality, especially in the Douro, where the wines are intense yet soft, rich and elegant. Duas Quintas Reserva typifies the character of 1994 in the Douro, as does Reserva Ferreirinha. Not surprisingly, 1994 produced some outstanding Ports. With heavy demand from the United States, opening prices rose considerably and have continued to soar. Dow, Fonseca, Graham, Taylor and Warre made wines that will stand the test of time.

1993

Portugal's *annus horribilis*: a wet spring led to uneven flowering, and this was followed by a relatively cool summer. The harvest was abnormally late, but as soon as picking began the heavens opened, turning the vineyards into a quagmire. Even the normally drought-ridden Alentejo suffered. The result was a puny crop (just 4.5 million hectolitres) of wine that most growers would rather forget. One rather foolhardy estate bottled some Vintage Port but otherwise 1993 was dire for all concerned.

1992

The winter of 1991–2 was unseasonably dry and the drought continued unbroken through most of the summer. Although the weather was not abnormally hot, substantial damage was inflicted on the south of Portugal, especially the Alentejo. As a result yields were substantially down on 1991, with total production amounting to 7.5 million hectolitres. In general, wines from the north are considerably better than those from the south, which tended to be overblown and unbalanced. Quinta da Gaivosa made an exceptional Douro red. Taylor and Fonseca both declared impressive Vintage Ports, preferring 1992 to 1991. Niepoort declared both years.

1991

A wet winter was followed by a dry, settled spring, and flowering took place in near-perfect conditions throughout the country. The summer was hot and dry, but mid-September rain in the north helped to swell the grapes. Hot weather returned for the harvest, causing problems for those without recourse to temperature control. The result was a large crop (9.6 million hectolitres) of generally good-quality wine. Some stunning wines were produced in Bairrada, somewhat harder and more structured in style than in 1990. In the Douro this was the first vintage for Niepoort's Redoma and Ramos Pinto's Duas Quintas Reserva, both of which were big, rustic reds in 1991. Ferreira bottled Barca Velha for the first time for six years (see page 210). 1991 was favoured by the majority of Port shippers for declaration over 1992. Croft, Dow, Graham, Niepoort and Warre produced powerful, well-structured vintage Ports for the medium to long term.

1990

Winter rains replenished the water table after a dry twelve months, but blisteringly hot weather during July and August brought on a drought in the south of the country. Rain in early September saved the day in the Douro. The best wines came from the coastal regions, whereas those from the interior and the south tended toward jamminess. Nonetheless there were some very impressive wines from Mouchão in the Alentejo and Valle Pradinhos in Trás-os-Montes. Bairrada was particularly successful in 1990 and Casa de Saima's monumental *garrafeira* is one of the greatest red wines that Portugal has ever produced. It will develop for a lifetime. There was no fully fledged vintage Port in 1990 but some appealing single-quinta wines were produced at Quinta do Bomfim (Dow), Quinta da Cavadinha (Warre) and Graham's Malvedos.

1987

A hot, dry summer was upset by wet weather during the harvest, but a number of shippers made some fine vintage Ports. A few opted for an outright declaration, but, perhaps sensing the impending global economic downturn, the majority opted for single-quinta Vintage Ports. Niepoort and Quinta da Eira Velha (Martinez) are well placed for drinking now and in future (to 2010 plus). In the Alentejo, look out for any stray bottles of Quinta do Carmo Garrafeira, which is outstanding.

1985

Well received by the trade when the wines were declared, 1985 has subsequently thrown up one or two unpleasant surprises. The best (Fonseca, Dow, Graham and Warre) are impressively ripe and well balanced, reflecting the near-perfect weather conditions during the harvest. Others, including some big names, are very disappointing. *Caveat emptor*. Ferreira bottled a rich but rather early-maturing Barca Velha.

1983

The year began badly with a long, cold winter and spring. Snow fell on the Serra do Marão as late as May 20. After a hot but unsettled summer, a fine September saved the day. Declared by the majority of shippers, 1983 has produced some firm, long-lived wines that have plenty of time left to run. Dow, Gould Campbell, Graham, Niepoort, Quarles Harris, Smith Woodhouse, Taylor and Warre are all powerful, muscular wines with the backbone to last until 2015 at least.

1982
A handful of shippers chose to declare 1982 in preference to 1983, leading to a so-called "split vintage". In retrospect they clearly made a mistake, for the wines are generally soft and early maturing. Drink soon.

1980
Overshadowed from the start by the 1977 (and subsequently by the 1983 and 1985), 1980 has become a "Cinderella vintage", whereas the 1985 at least has turned into a rather ugly sister (see above). The growing season was variable, but the weather was good during the harvest. Despite some low sugar readings, 1980 produced some attractive, balanced wines for the medium to long term. Dow, Graham, Niepoort, Smith Woodhouse, Taylor and Warre are drinking well now and will continue to develop well until 2010 at least.

1977
Fine weather during the harvest produced some impressively deep-coloured wines in spite of a rather cool summer. Hailed as a "classic" when it was declared in 1979, 1977 was compared in stature with 1963. The wines have developed rather faster than expected, and although Fonseca is an all-time great, many '77s are fully ready to drink and even looking a little tired around the edges. No match for 1963 (or 1966) in my opinion.

1975
Christened the *Verão Quente* (hot summer) because the thermometer and the political temperature both rose sharply, 1975 produced some soft, easy-going vintage Ports which are fully ready to drink. Do not keep other than for academic interest.

1970
Underrated (and undervalued) from the start, the hot, dry summer of 1970 produced some outstanding vintage Ports that have subsequently stood the test of time. Although there is some bottle variation (this was

the last vintage to be bottled both in Oporto and the UK), there is a long list of impressive wines: Cálem, Delaforce, Dow, Fonseca, Graham, Kopke, Niepoort, Noval Nacional and Taylor. Delicious to drink now, the majority will keep until 2020 at least.

1966
Despite some rain during the harvest, 1966 produced powerful wines, the best of which compare with 1963. Quinta do Noval Nacional is truly magnificent, as are Dow, Fonseca, Graham and Taylor. No hurry to drink: the best will keep for a lifetime or more.

1963
A textbook growing season in northern Portugal, with a long, warm summer followed by a little light rain in mid-September that helped to swell the grapes just before the harvest. The wines are good across the board, with layer upon layer of ripe fruit backed by powerful tannins. Some are only just ready to drink and most will last for decades to come. Cockburn, Croft, Dow, Fonseca, Graham, Quinta do Noval Nacional, Taylor and Warre are superb. No other Port vintage since 1963 has quite such an extensive roll of honour.

3

Atlantic Wines

The coldest winter I have ever spent was a summer in San Francisco.

MARK TWAIN

As far as I am aware, Mark Twain never visited Portugal, but his observation on the weather in San Francisco might equally apply to Oporto. Substitute the Atlantic for the Pacific and the reasons for this climatic anomaly are much the same. During the height of summer the waters of the north Atlantic are still so cold that they cause a bank of fog to build up just offshore. It lurks there after sundown and rolls in silently during the early hours, the only noise being the sad boom of the foghorn on the *molhe* (breakwater) at the mouth of the Douro. Like the Golden Gate in San Francisco, the narrow estuary serves to funnel the fog upriver. Occasionally it will cover more than half of northern Portugal, reaching eighty kilometres inland before gradually retreating back toward the coast as the sun burns through. However, in high summer the coastline from the Aveiro lagoon to the mouth of the River Minho and beyond is often shrouded in clammy fog until midday or mid-afternoon.

The Atlantic Ocean exerts an influence over Portugal in its entirety. Even the Alentejo, one hundred kilometres (sixty-two miles) or more from the coast, is to some extent under the sway of the prevailing Atlantic westerlies. But the oceanic influence is strongest on the *litoral*, a narrow strip of country twenty to sixty kilometres (twelve to thirty-seven miles) wide extending from the northern frontier with Spain 400 kilometres (248 miles) south to the outskirts of Lisbon. The *litoral* is shaped by a series of interlocking river basins. The lower reaches of the Minho, Lima, Cavado, Ave, Douro, Vouga, Mondego and the *ribeiras* that drain the hills of Estremadura provide ample sites for cultivating vines. But it is the

Northern Portugal

climate that is the unifying factor for a seemingly disparate group of wine regions with varying fortunes. In the north lies Vinho Verde, the most Atlantic of all Portuguese wines, occupying an area of granite scenery that feels part of northern Europe. It merges almost imperceptibly with Lafões on the River Vouga, which leads to Bairrada, an inveterate wine region that (weather patterns permitting) is capable of greatness. The university city of Coimbra provides a gap before vineyards recommence with a vengeance. Estremadura, Portugal's largest wine region in terms of output, begins in the hills just north of the city of Leiria and stretches down the coast into the Lisbon suburbs. These suburbs engulf (or threaten to engulf) three very different but historic enclaves – Colares, Carcavelos and Bucelas – the first of which certainly merits a protection order to save it from the speculators.

Over a third of Portugal's wine comes from these vineyards but, due to the unpredictability of the climate, both quantity and quality vary alarmingly. Rainfall, perhaps the most representative measure of climatic differentiation within Portugal, is high throughout, from 800 millimetres (31.5 inches) per annum north of Lisbon up to 2,900 millimetres (114 inches) in the mountains south of the River Minho. Timing is everything. Most rain falls in winter, but drab, damp weather in May and June is not uncommon and will reduce yields to paltry levels at the same time as provoking disease. There's a proverb that highlights this risk: *Maio e couveiro não e vinhateiro* ("May is a month for cabbages but not vines"). However, late spring frost, a problem in the mountain valleys, is rarely a threat on the coast. High summer is usually dry – dry enough to cause hydric stress in those vineyards rooted in shallow granite soils but with sufficient moisture in the atmosphere for disease still to be a problem. Severe stress causes the vine to shut down, which means that the vine leaves curl and the grapes cease to ripen evenly. This difficulty is summed up in another local saying: *Em Agosto secam os montes, em Setembro as fontes, em Outubro tudo* ("In August the hills dry up, in September the springs, in October everything"). However, during September growers play an increasingly tense waiting game, balancing the ripening of their grapes with the looming threat of autumn rain. The summer weather often breaks during the September equinox, and the expectation of a fine crop can be cruelly dashed at the last minute when the heavens open and the rain continues to pour down for the two or three weeks pencilled in for the harvest.

After years like 1988, 1993, 1998 and 1999, it is little wonder that growers on Portugal's Atlantic seaboard are tempted to pick early, often before their grapes have reached optimum ripeness.

Atlantic Portugal is undoubtedly a challenging place to grow grapes and make wine, but thankfully there is an increasing number of producers who feel that it is worth the effort. Although the total vineyard area may be shrinking as vines are uprooted and licences transferred to the newly fashionable wine regions inland, there are growers who are prepared to take the time out and discover their own *terroir*. "This", as one quality-conscious grower in Estremadura emphasized, "is not the place to be an absentee farmer." The variability of the weather means that snap decisions have to be taken in the vineyard in order to protect the crop and produce worthwhile wine. There are some extremely worthwhile wines – red, white and occasionally fortified – being made all the way down the Atlantic seaboard, with the added advantage that some of those producers who have found the right formula are able to turn out volume at a keen price.

With few exceptions the wines from Portugal's *litoral* share a family resemblance. Levels of alcohol are never head-splittingly high and there is always a streak of nervy acidity never very far from the surface. The Portuguese use the word *astringente* (astringent) not as a pejorative term but in its positive sense. It describes that combination of firm tannin and acidity that is the hallmark of Portugal's best Atlantic reds. Astringency gives the wines longevity, equalled perhaps only by the finest Bordeaux. In fact there can be a real affinity with Claret, a trait that was not overlooked during the phylloxera years, when this part of Portugal supplied the French with large quantities of red wine. It has taken more than a century for wine producers in Vinho Verde, Bairrada and Estremadura to rekindle their own pride. Sometimes this is misplaced, either in cooperatives who really believe that they are making the world's best wine or in producers who try to command a high price for something mediocre. But there are people who are getting the balance right: in the vineyard, in the winery and in their sales and marketing. In general, they are the ones who have been prepared to reunite the vineyard with the bottle, seeing things through from the setting out of a new vineyard to presenting their wine at a tasting in Lisbon, London or New York. Although it is impossible to govern the climate, the key to making good wine in Atlantic Portugal is to be in complete control.

I. VINHO VERDE

The coastline north of Oporto is aptly titled the Costa Verde ("green coast"). Behind the white sandy beaches, a barrier of aromatic pine and eucalyptus yields to a riot of vegetation like a kitchen garden gone to seed. Go into a restaurant on the Costa Verde and you will find *caldo verde*, "green broth" made from the local cabbages which are capable of growing 1.8 metres (six feet) high. Casting a shadow over cabbage fields, paths and byways is a giant network of pergola-trained vines producing Vinho Verde, or "green wine".

It comes as something of a surprise to find that about one-third of the production of Vinho Verde is inky red rather than pale, green-tinged white. The name originates not from the colour of the wine in the glass but from the need to drink Vinho Verde young, in its first flush of youth. Many restaurant wine lists still make the broad distinction between *vinhos maduros* (so-called "mature" wines) and Vinhos Verdes, a tradition harking back to the days when Vinho Verde was the only fresh, early drinking style of wine available in Portugal. Investment in stainless-steel technology has meant that fresh, fruit-driven wines can now be made almost anywhere, but Vinho Verde with its own DOC has held onto its identity, producing predominantly dry, spritzy wines with searingly high acidity (6 grams/litre is the minimum) and low alcohol (8.5–11.5 per cent). This is partly a reflection of the cool, damp climate in north-west Portugal, partly of the stringent regulations that govern the production of Vinho Verde. Where other wine regions in Portugal have moved on, Vinho Verde has stayed much the same, shifting from rasping red to frail white and back again, according to fashion. As a result of competition from elsewhere, Vinho Verde lost much of its popular appeal during the 1990s, even in its native territory.

The region producing Vinho Verde is the largest DOC in Portugal. It stretches from Melgaço on the River Minho in the north all the way down the coast through Oporto almost to the banks of the Vouga south of Vale de Cambra. Most of the region corresponds to the province of Entre-Douro-e-Minho ("between the Douro and Minho"), an area sweepingly referred to as "the Minho". The vineyards are to be found concentrated along the rivers that drain the mountains of Trás-os-Montes inland. From north to south these are the Minho (which forms the frontier with Spain),

Vinho Verde: espigueros *(granaries) and cabbages*

Lima, Cavado, Ave, Douro and its tributaries the Tamega and Paiva. Vines peter out above 800 metres (2,624 feet) or so and the high country is mostly given over to forestry.

Vinho Verde country is the cradle of Portugal. Guimarães was the nation's first capital, from where the Christian kings launched their attacks on the Moors, driving them southwards until Portugal gained its present elongated shape. The Minho was also one of the first tracts of mainland Portugal to produce wine for export. When the English shied away from all things French in the sixteenth century, they sourced wines from Monção and Viana do Castelo, the closest seaports to Blighty. The strong link between the people and the land in north-west Portugal makes for a conservative attitude. The bells of chapels and churches ring out all over the countryside, a mark of the deep Catholicism that pervades these parts. The revolutionary military who ran the government in Lisbon during the summer of 1975 received short shrift from the folk of the Minho. The backlash that spread through the country in the autumn began with the burning of the Communist Party headquarters in Vila Nova de Famalicão.

With the economic recovery that followed the revolution, the landscape of Vinho Verde has become increasingly chaotic. Home to around 3.5 million people, it is the most densely populated part of rural Portugal. The region now includes some of the most industrialized areas of the country cheek by jowl with some of the most Arcadian. Agriculture vies for space with houses and light industry. Textiles, shoes, timber and furniture are the mainstay of the local economy alongside a polyculture of different crops. Maize, cabbages, a cow, a goat and some vines can often be seen co-existing on the same tiny plot. Eking out the last drop of goodness from the generally poor granite-based soils, vines seem to take up the very last spare inch of space, forming the hedgerows between fields, running along railway lines, over roads and infiltrating back gardens. It is not uncommon to see a line of washing strung out beneath the vines.

It is impossible to assess just how much land is occupied by vineyard in the Minho. The official figures record over 100,000 vineyards, taking up just over 59,000 hectares, but the real total is almost certainly 10,000 hectares more. For every hundred farmers in the region, ninety count themselves as vine growers, and in spite of the rampant industrialization in recent decades around Famalicão, Santo Tirso and Guimarães, over a quarter of the workforce is still engaged in agriculture. Ninety per cent of the holdings are fewer than five hectares in extent and the vast majority are minifundios, little bigger than a suburban back garden.

In order to make the most of this cramped environment, vines have been trained to grow high above the ground, leaving space for other forms of land use underneath. In the past vines would climb like beanstalks up the trunks of chestnut, elm, cherry or poplar trees, the canopy of the vine draped from one tree to another. This impractical method of cultivation, known as *enforcado* ("hanging"), has largely been abandoned, but it is not uncommon to see an extension of this system known as *arejão* or *arjoado* ("aired" or "ventilated"). Four or five wires are stretched between small trees or tall pillars, and vines planted two or three metres (seven or ten feet) apart grow vertically to form a dense screen up to six metres (twenty feet) in height. Much more widespread are the pergola-trained vines known as *vinha ramada*. Stout granite posts around three metres in height support a horizontal wire trellis. This in turn supports the vine canopy and the heavy bunches of grapes that hang beneath. Vinha ramada has a distinctly ornamental look, resulting from the fact that during the Salazar era, when feeding the nation became a priority, vines could only be planted in the Vinho Verde region for "decorative purposes". This drove smallholders to coax as much yield as they could from their supposedly "decorative" vines and did nothing to advance the quality of Vinho Verde.

Apart from maximizing the use of space, high-trained vines have a number of other advantages. The climate in Vinho Verde country is challenging to say the least. The humid westerlies that sail over the Atlantic are forced to rise and condense when they reach the Iberian landmass. Annual average rainfall varies from 1,200 millimetres (47 inches) on the coast to as much as 2,900 millimetres (114 inches) on the Serras of Peneda and Gerês inland. Most of the rain falls in the winter months, but the occasional wet spring and summer creates havoc during flowering and necessitates regular treatment against mildew and oidium. It is not uncommon to have to carry out twelve or more spraying operations in a season. The summer warmth that creates the conditions for olive trees, kiwis and oranges to flourish alongside vines also provokes fungal disease. Raising the canopy above the ground helps the air to circulate freely and reduces the risk of rot or, in the mountain valleys, damage from late spring frosts. But these practical advantages are increasingly outweighed by problems. Since the phylloxera epidemic in the late nineteenth century, vine varieties have been selected for their vigour and yield rather than the intrinsic quality of their fruit. Vigorous plants (including many direct producers and hybrids) produce grapes that are low in sugar and high in acidity, particularly as the dense thicket of leaves shades the bunches from exposure to the sun.

In the 1970s, with the relaxation in the legislation that followed the revolution, a number of growers began to abandon the labour-intensive pergolas in favour of another form of training, namely the *cruzeta*. Four vines are planted around the base of a wooden, cement or granite pole, two metres (seven feet) or so in height. A crossbar (hence the name *cruzeta*) 1.5 to 1.8 metres (five to six feet) in width supports two lateral wires along which the vine's fruit-bearing arms are trained to give the plant a semblance of order and shape. Planted in rows and spaced to allow tractors to pass in between, *cruzetas* permit a certain amount of mechanization, but they have not been popular with growers, who find them troublesome and expensive to maintain. Most of the larger growers have now moved on to a more straightforward system of training, *cordão simples*, with vines supported on a vertical cordon 1.5 metres (five feet) in height. This facilitates mechanization, to the extent that one property, Quinta de Aveleda near Penafiel, is now able to harvest by machine. According to the owner, António Guedes, one mechanical harvester is able to carry out the work of sixty men: a considerable feat in an area where agricultural labour is in increasingly short supply. At a density of 1,500 to 2,000 vines per hectare (compared to the 500 vines per hectare or less that was usual in the past), cordon planting has helped to improve the quality of the wine. Better exposure is producing grapes with higher levels of sugar and lower acidity, bringing some growers into conflict with the authorities, who have continued to insist on a maximum level of alcohol of 11.5 per cent by volume.

Sub-regions

The Vinho Verde region divides into six officially recognized sub-regions, each of which produces a distinct style of wine based on a different mix of grapes. (The characteristics of the varieties themselves are covered in detail in Chapter 2).

MONÇÃO

In the extreme north along the River Minho, Monção takes in the municipalities of Monção and Melgaço. Like Galicia immediately to the north, the growers around Monção have become so possessive about the Alvarinho grape that the authorities have effectively prohibited it from being planted anywhere else. As a result the countryside around Monção and Melgaço now has a dynamic all of its own, and Alvarinho wines (still technically classed as Vinhos Verdes) are subject to separate legislation stipulating 11.5 per cent as the minimum level of alcohol by volume. Most Alvarinhos typically ripen to give 12.5 or 13 per cent; the Trajadura grape is also planted in the region and the two varieties are frequently blended to produce a lighter style of wine. Two distinct styles of pure, varietal Alvarinho have emerged. Those from the stony alluvial soils tend to be the richest and most aromatic, whereas those from the granite are more subdued. Although no distinction is made on the label, Alvarinho from Melgaço upstream tends to have more nervy acidity, whereas that from Monção produces wine which is softer and rounder. A well-managed cooperative at Monção blends wines from both districts.

LIMA

The Lima sub-region embraces the municipalities of Viana do Castelo, Ponte de Lima, Arcos de Valdevez and Ponte de Barca either side of the River Lima. Cut off from the urban areas to the south by a chain of mountains, it is the most rural part of the Vinho Verde region. Pergola-trained vines thread their way through the countryside, gradually petering out as they ascend the inhospitable slopes of the Serra da Peneda. The municipality of Ponte de Lima is the heart of the region, with more individual growers than any other: 6,000 in total, farming an average of 0.4 hectares each. The leading vineyards are planted mainly with Loureiro, which produces light, fragrant, minerally Vinho Verde. Wines from the few outcrops of schist south of the Lima tend to be finer and more aromatic than the lighter wines from the granite-based soils that predominate throughout the Vinho Verde region.

BRAGA

To the south, Braga is the largest of the six sub-regions, with 15,000 hectares of vines. It takes in two river valleys, the Cavado and the Ave, and eleven municipalities: Esposende, Barcelos, Vila Verde, Amares,

Braga, Povoa de Lanhoso, Fafe, Guimarães, Vila Nova de Famalicão and Santo Tirso. This is one of the most industrialized parts of Portugal, with ostentatious houses built alongside the main roads by the new middle classes, showing off their possessions to all who pass by. There are pockets of beautiful countryside seemingly untouched by the passage of time. Dominated by co-ops, the Braga sub-region is also home to some substantial family estates, many of which are being revitalized. Loureiro has emerged as the best grape variety, although there are substantial quantities of Azal, Paderná (aka Arinto) and Trajadura as well as the ubiquitous red Vinhão.

BASTO

Due east of Braga, Basto takes in the Tamega Valley upstream from Amarante and the slopes of the Serra do Alvão. Off the beaten track, this is the most mountainous Vinho Verde sub-region and also one of the most attractive to visit, with terraced smallholdings and vines strung out between the trees. Four municipalities make up Basto: Celorico de Basto, Cabaceiras de Basto, Mondim de Basto and Ribeira de Pena. White wines are based on Azal, Batoca and Paderná, but there is still a large quantity of red emanating from Borraçal, Espadeiro, Padeiro de Basto, Rabo de Ovelha and Vinhão.

PENAFIEL

Even more urbanized than Braga is Penafiel, which extends almost into the suburbs of Oporto. Five municipalities – Penafiel, Lousada, Paredes, Felgueiras and Paços de Ferreira (the latter better known for the manufacture of furniture than wine) – nonetheless manage to shoehorn in 10,000 hectares of vineyard between them. Azal and Paderná are the principal white grapes, with Loureiro and Trajadura confined to the larger estates. Borraçal, Espadeiro and Vinhão make up the red. Penafiel includes two giants of Vinho Verde: Quinta de Aveleda and the Adega Cooperativa de Felgueiras.

AMARANTE

With nearly 8,000 hectares of vines, Amarante has more vineyard than any other single municipality. Along with neighbouring Marco de Canaveses (birthplace of Carmen Miranda), it produces large amounts of red Vinho Verde, mostly from Vinhão. White wines derive almost exclusively from Azal and Padernã.

OTHER AREAS

A further sixteen municipalities fall outside these officially designated sub-regions, the most significant of which are those along the River Douro from Castelo de Paiva to Resende, which make a speciality of red Vinho Verde from Amaral, better known locally as Azal Tinto. Baião, almost in the Douro demarcation itself, makes an atypically full, alcoholic style of white Vinho Verde from the Avesso grape.

Late September brings the narrow lanes of Vinho Verde country to a crawl as carts and trailers groaning with grapes wend their way to the nearest winery. Normally, October 5 marks the height of the harvest. This coincides with a national holiday, *Dia da Republica*, allowing entire families to go back to their rural roots and pick grapes. Unfortunately, October 5 also frequently coincides with a break in the weather, and it is by no means uncommon to see long lines of tractors queueing in the rain while the grapes receive a generous dousing, further diluting the crop.

The production of Vinho Verde falls into two camps. Until the 1950s, Vinho Verde was a cottage industry where wines were made in small stone *adegas* or back parlours all over the region. Vinification still takes place on this scale, with the grapes trodden and fermented in stone *lagares*, after which the wine (mostly red) is run off into old wooden casks. Either shortly after the end of the alcoholic fermentation or in the spring after the harvest, the malolactic begins, converting harsh malic acid into the softer lactic acid. Carbon dioxide is generated by this process and some of this is retained in the wine, giving it a natural spritz or sparkle. This is the origin of Vinho Verde: an astringent, hazy, scrumpy-style wine that is also inherently unstable. It can be found served fresh and frothing from the cask in private houses or roadside *tascas* in the more remote parts of the region.

With the drive to make wine for export in the 1950s and 1960s, Vinho Verde came to be made on a much larger scale. In the co-ops and centralized wineries that date from this era, the grapes are crushed or pressed mechanically (often in continuous presses) and the must is fermented either in lined cement vats or, since money flowed in from the EU, in temperature-controlled stainless steel. Once the sugar in the grapes has fermented to alcohol, all white wines are dosed with sulphur dioxide to prevent the malolactic from taking place. This not only helps to prevent oxidation but also preserves much of the primary fruit character that would be otherwise lost during the malolactic. With this in mind, bottling takes place early, either in the late winter or early spring. The characteristic spritz now results from an injection of CO_2 shortly before the wine is bottled, but many red Vinhos Verdes still gain their *pico* or effervescence from the malolactic in the traditional way.

The local perception of Vinho Verde is that it is a bone dry wine, red or white, made to be drunk in the year after the harvest. For this reason, few bottles carry the year of the vintage on the label. Red Vinho Verde is still popular in the Minho, where it cuts through the richness of the local food. With its rasping astringency, it is something of an acquired taste, famously described by wine writer Oz Clarke (a fan) as akin to drinking cold tea through sandpaper! The Vinho Verde prepared for overseas markets is mostly white and is bottled with up to 15 grams/litre of residual sugar, frequently accompanied by a heavy-handed dose of sulphur dioxide as a belt and braces precaution against oxidation and/or secondary fermentation. As a result of poor stock rotation, many Vinhos Verdes remain for too long on brightly lit supermarket shelves and end up being both sulphurous and oxidized. Consequently, much of the Vinho Verde consumed abroad is far removed from the crisp, minerally dry white wine that is drunk with fresh shellfish in the *marisqueiras* that line the beaches of the Costa Verde.

Producers

There are literally thousands of Vinho Verde producers scattered all over the region. The Oporto-based Regional Commission lists over three hundred, including twenty-two cooperatives, but there are many more making a few pipes of wine for family and friends. Most Vinho Verde is bottled and sold by large, privately owned merchant firms who either make wine from their own grapes or (more commonly) buy in wine from the cooperatives. In common with the rest of Portugal, since the early 1980s there has been a revival in small-scale production as the larger single estates or quintas have benefited from EU finance to invest in their own production and marketing. Together they account for about two per cent of the region's total production. I have restricted the producers

covered in this book to those, either co-ops, private firms or single quintas, with a profile on the domestic and/or international market. Names
accompanied by an asterisk (*) form part of the *Rota dos Vinhos Verdes*
(Vinho Verde Wine Route) and are open to receive passing visitors. Some
are inevitably better geared up for visitors than others.

QUINTA DE ALDERIZ

Soc Agric da Casa Pinheiro Lda, 4950 Monção

Although by no means the most expressive of wines from Monção,
Anselmo Mendes ("Mr Alvarinho") succeeds in producing one of the
purest Alvarinhos from this ten-hectare estate with a small modern winery. The wine is restrained and minerally, with plenty of fine fruit and a
long steely finish. The florid label, on the other hand, doesn't win many
friends!

QUINTA DO AMEAL

Refoios do Lima, 4990 Ponte de Lima

Practically abandoned until the 1990s, Quinta do Ameal, deep in the
Lima valley, has been completely replanted and restored by Pedro Araújo,
brother of the owner of Quinta de Covela (see page 145). The vineyard
extends to thirty-five hectares, not inconsiderable in the context of the
partilhas ("sub-divisions") of the Vinho Verde region. Made entirely from
Loureiro, Quinta do Ameal is one of the best expressions of this variety,
with a fresh, green, grassy character that just hints at Riesling. Breaking
with convention, it is bottled in a Bordeaux bottle.

QUINTA DA AVELEDA*

Aveleda – Sociedade Agricola e Comercial de Quinta da Aveleda SA,
4560 Penafiel

Aveleda is a calm oasis amid Oporto's chaotic hinterland. Fantastic
gardens with avenues, pools and fountains surround the seventeenth-
century manor house. Hidden amongst the oak trees and giant camellias
is one of Portugal's leading privately owned wineries, bottling around
eight million litres of wine a year, making Aveleda the largest shipper of
Vinho Verde. The estate belongs to the Guedes family, cousins of the owners of Sogrape, and until 1979, when a domestic dispute intervened,
Aveleda was part of the Sogrape corporation.

The vineyards at Aveleda are the largest and most advanced in north-west Portugal. As far back as 1860, Dom Manuel Pedro Guedes began batch-planting vines by variety as opposed to the muddled interplanting of different grapes that continued to take place elsewhere for at least another hundred years. In the twenty-first century, Aveleda is the only property in the Vinho Verde region to be almost completely mechanized. With over 200 hectares of vineyard, Aveleda is far removed from the cabbage patch league.

A number of very different wines are made here. The light, spritzy, off-dry Casal Garcia is the main brand. Made from grapes grown on the estate and purchased from local farmers, it is the single best selling Vinho Verde, with sales amounting to around five million litres per annum. Aveleda and Quinta da Aveleda are two distinct wines made from a higher percentage of Loureiro and Trajadura. The first is off-dry and geared to export markets, whereas the second is classic Vinho Verde: bone dry with crisp, green apple aromas and flavours. Aveleda has also introduced three varietal wines, from Loureiro, Trajadura and Alvarinho respectively. The latter, with aromas of jasmine and flavours of peach, is one of the best of the genre. The range is capped by Grinalda, an expressive, floral blend of Trajadura and Loureiro from grapes grown entirely on the estate. There is also a good, dark, rasping red Vinho Verde; the sort of wine you could use to fill a fountain pen! To complete the picture Aveleda also produces cheese and one of Portugal's best *águardentes*, Adega Velha.

The Aveleda estate is open to passing visitors. It is well worth leaving the frightful A4 motorway to taste the wines and seek refuge in the gardens. Look out for the high-rise goat house.

BORGES

Sociedade dos Vinhos Borges SA, Rua Infante Dom Henrique, 421, Apartado 18, 4439 Rio Tinto

From the mid-1970s to the late 1990s this well-known Portuguese firm went to hell and, but for the last-minute intervention of industrialist José Maria Viera, might never have come back. Borges and Irmão was nationalized along with the bank of the same name during the 1975 revolution and has taken twenty-five years to regain a sense of direction. With interests throughout the north of Portugal, the company has decamped from its historic HQ in Vila Nova de Gaia to the Torrié coffee factory at Rio

Tinto ("red river") just outside Oporto. It is one of the largest exporters of Vinho Verde (much of it for supermarket own label), but sales of Gatão, once the largest single Vinho Verde brand, have declined considerably during the years of upheaval. The company has diversified, with a single-quinta Vinho Verde (Quinta de Simaens) being joined by wines from the Douro (Perola and Lello), Dão (Meia Encosta) and Quinta de Aguieira (a Dão single quinta). In the past, winemaking has been distinctly patchy, but with renewed investment in the company's Lixa winery, under the guidance of Anselmo Mendes, this looks set to improve.

SOLAR DAS BOUÇAS
Prozelo, 4720 Amares
One of the first single-estate Vinhos Verdes, this property on the banks of the River Cavado north of Braga was the subject of considerable invest-ment by Port shipper Quinta do Noval. When Noval was sold to AXA, Bouças remained with the van Zeller family. With thirty hectares of vine-yard, Solar das Bouças is a fragrant Loureiro-based wine with a good track record.

PALÁCIO DE BREJOEIRA
Pinheiros, 4950 Monção
This grandiose nineteenth-century palace just outside Monção only began making its own wine in 1976, but quickly established its reputation as a "first growth" among Vinhos Verdes, with a price to match. The wine is the creation of Maria Hermina Pães, the redoubtable owner of this impressive but gaunt property, which even boasts its own private theatre. Made entirely from Alvarinho, for almost two decades Brejoeira was, undeni-ably, one of Portugal's finest wines. Over recent years, however, standards seem to have slipped as the competition among Alvarinhos has increased.

QUINTA DA FRANQUEIRA*
Lugar de Pedrego, 4750 Barcelos
The English have not been identified with Vinho Verde since the seven-teenth century, when they ceased shipping wine from Viana do Castelo and Monção and moved to Oporto. However, in 1980 Piers Gallie set about planting six hectares of vines on his family property, an old monastery near Barcelos. Made from a blend of Loureiro, Trajadura and a tiny quantity of

Azal, Quinta da Franqueira is a consistently well-made Vinho Verde with fresh, grapefruit-like flavours and steely acidity. The Gallies have opened their home to *turismo de habitação* and invite guests for Earl Grey tea, chocolate cake or a glass of their own Vinho Verde.

QUINTA DE LUOU*
Quinta de Luou – Sociedade Agricola Lda, Sta Cruz de Lima,
4990 Ponte de Lima

This estate is located in one of the most beautiful parts of northern Portugal, off the beaten track in the Lima valley. The eighteenth-century manor house seems to have hardly changed since it was built, and it has been inhabited by the Malheiro Reymão family for over a century. Under the auspices of Gaspar Malheiro Reymão, Luou was one of the first estates to bottle and market its own wine, beginning in 1985. The vineyard, planted on *cruzetas*, and winery now look rather dated, but José Ferrão, consultant winemaker for a number of single estates, succeeds in making an authentic, very crisp, restrained Vinho Verde from Loureiro (seventy-five per cent) along with Trajadura and Paderná.

QUINTAS DE MELGAÇO*
Quintas de Melgaço – Agricultura e Turismo SA, Ferreiros de Cima, Alvaredo, 4960 Melgaço

A consortium with 150 members, Quintas de Melgaço is the source of some of the best Alvarinho. Much is sold to firms looking for own label Alvarinho (where much depends on subsequent handling and bottling), but Quintas de Melgaço produces its own peachy wine named QM. Anselmo Mendes is in charge of the winemaking.

ADEGA COOPERATIVA REGIONAL DE MONÇÃO*
Cruzes, Macedo, 4950 Monção

Established in 1958, Monção is one of just a handful of well-run cooperatives in Portugal. It operates from surprisingly old-fashioned premises just south of the town and draws in grapes from 1,600 growers in the municipalities of Monção and Melgaço. The Monção Cooperative is the single largest producer of Alvarinho, accounting for more than half the production of the Monção sub-region. In common with most cooperatives, grapes are selected by their sugar reading rather than *terroir*. Those with a potential alcohol level in excess of 11.5 degrees are directed into a pure, peachy Alvarinho called Deu-la-Deu. Grapes that fail to make the grade are blended with fifteen per cent of Trajadura in a more delicate, appley dry white known as Muralhas de Monção. It is a testament to the success of the Monção Co-op that "Muralhas" is one of the most reliable and best-known Vinhos Verdes in the thousands of fish restaurants that line the coast of Portugal from Lisbon to the Minho. A lighter wine named Danaide, a fifty-fifty blend of Alvarinho and Trajadura, soaks up the remaining grapes. In successful years, when red grapes achieve a potential alcohol level of at least 10 degrees, Danaide tinto, made mainly from the locally named Negrão (Vinhão) grape, completes the range of wines from this efficient *adega*. A number of well-known firms source their Alvarinho wines from the Monção co-op, but much depends on subsequent handling.

MUROS DE MELGAÇO
Anselmo Mendes, 4960 Melgaço
This is an example of Portugal's so-called "garage wines". Anselmo Mendes produces a few casks of wine from Alvarinho grown on his own 1.5-hectare property overlooking the Minho Valley. I prefer Alvarinho pure and simple, without recourse to barrel fermentation in oak, but his wine is well made nonetheless.

QUINTA DO MINHO*
Quinta do Minho – Agricultura e Turismo, Lugar do Barrio, Lanhoso, 4830 Povoa de Lanhoso
The solid baroque manor house at Quinta do Minho lies in ruins, but alongside is a modern winery with a capacity greatly in excess of that required for the thirteen hectares of vines planted on the estate. Quinta do Minho buys in grapes from growers throughout the Braga sub-region and produces a light, minerally wine named Vinha Verde ("Green Vine") from Loureiro and Trajadura. Off-dry but balanced with grapefruit flavours, it is one of the most consistently reliable of all the big Vinho Verde brands. Quinta do Minho also produces a pure, appley Loureiro from grapes grown on the estate and a slightly fuller, late-harvest wine picked in mid-November called Colheita das Netas. Unusually for a white Vinho Verde, the CO_2 spritz in the wine originates from the malo-

lactic fermentation, which takes place in bottle. Another white wine, Gabia, is made from Alvarinho grapes bought in from Melgaço. Vinified at Povoa de Lanhoso, which is well outside the authorized sub-region, Gabia does not qualify as an Alvarinho and as a result of barrel fermentation followed by twenty-one months' ageing in oak, this soft, smooth dry white does not bear much resemblance to a Vinho Verde and is bottled as a *vinho de mesa*. This inventive producer has been pioneering a revival of Vinho Verde tinto, and APS, named after the founder of the estate, António Pires da Silva, is a deliciously rasping red made mainly from Vinhão with herbal, berry fruit flavours. The cork is firmly wired down, which hints at the lively spritz resulting from malolactic fermentation in bottle. This is a wine that would go well with *rojões a moda do minho* (a hearty pork casserole) or locally caught lamprey.

QUINTA DA PEDRA
Vinompor, Troviscoso, 4950 Monção
One of the largest producers of Alvarinho, Quinta da Pedra has thirty hectares of vineyard on stony soils (hence the name) near Monção. This fresh but rather simple, minerally Alvarinho is one of very few Vinhos Verdes to be certified as a Vinho Ecologico. A second label, Senhoria, is a blend of Alvarinho and Trajadura.

ADEGA COOPERATIVA DE PONTE DE LIMA*
Rua Conde de Bertiandes, 4990 Ponte de Lima
Portugal has, in general, been poorly served by cooperatives, but Ponte de Lima is an honourable exception. Under the guidance of the elected president, Gaspar de Castro Pacheco, the membership of Ponte de Lima co-op has expanded greatly from just thirty growers at its foundation in 1963 to nearly 2,000. Unlike some of the flyblown co-ops elsewhere, Ponte de Lima has a smart, corporate air and the president sits in a big leather chair rather like the chairman of a multinational. Producing an average of around 6,000 pipes (3.3 million litres) of wine a year, 4,000 of which are white and 2,000 red, Ponte de Lima is the largest single producer of Vinho Verde, selling large quantities of wine to other firms. Its range of wines is simple: a straightforward minerally white blended from Loureiro, Padernã, Trajadura and Esganinho, a fragrant varietal Loureiro and two inky reds made mainly from Vinhão. The co-op is justifiably

proud of its so-called *tinto lavrador* ("worker's red"), a deliciously sappy-spicy wine with an aroma of pepper and blackberries bottled at 2 kilo-grams (4.4 pounds) of pressure. Portugal could do with more co-ops like Ponte de Lima.

PROVAM*

Provam – Produtores de Vinhos Alvarinho de Monção, Cabo, Barbeita, 4950 Monção

Provam is the rather lacklustre name for a group of ten growers who decided to form a private consortium in 1992. The wines are made by Anselmo Mendes, a young winemaker who has quickly established a rep-utation for Alvarinho. Portal de Fidalgo is a long, steely pure Alvarinho, whereas Varanda do Conde blends Alvarinho with Trajadura. Vinha Antiga exposes Alvarinho to new oak both during fermentation and for around eight months before bottling. It is appreciated by some, but to my mind it lacks the freshness and immediacy of the early bottled wines.

SOLAR DE SERRADE

Mazedo, 4950 Monção

This baronial property outside Monção has been converted to receive paying guests (*turismo de habitação*) and provides a good base for visiting the Minho Valley. With eighteen hectares of vines on granite soil, it also makes a sub-tropical but slightly earthy varietal Alvarinho.

CASA DE SEZIM*

Sezim – Sociedade Agro-Pecuaria Lda, Nespereira, 4810 Guimarães

The ancestral home of the Pinto de Mesquita family since 1376, Casa de Sezim is a well-proportioned eighteenth-century house in the outskirts of Guimarães, Portugal's first capital city. The property is protected from the encroaching suburbia by eighty-five hectares of park, which includes twenty hectares of vineyard planted with Loureiro, Trajadura and Padernã in roughly equal proportions. The wines are made by José Paulo Pinto Mesquita in a well-equipped modern winery. The mainstay is a crisp, fragrant dry wine made from all three grape varieties, its aromatic qualities enhanced by exposing Loureiro and Trajadura to a short period of maceration on the skins. The family is also experimenting with a barrel-fermented wine made from Loureiro and Padernã.

Casa de Sezim is open all the year round to paying guests (*turismo de habitação*). It is worth asking to see the main rooms of the house, which are adorned with some particularly fine hand-painted panoramic wallpapers dating from the early nineteenth century.

Casa de Sezim

QUINTA DE SOALHEIRO*
António Esteves Ferreira, Charneca, Alvaredo, 4960 Melgaço
Quinta de Soalheiro produces a varietal Alvarinho named Soalheira, the first such wine to be made in Melgaço. Perhaps because the vines are well established, having been planted in 1974, Soalheira is consistently one of the best of the genre: quite full and peachy but fine, and balanced by the steely acidity that seems to be prevalent in the wines of Melgaço. Soalheira regularly captures the ethereal jasmine-like fragrance that is the hallmark of good Alvarinho. The title Quinta de Soalheira is reserved for an oak-aged Alvarinho that transforms jasmine into smoky bacon crisps! The property also makes an *espumante* (see Chapter 8).

SOGRAPE
Correspondence address: Sogrape Vinhos de Portugal SA, Aldeia Nova, Apartado 3032, 4431 Avintes
After the family rupture with Aveleda in 1979 which left Sogrape (Portugal's largest wine producer) without a Vinho Verde, Fernando Guedes bought the Honra de Azevedo estate near Barcelos and set about making their own competing brand. Sogrape's Gazela is now the second largest brand of Vinho Verde after Aveleda's Casal Garcia. Off-dry, with 12 grams/litre residual sugar left behind to counteract the acidity, it is one of the most reliable of all the big brands of Vinho Verde, favoured by Portuguese and foreigners alike. A wine named Chello is its bone-dry

counterpart. Sogrape also produces Quinta de Azevedo, a single-estate Vinho Verde from Loureiro and Paderná, and Morgadio de Torre, a pure Alvarinho from Monção.

SOLOURO*
Solouro – Sociedade Agricola do Louro SA, Rua Padre Domingos Joaquim Pereira, 1122, 4760 Louro

Mesa do Presidente is the principal brand name for this large firm bottling Vinho Verde near Famalicão. In my experience the wines are somewhat unreliable.

QUINTA DE TAMARIZ*
Sociedade Agricola da Quinta de Santa Maria SA, São Miguel de Carreira, 4775 Barcelos

António Vinagre has an unfortunate surname, given that he is a leading promoter of Vinho Verde, with three separate estates. During the 1980s he restored the vineyards at Tamariz, replacing the *vinha ramada* with vines trained on cordons. The wine with its distinctive, scented aroma is now made almost entirely from Loureiro. Two other family properties, Quinta da Portela and Quinta do Landeiro, produce lesser wines from a traditional mix of Vinho Verde varieties.

PAÇO DE TEIXEIRÓ*
Montez Champalimaud Lda, Teixeiró, Baião, 5040 Mesão Frio

Closer to the Douro than to the heart and soul of Vinho Verde, Paço de Teixeiró belongs to Miguel Champalimaud, who also owns nearby Quinta do Côtto, over the border in the Port wine region. Twelve hectares of terraced vineyard hewn from the schist are planted mainly with the Avesso grape, which makes an unusually soft, ripe style of wine with a mature, almost buttery character from ageing in new wood. At 11 to 11.5 per cent alcohol by volume, it only just qualifies as Vinho Verde.

TORMES*
Fundação Eça de Queiroz, Quinta de Vila Nova, Tormes, 4640 Santa Cruz do Douro

Made famous by the nineteenth-century novelist Eça de Queiroz, the Quinta de Vila Nova, or "Casa de Tormes" as it is better known, is now a charitable foundation open to the public as a museum. Situated high above the River Douro, the estate was the setting for the novel *A Cidade e as Serras* ("The city and the mountains"), in which Eça de Queiroz eulogizes the wines of Tormes:

> *O vinho de Tormes, caindo de alto, da boujada infusa verde – um vinho fresco, esperto, seivoso, e tendo mais na alma, entrando mais na alma, que muito poema ou livro santo . . .*
> The wine of Tormes, falling from on high, a bulging green flagon – a fresh, sharp, sappy wine – is more soulful, enters more into the soul than many poems or holy books . . .

But for the granite, the terraced vineyards below the house look as though they belong to the Douro rather than to the Vinho Verde region. Some of the older vines are still ungrafted. The grapes, mostly Avesso with a little Padernã, are brought to a small, modern winery on the property, where they are pressed and fermented in stainless steel, the old granite *lagar* having been retained as a museum piece. I could not be as effusive as Eça de Queiroz about the wines of Tormes, but they are crisp, steely and cleanly made, with a lemongrass character.

VERCOOPE*
União das Adegas Cooperativas da Região dos Vinhos Verdes, Gandra, Agrela, 4780 Santo Tirso

Vercoope is the brand name of the Union of Vinho Verde Cooperatives. This is an amalgam of eight co-ops in the southern half of the Vinho Verde region, at Felgueiras, Amarante, Paredes, Guimarães, Vale de Cambra, Famalicão, Braga and Vila Verde, which together produce about seven million litres of wine per annum. Some, like Felgueiras, are well equipped and turn out fresh, clean, spritzy wine. However, my abiding memory of visits to these co-ops is seeing queues of tractors waiting to deliver grapes in the pouring rain. Quantity rather than quality is the abiding consideration.

CASA DE VILLAR
Aparecida, 4620 Lousada

Rui Feijó managed the first cooperative in Vinho Verde, at Lousada, and cultivated the vineyard on his family estate in the Sousa valley. In 1984 his son Rui Graça Feijó returned from reading history at Oxford and began to restore the estate, eventually parting company with the co-op in 1989. His range of wines now goes way beyond bog-standard Vinho Verde and includes a rosé from Espadeiro and a varietal Avesso, as well as wines from Alvarinho, Trajadura and Loureiro. Vinha da Senhora, a partially barrel-fermented wine made from Alvarinho and Loureiro, falls outside the Vinho Verde remit and is classified as a Vinho Regional (see below). The classic wine from the quinta is Casa de Villar, a clean, steely, blended Vinho Verde with aromas akin to an orchard. The property also bottles a good forty year old *águardente* named Conde de Carreira.

OTHER PROMINENT SINGLE QUINTAS

Paço d'Anha, Vila Nova d'Anha, 4900 Viana do Castelo*

Casa de Cabanelas, Cabanelas de Baixo, 4650 Bustelo*

Casa de Compostela, Requião, 4760 Vila Nova de Famalicão

Casa de Laraias, Travanca, 4605 Vila Meã*

Casa do Largo, Livração, 4630 Marco de Canaveses

Quinta do Miogo, S João da Ponte, Campelos, 4800 Guimarães

Quinta da Pena, S Paio da Pousada, 4700 Braga

Quinta de São Claudio, São Claudio de Curvos, 4710 Esposende

Terras da Corga, Quinta do Paço, Lago, 4720 Amares*

Casa do Valle, Moimenta, Cavez, 4860 Cabaceiras de Basto*

Casa de Vila Boa, Vila Boa de Quires, 4630 Marco de Canaveses

Quinta Villa Beatriz, Vila Seca, Santo Emilião, 4830 Povoa de Lanhoso*

II. MINHO

The regional wine category Minho (originally Rios do Minho) embraces the entire Vinho Verde region and a little more besides. The rules are much less prescriptive than those applied to Vinho Verde, permitting all the authorized Vinho Verde grapes (including Alvarinho) as well as non-indigenous varieties like Chardonnay, Chenin Blanc, Riesling, Cabernet Sauvignon and Merlot. As with Vinho Verde, the minimum alcohol level is set at 8.5 per cent by volume, but there has never been a maximum. As a result, Vinho Regional Minho has become something of a catch-all designation for those wines that fall outside the strictures of Vinho Verde. Although a large number of producers are registered as producers of Minho wine, there are in practice very few wines on the market. Casa do

Valle makes a rosé, Quinta de Lourosa a Touriga Nacional/Merlot and Casa de Villar produces a wine from barrel-fermented Alvarinho and Loureiro (Vinha da Senhora). The best-known producer so far is Nuno Araújo, whose well-stocked private cellar seems to inspire the wines of Quinta de Covela, a property whose entire production is Vinho Regional.

QUINTA DE COVELA
São Tomé de Covelas, 4640 Baião

Situated in a natural amphitheatre overlooking the River Douro, Quinta de Covela belongs to a *terroir* all of its own, the transition between Vinho Verde and Douro. Since 1988, Nuno Araújo has restored the vineyard, planting small parcels of different vines, both indigenous and foreign. Alongside the local Avesso there were at the last tally plots of Riesling, Gewürztraminer, Sylvaner, Sauvignon Blanc, Chenin Blanc and Viognier as well as Cabernet Sauvignon, Cabernet Franc and Merlot – all this on eighteen hectares. Covela produces five different wines, all of them Vinho Regional Minho. The three whites range from Campo Novo (pure Avesso) through Quinta de Covela, an eclectic blend of Chardonnay, Gewürztraminer and Avesso, to Covela, made from barrel-fermented Chardonnay and Avesso. The red Covela combines Touriga Nacional with slightly herbaceous Cabernet and Merlot. There is also a *palhete* or rosé. Expect more and ever better wine from this innovative property.

III. LAFÕES

The region of Lafões is a zone of transition between Vinho Verde, Bairrada and Dão. Its axis is the narrow valley of the Vouga, along which are the towns of Oliveira de Frades, Vouzela and São Pedro do Sul, where there are thermal springs. Soils vary between granite and localized outcrops of schist. The majority of the wines are light, acidic reds with a distinct resemblance to red Vinho Verde, even though the grapes include Jaen and a somewhat mysterious variety known locally as "Tourigo". Whites made from Arinto, Cerceal, Dona Branca, Esgana Cão and Rabo de Ovelha are generally low in alcohol, acidic and spritzy like Vinho Verde. There is a story that Lafões wanted to become part of the Vinho Verde DOC but was refused admission. Production is centred on the cooperative at São Pedro do Sul and there is one brave soul near by at Quinta da Comeda making an organic wine from twenty-two hectares of vines. With rainfall totalling 2,000 millimetres (79 inches) per annum, Lafões does not seem to be the obvious place to dispense with systemic sprays in the vineyard.

IV. BAIRRADA

Bairrada makes the best and worst of wines. The Atlantic climate and a single red grape conspire to produce wines that range from being powerful, bold and long-lived to lean, mean and vegetal in style. The chief culprit is a capricious variety known as Baga. This four-letter word means "berry" in Portuguese and, owing to the variety's inclination to rot, is often uttered by winemakers in much the same way as the English expletive. However, Baga's dissemination is such that it makes up ninety-five per cent of all the red varieties and eighty per cent of all the grapes growing in the region.

Baga predates Bairrada, a region whose definition has long been open to debate. The Romans grew vines south of Anadia in the country that has subsequently become the heart of the region, and in the tenth and eleventh centuries AD, as Portugal began to emerge as a nation, modern-day Bairrada marked the borderlands between the Christian and the Moorish occupation. As the Christians forged their way south, Bairrada became an important source of wine for the nearby city of Coimbra. Special privileges were granted to the wine growers around Horta, Mata, Tamengos and Aguim, villages that have been at the centre of the many subsequent attempts at demarcation.

Bairrada suffered a major setback at the hands of the Marquês de Pombal, prime minister during the reign of José I (1750–77). In a super-human effort to protect the quality and authenticity of Port, he ordered that the vineyards of the Bairrada region be uprooted and replaced with other crops. After Pombal's removal from office in 1777, vines were replanted, but his action has never been entirely forgotten and growers in the region still bear a grudge against those in authority. As recently as 1998, Luís Costa, one of the two brothers owning Caves São João, wrote: "At a time when democracy and freedom are proclaimed throughout the civilized world, the Bairrada winegrower is still shackled by political power which treats him as though he has only arms, forgetting that he also has a head." In Bairrada, bureaucracy still rules OK and it is hardly surprising that an increasing quantity of wine is being bottled under the less rigorous designation of Vinho Regional Beiras.

The first attempt at demarcating Bairrada came in 1866 when António Augusto de Aguiar produced a map defining the region according to the quality and character of its wines. Taking his lead from Pombal's earlier demarcation of the Douro, he designated the country centred on the town of Mealhada as being capable of producing red "export wines" (that is, the best quality), with the land to the north between Óis de Bairro, Mogofores and Anadia as the area suitable for white wines. The remainder of the country, stretching from Anca in the south to Oliveira do Bairro in the north, was designated merely as *consumo*.

The onset of phylloxera halted attempts to define Bairrada, but in the early years of the twentieth century a number of authorities pitched into the debate over demarcation. Cincinnato da Costa, Goncalves Perriera, Amorim Girão and Mario dos Santos Pato all advocated rather broader boundaries, each taking into account the extent of the limestone-based soils in the region. It is revealing that all of them excluded the sandy soils of Gandara to the west, with Amorim Girão advocating that Gandara should be an entirely separate region.

In spite of these valiant attempts at demarcation – or perhaps because of the inability of the growers to agree – the authorities chose to ignore Bairrada. It was only in 1975, in the midst of post-revolutionary fervour, that a working party was set up to fix the boundaries of a new demarcation. Perhaps seeking to appease all concerned, the working party opted for a broad demarcation that finally entered the statute books in 1979. In 1991, after Portugal's accession to the EU, Bairrada was among the first wave of regions to be elevated to DOC status.

Modern-day Bairrada is framed by the River Vouga to the north, the Mondego to the south and the Serras of Caramulo and Buçaco to the east. But for a strip of pine forest to the west, Bairrada would reach the Atlantic coast. The region itself is drained by three small rivers, the Certima, Agueda and Varziela, which flow northwards into the Aveiro lagoon. The lie of the land varies from 500 metres (1,640 feet) above sea level on the *serra* foothills to just forty metres (131 feet) adjacent to the coast. Most of the vineyards are to be found on relatively flat land at an altitude of 70–120 metres (230–394 feet) in the broad valley of the Certima, the river that links the municipalities of Mealhada, Anadia and Oliveira do

Bairro. This corresponds to an area of Jurassic and Triassic limestone giving rise to soils of calcareous clay. It is generally accepted that these soils produce red wines with the greatest structure and longevity, whereas those from the more sandy soils to the west tend to be lighter and more aromatic. As cooperatives have lost some of their grip on the region over recent years, there is a determined move toward the production of site-specific wines, of which Luís Pato (see below) is perhaps the principal exponent.

The Portuguese word for clay is *barro*, which may be the origin of the name Bairrada. Another school of thought suggests that the name derives from the word *bairro* meaning settlement or quarter. Whatever the truth, a maze of narrow lanes links the industrious little villages (many bearing the name "Bairro") that eke a living from Bairrada's rich clay soils. The DOC region covers a total of 110,000 hectares, of which roughly 15,000 are planted with vines. The rest of the landscape is shaped by a variety of crops – olives, maize, potatoes and rice – as well as tall pine and eucalyptus that sway in the Atlantic breeze. In common with most of the northern *litoral*, Bairrada is fairly densely populated and the countryside has been broken down into thousands of small plots, ninety-eight per cent of which are less than a hectare in size. Owing to a lack of investment, many of the region's vineyards are over fifty years old and octogenarian vines are still by no means uncommon. A programme of replanting and restructuring in the 1990s has helped to increase the economic viability of some vineyards, but many growers have abandoned the land altogether in recent years, preferring more sedentary jobs in the light industries that have sprung up in the area.

Bairrada is unique in Portugal in that it is almost completely dominated by one grape (compared with the eighty or so varieties found in the Douro). Apart from Baga, there are small quantities of Câmarate (still known locally as Castelão Nacional), Jaen and Touriga Nacional. There are also scattered plots of Cabernet Sauvignon and Merlot, but as neither of these grapes is as yet officially recognized by the Regional Commission, they come under the designation of Vinho Regional Beiras. This strikes me as being rather short-sighted, as both these grapes perform relatively well in Bairrada and could easily be used to enhance the reputation of the region's wines. There's nothing New World about Bairrada Cabernet, which, shaped by the cool Atlantic climate, produces wines that are very Bordelais in style. White grapes make up twenty per cent of the total vineyard, much of which is directed to making *espumante* (sparkling wine). Maria Gomes (aka Fernão Pires) is the principal variety, but the best in terms of quality is Bical, which on its own has the capacity to make some long-lasting wines. There are also plots of Cerceal, Arinto and Rabo de Ovelha.

The weather in Bairrada is some way short of ideal for growing grapes. At best it can be described as unreliable. Prevailing winds from the northwest bring an average of 800 to 1,200 millimetres (thirty-one to forty-seven inches) of rain a year, which falls mostly during the winter months. Summers tend to be warm and relatively dry, without the extreme heat that is often encountered in the mountain regions inland. However, the rain-free period is relatively short and growers often face a race against time to ripen grapes before the autumn rains blow in from the Atlantic in late September or early October. As a result the harvest often takes place in torrential rain. The clay soils are easily waterlogged and if the rains arrive too early (as was the case in 1998, 1999 and 2002) the Baga grape begins to rot on the vine before it is fully ripe. Better vineyard practices (including work on clonal selection and canopy management) would almost certainly help to promote earlier ripening. But some larger producers like Caves Aliança have been turning their back on Baga in favour of Cabernet, Merlot or Câmarate, which ripen earlier than Baga and are therefore less likely to be picked in the rain. Nevertheless, Bairrada can honestly claim just three or four good vintages a decade, although, rather like Bordeaux, many growers and winemakers might protest otherwise.

Two distinct schools of winemaking have evolved in the Bairrada region. There are the traditionalists who still tread grapes by foot and ferment the grapes, stalks and all, in stone *lagares* without recourse to temperature control. These dark, fiercely tannic wines are left to develop for a varying amount of time, often up to two years, in old wood before bottling. In spite of these age-old techniques, when the Baga is fully ripe some of the finest red wines in the Bairrada region (and occasionally in Portugal as a whole) are made in this way. In ripe vintages, undiluted by rain, these wines combine depth and concentration with the haunting, wild berry fruit character of Baga. With an alcoholic strength of 13 to 14 per cent by volume, traditional red Bairrada has a peculiar affinity with good Californian Zinfandel. A consultant winemaker named Rui Moura

Alves is responsible for nearly all the region's best traditional wines. Operating on a much bigger scale, the cooperatives and larger private winemakers tend to destem the entire crop before fermenting on the skins in temperature-controlled stainless steel, the better quality wines being aged in new French oak. A few companies seeking exposure in price-sensitive overseas markets flavour their wines and cut corners by adding oak chips. But Baga is nothing if not a chameleon and large quantities of grapes are bought by Sogrape to produce millions of litres of Mateus Rosé (see Chapter 7).

Producers

The cooperative movement is firmly embedded in Bairrada, but is nowhere near as dominant as it is in neighbouring Dão. By far the largest co-op is that at Cantanhede, but there are others at Mealhada, Vilarinho de Bairro, Souselas and Mogofores, which together produce about forty per cent of the region's wine. Bairrada's cooperatives are no better and no worse than those elsewhere in Portugal, and some continue to turn out fairly unpleasant wine. José Neiva of DFJ Vinhos works with the co-op at Vilarinho de Bairro, which is probably the best, producing red and white wines under the name Bela Fonte, and Peter Bright works with Cantanhede to produce a varietal Baga. All these wines are bottled under the designation "Vinho Regional – Beiras". Many small growers still retain a considerable amount of wine for local consumption but, since the early 1980s, a number of properties have begun to bottle their own site-specific wines. Together they account for a surprising thirty-five per cent of total production. In the 1920s and 1930s a large number of merchants established so-called *caves* in the region. Some of the big names in Bairrada, such as Caves Irmãos Unidos (now Caves São João), Caves do Barrocão, Caves Messias, Caves Aliança, Caves Valdarcos, Caves Solar de São Domingos and Caves Borlido, date from this era. They have been joined by other *caves*, which sometimes buy in wine from the cooperatives and small growers but increasingly produce an ever greater proportion of their own wine. These privately owned firms, whose wines are those most frequently seen on export markets, account for about a quarter of Bairrada's total production. Producers marked with an asterisk (*) are on the *Rota do Vinho da Bairrada* and are open to passing visitors.

QUINTA DE AGUIEIRA

Correspondence address: Aveleda – Sociedade Agricola e Comercial da Quinta da Aveleda SA, Apartado 77, 4560 Penafiel

Aveleda have ventured outside the Vinho Verde region and acquired a property in Bairrada. Under the supervision of Bordelais winemaker Denis Dubourdieu, they have produced two white wines: a floral blend of Bical and Maria Gomes and a restrained barrel-fermented Chardonnay. Reds from Touriga Nacional and Cabernet Sauvignon will follow.

CAVES ALIANÇA*

Rua do Comercio, Apartado 6, 3781 Sangalhos

Established in 1927, Caves Aliança belongs to the first wave of the Bairrada *caves* and is now one of the largest producers in the region. This family-owned company invested heavily in a new winery in the 1980s and has subsequently diverted its attention to viticulture. Aliança now has holdings in Trás-os-Montes, the Douro, Dão and Alentejo as well as Bairrada, amounting to 350 hectares in total. Alongside Sogrape, Caves Aliança has the most international outlook of all the wine producers in the region and this is reflected in its sales, over half of which are on export markets. Under the direction of Mario Neves and winemaker Francisco Antunes, Aliança was the first company in Bairrada to move toward a more modern style of winemaking. Bordeaux consultant Michel Rolland has been recruited to accelerate this process, and Aliança is making a range of ever more accessible wines. Its somewhat light, insubstantial Bairrada now takes second place to a range of wines bottled as Vinho Regional Beiras under either the Tabor or Galeria labels. Baga is gradually being usurped by Cabernet Sauvignon, either as part of a minty blend in Aliança Classico or as a good Bordeaux lookalike in Galeria Special Selection. The Galeria range also includes a dry rosé and well-priced white varietals made from Bical and Chardonnay. Aliança owns Quinta das Bacelladas, a property in the Bairrada region, but, because it is planted with Cabernet Sauvignon and Merlot, its wines qualify as Vinho Regional. Aliança uses both French and American oak, but under the guidance of Michel Rolland the emphasis is becoming increasingly French. Caves Aliança also has interests near Borba in the Alentejo (see page 271).

QUINTA DAS BÁGEIRAS
Mario Sergio Alves Nuno, Fogueira, 3780 Anadia

This twenty-one-hectare estate in the heart of the Bairrada region has been tended by three generations of the Alves Nuno family. Until 1989 they sold the majority of their wine to Caves São João, but Quinta das Bágeiras has now established a good reputation in its own right making *espumante* and *águardente* as well as red and white Bairrada. Six hectares of old vines (over seventy-five years old) form the core of the red Quinta das Bágeiras, which is foot-trodden and fermented in *lagar*. The wines bear the hallmark of winemaker Rui Moura Alves. They are tight-knit and dense in style, particularly in ripe years like 1995 and 1997 when the cream of the crop is bottled as a *garrafeira*. Bágeiras wines sometimes show a hint of aromatic resin, which is perhaps not surprising as the vineyards are close to eucalyptus plantations.

QUINTA DE BAIXO
Sociedade Agricola, Quinta de Baixo, Corinha, 3060 Cantanhede

Located on the best Bairrada *terroir*, the wines from Quinta de Baixo have long been sold in bulk to appreciative customers, including the late José dos Santos at the Buçaco Palace Hotel. José Povoa has now taken to the cellar as well as tending seven hectares of old vines. The wines are made under the guidance of Rui Moura Alves and are only bottled when they are good enough to qualify as *reservas* or *garrafeiras*. The remainder of the wine continues to be sold off in bulk.

QUINTA DO CARVALINHO*
Ventosa do Bairro, 3050 Mealhada

António Navega has restored a property purchased by his great-grandfather in 1890 and released the first estate-bottled wine from Carvalinho a century later. Twelve hectares are planted with Baga, accompanied by Cabernet Sauvignon, Merlot and Syrah. The house on the estate is now run as a hotel.

CAVES MESSIAS*
Sociedade Agricola e Commercial dos Vinhos Messias SA, Rua Commendador Messias Baptista, 56, Apartado 1, 3050 Mealhada

The Messias family has interests throughout the north of Portugal, but its base is the town of Mealhada, where it has adapted an old cinema for storing and ageing wine. Messias owns around 160 hectares of vineyard, nearly half of which is at Quinta do Valdoeiro on the foothills of the Serra do Buçaco. Here they produce a range of single-quinta wines, both blends and varietals, with local grapes supplemented by Chardonnay and Cabernet Sauvignon. Although Messias Bairradas tend to be quite traditional, the somewhat variable rustic wines of the past have become fresher and more fruit-driven in style.

LUÍS PATO*
Óis de Bairro, 3780 Anadia

Luís Pato has done more to put Bairrada (and perhaps Portugal) on the international map than any other winemaker. But owing to a disagreement with the regional commission in 1999, he has decided to remove the name "Bairrada" from his labels and bottle his wines henceforth as plain Vinho Regional. Pato only began to bottle wines under his own label in 1980, after he inherited seventy hectares of vines from his father, and he has worked tirelessly to promote his own good name (which translates as "duck") ever since. After a decade or more of trial and error, Pato has established a successful formula based on the local *terroir*. He is forever comparing and contrasting wines from the region's "sandy-clay" and "chalky-clay" soils. With over twenty plots of vines scattered around Bairrada, Pato reserves the sandy soils for white wines and a few lighter reds, whereas the heavier clays produce an ever increasing range of full-bodied red wines. His most impressive wines are those bottled individually by vineyard. Yields are kept low and the wines, based predominantly on Baga but with some Touriga Nacional and Tinto Cão, are dense, ripe and peppery. A confusing array of labels reflects the many different plots of vines. Vinha Barrosa is a plot of seventy-year-old Baga near the village of Aguim, and Vinha Pan (short for Panascal) is a plot of younger but still low-yielding Baga. These labels have subsequently been joined by Vinha Barrio and Quinta do Moinho at São Lourenço de Bairro. Pride of place goes to Pato's Pé Franco, made in minuscule quantities from one hectare of ungrafted Baga planted back in 1988. With a yield typically as low as eight hl/ha, Pé Franco is a dark, impenetrable red with massive concentration of flavour. This has all the makings of a Bairrada *grand cru* but only if Pato consents to put the region back on the label.

CAVES PRIMAVERA*

Caves Primavera Lda, Rua das Caves, Agueda de Baixo, 3750 Agueda

Primavera was established toward the end of the Second World War, primarily as a bulk business selling wines to Portuguese Africa. When the colonies gained their independence in 1975, the rug was pulled from underneath Caves Primavera and it had to reinvent itself. With EU help it established a new winery and bottling line and now produces a range of simple, clean wines from Baga as well as blends from Baga/Cabernet Sauvignon and Bical/Chardonnay that qualify as Vinho Regional Beiras. All Primavera's wines are on the light side and do not stand up to extended ageing in bottle.

CASA DE SAIMA*

Casa Agricola de Saima Lda, Saima, 3780 Anadia

With cellars underneath a modest pink house, Dr Carlos Almeida e Silva farms twelve hectares of vineyard split between various plots in Saima, Fogueira, Paraimo, Ancas and São Mateus. The more sandy soils are planted with white grapes – Bical, Maria Gomes and Cerceal – which produce fragrant, steely-dry white wines with the capacity to age in bottle. A pure Bical made in 1981 and uncorked sixteen years later had developed a petroleum quality, not dissimilar to a well-made Riesling. Saima has also planted a small quantity of Chardonnay. The red varieties, essentially Baga with around ten per cent of Castelão and Tinta Pinheira, are planted on the clay-limestone soils. The red wines are uncompromisingly traditional in style, fermented in stone *lagares* without destalking and aged for up to three years in old wood prior to bottling. In years that are less than fully ripe, the wines can taste somewhat hard and green when young but usually grow in stature in bottle. *Garrafeiras* (adorned with a cork label) prove that Baga really is capable of making great wine, particularly in 1990, when Casa de Saima produced one of Portugal's best reds: dense, structured yet fleshy and intense. These wines have the capacity to age for three decades or more. The winemaking at Casa de Saima is the responsibility of Rui Moura Alves.

CAVES SÃO JOÃO*

Sociedade dos Vinhos Irmãos Unidos Lda, São João de Anadia, 3780 Anadia

Formerly known by the name Irmãos Unidos ("united brothers"), Caves São João was founded in 1920 by three brothers: Albano, José and

Manuel Costa. Remarkably, given Portugal's Napoleonic laws of inheritance and a few old-fashioned family disagreements, the company is still controlled and run by two brothers, Alberto and Luís Costa, and Luís's son Manuel Zé. The company gained its reputation for quality in the late 1950s with the release of Frei João Bairrada in 1959 followed by Porta dos Cavaleiros, Dão, in 1963. These wines are firmly established in the national psyche, mostly because of their unwavering commitment to the best traditional standards of winemaking during a time of enormous change. *Reservas*, distinguished by their cork labels, are solid, structured wines with the capacity to age for three decades or more. Proof of this came when I recently uncorked a bottle of 1966 Frei João Reserva which was still deep in colour, retaining its alluring wild berry fruit perfume and flavour – a truly thrilling red wine. Although Caves São João might at first appear to be stuck in a time warp (there is not a computer in sight), the company has changed direction again since 1972 when it purchased Quinta do Poço do Lobo ("wolf's well estate") near Cantanhede. Initially planted with Baga, Câmarate, Moreto and Arinto, the Costa brothers have, somewhat surprisingly, added both Chardonnay and Cabernet Sauvignon. Both are bottled as varietals but fall outside Bairrada's DOC legislation. Rui Moura Alves is the winemaker who oversees this eclectic range of wines.

SIDONIO DA SOUSA*
Ducelineia Santos Ferreira, Largo da Vila, 3780 Sangalhos
This family property includes a venerable old vineyard planted on a former brickyard. One plot of vines is octogenarian, the other centenarian, pruned by the traditional *taça* (gobelet) method. Dark, dense red wines are made under the guidance of Rui Moura Alves in an old stone *lagar* at Sangalhos.

CAVES VALEDARCOS
Malaposta, 3780 Anadia
This, one of the traditional Bairrada *caves*, is best known as a producer of *espumante* (sparkling wine). However, under Rui Moura Alves, who has bought a share in the company, Caves Valedarcos has been identifying small growers, many of whom still retain their old stone *lagares*, and bottling the wines separately. The *garrafeiras* are impressive.

OTHER SIGNIFICANT PRODUCERS OF BAIRRADA

Caves Acácio – Vinhos de Portugal SA: Avenida Jorge Correira, 631, Apartado 1503, Miramar, 4406 Arcozelo

Caves do Barrocão Lda: Apartado I, Paraimo, 3780 Sangalhos*

Caves Borlido Lda: 3780 Sangalhos

Caves Fundação Lda: Sua Salvador Allende Lt. 104, 2685 Sacavem

Caves Imperio SA: Apartado 9, 3781 Sangalhos

Caves Monte Crasto – Vinhos Justino de Sampaio Alegre SA: 3781 Anadia

Caves Neto Costa SA: 3780 Anadia

Caves do Solar de São Domingos: Apartado 16, Ferreiros, 3780 Moita*

Vinexport – Caves de Coimbra, Trouxemil, Apartado 154, 3001 Coimbra*

V. BUÇACO

The Serra do Buçaco rises out of the coastal *litoral* and marks the division between the Atlantic vineyards of Bairrada and the mountain vines of Dão. Unlike that of either of these regions, the name Buçaco does not appear on any of the official Portuguese wine maps, yet it is synonymous with some of Portugal's most distinguished red and white wines. Set in a forest, just below the "damned long hill" where Wellington fought one of the most decisive battles in the Peninsular War, is the Palace Hotel. It is one of the few hotels that really deserves the name, for this extraordinary neo-Manueline building was intended as a palace for Portugal's penultimate king, Carlos I. He was assassinated in 1908 and his second son, Manuel II, abdicated before the building was finished. Since 1917 Buçaco has been leased by the state to Alexandre d'Almeida, a company running a small chain of hotels in Lisbon, Carcavelos, Coimbra and nearby Curia. Buçaco is the jewel in the crown and surely one of the most remarkable hotels in the world.

Time stood still at Buçaco, and during the Salazar years the hotel became a magnet for visiting heads of state and dignitaries. Agatha Christie, Cole Porter, Amalia Rodrigues, Douglas Fairbanks and Alec Guinness were among the hotel's many "celebrity" guests. Apart from the peace, solitude and old-fashioned quality of service, wine became an important attraction at Buçaco, particularly as the company began to make and bottle its own red, white and rosé to serve exclusively in the hotel dining room. Much of the hotel's more recent reputation can be

Mosaic façade on the Convent of Buçaco

credited to the legendary José dos Santos, who managed the hotel from 1952 until shortly before his death in 1995. "Senhor Santos", as he was known with respect by guests and staff alike, began working at Buçaco as a bell boy in 1934 and rose through the ranks to control the hotel with quiet but omnipresent authority. Buçaco wine became his concoction, upheld since 1969 by *mestre de cave* ("cellar master") Silverio Pires.

Buçaco's wines ostensibly originate from nine hectares of vines planted alongside the other Palace Hotel belonging to Alexandre d'Almeida – in the nearby spa town of Curia – but wines from other producers in Dão and Bairrada are used to supplement production. I strongly suspect that Caves São João and Quinta do Baixo in Bairrada and the Santos Lima family at Silgueiros in Dão have all played their part in the blending of Buçaco over the years. The Baga grape is a major component in red Buçaco, but the wines have a habit of changing somewhat in style from year to year, depending on the proportion of Dão and/or Bairrada in the wine. The wines are aged in cavernous cellars immediately below the entrance hall to the hotel. After spending around three years ageing in vats made from oak grown in the Buçaco Forest, the wine is bottled by hand without any fining or filtration. The bottles (many of which are hand blown) are reused, as they rarely, if ever, leave the hotel dining room. They are washed in sand and sealed with a pungent beeswax made by the hotel. Stocks of old Buçaco wines amount to 200,000 bottles, and the hotel lists wines dating back to 1945 for the reds and 1944 for whites. The oldest bottles in stock include the 1927 and a bottle of the first ever Buçaco wine, dated 1917, that is reputedly kept at Curia. The label has remained the same ever since.

I have tasted Buçaco's wines, red and white, on a number of occasions, both with the late Sr Santos and his successor João Castro Ribeiro. Provided you have the confidence to reject the occasional inconsistent bottle, there are some extremely impressive, reassuringly old-fashioned wines to be drunk from the hotel's wine list, and the odd bottle occasionally escapes to auction at Christie's in London. It is well worth making the trip to Buçaco, both to experience the remarkable idiosyncracies of the hotel and the unique character of the wine. The following reds are among the best Buçaco wines that I have tasted (with my own star grading out of a maximum of five):

1992 deep, tight, concentrated berry (Baga fruit). Ripe tannins. Needs time to develop and soften. ***
1989 herbal with a hint of eucalyptus, soft, broad, middle-distance wine. Good now but not for the long term. ***

1985 deep colour, savoury, meaty, but with a slight *rancio* character. Broad, fleshy and expansive. ***

1983 still deep in colour but mature and slightly musky on the nose. Still retaining its fresh berry-like fruit and firm tannins with a somewhat rustic backdrop. Having tasted this wine on a number of occasions, beware of significant variation from bottle to bottle.

1970 surprisingly deep, youthful colour for a wine of this age; rich and concentrated both on the nose and palate with an explosive peacock's tail of a finish. Still tannic and solid after all these years. ****

1962 massive colour, wonderful mulberry fruit, and a big, ripe, intense flavour. One of the very best Buçaco wines that I have tasted – it was apparently the favourite of the late Americo Tomás, the president of Portugal deposed in the 1974 revolution. *****

1959 now brick red with an amber rim; cedarwood aromas with ripe, claret-like concentration and finesse. ****

Other good years include 1945, 1958, 1977 and 1988.

Some of Buçaco's white wines are as remarkable as the reds, if not more so. They are made from locally grown Bical supported by Maria Gomes, Arinto and sometimes the merest hint of Moscatel. Aged for a year in wood before bottling, the best white wines develop in the most extraordinary way, taking on a peachy depth in bottle. Among the finest that I have tasted are:

1992 very crisp, clean, tight and green when I tasted it in 1996. The flavour seems dominated by Bairrada's Bical grape which suggests that it will develop well. ***

1991 deep, golden colour partly oxidized nose suggesting walnuts. Nutty, peachy flavours and a hint of resin lends further complexity. Totally different in style from 1992. **

1985 deep, golden colour; dried apricots, peaches and walnuts in the characteristic Buçaco mode; fully mature but a tang of citrus-like acidity keeps the wine alive. Toast and butter finish. ****

1966 deep gold; remarkably fresh aromas with richness and complexity akin to Condrieu; clean, restrained lemony fruit with underlying richness and texture and a touch of casky oak. Fresh, lingering length. *****

Other good years for white Buçaco include 1944, 1967, 1982 and 1990.

VI. BEIRAS

This huge Vinho Regional spans both the Atlantic *litoral* and the mountains inland. In its Atlantic context, Beiras is largely a conduit for declassified Bairrada, mostly from the cooperatives. Bright Bros and DFJ Vinhos both bottle large volumes of varietal Baga wines with the

Beiras designation. However, out of sheer frustration with the authorities, Luís Pato has decided to bottle all his wines as Vinho Regional Beiras, despite the fact that they qualify as Bairrada (see entry above). One other property, well outside the confines of Bairrada, also deserves mention. More information on the Beiras Vinho Regional can be found on page 237.

QUINTA DE FOZ DE AROUCE
3200, Lousã

Bairrada's Baga grape spills over the border into the countryside around the university city of Coimbra and is even found as far south as Estremadura and the Ribatejo. Planted in schistous soils at this property on the foothills of the Serra da Lousã, Baga produces a firm, fleshy red wine retaining its characteristic wild fruit aroma but shedding much of the hard astringency that frequently makes Bairrada so unapproachable in its youth. Much is down to the skill of consultant winemaker João Portugal Ramos, who journeys north from his home in the Alentejo to make wine for his father-in-law at Foz de Arouce. Vinification is a blend of old and new, with a proportion of the crop being fermented in *lagar* and the remainder in stainless steel. The wine then spends a year in new Portuguese oak, which adds a spicy veneer to the underlying concentration of fruit.

VII. ESTREMADURA

Every major wine-producing country has a need for volume. France draws on the vast swathe of vineyard that covers the Midi, Spain has an ocean of vines in La Mancha, and in Portugal the largest single wine-producing region in both quantity and area is Estremadura. Supported in part by the adjoining Ribatejo (see page 242), Estremadura has long been something of a paramour among wine regions. The wines enjoyed a brief vogue in the United Kingdom following the Peninsular War, when Wellington's troops were stationed in the region, leaving behind the celebrated defensive lines of Torres Vedras. Later in the nineteenth century Estremadura fell into bed with France, shipping "neutral tasting red wines . . . for mixing with the pale and poorer growths of the northern wine-growing departments", according to Henry Vizetelly, who visited the region at the time. When, post-phylloxera, the Midi took over this role, Estremadura turned to distillation. High yielding white grape varieties supplanted red and every major property was equipped with a still to produce the grape spirit used to fortify Port. After the Second World War the emphasis shifted overseas again, when huge cooperatives were built to slake the thirst of Portugal's African colonies. This came to an abrupt end in the aftermath of the 1974 revolution, when the colonies gained their independence, and by the late 1970s producers in Estremadura were reduced to selling wine in bulk to the Soviet Union for a fraction of an escudo a litre. The only market to remain loyal throughout was nearby Lisbon, which continues to absorb a huge amount of wine from Estremadura. One cooperative even operates its own retail outlets, selling wine in five-litre *garafões* in the working-class *bairros* on the north side of the city.

Until the early 1990s the wines of Estremadura were almost completely anonymous. The region was known colloquially as the Oeste (pronounced as a rather drunken "wesht"), an apt description for this narrow band of rolling country which extends along the west (*oeste*) coast of Portugal from Pombal just south of the River Mondego to the Tagus estuary. The entire region includes around 50,000 hectares of vineyard, a fifth of the national total, but less than a third of this qualifies for either DOC, IPR or Vinho Regional status. Although the proportion of wine entitled to these geographic designations is on the increase, the majority of wine from Estremadura is still sold as ordinary, anonymous *vinho de mesa* (table wine) with nineteen cooperatives producing the lion's share. These lowly establishments have undergone something of a transformation in recent years and, with a certain amount of external supervision, are capable of producing some inexpensive and reasonably characterful wines. Sogrape and Lancers have both sourced wines here in the past to supplement their brands of rosé, and Peter Bright and José Neiva of DFJ Vinhos currently work closely with a number of co-ops, bottling wines for export under their own labels. Some Estremadura cooperatives on the other hand continue to live in a little world of their own, convinced that they make great wines when in reality much of what they produce is close to undrinkable. A number still insist on making red wines by means of a somewhat bizarre 1960s contraption known as *vinificação continua* ("continuous vinification").

The Estremadura Vinho Regional is officially divided into two, with wine from the northern part of the region, around Alcobaça and Leiria, entitled to the designation Alta Estremadura. But most of the vineyards are planted in the south, in the undulating country around Torres Vedras, São Mamede de Ventosa, Bombarral and Cadaval: four small communities which play host to the largest cooperative wineries in Portugal. In order to make sense of Estremadura in quality terms (and there is quality wine to be had), one should draw the dividing line north–south rather than east–west. Starting with the Serra do Sicó in the north near Pombal, a line of hills and mountains heads diagonally south through the Serras Aire, Candeiros and Montejunto, culminating in Byron's "glorious eden" of the Serra de Sintra due west of Lisbon. Rising to a height of just over 650 metres (2,132 feet), these limestone mountains have always been of strategic significance, supplying water to the capital and, in the case of the Serra de Montejunto, ice to the eighteenth-century court. The locals know Montejunto as the Serra de Neve ("snow mountains"), because its denuded limestone peaks appear to be snowcapped the whole year round. With annual rainfall rising to 1,300 millimetres (fifty-one inches) in places, the climate on the western side of the mountains is strongly influenced by the Atlantic Ocean. With the possible exception of Colares (see page 175), the wines from the coastal strip extending from Sintra through Torres Vedras, Óbidos and Alcobaça to Leiria and Pombal are often on the light side and can be thin and acidic in the manner of basic Vinho Verde. When the Vinho Verde region suffered a serious collapse in production at the height of its popularity in the late 1980s, the cooperatives in the so-called Oeste surreptitiously made up the shortfall. The legacy lives on in wines designated *vinho leve* (light wine), which have an alcohol level of 9.5 per cent by volume.

It is the country east of the *serras* bordering on the Ribatejo that is capable of making good wine, and during the 1990s a number of quintas have become sufficiently well established to prove the point. Among the many DOC and IPR regions delimited within Estremadura in the early 1990s, Alenquer is the only one with any real pretensions to quality so far, but there are parts of Arruda, Óbidos and the obscure Encostas de Aire that are sufficiently sheltered from the Atlantic to produce fine, well-balanced wine.

Much of Estremadura is still hampered by the type of viticulture where growers tending their small plots put quantity before quality. In the 1960s, when the cooperative movement was at its height, volume production was officially encouraged by the authorities, who devised high yielding hybrid grape varieties like Seara Nova ("new harvest"), Vaca Leiteira ("milk cow") and Carrega Burros ("load the donkeys") that did nothing to improve the quality of Estremadura's wines – in fact, quite the reverse. Although these grapes are mostly outside the legislation covering the DOCs and Vinho Regional, there is still plenty of hybrid vineyard awaiting so-called "reconversion" to better varieties. The principal grape varieties in Estremadura are Vital, Jampal, Tamarêz, Arinto and Fernão Pires for the white wines and Câmarate, Tinta Miuda, Preto Martinho and Castelão for the reds. Each of these grapes is profiled in Chapter 2. Fortunately, the Vinho Regional casts a much wider net than the DOCs and there are plenty of other promising varieties, including Alvarinho, Chardonnay, Viognier, Touriga Franca, Touriga Nacional, Tinta Roriz and Cabernet Sauvignon, that are being planted by enterprising growers.

With a notoriously variable climate, Estremadura is not a place for absentee farmers. The harvest stretches over a long period, beginning as early as mid-August for Alvarinho and Chardonnay and extending well into October for Tinta Miuda, which is always the latest grape to ripen. As with so much of Atlantic Portugal, Estremadura runs the risk of contracting widespread rot if the weather breaks (as it almost invariably does) around the time of the September equinox.

Sub-regions
Within Estremadura there are eight separate DOCs and two IPRs. Bucelas, Colares and Carcavelos on the edge of Lisbon each have their own historical background and merit separate entries (see pages 172–82). Lourinhã, west of Óbidos, is demarcated purely for brandy. Taking the region from north to south, the following regions are beginning to appear on labels.

ENCOSTAS DE AIRE (IPR)
The largest of Estremadura's DOCs and IPRs, Encostas de Aire is the least known, with a tiny area of vineyard currently fulfilling the criteria for designated quality wine. The region covers the calcareous slopes of the

Serras de Sicó and Aire east of Leiria and Pombal through Batalha, Vila Nova de Ourem, Fatima and Porto de Mós. Crazy yields of eighty hl/ha are permitted under the local legislation. White wines from Arinto, Fernão Pires, Malvasia (the rules do not specify which), Tamarêz and Vital are less distinguished than reds from Baga, Castelão and Trincadeira Preta. Rui Moura Alves (Bairrada's "Mr Baga") makes a red wine from the Baga grape at Quinta da Sapeira near Leiria.

ALCOBAÇA (IPR)
Although this region has officially existed as an IPR since 1989, no wine has yet been produced under the Alcobaça name. The permitted grapes are the same as those in Encostas de Aire (above), but the region being closer to the Atlantic, the climate favours quantity rather than quality and nearly all the production is undistinguished *vinho de mesa* (table wine). The IVV (*Instituto da Vinha e do Vinho*) has its out-of-town headquarters in the quiet monastic town of Alcobaça and maintains a museum of wine-related artifacts and paraphernalia.

ÓBIDOS
The walled town of Óbidos, a magnet for tourists, overlooks rolling country that is awash with vines. The village of Gaeiras, along with two giant cooperatives at Bombarral and Cadaval, are the principal wine-making centres. Yields of up to ninety hl/ha are permitted for white wines from Vital, Arinto, Fernão Pires and Rabo de Ovelha, with seventy hl/ha for reds from Castelão, Bastardo, Tinta Miuda and Câmarate. There is a hint of quality here (see Companhia Agricola do Sanguinhal below), but for the moment it remains a hint.

TORRES VEDRAS
Torres Vedras had a notorious start to life in 1989 when it was simply designated "Torres" and was immediately challenged by Miguel Torres of the much more famous family winery in Penedés, Spain. Sense finally prevailed and the name "Vedras" was added, which is, after all, the name of the town. Wellington's defensive lines of Torres Vedras can still be made out on the surrounding hills. The town itself plays host to the Regional Commission – which operates from a building of Salazarist architectural proportions – as well as to the huge Torres Vedras coopera-

tive. There are large and somewhat depressing co-ops near by at Carvoeira, Dois Portos and São Mamede de Ventosa. The vineyards stretching from the footslopes of Serra de Montejunto to the coast are mostly planted with high yielding white grapes, with Seara Nova among those recommended. At ninety hl/ha, Torres Vedras and Óbidos share the highest maximum yields permitted in Portugal. With the exception of one or two admirably inexpensive red wines made under the auspices of José Neiva (see DFJ Vinhos below), Torres Vedras has little to offer except volume.

ALENQUER

Sheltered from the Atlantic westerlies by the limestone hulk of the Serra de Montejunto, Alenquer presents a very different picture from Torres Vedras, which lies over the hills but not so far away. This is good fruit growing country, known for apples and pears, which is seen by some as a condition for producing good grapes and thereby balanced wine. It is no coincidence that nearly all Estremadura's best wine producers are clustered around the quiet whitewashed town of Alenquer. Physically, the region is anything but uniform, with rolling limestone hills to the west and an alluvial plain stretching to the Tagus in the east that is closer in character to the Ribatejo than Estremadura. The grape varieties permitted in Alenquer are similar to those elsewhere: Arinto, Fernão Pires, Jampal and Vital for white wines and Castelão, Câmarate, Trincadeira Preta, Preto Martinho and Tinta Miuda for reds. Castelão, Trincadeira and Tinta Miuda are all capable of making quality wines if yields are kept in check, but many of the local producers are working outside the DOC with grapes like Chardonnay, Cabernet, Syrah, Touriga Nacional and Tinta Roriz. Unless the DOC becomes more inclusive, Alenquer will find itself relegated behind Vinho Regional Estremadura. The region is likely to alter significantly when Lisbon's new airport is built at Ota, ten kilometres (6.2 miles) north of Alenquer. Having been discussed for decades, it is expected to be complete by 2010.

ARRUDA

The last piece in the complex jigsaw of DOC and IPR regions fits tightly in between Alenquer, Torres Vedras and Bucelas. It is named after the dozy little town of Arruda dos Vinhos, where wine is so important that it is even incorporated into the name. The surrounding hills, topped by windmills, are some of the most intensively cultivated in Portugal, yielding large quantities of grapes, the bulk of which is vinified at the reasonably well-run local cooperative. Fortuitously for Arruda but unusually for Estremadura, red wine predominates here, with Castelão, Câmarate, Preto Martinho and Tinta Miuda the principal grapes. The wines rarely show anything like the same class as those of Alenquer to the north, but are light, peppery and early maturing. Arruda has therefore become the source of many a wine bottled under a proprietary label.

Producers

Estremadura produces around twenty per cent of Portugal's wine, mostly from seventeen cooperatives. Although some of these establishments are managed much more efficiently than others, there is little to be gained from profiling each of them here. The following count among the growing band of independent producers placing an increasing emphasis on quality. Nearly all are in or around Alenquer. Properties marked with an asterisk (*) form part of the *Rota dos Vinhos do Oeste* (Oeste Wine Route) and are open to passing visitors.

Estremadura: balões or *"mammas" for bulk wine storage*

QUINTA DE ABRIGADA*

Quinta de Abrigada – Sociedade Agricola, Rua Francisco Pinheiro Gorjao, 2580 Alenquer

Abrigada enjoys a privileged position at the foot of the Serra de Montejunto. It is well protected from the Atlantic westerlies and well situated to take advantage of the new airport scheduled to be built at Ota, just five kilometres away. This noble property once belonged to Pedro Alves Cabral, the navigator who discovered Brazil, and was among the first in the region to make and market its own wines, from around fifty hectares of vineyard growing on alluvial soils. Castelão, Câmarate, Trincadeira, Tinta Miuda and Alicante Bouschet combine to produce sound but occasionally impressive red wines, especially the *garrafeiras* aged in Portuguese oak, which develop well in bottle. But wine seems to have been demoted into second place now that a golf course and hotel are being built on the estate, and I have found recent vintages of Abrigada tasting rather hard, herbaceous and astringent. Whites from Fernão Pires, Arinto and Vital are clean and light but somewhat extractive. Vinha Nobre, Raizes and Gorjão are the labels awarded to Abrigada's best red wines, with Terras do Rio and ABA de Serra as second labels.

QUINTA DO CARNEIRO*

Sociedade Agricola do Carneiro, 2580 Alenquer

Situated on flat, fertile land close to the Tagus near Carregado, Quinta do Carneiro appears to belong to the Ribatejo rather than to Estremadura, but it is nevertheless just within the Alenquer DOC. The property has been completely restored since 1990 and the forty-five-hectare vineyard, planted with a wide range of grapes, is fully mechanized. Yields are high, reflected to a certain extent in the wines, some of which are on the light side, although all are fruit-driven and well made. Vinhas do Carneiro is the name given to a duo of simple but inexpensive red and white wines made from lesser grapes, with Quinta do Carneiro reserved for a more complex mid-weight red blended from Castelão, Trincadeira and Cabernet. The somewhat confusing range extends to Castas de Carneiro, a fifty-fifty blend of either Castelão/Tinta Roriz or Roriz/ Trincadeira, and culminates in Pactus, two ripe flavoured, balanced varietal reds from Cabernet and Tinta Roriz.

QUINTA DA BOAVISTA – CASA SANTOS LIMA*

Casa Santos Lima – Companhia Vinhas SA, Quinta da Boavista, Aldeia Galega, 2580 Alenquer

It is difficult to put a title on this entry, as the wines from this substantial estate are bottled under a variety of names not including that of the quinta itself. One hundred and fifty hectares of well-situated, rolling vineyard are planted with all the traditional local grape varieties as well as Touriga Nacional, Touriga Franca, Tinta Roriz, Cabernet Sauvignon, Merlot, Chardonnay and Moscatel. The wines bear the hallmark of José Neiva (see DFJ Vinhos), who is responsible for the vinification, and have an ease and approachability about them that is uncommon in the region. For all this, the winery is not particularly up to date, although it has the distinct advantage of having detached cement vats (as opposed to the interlinked vats in cooperatives), which is helpful for temperature control. Palha Canas is probably the best known of Boavista's wines: a lemony dry white from Arinto and Fernão Pires and a fleshy, satisfying red, flattered by new oak, made from Castelão and the two Tourigas. Reds with a similarly attractive *confit* of fruit go under the names Quinta da Espiga, Quinta dos Bons Ventos and Quinta de Setencostas. They might not impress the more diehard Portuguese critics but, adorned with simple, eye-catching labels, they are very much in tune with the international market. Casa Santos Lima is reserved for a series of well made though not particularly expressive varietals from Chardonnay and Fernão Pires through Câmarate, Trincadeira, Castelão, Cabernet, Merlot, Touriga Nacional, Touriga Franca and Tinta Roriz. These final three grapes go in roughly equal proportions into a red called Touriz, with characteristically approachable fruit and a hint of toasty oak.

QUINTA DE CORTEZIA

José Miguel Catarino, Aldeia Gavinha, 2580 Alenquer

Miguel Catarino trained at Montpellier University, where Professor P Truel conducted one of the first and most comprehensive of recent studies of the native Portuguese grape varieties. He took on Cortezia in 1988, when the property (like so much of Estremadura) was in a sorry state, and began a fifteen-year restoration plan. The vineyard was completely grubbed up and local grapes like Castelão and Tinta Miuda were jettisoned in favour of Touriga Nacional and Tinta Roriz, with small plots of Merlot, Cabernet Sauvigon and Chardonnay planted as a "reference point" for the native varieties. Catarino put the vineyard first in his priorities and, in the absence of a well-equipped *adega*, the early wines have been made by Caves Aliança. They show great potential, with powerful aromas and flavours offset by new French and American oak. Touriga Nacional has proved particularly impressive, combining both structure and finesse. Miguel Catarino's Cortezia is a world away from the thin, stretched Castelão-based wines of yesteryear.

DFJ VINHOS
c/o Quinta da Fonte Bela, Valada, 2070 Cartaxo

Dino Ventura, Fausto Ferraz and José Neiva are the names behind the initials DFJ, one of the most successful wine ventures in Portugal. The wines are much less well known on the domestic market than they are in the UK, where Neiva and his partners have succeeded in exporting reasonable quality at an acceptable price. He justifies this with his own parable: "The world has two classes: rich and poor. There are more poor than rich and my intention is to make good wines for the poor – the best wines drunk by as many people as possible." It sounds to me like a good formula for getting rich! Although DFJ is based in the Ribatejo (see page 249), Neiva's family estate is Quinta do Porto Franco at Atalaia near Alenquer. The property used to belong to the Visconde de Chanceleiros – who is credited with having introduced American rootstock to Portugal in the wake of phylloxera – and was bought by the Neiva Correira family in 1918. Vineyards extend to 155 hectares and are now completely adapted to mechanized harvesting. The winery was constructed in 1923 (one of the first built from cement), but like that of Casa Santos Lima (see above), has been cleverly adapted by Neiva for the twenty-first century. DFJ produces a huge range of wines, all of which tend to reflect the hand of the winemaker rather than the intrinsic character of the grape or *terroir*. Given the rather emaciated character of many Estremadura wines, this is no bad thing, for Neiva's wines are nothing if not accessible and easy to drink. The DFJ range is never static, and includes bargain basement wines made by the local co-ops under Neiva's supervision and bottled under a variety of labels, of which Ramada is probably the best known. Wines from Estremadura include Manta Preta, a smooth blend of Touriga Nacional and Tinta Roriz, and an eclectic range known as

Grand'Arte representing a blend of Chardonnay and Alvarinho as well as varietal wines from Touriga Franca, Alicante Bouschet and Trincadeira. Caladoc (see page 67) is a varietal newcomer.

QUINTA DO MONTE D'OIRO
José Bento dos Santos, Freixial de Cima, 2585 Olhavo

The single-street village of Freixial de Cima is a strange place to find a bottle of Chapoutier's wonderful Hermitage Le Pavillon, but then José Bento dos Santos is an exceptional man. An industrialist whose passion for fine food and wine has turned into a fervour, Bento dos Santos has amassed one of the finest private cellars in Iberia. His enthusiasm for the Rhône extends to the vineyards at Monte d'Oiro ("hill of gold") where, in 1992, he began planting Syrah with clones directly imported from France. At the time it was a brave (some might say foolhardy) move, but it has certainly begun to pay dividends. Two wines, Quinta do Monte d'Oiro and a "second wine" entitled Vinho da Nora are distinctly north-ern Rhône in style, combining peppery aromas with dark chocolate con-centration. They are emphatically Syrah, as opposed to the Shiraz-style wines from the warmer Ribatejo and Alentejo. The wines are impressive by any standard and are well on the way to being the best manifestation of Syrah in the Iberian peninsula, proof that Estremadura is capable of making world-class wine. Viognier is Bento dos Santos' next challenge.

QUINTA DE PANCAS
Sociedade Agricola Porto de Luz, Quinta de Pancas, 2580 Alenquer

Along with Abrigada, Pancas was the first of the new generation of quality quintas in Estremadura, and it continues to be one of the leading estates in the region. The forty-five-hectare vineyard overlooking the seventeenth-century manor house at Pancas was in a poor way when the Guimarães family took over the property in 1973, but Joaquim Guimarães has now revitalized the entire estate, recently adding a new winery. Local grapes like Arinto and Castelão have been joined by Chardonnay, Cabernet Sauvignon, Merlot, Syrah, Tinta Roriz and Touriga Nacional. João Portugal Ramos, who did so much to develop the wines, has been replaced by the talented young winemaker Rui Reguinga. Quinta Dom Carlos (made by Reguinga at Pancas) is pure Arinto and one of the best of the genre, with a delicate leafy character that is the hallmark of this grape. Reguinga is also blending Arinto with Chardonnay and making a pure Chardonnay, part fermented and aged in new oak. There are two varietal Cabernets, including a wine designated "Special Selection" that is more New World than Bordelais. Tinta Roriz and Touriga Nacional make impressive varietal "Special Selection" wines and both gain a certain elegance from being planted in a cooler maritime clime. There is also some Syrah, which is blended with Cabernet to good effect in a wine called Marques de Valada. A second wine from Pancas, Quinta de Parrotes, based mainly on Castelão with a small proportion of Cabernet, is lighter in style, with peppery, black cherry fruit. The wines from Quinta de Pancas just keep on improving with every new release.

COMPANHIA AGRICOLA DO SANGUINHAL LDA*
Carlos João Perreira da Fonseca, Quinta das Cerejeiras, 2540 Bombarral

Abel Perreira de Fonseca was an important shipper in the nineteenth century, with cellars in Lisbon and Torres Vedras, the latter now sadly demolished. In 1936 the firm was sold by the family, which retained one hundred hectares of vineyard at Bombarral. The estate divides into three: Quinta das Cerejeiras produces red and white DOC Óbidos wines, Quinta do Sanguinhal with forty hectares of vineyard is the family's elegant eighteenth-century home, and Quinta do São Francisco with fifty hectares serves as the production centre for the company. The impressive winery with a museum of wine artifacts dates from the 1870s. Sanguinhal produces a wide range of wines. Reds based on Castelão and Tinta Miuda tend to be more impressive than the whites which, though cleanly made, are somewhat dull. Wines from each of the properties are bottled separately, the best of which is the Quinta das Cerejeiras Reserva (with its distinctive yellow label), which develops a wonderful leathery quality after ten years maturation in wood and bottle. Reds from the São Francisco and Sanguinhal are similarly well made, with lively, balanced morello cherry fruit tempered by maturation in different types of oak. Quinta do São Francisco is also the source of some fascinating *solera*-matured *licoroso* (fortified) wines. The dry white from a base of Fernão Pires, Arinto and Vital tastes rather like an old White Port sharpened up by crisp acidity. The red, with its amber hue and flavours of candied peel, resembles a good if rather rustic tawny. There is also a fragrant Quinta do São Francisco fortified Moscatel and a number of good *bagaçeiras* (marc) and brandies. For those with a penchant for traditional Portuguese wines, Sanguinhal deserves to be (re)discovered.

VIII. BUCELAS

Of the three historic wine regions within so-called *Grande Lisboa* ("Greater Lisbon"), Bucelas has retained the most in terms of heritage. Despite being situated fewer than twenty-five kilometres (15.5 miles) from the Praça do Comércio, the hub of the capital, Bucelas still has a rural feel. The place is much as Henry Vizetelly described it in the 1870s, with its "shabby little *praça* or public square, bordered by a few trees", the village having "straggled from the valley half way up the adjacent hills". Only the drone of the CREL, Lisbon's orbital motorway, denotes the proximity of the conurbation. Although production techniques have changed radically, Bucelas wines are also much the same as they were in Vizetelly's day: "Fresh in flavour with a slight greenish tinge of colour and in many respects the counterpart of a youthful hock."

Bucelas has always been an enclave for white wine. Arinto, a grape that has travelled far and wide in Portugal, is the *ex libris* of Bucelas and must legally make up at least seventy-five per cent of any blend. Although Arinto carries sufficient acidity in its own right (and, perhaps for this reason, was once thought to be related to Riesling), it is supported by the ferociously acidic Esgana Cão ("dog strangler") and the tamer Rabo de Ovelha ("ewe's tail"), all three of which are profiled in Chapter 2. Red grapes are also planted in Bucelas (mostly Castelão), but these only have the right to produce Vinho Regional Estremadura.

The region was first demarcated in 1907 and spans the valleys of the River Trancão and Ribeira de Bemposta between the villages of Bucelas, Fanhões and Santo Antão do Tojal. A range of limestone hills rising to 350 metres (1,148 feet) above sea level protects the vineyards from the maritime fogs that seep into the Tagus estuary. Bucelas has a long and distinguished history. It is thought by some to have been the wine referred to as "Charneco" in Shakespeare's *Henry VI, Part II*, but this is open to interpretation (see page 9). The wine gained popularity following the Peninsular Wars, when it was frequently listed by English wine merchants as "Portuguese Hock", an appellation that would appal the Brussels bureaucrats of today. Sandeman, which owned cellars at nearby

Cabo Ruivo, was the largest shipper of Bucelas for a time with a brand called "El Rey – Royal Bucellas Hock". This by all accounts was a pure, unfortified wine with the capacity to become "ethereous" with age. Much Bucelas was either fortified or, according to Vizetelly, "plastered, sweetened and coloured by artificial means". As late as 1893, the London wine merchant Hedges and Butler listed "Bucellas" alongside Madeira, Malaga, Lisbon and Calcavella, suggesting that the wine was probably fortified to a similar strength. Adulteration and sharp practice undoubtedly hastened the region's demise. The vineyards lost ground to market gardens following phylloxera, and by the 1970s there was just one producer of Bucelas remaining. But unlike Colares and Carcavelos, both of which have been driven close to extinction, Bucelas has staged a surprising recovery. Where twenty years ago it was hard to spot a vineyard, there are now 170 hectares in the region. During the period of replanting it is encouraging to see that the vineyards have moved off the alluvial soils where they were in the nineteenth century and onto the hillsides.

Producers

An asterisk (*) indicates that the producer is on the Rota dos Vinhos de Bucelas, Carcavelos and Colares and is geared to receiving passing visitors.

QUINTA DO AVELAR
Freixial, 2670 Bucelas
Grapes from the vineyards of Quinta de Avelar used to be sold to Caves Velhas until Nuno Barba bought the property with the profits from his poultry farm near by. Avelar was one of the first in the region to install stainless steel and Barba describes the style of his wines as being somewhere between a traditional *vinho maduro* ("aged wine") and a Vinho Verde. The property produces two wines, one a blend of Arinto, Esgana Cão and Rabo de Ovelha, the second a pure Arinto. Both are fresh, slightly floral and lemony, with a sub-tropical finish akin to lemon meringue pie.

QUINTA DA MURTA
Francisco Castelo Branco, Casal do Mato, Apartado 736, 2670 Bucelas
A joint venture with Port shipper Cockburn at the outset, Francisco Castelo Branco replanted fifteen hectares of vineyard close to the village

of Bucelas. Now operating on its own, Murta produces a crisp, citrusy wine made mostly from Arinto with token amounts of Esgana Cão and Rabo de Ovelha.

CAVES VELHAS*
Caves Velhas SA, Rua Professor Egas Moniz, 2670 Bucelas

For many years Caves Velhas (also known locally by its previous name, Caves Camillo Alves) was the only producer of Bucelas. The wines were never much of a showcase for the region, combining heavy-handed traditional vinification with characteristically high levels of acidity. Now belonging to Centralcer, one of Portugal's largest breweries, Caves Velhas has undergone a mutation, shedding its old wood in favour of stainless steel. The company now produces four different styles of Bucelas, mostly from forty hectares of vineyard at Quinta do Boição. Two wines are made in a semi-traditional style (including a *garrafeira*): there is an opulent, tropical varietal Arinto and a soft but rather ponderous oak-aged wine made from grapes grown exclusively at Quinta do Boição. Caves Velhas also bottles a sturdy but somewhat old-fashioned red named Romeira, which is made predominantly from Castelão grapes sourced south of the Tagus in Palmela. The company acts as a large *négociant*, bottling wines from the Ribatejo, Alentejo, Bairrada, Dão and Douro. Caves Camillo Alves, established in Bucelas in 1881, is reserved as a label for inexpensive wines sold either in *garafão* or tetrapak.

QUINTA DA ROMEIRA
Companhia das Quintas, 2670 Bucelas

Amid jokes about chaptalization, Alcantara Agricola, a Portuguese subsidiary of Britain's Tate and Lyle sugar company, bought 140 hectares of well-drained land on the so-called *meia encosta* ("halfway up the slope") between Bucelas and Alverca in 1987. The property has now been sold on to a group of independent investors that owns a number of wine-producing properties throughout Portugal. These include Quinta do Cardo in Beira Interior (see page 236) as well as new vineyard properties in the Douro and Alentejo, Quinta Cova Barca and Farizoa. Quinta da Romeira itself has expanded quickly to become the largest single producer of Bucelas, with 80 hectares of vineyard mostly planted with Arinto, although there are plots of Touriga Nacional, Cabernet

Sauvignon and Merlot alongside. The remains of Wellington's defensive lines can still be made out on the hillside above the vines. Consultant winemaker Nuno Cancela de Abreu employs a short period of skin maceration to coax as much aroma and flavour as possible from the Arinto grape before fermenting Romeira's principal wine, Prova Regia, in stainless steel. A smaller quantity of wine is fermented in new French oak. Softer and more appealing to most palates than Prova Regia, it is bottled under the name Morgado de Santa Catherina. A wine named Quinta da Romeira is made exclusively for export markets, whereas Tradição, a blend of eighty per cent Arinto with twenty per cent Esgana Cão and Rabo de Ovelha, is destined for the home market. Romeira also produces a series of eye-catching varietals entitled "Perfumes de Romeira" that include wines made from Sauvignon and Riesling. All of Romeira's wines are well made and represent the best that modern-day Bucelas has to offer.

IX. COLARES

Gazing down at a few gnarled old vines on the clifftops west of Lisbon, it is hard to believe that Colares used to be a name to be conjured with alongside Bordeaux. The vineyards that earned their fame by surviving phylloxera in the late nineteenth century have now all but succumbed to the commercial pressures of the twenty-first century. But if, like me, you are an incurable wine romantic, it is worth journeying to this windswept stretch of coastline close to Europe's westernmost point to pay homage to the remains of this once great wine region.

It is not easy to pinpoint the vineyards of Colares. The village that lends its name to the wine has always been some distance from the prime *terroir*, which is located on the dunes between Praia das Maçãs ("apple beach") and Magoito. There were also a few scattered plots of vines making lesser wines on the foothills of the Serra da Sintra at Almoçageme near Cabo da Roca and on the Encosta de Monsarrate, but these have been abandoned. At the beginning of the 1930s Colares claimed over 1,800 hectares of vineyard (including a large plot belonging to José Maria de Fonseca), but over the ensuing decades this has been whittled away to just two or three sites which together make up fewer than fifty hectares of vines. The chequerboard of tiny plots, each protected from the Atlantic westerlies by low walls or bamboo windbreaks, has largely been usurped by smart seaside villas and weekend apartments.

The legacy of this traditional form of cultivation is to be found between the villages of Fontanelas and Magoito and the sea. Here on the sand, one hundred metres (328 feet) or so above the Atlantic swell, are a handful of plots still dutifully tended in exactly the same way as they have been for centuries. Vines were already planted here when Afonso Henriques became Portugal's first king in the twelfth century and, in 1154, soon after his forces had captured Lisbon from the Moors, he paid tribute to the wines. The Ramisco grape, which is still unique to Colares, was subsequently eulogized on many occasions, but the vine gained international renown in the second half of the nineteenth century when it survived the ravages of phylloxera virtually unscathed. This *vinifera* variety continued to grow on its own roots, protected from phylloxera by a layer of pure sand which meant that the pestilential phylloxera louse was unable to complete the most injurious part of its life cycle below ground.

In the 1880s and 1890s the red wines of Colares were regularly compared with those of the Médoc (although Vizetelly describes them variously as having the character of a "full bodied Beaujolais" or a "thin Burgundy"). The perfumed Ramisco grape in its own Atlantic *terroir* certainly produced wines of considerable style and finesse. But the subsequent popularity of Colares both in Portugal and overseas led to a great deal of fraud, and grapes found their way to the region from vineyards elsewhere in Estremadura, far from the clifftop soils. Colares was delimited in the first wave of Portuguese demarcations in 1908, but the abuse continued and prices began to fluctuate wildly according to supply and demand. The region was badly hit by the sudden collapse of the Brazilian market in 1930, when the new ruler, Getúlio Vargas, placed an embargo on wine imports and made outstanding payments impossibly difficult to effect. Azeitão-based José Maria da Fonseca, which was exporting 35,000 bottles of Colares a year to Brazil, was forced to sell its vineyards in the region.

In the same year the *Estado Novo* stepped in and prohibited the blending of wine from the so-called *chão de areia* ("sandy ground") with that from the *chão rijo* ("hard ground"). A year later the government established the *Adega Regional de Colares*, effectively a cooperative, which within four years of its creation claimed 507 out of a total of 690 hard-pressed growers in the region as members. Intended as a voluntary association, the *Adega Regional* eventually gained a monopoly over Colares. From the mid-1930s until Portugal joined the EU in 1986, all grapes grown within the Colares region had to be delivered to the *Adega Regional* at Banzão to be turned into wine. The *adega* was poorly equipped, even by the standards of most Portuguese cooperatives, and the wines became increasingly standardized. Although a number of private producers continued to bottle Colares under their own name, by the 1970s the wines of this once great region were literally a pale imitation of those a century earlier. The growers regained their freedom in 1990, but there was little left to salvage. Despite a valiant attempt to revive Colares (backed indirectly by Allied Domecq), the protracted and seemingly terminal decline continues unabated. Although the *Adega Regional* continues to produce small quantities of wine, much of the cavernous building has been made over as an auditorium for summer concerts.

The scant remnants of the traditional Colares vineyards deserve to be given World Heritage status. The topsoil is composed of fine sand ranging in depth from to one to seven metres (three to twenty-three feet),

Colares: pines, vines and sand

below which is a layer of clay. When the vineyards were planted, huge trenches were dug through the sand in order to anchor the roots of the young vine canes in the clay below. Owing to the tendency of the sides of the trench to collapse without warning, vineyard workers would wear baskets over their heads to protect themselves against instant suffocation. Once the trench was filled in the vines themselves would clamber over the sand like giant spiders. At intervals the branches were then pegged down and layered to give rise to what appeared to be up to half a dozen independent plants all rooted on a single mother vine. Consequently, six years after planting a hectare of 1,200 vines, the number would have multiplied to at least 4,000.

The vineyards that remain look rather like an unkempt kitchen garden. The vines, many of them centenarian and all still ungrafted, are protected from the relentless Atlantic breezes by a few stunted apple trees and a network of windbreaks woven from local bamboo. During the growing season, when the branches became laden with fruit, stout bamboo supports known as *pontões* were inserted under the vine to prevent the bunches from being scorched on the burning sand. The growers are not unlike the vines. A few bent old men still toil in their tiny vineyards. But with yields low by any standards – well below the maximum permitted fifty-five hl/ha – their sons have left the vineyards to find more profitable and less arduous work, such as building the seaside villas that are springing up along this wild and beautiful coast.

Colares was all but lost until the late 1980s when a local producer, Tavares & Rodrigues, planted twelve hectares of Ramisco in the pine woods inland from the village of Azenhas do Mar. The sand was excavated by a mechanical digger and the vines have been planted, pruned and trained in an orderly manner to allow for mechanization. With screens of plastic netting taking the place of the traditional bamboo windbreaks, it looks quite futuristic for somewhere as conventional as Colares.

Three different types of wine are permitted to use the name Colares: two styles of red and one of white. The most highly prized Colares comes exclusively from the *chão de areia*. Here the Ramisco grape must make up at least eighty per cent of the blend, giving true Colares its perfumed raspberry and morello cherry character. Other varieties (mostly Castelão, Parreira Matias and Tinta Miuda) may be added to fill out the blend. The wines are austere and tannic when young and it was customary to give them time in bottle (at least ten years) to shed their initial astringency. Since the 1970s Colares has been so lean and a stringent in style that the fruit has frequently dried up before the tannins have softened. However, a vertical tasting of Colares organized by Dirk Niepoort in 2001 revealed wines from the 1960s, 1950s and 1940s that were still in tolerably good condition, with characteristically perfumed aromas, linear tannins and some enticingly fine but fragile fruit remaining. In those days DJ Silva, Paulo da Silva "Chitas" and Viúva Gomes all bottled wines to a high standard.

A small quantity of a second and much less esteemed red wine comes from the *chão rijo*, on the largely calcareous soils away from the coast. These are heavier, sturdy wines made from a number of grapes more productive than the low yielding Ramisco. Blending them with the *chão de areia* wines is still technically forbidden, but they may occasionally be bottled under a separate label with the designation Colares-Chão Rijo. There is also a small amount of white wine made from ungrafted Malvasia (although the type of Malvasia is not specified). Hampered by archaic winemaking, these wines were never particularly impressive, but it was just possible to detect a flicker of freshness and a saline quality in a 1960 white from Viúva Gomes tasted in 2001.

Producers

The bulk of Colares is still produced by the *Adega Regional*, whose cellars have not changed much since it was established in the 1930s. The wines used to be foot-trodden in *lagar* but nowadays they ferment on the stalks in large wooden vats without temperature control. The local legislation specifies a minimum ageing requirement of at least eighteen months for reds and six months for whites, which takes place in old oak casks ranging in size from four to fourteen thousand litres. The wines are either bottled *in situ* or returned to the grower who delivered the grapes to the *Adega Regional* at the outset. A number of firms associated with Colares have become history. DJ Silva and Tavares & Rodrigues are no longer and the huge winery belonging to Caves Visconde de Salreu is now used for storage by Adegas Beira Mar (see below). One of the greatest names of Colares, Viúva ("widow") Gomes, bottled some excellent wines until they ceased trading in the 1970s and bottles from a consignment of wine from 1965, 1966 and 1967 discovered in cellars near Colares fire-station can still be found on sale. But as always with wines of this age, *caveat emptor!* Viúva Gomes started up again in 1989 under the Beata family but the wines are not particularly impressive. Over the last century, just one producer has kept his head above water in Colares.

PAULO DA SILVA "CHITAS"
António Bernardino Paulo da Silva "Chitas", Adegas Beira Mar, 2710 Azenhas do Mar

It takes only one look at Paulo da Silva's tidy, old-fashioned office to realize that he is the sort of proud, fastidious character who has kept Colares going for so long. His family has owned Adegas Beira Mar ("cellars beside the sea") since the turn of the century, together with four hectares of vines at Magoito along the coast. Sadly he has no one to succeed him in the business. Helped by his wife, da Silva bottles Colares as well as a range of wines from locally grown grapes bought in from outside the region. The full-flavoured Casal de Azenha and the lighter though fragrant Beira Mar are worth seeking out, even if you sometimes have to exercise your imagination to believe the vintage dates on the label. His Colares wines from the 1970s had a vestige of the wild berry fruit character of Ramisco but, reflecting the standards of winemaking at the *Adega Regional*, subsequent vintages have proved to be rather hard and astringent.

X. CARCAVELOS AND "LISBON"

There was a time when vineyards penetrated deeply into Lisbon's tightly drawn city boundaries and wines were made where washing now hangs in tall streets. There were two well-known wines from Lisbon's so-called *Termo* ("city limits"). To the north-east was an area described by Vizetelly in the 1870s as "a succession of hills and dales" with "ample sites for the cultivation of the vine". Here, villages like Câmarate, Olivais, Sacavém, Frielas and Apelação were important wine-producing centres in the eighteenth and nineteenth centuries, progenitors of a fortified wine called "Lisbon" which briefly rivalled "Oporto" or Port. Much of this land has now been absorbed by the airport and surrounding suburbs, but the remains of an eighteenth-century quinta can still be seen just in front of the entrance to the main terminal. The only vineyard remaining within Lisbon's city boundary is one belonging to the *Instituto Superior de*

Agronomia at Tapada de Ajuda, which can be clearly seen from the Ponte 25 de Abril that crosses the Tagus.

Further west, a wine called Carcavelos still struggles to survive. Known in the eighteenth century as "Calcavella", this was a rich, amber-coloured fortified wine that regularly appeared alongside Lisbon at Christie's early London auctions. The two wines were probably very similar in style, for John Croft, writing in 1788, described 4,000 to 5,000 tuns (40,000 to 50,000 hectolitres) of "Lisbon" being imported to England "all promiscuously called Calcavella". Such deceit was tacitly encouraged by the Marquês de Pombal, who owned a substantial country estate at nearby Oeiras. Although he acted to protect the authenticity of Port, Pombal deliberately flouted his own rules and insisted on blending Carcavelos with Port to enhance the colour and flavour of the wine. A consignment of Carcavelos was sent by José I to the court of Peking, no doubt at Pombal's instigation.

Carcavelos continued to be shipped to England during the nineteenth century and, like so many of the wines around the Lisbon region, enjoyed a period of vogue in the aftermath of the Peninsula War. The region suffered from phylloxera, which put paid to exports. Production fell to just twelve pipes (6,600 litres) in 1867, but by the 1930s it had recovered to reach over 40,000 litres of wine a year. Carcavelos was demarcated in 1908 to take in the then villages of Oeiras, São Domingos de Rana and Carcavelos itself, all of which had substantial areas of vineyard. Now a DOC, the boundaries of the area are still intact but are all but meaningless. Since the 1950s quintas with bucolic names like Quinta de Bela Vista and Quinta das Rosas have been transformed into housing estates as Lisbon has expanded along the Tagus estuary. There is one development named Bairro Além das Vinhas ("estate beside the vines"), even though the vines are no longer present. A new vineyard was planted in the 1980s at Quinta dos Pesos at Caparide on the edge of the region but, of the traditional Carcavelos quintas, only one – Quinta do Barão – just about remains. A new feeder road cuts straight through the property, and on June 23, 2001 the weekly newspaper *Expresso* announced that this historic estate, which once belonged to the Counts of Riba d'Ave, is shortly to be developed. A token area of vineyard may survive but, if the plans go ahead, it will be completely encased by gawping blocks of flats.

It is now hard to find an example of traditional Carcavelos wine. At the last count just three small producers remained. The *Estação Agronomica Nacional* at Quinta do Marquês, Oeiras, bottles a rather dull, raisiny Carcavelos under the name Quinta de Cima. The estate which used to belong to Pombal, is open to passing visitors. There are two other properties which are not open to the public: Quinta dos Pesos which has just three hectares and a seminary named Quinta da Ribeira de Caparide which still produces a small amount of Carcavelos wine.

Carcavelos may be made from both red and white grapes: Castelão and Preto Martinho alongside Boal Ratinho, Arinto and Galego Dourado. Of these, Galego Dourado seems to be the most distinguished and is almost certainly unique to the region. In the past the grapes were foot-trodden in *lagar* and fermented dry before being fortified with grape spirit up to at least 17.5 per cent alcohol by volume. According to António Maria de Oliveira Bello, who described Carcavelos toward the end of its heyday, the wine was produced in two styles: *seco* and *meio seco*. The former was apparently sold with a minimum of eighteen years of age and the latter with eleven. Both are described as *aveluado* ("velvety"). Nowadays the Carcavelos that remains is medium dry, sweetened with a small amount of *vinho abafado* (grape must preserved with the addition of alcohol) added after fermentation. This gives the wine ten to fifteen grams of residual sugar and a vaguely sweet, raisiny aftertaste. A minimum of two years in large oak casks adds a slight nutty complexity to the wine, much of which is blended and aged in *soleras*. There seems to be no such thing as vintage Carcavelos. The only Carcavelos I have tasted that more than hints at past glory is a wine from Quinta de Bela Vista at Sassoeiros, a property that fell prey to the developers in 1969 and is now occupied by high-rise blocks named Torres Bela Vista. Made almost exclusively from Galego Dourado, this blend of wines from vintages in the 1940s to 1960s has a pale, amber-gold colour with delicate caramelized aromas and a rich yet off-dry flavour akin to a well-aged Oloroso Sherry. On the finish it has something that many fortified wines lack: crisp acidity. Bottled in 1990, 12,000 bottles of this remarkable old wine are still in existence, held by the Companhia Agricola de Sanguinhal at Bombarral (see page 171). There are other relics available, mostly at a price that is not matched by quality.

4

Mountain Wines

The mountains of north and central Portugal are but a small segment of the great *sierras* and *serras* that surround the Iberian *meseta*. They skirt the Biscay coast as the Cordillera Cantabrica and curve south through Galicia and León before heading into the Portuguese interior. These mountains mark an important climatic transition between Atlantic and continental Iberia. On the *meseta*, the vast tableland at the centre of Spain with its bleak horizons, they talk of *nueve meses de invierno y tres de infierno* ("nine months of winter and three of hell"). When the arid wind blows from the east into the mountains of north and central Portugal, they mutter *nem bom vento, nem bom casamento vem de Espanha* ("neither good winds nor good weddings come from Spain"). In the spirit of European cooperation, the saying has been shortened to *nem bom vento* but the sentiment remains much the same.

Many of Iberia's best wines are to be found on the leeward side of this band of mountains. Rioja Alta and Alavesa, the two best sub-regions, are in the rain shadow of the Sierra de Cantabria. Ribera del Duero benefits both from shelter and altitude and there is as yet untapped potential in the mountains of Galicia and León. Port, Portugal's best-known wine, is very much a product of the steady climatic transition from Atlantic to continental-Mediterranean, and the unfortified wines of the Douro, Dão and certain parts of Beira Alta and Beira Baixa all have the potential to be world class.

Portugal is top-heavy with mountains. They drive a wedge through the north of the country, subsiding just south of the Tagus with the Serra de São Mamede near Portalegre. Rainfall, high on the coast, rises significantly on the windward slopes before diminishing sharply on the leeward side. A total of just 300 millimetres (12 inches) per annum, perennial drought, is not uncommon in places along the Spanish frontier. The *planalto* or high plain in the farthest north-east corner of the country is really an extension of the meseta, a word that is rarely used in Portuguese, and is known by the provincial name of Trás-os-Montes ("behind the mountains"). This remote region with its cold winters and hot summers is sealed off from the Atlantic by a sequence of granite *serras* reaching up to 1,500 metres (4,920 feet) in the Gerês. Trás-os-Montes ends at the River Douro, which cuts a deep scar through the north of Portugal. Although it has never been recognized as a single administrative region, the upper Douro has a strong territorial claim of its own. Where the river flows through the slate-like schist, the Douro and the lower reaches of its tributaries the Corgo, Varosa, Tavora, Torto, Pinhão, Tua and Coa collectively form one of the world's most dramatic vineyard regions, demarcated both for Port (*Vinho do Porto*) and unfortified Douro wines.

The vineyards on the south side of the Douro belong to the Beiras, a huge slice of central Portugal split into three. The land rises steeply into Beira Alta, and although grapes for sparkling wines are grown on the so-called altos above Lamego, much of the country south of the Douro is too high and too sheer, even for vines. A thousand metres (3,280 feet) is about the limit. The giant massif of the Serra da Estrela rises to a height of 1,993 metres (6,537 feet) – the highest point in Portugal – and the land around the city of Guarda to the north-east is bleak, windswept and barren. The granite soils are frequently too poor and shallow to support viticulture, but there are outcrops of schist on the *planalto* north of Pinhel where a handful of growers are starting to prove that vines can be cultivated to good effect. The area has been awarded its own DOC: Beira Interior.

The Mondego, the largest river entirely within Portugal, bubbles up as a spring in the Serra da Estrela and loops round the northern flank of the mountains, carving a broad basin to the south of Viseu. This region takes its name not from the mighty Mondego but the diminutive River Dão, which rises near Trancoso and crashes over granite boulders until it joins the Mondego downstream from Santa Comba Dão. Hemmed in by mountains, Dão is in the middle of the Atlantic–continental climatic transition. It has traditionally been the repository of some of Portugal's finest red wines, which after half a century of decline are undergoing a timely revival.

Lazy "z" bends in the mountains of northern Portugal

East of the Serra da Estrela the watershed is that of the Tagus, and the upper reaches of the River Zêzere define another basin known as Cova de Beira. This is the heart of Beira Baixa ("lower Beira"), a province that extends all the way down to the River Tagus, south of Castelo Branco. Cova de Beira is a good fruit-growing area that is slowly turning to wine, also under the DOC of Beira Interior. But much of the wine from these newer regions is bottled as Vinho Regional, Beiras. This huge and somewhat disparate designation covers almost the entire province, from all but the very highest mountain peaks right down to the coastal *litoral*.

I. PORT

Vinho do Porto, Vin de Porto, Porto, Port Wine; Port takes its name from Portugal's second largest city, Porto (Oporto in English). It is a curious paradox that, nowadays, very little wine flows through the place, and Port is much more closely identified with the adjacent city of Vila Nova de Gaia and "the Douro", a loose description given to 250,000 hectares of mountainous country inland. The River Douro forms the axis of this, one of the oldest demarcated wine regions in the world, which commences about sixty kilometres (thirty-seven miles) upstream from Oporto as the crow flies and extends another ninety kilometres (fifty-six miles) eastwards to the frontier with Spain. The river used to be the conduit for wine to reach the coast, and Oporto on the narrow estuary was little more than the seaport from which Port wine gained its worldwide reputation. Names like Cockburn, Croft, Graham and Taylor are so synonymous with Port that many people would find it hard to pinpoint its origin.

Port is very much a product of the mountains of northern Portugal and the climatic transition therein. To the north the Serras de Alvão, Padrela and Bornes shield the Douro region from the cold northerlies, whereas to the west the 1,400-metre (4,592-feet) massif of the Serra do Marão casts a rain shadow over the entire region. Travelling by road to the Douro, it is not uncommon to leave Oporto shrouded in Atlantic mist, traverse the mountains of Marão in a downpour and descend the other side in bright sunshine.

Whereas the greater part of northern Portugal is granite, the country either side of the upper Douro corresponds with an outcrop of schist. This foliated, slate-like rock fractures vertically, allowing the penetration of roots to depths that would be impossible within the granite. Over the years, the surface has been worked into a coarse soil. Lumps of schist on the surface shine almost like polished steel in strong sunlight, radiating heat and limiting erosion during heavy winter downpours. Over time, the schist weathers into a fine silt-like dust, clouds of which billow up from trails and tracks, covering vehicles in the summer months.

The land either side of the Douro is very steeply inclined and has been sculpted into narrow step-like terraces in order to support rows of vines. It is hard to imagine a more challenging place in which to grow grapes and, over recent decades, methods of cultivation have evolved to take account of rising costs. The traditional terraces (*socalcos*) with their high retaining walls are expensive to maintain and are almost impossible to mechanize. Only man and mule have the dexterity to gain access. In the 1970s a new form of terracing was devised whereby steeply inclined earth ramps known as *patamares* took the place of troublesome walls. A network of tracks running diagonally across the slope allows small, specially adapted tractors to gain access to the flat surface of the terrace. Although these terraces were widely adopted by growers under the World Bank-financed PDRITM scheme in the 1980s, they have a number of drawbacks. Chief among them is the lower vine density. Whereas Douro vineyards were traditionally planted at densities of 5,000–6,000 vines per hectare, *patamares* only achieved densities of 3,500 vines per hectare. The wider spacing induces greater vigour in the individual plants. This makes the vineyard difficult to manage as well as producing excessive shade, with consequent effects on the quality of the fruit. In the late 1970s and early 1980s, Ferreira and Ramos Pinto, which own two adjacent quintas in the Torto valley, began laying out their rows of vines up and down the slope as opposed to planting them parallel with the contours. Known as *vinha ao alto*, this system of cultivation permits densities of 5,000 vines per hectare as well as limited mechanization. Tracks that cross the slope at right angles to the rows of vines give access for tractors equipped with winches for ploughing or giant cannons to spray against disease. Taylor and Fonseca, both enthusiastic converts to *vinha ao alto*, have taken this a stage further, using ATVs (All Terrain Vehicles) to speed up treatment of their vines. *Vinha ao alto* has certainly transformed the landscape in parts of the Douro, and although it is still challenging to cultivate, a number of producers have come to recognize that planting up-and-down produces the best quality wine.

Sub-regions

First demarcated by the Marquês de Pombal in 1756 (see page 15), the Port wine region is now divided into three semi-official sub-regions.

BAIXO CORGO

This is the westernmost of the sub-regions, in the shadow of the Serra do Marão around the city of Régua. With an annual rainfall of about 900–1,000 millimetres (thirty-five to thirty-nine inches), the Baixo Corgo is the wettest and coolest part of the Douro demarcation and therefore tends to produce large volumes of relatively insubstantial wine, destined to become inexpensive Ruby and Tawny Port. Covering a total area of 45,000 hectares, it is still the most intensively planted of the three sub-regions, with over a third under vine.

CIMA CORGO

Above the River Corgo, which joins the Douro just upstream from Régua, the Cima Corgo, centred on the small, scruffy town of Pinhão, is the heart of the demarcated region. The rainfall here averages 700 millimetres (twenty-eight inches) and summer temperatures are correspondingly higher. The Cima Corgo embraces 95,000 hectares and has vineyards that tend to be larger than those downstream but which cover just over a fifth of the total land area. All the main Port shippers own properties in the Cima Corgo, either alongside the Douro or on one of the tributaries, the Tedo, Tavora, Torto, Pinhão and Tua. Wines from these vineyards form the basis of the finest quality Ports: Vintage, Aged Tawnies and Late Bottled Vintage (LBV).

DOURO SUPERIOR

The most easterly sub-region is a relative newcomer to Port, having been hampered for centuries by poor communications. The Douro Superior is the largest of the three, covering 110,000 hectares, of which less than a tenth is planted with vines. The climate is marked by continental extremes, with bitterly cold winters and blistering summers when the thermometer frequently exceeds 40°C. Rainfall near the Spanish border is as low as 400 millimetres (sixteen inches), meaning that some growers have to resort to irrigation in order to make up for the natural deficit. But these natural drawbacks are more than compensated for by the fact that the easterly reaches of the Douro are flatter than the Cima Corgo. In the right location, vineyards of the Douro Superior are capable of producing some powerful, premium quality wines.

The topography of the Douro is the *raison d'être* of a complex vineyard classification system used to regulate the production of grapes from a total of 33,000 individual growers. Each and every vineyard plot is graded according to a scale of positive and negative points based on twelve physical variables:

Altitude: more points for vineyards at lower levels, with properties above 650 metres (2,132 feet) effectively prohibited from producing Port. The maximum is 240 positive points, the minimum minus 900.

Locality: the entire region is divided into five sections, with the most points awarded to vineyards in the heart of the Cima Corgo around Pinhão. The maximum is 600 positive points, the minimum minus 50.

Productivity (yield): based on the principle that productive vineyards produce poorer wine. The maximum is 120 positive points, the minimum minus 600.

Soil type: schistous soils are awarded a maximum of 100 positive points, with a minimum of minus 400 for vines grown on alluvium.

Vine training: vines trained close to the ground (up to 0.8 metres/2.6 feet) are awarded a positive score of 100 points, but high trained pergolas (as used in Vinho Verde) are completely excluded from the production of Port.

Grape varieties: there are over eighty grape varieties growing in the Douro and these were originally classified into five groups, ranging from 150 points for grapes described as "very good" to minus 300 for those described as "bad". Nowadays the system has been simplified into varieties that are "recommended" or merely "authorized". Fourteen white varieties are recommended and fifteen red. The acknowledged top five red varieties planted in varying proportions in all the newer vineyards are (in order of importance): Touriga Franca, Tinta Roriz, Tinta Barroca, Touriga Nacional and Tinto Cão. These and the other Douro grape varieties are described in Chapter 2.

Angle of inclination (slope): on the basis that the best wines come from well-drained slopes, no points are awarded to vines growing on flat land and up to 101 points for a vineyard on a slope in excess of thirty-five degrees.

Aspect and exposure: depending on the locality (see above), minus 40 points may be awarded to a north-facing vineyard in the cooler Baixo Corgo, whereas a positive score of 100 may go to a south-facing site in the Cima Corgo.

Stoniness (soil texture): stony soils that retain the heat are awarded up to 80 points, but no score is given to a soil lacking in stone.

Age of vines: older vines generally yield less but produce more concentrated wines. Vineyards less than four years old are excluded from Port production, those between four and twenty-five years old receive 30 points and those over twenty-five years get 60 points.

Shelter: sheltered sites are awarded a maximum of 60 points whereas the most exposed receive no points at all.

Vine density: on the basis that density helps to control vigour, vineyards planted at higher densities (up to 5,700 plants per hectare) receive a maximum of 50 points.

Taking these variables into account, each and every vineyard plot (and there are 140,000 altogether) is recorded on a *cadastro* or register. After a certain amount of number crunching, each holding is classified according to the total number of points as follows:

Class A: 1,201 points or more
Class B: 1,000–1,200 points
Class C: 801–1,000 points
Class D: 601–800 points
Class E: 401–600 points
Class F: 201–400 points

This classification system forms the basis of the annual authorization or *benefício*. Taking into account the previous year's sales and the stocks of wine held by the Port shippers, the Oporto-based Port Wine Institute (IVP) sets a figure for the total amount of grape must within the demarcated region that may be fortified to make Port. Licences are then handed out to individual growers on the basis of the points system outlined above. The theory behind this system is that those vineyards with higher grades (A and B) are thereby able to fortify a greater proportion of their wine to make Port than properties rated C, D, E and F. The *beneficio* also helps to keep the supply of Port roughly in line with demand.

When the harvest begins in late September, the vineyard terraces suddenly come to life. Even the smallest sound has a strange resonance in the Douro and the babble of the pickers can be heard across the valley. In spite of the many changes that have taken place in the vineyards over recent years, the vintage or *vindima* is still a manual undertaking, celebrated by folk from the outlying villages who find work in the vineyards, often on the same property each year. Winemaking used to be a largely manual undertaking as well – or, more accurately, it was a process primarily undertaken by foot. At the end of a long, hot day in the vineyards each member of the gang or *roga* of pickers dons a pair of shorts to tread the grapes in rectangular stone tanks known as *lagares*. For the first two or three hours the roga links arms and marches slowly backward and forward thigh-deep through the purple mass of grapes in a ritual known as the *corte* ("cut"). At the end of this, *liberdade* ("liberty") is declared, indicating a free-for-all with dancing in the *lagar* until midnight, when the members of the roga return to their dormitories to sleep off a hard day's work.

The principle behind this seemingly archaic method of winemaking is expediency. Unlike most red wine, which is fermented in contact with the grape skins over a period of ten days or more, Port as a sweet, fortified wine has a relatively short period of skin contact. Depending on the speed of fermentation, Port may be run off from the skins and fortified with seventy-seven per cent strength spirit (*águardente*) after just two or three days, thereby leaving the required amount of natural residual sugar in the wine. In order to coax the necessary colour, flavour and tannin structure from the grapes, the extraction process needs to be vigorous. Hence the need for the *roga* – one or two people per 550-litre pipe of must – to tread the grapes thoroughly before the fermentation begins.

Although many of the finest Vintage Ports are still foot-trodden in the time-honoured way, the mass emigration that afflicted rural Portugal in the 1960s nearly turned the *lagar* into a museum piece. Sensing the impending crisis, the major shippers hastily constructed centralized wineries to which outlying quintas could deliver their grapes to be made into Port. One or two shippers tried to automate their *lagares* using the ill-fated *movimosto* system, but with little or no electric power available at the time, the majority opted for a system known as autovinification. This self-perpetuating process relies on the build-up of carbon dioxide (a by-product of the fermentation) within a sealed unit. The pressure within the vat forces the fermenting grape must up into an open holding tank above. Once a certain pressure has built up inside the vat, the carbon dioxide escapes through a calibrated valve and, no longer supported by the pressure below, the fermenting must falls back inside the vat spraying the cap of grape skins below with considerable force. When fermentation is in full flow, this cycle takes place every fifteen to twenty minutes, day and night.

The early autovinification vats were square in shape, built of cement and with roughly the same capacity as a traditional *lagar*. In warm years the ferment would frequently overheat, whereas in cold weather, without the human warmth of twenty or thirty legs in the grapes, a few days could elapse before the must started to ferment and the autovinification process commenced. In the 1980s a number of modifications were made to the autovinification system that ensure its survival today. Stainless steel was introduced and the new cylindrical autovinifiers were equipped with temperature control. Since the mid-1960s the Symington-owned houses have largely stuck to autovinification, whereas others, notably Croft, Ferreira and Taylor/Fonseca, have devised their own methods along much the same lines. But in the late 1990s there was something of a return to treading, either by human foot in *lagar* or using automated ("robotic") treaders. Quinta do Noval were the first to adapt an existing *lagar* to a robotic treader, but the Symington family have devised an entirely new stainless-steel *lagar* which can be programmed to tread the grapes day and night. These have been installed at Graham's Quinta dos Malvedos and there are some at the Symingtons' central winery, Quinta do Sol. With labour once again in short supply in Portugal's booming EU-financed economy, it is likely that these robotic *lagares* will become a more common sight in the Douro and elsewhere for the production of high-quality wine.

Port spends its first winter in the Douro, during which time the wines "fall bright" as sediment and natural tartrates fall to the bottom of the vat. A month or two after the conclusion of the harvest the *lota* begins, with wines being classified and blended according to their potential quality. This is no mean task, for a large shipper making a complete range of Ports may end up with 400–500 lots. In the spring after the harvest, the wines start to be shipped downstream to complete their maturation in the relatively cool coastal climate of Vila Nova de Gaia. Until as recently as the 1960s, the wines made their way downstream by boat but nowadays road tankers choke the narrow lanes in the Douro and Vila Nova de Gaia. The wines are housed in long, low buildings known in English as "lodges" or in Portuguese as *armazens*. Below the network of long red roofs that make up the *entreposto* ("entrepôt") of Vila Nova de Gaia are a variety of different wooden vats and vessels, with the larger examples (*balseiros* and *toneis*) reserved for wines destined for bottling after two or three years (Ruby, LBV and Vintage) and the casks known as *pipas* ("pipes") for wines intended for longer ageing (Aged Tawnies and Colheitas). The flavour of new oak is not a desirable characteristic in Port, and most of the vats and casks are made from well-seasoned wood, either oak, Brazilian mahogany or (occasionally) Italian chestnut.

Port styles

Most Ports are complex blends, or even blends of blends, and all the major Port shippers employ an experienced taster to maintain and develop the house style. He (for they are nearly all men) dwells in a room that has a superb view of Oporto on the opposite side of the river and thus captures the north light. Colour is a vitally important indicator of style and it is no coincidence that the names of two major categories of Port – Ruby and Tawny – reflect the maturity and hue of the wine.

In spite of the proliferation of different styles of Port since the 1960s, there are still two fundamental categories of wine. Wood-matured Ports are those that mature in bulk (either in wood, cement or stainless-steel vats) and are bottled only when they are judged to be ready for drinking. This category includes all Ruby, Tawny and White Ports as well as the majority of LBV. Once in bottle these wines will keep for a year or more, but are not intended to be aged over the medium to longer term and are generally bottled with a stopper cork. Having been fined and filtered before bottling, they do not need to be decanted before serving.

Bottle-matured Ports are those that are bottled relatively early. Compared to wood Ports, which age in a controlled oxidative environment, bottle-matured wines develop in reductive conditions that slow down the ageing process. This category includes all Vintage Port (and single-quinta Vintage), Crusted Ports and some LBVs (usually designated as "traditional" or "bottle-matured"). Bottle-matured Ports are not generally subject to any fining or filtration and therefore throw a sediment or "crust" in bottle; thus they should be decanted before serving. They are mostly bottled in opaque glass to protect them from the light and with a driven cork, and should be stored laying down in cool conditions.

The Port Wine Institute (IVP) has its own categorization of Port which is written into the statutes. Anything other than Ruby, Tawny and White Port, which together account for around ninety per cent of the trade in terms of volume, belongs to a *Categoria Especial* ("special category"). This embraces Vintage Port, LBV, so-called "Vintage Character"/reserve Ruby, Aged Tawnies (that is, those bottled with an indication of age, such as twenty, thirty, forty and over forty years old) and Colheita. The rules that accompany the Special Categories are considerably more exacting and the wines are regularly and randomly monitored by the IVP.

RUBY

Named after its youthful colour, Ruby is the simplest and can be one of the most satisfying styles of young Port. The wines chosen to make up a Ruby usually present a deep colour, straightforward fruity aromas, some body and structure but not too much in the way of tannic grip. Ruby blends are generally made up from more than one year, aged in bulk for up to three years and bottled young to capture the strong, fiery personality of young Port. Cockburn, Dow, Sandeman and Smith Woodhouse all bottle reliable, straightforward Ruby Port.

TAWNY

The word "Tawny" is attached to two very different styles of Port. It implies a wine that has been aged in wood for longer than a Ruby until it takes on an amber-tawny hue. But much of the "Tawny Port" that reaches the shelves today is no older than the average Ruby and it is not uncommon to see the two wines standing side by side at the same price. These inexpensive Tawnies are generally made from lighter wines from the Baixo Corgo, often further diluted with some White Port so that they take on a pinkish tinge. Heavy fining may also be used to adjust the colour. Many wines spend a summer up in the Douro being *estufado* ("stewed") in cement *balões* by the ambient heat and, as one shipper admitted candidly, these Ports see wood by accident rather than by design! The resulting wines usually display a slightly brown tinge on the rim but lack the freshness and vibrancy usually associated with young Port. Often drunk as an aperitif, these so-called "Tawnies" have a popular following in France.

WHITE PORT

There is an old adage that Port has two duties: the first is to be red and the second is to be drunk. Having tasted so many dull, insipid White Ports I am more than inclined to agree. Although handling has improved in recent years, characterless grape varieties and heavy-handed vinification methods are still largely to blame. Wood ageing lends character to White Port, but most wines are left in lined cement or stainless steel and bottled after eighteen months to two years. The honourable exceptions are Barros, Churchill, Niepoort and Quinta de la Rosa, all of whom bottle excellent traditional dry White Ports which have turned golden amber with age and picked up an incisive, nutty character from the wood. White Port is usually served chilled as an aperitif, either on its own or with a twist of lemon peel to sharpen up the flavour, accompanied by a bowl of salted almonds. Some shippers pour White Port over ice and turn it into a long drink with tonic water, adorned with a slice of lemon or a sprig of mint.

RESERVE ("VINTAGE CHARACTER")

Vintage Character became Port's great misnomer and the name, though not the category, is being phased out. The wines are not the product of a single year and few share much of the character or concentration of a true Vintage Port. The style is nonetheless highly laudable and results from the blending of young Ports of a higher quality than those used for standard Ruby, with an average age of between three and five years. The greater part of the blend is likely to be aged in wood, although shippers are looking to select well-structured wines with a ripe, primary fruit character that have mellowed more than a standard Ruby. Like Ruby, Reserve or Vintage Character Port is ready to drink as soon as it is bottled and is not intended for laying down. This category includes some of the best-selling Ports on the UK and North American markets. Cockburn's Special Reserve, Dow's Trademark, Fonseca Bin 27, Graham's Six Grapes, Taylor's First Estate and Warre's Warrior are among those with the most depth and character.

LATE BOTTLED VINTAGE (LBV)

LBV means what it says: a wine from a single year bottled between four and six years after the vintage (compared to a maximum of two years for Vintage Port *per se*). Although Taylor's claim to have invented the style, it evolved largely by default and has proved to be hugely successful in English-speaking markets where the word "Vintage" undoubtedly commands a premium. In order to prevent too much oxidative character from entering the blend, wines destined to become LBVs are kept in large vats (either of wood or stainless steel) until they are bottled, between July 1 in the fourth year after the harvest and December 31 in the sixth year. Two very different styles of LBV have now evolved. Most producers followed Taylor's in filtering and cold stabilizing their wines before bottling in order to prevent the formation of a sediment, thereby removing the need to decant. Graham and Taylor are the leading exponents of this style. Since the 1990s there has been a trend toward so-called "traditional" LBV, bottled without any filtration or treatment. Usually produced from a good, undeclared harvest, in order to qualify for the traditional/bottle-matured designation the wine must spend an extra three years in bottle before being released. Bottled with a driven cork (as opposed to the stopper corks used for filtered LBVs), these wines will often continue to improve in bottle for another four to six years and the best share something of the depth and intensity of a true Vintage Port. Burmester, Churchill, Ferreira, Niepoort, Smith Woodhouse and Warre all bottle good unfiltered LBV.

CRUSTED

So called because of the deposit or "crust" that the wine throws in bottle, Crusted Port is a fairly recent creation that has earned itself the epithet of "poor man's Vintage Port". Although the coveted word "Vintage" does not appear anywhere on the label, Crusted Ports are much closer in style to Vintage Port than either "Vintage Character" or most LBV, presenting a dense, concentrated wine for a fraction of the price. Wines from two or three harvests are aged in wood for up to two years and bottled without any fining or filtration. The only date that is of any significance is the year of bottling that appears on the label. The wine may only be released after spending at least three years in bottle, by which time it is usually quite approachable, having developed the ripe aromas characteristic of a Vintage Port as well as a substantial crust. Dow is the leading producer of Crusted Port.

TAWNY WITH INDICATION OF AGE

The majority of "true" Tawny Ports are bottled with an "indication of age". "Ten", "twenty", "thirty", "forty" and "over forty years old" are the designations officially permitted by the IVP. These are merely approximations, as all Tawny Ports with the exception of Colheita (see below) are complex blends of wines from a number of different years. Wines set aside to become part of this chain of old Tawnies are selected from among the finest Ports only after making up the potential Vintage or Single Quinta Vintage *lotes*. By their very nature, the component wines are mostly sourced from A- or B- grade vineyards in the Cima Corgo or Douro Superior. Individual shippers look to maintain different house styles, but on the whole the young wines destined to develop into mature Tawnies combine stature and structure with elegance and finesse. The refined complexity of a well-aged Tawny befits the climate and temperament of the Douro better than the hefty, heady character of bottle-matured wines, which are better suited to cooler climes. Indeed, a glass of Tawny served cool from the fridge is positively refreshing either as an aperitif or after a lunch in the heat of the day. Barros, Burmester, Ferreira, Fonseca, Kopke, Niepoort, Ramos Pinto and Sandeman are specialists in fine, well-balanced Tawnies at various levels of age.

COLHEITA

Often misunderstood, the Portuguese word *colheita* (pronounced col-yate-a) means "harvest" and by extension can be confused with "vintage". Like Vintage Port, Colheitas are the product of a single harvest, but the wines are aged in wood for a minimum of seven years, by which time they have begun to take on an oxidative, Tawny character. In practice most Colheitas are aged for considerably longer, the casks or vat being racked and topped up periodically (in theory with the same wine) to replace that lost by evaporation. The wines take on secondary aromas and flavours, losing colour and gaining in richness, sweetness and intensity the longer they mature in wood. Without recourse to blending and refreshing, some Colheitas look distinctly tired by the time they come to be bottled and in comparative tastings they tend to fare less well than aged Tawnies. Two dates appear on the label: the date of the harvest (*colheita*) and the date of bottling. The latter is significant, as the wine will not generally improve in bottle (although after prolonged oxidative ageing in wood it won't deteriorate that quickly either). Cálem, Barros, Burmester, Dalva, Krohn, Kopke, Noval and Niepoort are specialists in this niche market.

VINTAGE

For many shippers, Vintage Port represents the very pinnacle of achievement. The British-owned shippers in particular have built their individual reputations on Vintage Port and, in spite of the reluctance of some Portuguese firms, the category has become a flagship for the entire trade. But all the approbation that surrounds Vintage Port belies the fact that it is one of the most straightforward of all Ports to produce. Wines from a single year are bottled, without treatment or filtration, after spending a maximum of two years ageing in bulk. The skill in producing a Vintage Port is in the selection of the finest grapes, picked at optimum ripeness after a successful growing season. To a certain extent this is predetermined, as most shippers know their own quintas as intimately as those belonging to their long-term suppliers. Many of the most successful Vintage Ports are therefore based year after year on grapes from the same plots of vines in the same properties. The grapes need to be very well worked during vinification, usually foot-trodden in a *lagar* or turned over in an autovinifier. After the harvest these Ports are put to one side and monitored as potential Vintage *lotes*. Under the rules set out by the IVP, the shippers have up to two years to decide whether to "declare" the wine as Vintage. Contrary to popular opinion, the declaration is a decision taken independently by each shipper. More often than not there is a natural consensus, but there are a number of recent examples of so-called "split declarations", where some leading shippers have opted for one year and others have plumped for another (for example, 1982–3 or 1991–2).

With the steady investment in temperature-controlled vinification that has taken place since the early 1980s, the production of high-quality Port is much less of a hit and miss affair than it was in the past. Unless the harvest happens to be a complete washout (as in 1993), wines of potential Vintage quality are now made nearly every year. Port shippers have consequently been faced with the dilemma of how to market wines from good interim years without undermining or diluting the reputation of Vintage Port per se. The collective solution to this problem has either been to declare these wines under a second label (Fonseca–Guimaraens, for example) or, more commonly, to bottle a Single Quinta Vintage Port. The IVP treats these in exactly the same way as fully declared Vintage Ports. In order to obtain approval for the description "Vintage", a sample of the wine must be submitted to the Institute between January 1 and September 30 in the second year after the harvest. The amount of stock must be registered and, pending the wine's approval by the *Câmara de Provadores* (tasting panel), a current account will duly be opened for it. The bottling may take place from as soon as the wine has been approved until June 30 in the third year after the harvest. In practice most Vintage Ports are bottled during the cooler spring months.

Once a Vintage Port has been bottled, it continues to develop and evolve over a period of fifteen or twenty years before it is considered as being ready to drink. After an initial burst of youth the wine tends to shut down and go through ten to fifteen years of spotty adolescence before it re-emerges as a mature and graceful adult. Wines from the very finest vintages will continue to develop over half a century or more. A brief guide to the main Port vintages, including recommendations on the leading shippers and quintas, can be found in the section on vintages at the end of Chapter 2.

Producers

The Port trade is dominated by brands: shippers that have become household names like Cockburn, Sandeman, Graham and Taylor. Until 1986 these and other major shippers effectively enjoyed a cartel, as all Port wine had to be traded through the bonded *entreposto* ("entrepôt") at Vila Nova de Gaia. The legislation now permits Port to be exported directly from the Douro region as well. A number of larger growers have taken advantage of this, but the pre-eminence of the shippers with their brands means that sales of wines directly from the quintas and cooperatives are still relatively small. Twenty-two cooperatives produce around thirty-five per cent of all Port, most of which is bought in by the shippers as the basis for their standard Ruby and Tawny blends.

The shippers themselves are subject to a certain amount of categorization. Since the Second World War there has been considerable amalgamation, with multinational companies buying up established names like Croft, Cockburn, Delaforce and Sandeman. Croft and Delaforce have now been acquired from Diageo by Taylor/Fonseca and the company has been renamed as the Fladgate Partnership. Sandeman has been sold by Seagram and now belongs to Sogrape, Portugal's largest wine producers, who also own Offley and Ferreira. Family-owned firms (some of which have been in continuous existence for three centuries or more) are the custodians, tending to look to the long-term future of the Port trade, whereas the multinationals (most of whom arrived in the 1960s and 1970s) have taken a rather more short-term approach. Nonetheless, the tunnel vision that afflicted many Port shippers in the past has gradually been eroded and Vila Nova de Gaia and the Douro are now firmly on the map for a growing number of itinerant winemakers and *aficionados*. There are just over a hundred shipping companies registered with the IVP and profiles of the major firms and their wines can be found in my companion volume to this book, *Port and the Douro*, also published by Mitchell Beazley.

II. MOSCATEL DE FAVAIOS

There are pockets of Moscatel (Muscat) all over the Douro, but the greatest concentration is to be found on the *planalto* around the towns of Alijó and Favaios. So far it has escaped the attention of the legislators and no DOC has ever been created, although a special sub-region (Moscatel de Favaios) has been under discussion for some years. The wine is made in much the same way as Port and production is centred on the local cooperative, which ages the wine for around three years in wooden *toneis* and *balseiros* ranging in size from 10,000 to 33,000 litres. Most Favaios wines share a similar rustic style, with rather cloying sweetness somewhat akin to Demerara sugar. Few are sold outside the locality.

III. DOURO

There used to be something of Samuel Johnson's "Claret for Boys, Port for Men" in the attitude to Douro wines. This is partly reflected in the lexicon. No one could quite decide how to distinguish unfortified red and white wines from Port, and they were often described by Port shippers as merely *consumo* or "table wine" (*vinho de mesa*). The task has been made easier since 1979, when "Douro" wines were awarded their own DOC, over two centuries after the Douro Valley was first delimited for Port.

Terraces at Quinta do Bomfim overlooking the Douro

Unfortified wines are hardly new to the Douro. Until the early eighteenth century, most of the wine produced in the region was fermented dry and bolstered with a small amount of fortifying spirit to lend stability for shipment abroad. The development of Port into a sweet, fortified wine is covered in Chapter 1, but even as late as the mid-nineteenth century

Joseph James Forrester – a leading Port shipper of the day – continued to advocate a return to dry, unfortified red wine. Forrester's style of Port was never accepted in the UK (then the only major market) for, as Oswald Crawfurd, the British Consul in Oporto, wrote in 1880: "The true point at issue has always seemed to me to be, not whether port can be made without the addition of distilled wine, but whether wine so made is worth making or worth drinking. Such wine is an unmarketable product, and I think deservedly so. It is a strong, rough and comparatively flavourless liquor. If a man were to add six drops of ink to a glass of very common red burgundy he would get something exceedingly like unfortified port." Anyone who tasted the rough and ready unfortified wine that used to be produced in the Douro before the relatively recent advent of stainless steel and temperature control would be in broad agreement with Crawfurd's conclusion. It is hardly surprising that for much of the twentieth century, *consumo*, "table wine" or call it what you will was accorded the lowliest status in the Douro caste system, with the best grapes reserved exclusively for the production of Port.

It is therefore all the more remarkable that in 1950 the technical director of Ferreira Port, Fernando Nicolau de Almeida, should take himself off to Bordeaux to study production techniques for unfortified wines. At first he found it hard to conceive how the Bordelais could possibly tread the grapes in huge wooden vats, but de Almeida soon found out that they employed softer, more gentle extraction methods. Inspired by this, he returned to his remote family quinta in the Douro Superior and began to put their ideas into practice using high-quality Port grapes. The story, recounted below, is a triumph of strength over adversity. Ferreira's Barca Velha was born in 1952 and quickly earned itself the reputation of being Portugal's uncrowned "first growth". Nowadays it commands a price in excess of many Vintage Ports.

Following the success of Barca Velha, other producers slowly began to sit up and take notice and, in the late 1970s and early 1980s, a flurry of new Douro wines appeared on the market. Initially they were viewed as no more than a by-product, made from poor quality grapes surplus to the annual Port *benefício*. Production techniques were outmoded, with vinification (often autovinification) geared toward the extraction of tannin for the production of Port. With a complete absence of temperature control the resulting wines were hard, stewed and astringent. There were exceptions. The Symington family, which has now launched its own range of Douro wines, was quietly stashing away a few bottles of Douro red for a number of years. Made from surplus grapes, a 1970 red produced at Quinta do Bomfim (tasted in 1998) still retained its deep colour and hugely powerful, sinewy tannins. It must have started out akin to "blackstrap", the derisive term used to describe the strong Douro reds exported to Britain in the early eighteenth century.

Douro wines were given a much-needed fillip by Portugal's accession in 1986 to what was then the European Community. This brought the necessary finance to one of the continent's poorest regions and, from one vintage to the next, many wineries were re-equipped with the latest in stainless-steel technology. There remained, however, a lack of technical expertise, not to mention winemaking flair, among producers blinkered by their total commitment to Port. "Why waste good grapes on *consumo* when you can make them into Port?" was a common cry well into the 1990s. Wild fluctuations in yield continued to compound the problem, meaning that in one year there might be a huge surplus of grapes for making Douro wine whereas in the next vintage there would be a shortage. Up to the mid-1990s Douro wines continued to be treated as something of an afterthought.

At the turn of the new century, however, Douro wines are being reappraised. Prompted by a younger generation of resourceful winemakers, many with experience abroad, a number of leading Port shippers are according ever greater importance to Douro wines. Financially, Douro wines are also adding up. With an increasingly appreciative audience in Portugal and a growing export market, many of the better Douro wines are commanding margins similar to or better than those of LBV Port. And for a number of growers with C- or D-grade vineyards in the Baixo Corgo, high-quality Douro wine seems to offer a more secure future than the vagaries of price-sensitive Port.

Contrary to the methods used to make Port (see pages 191–193), the successful vinification of red Douro wine revolves around the need to tame the tannic excesses of the native grapes. With gentle handling, three of the five grape varieties planted under the PDRITM project of the 1980s – Tinta Roriz, Touriga Nacional and Touriga Franca – have proved to be eminently suitable for quality Douro reds. Tiny quantities of Cabernet Sauvignon have crept into the region, but its use is only permissible in a second category of wines bottled under the uninviting name of the Vinho Regional: Trás-os-Montes/Terras Durienses. The attributes of each of the Douro's many grape varieties are covered in some detail in Chapter 2.

The burgeoning market for Douro reds along with a number of small harvests has increased the competition for grapes. Most Douro wine-makers source grapes from more temperate locations, either downstream from Pinhão or from the so-called *meia encosta* ("half slope") at altitudes of 300–400 metres (984–1,312 feet). Grapes from the Douro Superior and the sheltered tributaries around Pinhão produce the most robust, concentrated wines, whereas those from the higher westerly margins of the region, on the *altos* around Lamego and Vila Real, lack the warmth and tend to produce thin, rasping wines sometimes more akin to Vinhos Verdes. There are so many different meso-climates within the Douro that there is an argument in favour of blending components from different areas. Just like a Vintage Port, this approach might produce a wine that is greater than the sum of its parts.

In their endeavour to produce softer, more supple red wines, most producers destalk the greater proportion of the crop once it reaches the winery. A number of notable single quintas continue to tread grapes in *lagares*, but the majority of producers have abandoned this and autovinification for Douro wines in favour of pumping over in stainless-steel fermentation tanks. Selected yeast cultures are generally favoured over wild yeasts, which frequently lead to stuck fermentations at higher levels of alcohol. Fermentation temperatures are generally controlled to between 24°C and 28°C (a few degrees lower than for Port) and macera-tion is increasingly carefully managed. Wines destined for early drinking remain on the skins for the duration of the fermentation (five days on average), whereas those destined for longer ageing generally undergo a period of *cuvaison* on the skins extending to fifteen or twenty days. Pressing has become much less extractive, and many producers have installed gentle pneumatic presses especially for the production of Douro wines.

White wines have largely been neglected in favour of red. Many of the Douro's white grapes are interplanted with red and the separation of the two is often too painstaking to be worthwhile. There are, however, promising local grape varieties like Viosinho, Gouveio and Rabigato, which, with careful handling, are capable of producing some fresh, fragrant dry wines. The best of these grapes tend to originate from the higher districts around Lamego, Vila Real, Alijó and São João de Pesqueira, where they retain a better acid balance than at lower altitudes. There is also a small amount of Chardonnay and Sauvignon Blanc, but like Cabernet these only qualify as Vinho Regional.

Hygiene has improved across the board and most wineries have now turned their backs on dirty old wooden vats in favour of stainless steel and new oak. Portuguese oak from Gerês and Trás-os-Montes was initially favoured and seemed to contribute a distinctive but not unpleasant green-vanilla character to some Douro wines, Barca Velha included. But with no forest management policy to speak of, oak is now virtually extinct in Portugal and producers are gradually turning to either French or American oak. Some have also used oak chips as a cheaper alternative to maturation in cask. Apart from Barca Velha, few Douro wines have much of a track record as yet, but the region's heavyweights probably have an inbuilt twenty- or thirty-year life span, parallel to that of Vintage Port.

Producers

There are so many small producers of Douro wine that it would be impossible to include them all in this chapter. Many of them have only been established since the successful 2000 vintage and have little or no reputation as yet. Apart from those described below, there are a number of young Douro wine makers who show real promise. Among these are Jorge Moreira whose new wine is known as Poeira, Jorge Serodio Borges and Sandra Tavares with a wine called Pintas, Bago de Touriga and Kolheita das Ideias both of which are masterminded by Luís Soares Duarte. These and others will doubtless merit their own entries in future editions of this book. However, the following producers are mostly well established and have a presence on both domestic and export markets.

CAVES ALIANÇA
Correspondence Address: Caves Aliança SA, Apartado 6, 3781 Sangalhos
Bairrada-based Caves Aliança (see page 151) buy in grapes to produce a middle-weight Douro red named Foral. Top of the range is the more substantial Foral Grande Escolha that is made from their own grapes grown on an A-grade quinta adjacent to Vesúvio in the Douro Superior.

BORGES

Sociedade dos Vinhos Borges SA, Rua Infante Dom Henrique, 421, 4435 Rio
Tinto

Having suffered a chequered history in recent years (see page 135),
Borges is well on the way to revival. The company was stripped of most
of its quintas but retained a winery near Vila Real, just ten metres (thirty-
three feet) from the DOC boundary. This is the source of a range of wines,
from an uninspiring white named Perola to reds bottled under the Lello
label. The straightforward Lello is light and rather herbaceous, but the
Garrafeira is full, leathery and rather astringent in the traditional style of
Douro reds. A Douro Reserva made from grapes sourced at Quinta da
Soalheira in the upper Torto is made in a more modern style, with firm
fruit offset by smoky new oak.

BRIGHT BROTHERS

Correspondence address: Bright Bros Vinhos Portugal Lda, Fornos de Cima,
Calhandriz, 2615 Alverca

With no vineyards of his own, Peter Bright scours the Douro for grapes
to produce red wine. In the past he has succeeded in producing large
quantities of vibrant fruity red, softened by a touch of oak, from excess
grapes at the Symington family's Quinta do Sol winery. Now that the
Symingtons have their own range of wines he buys grapes from Quinta
dos Frades, an impressive property on the south side of the river midway
between Régua and Pinhão. Here he makes two bigger, altogether more
serious wines than Bright Brothers Douro. Torcular is a wine made
entirely from *lagar*-fermented fruit bottled without any exposure to
wood. TFN is a solid blend of Touriga Franca and Touriga Nacional that
is lent a toasty character from short ageing in French oak barriques.

BURMESTER

JW Burmester & Ca Lda, Rua de Belmonte, 39, 4050 Oporto

Casa Burmester is a solid blend of Tinta Roriz and Touriga Franca aged
for between six and nine months in wood. Tavedo (named after the rivers
Tavora and Tedo) is a lighter style of wine mainly based on Roriz with a
small quantity of Touriga Nacional. Both wines are made at Burmester's
Quinta Nova between Régua and Pinhão.

QUINTA DO CACHÃO

Correspondence address: Sociedade Agricola e Commercial dos Vinhos Messias, Rua Commendador Messias Baptista, 56, Apartado 1, 3050 Mealhada

Port shipper Messias owns a 200-hectare property at Ferradosa in the Douro Superior which is the source of both fortified and Douro wine. A blend of four of the top five Douro grape varieties makes a vibrant if slightly rustic single-quinta red, and since 1996 Messias has produced a pair of deep-coloured Touriga Nacional and Tinta Roriz varietals made from grapes grown on the estate.

CALÇOS DA TANHA

Manuel Pinto Hespanhol, Vilarinho dos Freires, 5050 Peso da Régua

Named after the traditional step-like terraces above the River Tanha, this thirty-five-hectare quinta produces both Port and Douro wine from a roadside *adega* bedecked with *azulejos* (traditional tiles) in the village of Vilarinho dos Freires. The range of Douro wines includes a clean but neutral dry white and a well-balanced red, both bottled under the Calços da Tanha label, and a firm-flavoured Reserva partly aged in Portuguese and French oak. Calços de Tanha is also producing a varietal range from Tinta Roriz, Touriga Franca and, unusually for the Douro, Tinta Amarela. Quinta da Vila Freire is a second, somewhat lighter, red.

CÁLEM

AA Cálem & Filho SA, Rua da Reboleira, 7, 4050 Oporto

From grapes purchased in the Baixo Corgo, Cálem produces a duo of Douro reds under the names Solar de Sá and Terras de Sá. The wines are aged in new Portuguese oak pipes (subsequently used for Port) but so far have tended to be rather hard and sappy.

CHURCHILL

Churchill Graham Lda, Rua da Fonte Nova, 5, 4400 Vila Nova de Gaia

Established as Port shippers in 1981, it has taken twenty years for brothers Johnny, Anthony and William Graham to launch their own unfortified Douro wine. The purchase of their first property, Quinta da Gricha, in 1999, gave them the opportunity to vinify small quantities of grapes from different parts of the region. As a result, the wines produced so far have varied somewhat in style with the 2000 showing considerable elegance and refinement. João Brito e Cunha (see Lavradores de Feitoria on page 212) is the consultant wine maker. Churchill's wines are well-priced, which makes a refreshing change from some of the greedy pricing of some producers in the Douro.

COCKBURN
Cockburn Smithes & Ca SA, Rua das Coradas, 13, Apartado 20, 4401 Vila Nova de Gaia

For many years Cockburn's Tuella remained a well-kept secret. Named after the company's quinta and *adega* at Tua, the wine is made from surplus grapes high in the Douro Superior at Vila Nova de Foz Côa. Tuella was first produced back in 1972 and until the late 1990s remained confined to the local market. The cleanly made dry white is less interesting than the red, which combines a ripe, leathery character with good depth, weight and texture. Tuella is far from being the finest red wine in the Douro, but it always represents excellent value for money.

QUINTA DO CÔTTO
Montez Champalimaud Lda, Cidadelhe, 5040 Mesão Frio

This imposing eighteenth-century property above the Baixo Corgo village of Cidadelhe is much admired as a producer of some of the finest red and white Douro wines. Port now takes second place in the hierarchy and the cream of the crop from this mainly C-grade vineyard is directed toward two Douro wines, Quinta do Côtto and Quinta do Côtto Grande Escolha. The straightforward red Quinta do Côtto is produced nearly every year from a blend of Tinta Roriz, Touriga Franca and Touriga Nacional. Since the mid-1990s, the quality of Quinta do Côtto has improved markedly: whereas in the past the wine had a mean streak, it has now grown up to be a refined Douro red with firm, ripe tannins and supple, plum-like fruit. But the real acclaim must be reserved for the Grande Escolha. Produced in the most successful years from the oldest vineyards on the property, it undergoes an extended maceration or *cuvaison* followed by eighteen months in new Portuguese oak. The resulting wines are hugely tight and concentrated when young, without any of the green, sappy character that sometimes originates from Portuguese casks. With age, Grande Escolha retains its extraordinary colour, fruit and structure, gaining character and complexity. To date, Grande Escolha has only been produced in the following years: 1980, 1982, 1985, 1987, 1990, 1994 and 1995. Quinta do Côtto also makes one of the few genuinely interesting white Douro wines.

QUINTA DE COVELOS
José Carlos de Morais Calheiros Cruz, Canelas, 5050 Peso de Régua

With a well-equipped stainless-steel winery, Covelos began making Douro wines in 1996 from a blend of Tinta Roriz, Touriga Franca, Touriga Nacional and Tinta Barroca from thirty-five hectares of vineyard. The reds produced to date are elegant in style with well-defined if sometimes slightly green fruit, aged in French, American and Portuguese oak pipes. Quinta do Redolho is a second label.

QUINTA DO CRASTO*
Sociedade Agricola da Quinta do Crasto, Gouvinhas, 5060 Sabrosa

One of the most spectacularly situated properties in the Douro is Quinta do Crasto, where the Roquette family produces some of the region's most alluring red wines. Nearly fifty hectares of vineyard are split between mixed plantings of old vines up to seventy years old and newer varietal planting that began in 1986. Port tends to play second fiddle to Douro wine, and Crasto's Australian winemaker, Dominic Morris, often has the pick of the crop. A proportion is still foot-trodden in traditional *lagares* but most of the wines are fermented in an impressive stainless-steel winery and finished in new oak. Starting out in 1994 with just one wine, Crasto's range has widened to include a *reserva* based on low yielding old vines and varietal wines selected from among Tinta Roriz, Touriga Nacional, Touriga Franca and Tinto Cão according to the year. Crasto succeeds in capturing the quintessence of Douro fruit tempered by judicious use of French or American oak. A combination of carefully chosen grapes and thoughtful, even-handed winemaking yields wines that are well structured and supple without being over-extractive, hard or tannic. Two wines named Vinha do Ponte and Maria Teresa are made from separate plots of seventy-year-old vines that might otherwise produce great Vintage Port. These dense, concentrated reds (Maria Teresa is the bigger of the two) stand to become Douro greats.

FERREIRA

AA Ferreira SA, Rua da Carvalhosa, 19–103, 4400 Vila Nova de Gaia

The late Fernando Nicolau de Almeida is the father of modern-day Douro wines. Ferreira's former chief taster and technician began making unfortified wine at Quinta do Vale Meão in the early days when there was no electricity (ironically there is now a hydroelectric station near by). Nicolau de Almeida had to be inventive. In order to combat the raging heat in the Douro Superior, he rigged up a Heath Robinson system of temperature control using blocks of ice insulated in sawdust that had to be brought up by train from Oporto. To date only thirteen vintages of Barca Velha have been produced (1952, 1954, 1958, 1964, 1965, 1966, 1978, 1981, 1982, 1983, 1985, 1991 and 1995), but over the years it has become much less of a hit and miss affair. Control of the winemaking has now passed to José Maria Soares Franco, and Barca Velha is now made at a new purpose-built winery at Ferreira's Quinta da Leda nearby. Tinta Roriz has traditionally formed the backbone of the wine blended with smaller quantities of Touriga Franca, Tinta Barroca and Tinta Amarela. More Touriga Nacional is gradually entering the blend, lending it more power and body. The grapes are destemmed and fermented in stainless-steel vats at around 25°C. Regular, carefully managed pumping over ensures that extraction is controlled according to the character of the grapes and vintage. After going through malolactic in the Douro, the wine is transferred to Ferreira's lodges at Vila Nova de Gaia, where it spends around eighteen months in new oak, formerly Portuguese, now French.

Adopting something of the philosophy of Vintage Port, Barca Velha is the product of an exceptional harvest and the wine is only released after spending seven or eight years in bottle. It starts out with the in-house designation of "Douro Especial" and the wine is continually reassessed before a decision is taken as to whether it should be launched under the Barca Velha label. Since 1962, wine that is not considered to be quite up to Barca Velha standards is declassified as Reserva Especial (renamed Reserva Ferreirinha in 1989). The two wines share an affinity, combining open, sweet, fragrant aromas with suave tannins, often a touch of euca-lyptus and dense, concentrated, almost minty fruit. Sometimes a slightly sappy undertone creeps in from Portuguese oak. After an apparent dip in quality in the 1980s, Barca Velha returned to form in 1991 with a power-ful wine that like earlier vintages has the capacity to develop in bottle for twenty or thirty years. The 1966 (tasted in 1998) is an extraordinary wine, still upright and concentrated with a touch of tobacco box and the long sinewy finish that has become Barca Velha's hallmark. Reserva Ferreirinha from years like 1980 and 1989 (nearly "declared" as Barca Velha) can be almost as impressive, showing similar build but without the "first growth" cachet or price.

Owned by Sogrape since 1987, Ferreira has released a number of other Douro reds. Of these, Quinta da Leda, Callabriga and Vinha Grande are the most impressive, all of which are firm, fruit-driven wines, having been released much earlier than either Barca Velha or Reserva Ferreirinha. Departing from tradition, Ferreira has also bottled a concentrated varietal Touriga Nacional from grapes grown at Leda. Ferreira's most popular red is a wine named Esteva after the gum cistus plant that fills the Douro air with its heady aromas during the summer months. Grapes are bought in from vineyards at the higher margins of the region and vinified at Quinta do Seixo in the heart of the Douro near Pinhão. Much the lightest and most accessible of Ferreira's red wines, it is regularly voted as "the best everyday red" by the readers of Portugal's consumer wine magazine *Revista de Vinhos*. A million bottles are produced each year. In a poor vintage, however, Esteva can taste somewhat insipid and weedy.

VINHA DO FOJO
Quinta do Fojo, Vale de Mendiz, 5070 Alijó

Brother and sister Jorge and Margarida Serodio Borges took over the running of two prime quintas, Fojo and Manuela, deep in the Pinhão valley, from their grandfather in the early 1990s. Without any newfangled varietal plantings to rely on, the quinta's *omnium gatherum* of grapes from old, low yielding vines are foot-trodden and fermented in traditional granite *lagares*. Initially the wines suffered from a lack of temperature control and in 1997 the crop was spoiled. This has now been overcome by the installation of a heat exchanger in the *lagares*. The property produces two wines that reflect the local *terroir*. Fojo is a powerful red with a huge tannic superstructure and liquorice-like intensity of flavour. Vinha do Fojo is somewhat lighter (although that is a relative term), with vibrant fruit and good balance, although both wines are somewhat encumbered by their hefty price tag. Since 1999, David Baverstock of Esporão in the Alentejo has been travelling up to the Douro to oversee the winemaking.

QUINTA DA GAIVOSA*

Domingos Alves de Sousa, Apartado 15, 5031 Santa Marta de Penaguião

Domingos Alves de Sousa is one of the largest vineyard owners in the Baixo Corgo, with five properties amounting to over 100 hectares. Since giving up his profession of civil engineering, he has established a winery at Quinta da Gaivosa, a large C-graded property near Santa Marta de Penaguião. Rather like Quinta do Côtto Grande Escolha (see above), Gaivosa is only made in the best years. The wine is produced from old mixed vineyards, some of which were planted more than seventy years ago, and is a solid, structured red softened by short ageing in new French oak. Sensing the growing interest in Douro varieties, Alves de Sousa has launched a series of red wines from Tinto Cão, Tinta Roriz and Touriga Nacional. A second wine, Quinta do Vale da Raposa, named after the adjoining property, is lighter, with ripe, damson-like fruit softened by short ageing in second-year oak. Since 1996 two other properties, Quinta das Caldas and Quinta do Estação, both immediately above the spa town of Caldas de Moledo, have begun to produce firm flavoured, spicy reds. A partly barrel-fermented white wine blended from grapes grown at Quinta da Gaivosa is, to my mind, much the least successful of Alves de Sousa's ever expanding range of innovative Douro wines.

LAVRADORES DE FEITORIA

Lavradores de Feitoria/Vinhos de Quinta SA, Rua Cidade de Espinho, 24, 5000 Vila Real

In an attempt to bridge the yawning gap between small growers and large shippers in the Douro, fifteen quintas have come together to form Lavradores de Feitoria. The idea is to pool their collective know-how "with the aim of adding value to Douro grapes". João Brito e Cunha is the chief winemaker for the Feitoria project and, as well as single-quinta wines, he intends to market varietal wines and blends from the different quintas, which are scattered throughout the three sub-regions that make up the Douro DOC. This ingenious and innovative project deserves to succeed.

NIEPOORT

Niepoort (Vinhos) SA, Rua Infante Dom Henrique, 39, 4050 Oporto

Making the most of a network of long-established contacts in the Douro, Dirk Niepoort has begun to produce remarkable Douro wines. After a few years of trial and error in the early 1990s, Niepoort wines have settled down to become potential challengers to the hegemony of Ferreira's Barca Velha. Made by Jorge Serrodio Borges (brother of Margarida Serrodio Borges at Quinta do Fojo), the wines have developed their own distinctive style. All are based on Niepoort's old vines from vineyards at Quinta do Carril and Quinta de Napoles on the lower reaches of the Tedo Valley, midway between Régua and Pinhão. Redoma, which began life as a big, rather rustic red, has recently emerged as a middle-to-heavyweight wine combining depth and finesse. Whereas the 1991 Redoma (tasted in 2000) was dense, uncompromisingly traditional and slightly high toned (perhaps closer in style to a top Alentejano red), the 1999 is more supple and approachable, with the morello cherry character of well-ripened Douro fruit. Batuta is Redoma's big brother, a deep, dense red based (unusually) on Tinta Amarela and aged for eighteen months in new oak. It has a peacock's tail finish akin to that of a fine Vintage Port. Quinta de Napoles, from the vineyard of the same name, is a composite blend of the main Douro varieties foot-trodden in *lagar* and aged in French oak for nine months. It combines depth and power with unusually voluptuous elegance. Like Batuta, Napoles should develop well in bottle over a ten- to twenty-year period. At the time of writing, a fourth red named Charme, made from eighty-year-old vines, is yet to be released, but is intended to be an exercise in finesse – "the Douro's Côte de Nuits", according to Dirk Niepoort. Niepoort has produced some of the Douro's most promising dry white wines, blended from Gouveio and Rabigato from grapes growing in old, low yielding vineyards on the *altos* near Alijó. Redoma Branco is barrel fermented in forty per cent new oak followed by a year on the lees, and the Reserva, from 110-year-old vines, spends eighteen months on the lees, mainly in new oak. Both wines have a semi-tropical peachy richness offset by a streak of acidity. The Reserva has the poise of a fine white Burgundy and qualifies, without doubt, as one of Portugal's most impressive white wines. See Chapter 7 for information on Niepoort's rosé wine.

QUINTA DO NOVAL
Quinta do Noval Vinhos SA, Avenida Diogo Leite, 256, Apartado 57, 4401 Vila Nova de Gaia

Noval began experimenting with Douro reds when Cristiano van Zeller was at the helm in the 1980s. Having made some "blackstrap" reds that were never released, Noval (under new management and ownership) has settled on a more approachable red named Corucho. The grapes (predominantly Tinta Roriz, Touriga Franca and Tinta Barroca) are sourced from a number of neighbouring A-grade properties near Pinhão. Vinified in stainless steel at Noval, Corucho is a firm, well-focused red with leathery tannins and ripe fruit.

POÇAS
Manoel Dom Poças Junior Vinhos SA, Rua Visconde de Devesas, 186, Apartado 1556, 4401 Vila Nova de Gaia

Family Port shipper Poças Junior has a duo of Douro wines which are the brainchild of its Bordeaux-trained winemaker Jorge Pintão. Both are well made but lack flair. The white wine is soft but rather flat, and the red (a blend of the five main Douro varieties) has a firm, ripe, dusty character from heavy tannin extraction. In a play on words, the wines have been christened Coroa d'Ouro ("crown of gold").

QUINTA DO PORTAL*
Sociedade Agricola Quinta do Portal SA, Celeiros, 5060 Sabrosa

Formerly belonging to Sandeman, Quinta do Confradeiro at Celeiros was bought by the Branco-Mansilha family from nearby Favaios and renamed Quinta do Portal. Huge amounts of capital have been sunk into a well-planned modern winery equipped with all the hi-tech toys needed to produce a modern, quality wine. The range is somewhat eclectic, but Reservas and Grande Reservas packaged in their own expensive bottles show considerable class, with a price to match. A Frenchman called Pascal Chatonnet, the self-styled "wine alchemist", has been guiding Portal through its early years and his knowledge is beginning to pay dividends.

PRATS AND SYMINGTON
Correspondence address: Travessa Barão de Forrester, Apartado 26, 4401, Vila Nova de Gaia

In 1998 the Symington family (owners of the Dow, Graham and Warre Port houses) joined forces with Bordeaux winemaker Bruno Prats, famous as the former owner of the St Estephe Second Growth, Cos d'Estournel. The following year a few experimental lots were made to identify the most suitable grape varieties and in 2000, happily a successful harvest, the first red wine was made by the new partnership. It was christened Chryseia, the Greek translation of Douro meaning "gold". Drawing on the Symington family's considerable vineyard holding, the wine is made mainly from Touriga Nacional and Touriga Franca with smaller quantities of Tinta Roriz and Tinto Cão. Bordelais vinification and *élevage* have produced a wine that is worlds away from the traditional Douro blackstrap which the Symingtons themselves made in the 1970s. Aged in French barrels of 400 litres (rather than the traditional 225-litre *barriques*), the oak is deliberately restrained and complements rather than dominates the soft, naturally sweet plummy fruit. The wine is undeniably impressive but it remains to be seen if Chryseia has the structure to develop over twenty years or more like the classic Douro reds from the 1960s, 1970s and 1980s. Offered through the Bordeaux Market, Chryseia has unsurprisingly achieved cult status in Portugal after just one vintage.

RAMOS PINTO
Adriano Ramos Pinto (Vinhos) SA, Avenida Ramos Pinto, 380, Apartado 1320, 4401 Vila Nova de Gaia

João Nicolau de Almeida seems to be taking over where his father Fernando (of Barca Velha fame) left off. Their backgrounds could hardly be more different. Whereas his father learned about wine on the hoof, João studied oenology at Bordeaux University and joined the family Port shipper Ramos Pinto in 1976. Sometimes betraying the countenance of a mad professor, João Nicolau de Almeida has an insatiable thirst for experimentation, having been one of the principal brains behind the Douro's red varietal breakthrough in the early 1980s (see page 54). He has now turned his attention to white varietals like Viosinho, Gouveio and Rabigato. Although on granite soils just outside the Douro demarcation, Quinta dos Bons Ares is a crisp blend of local white varietals lifted by a little grassy Sauvignon Blanc. A red from the same property combines Touriga Nacional with Cabernet Sauvignon. Both wines are classified under the Vinho Regional, Trás-os-Montes/Terras Durienses. The Douro is represented by the red Duas Quintas. It combines the fruit of two very different properties (hence the name "two quintas"). The wild and remote Quinta da Ervamoira in the Douro Superior provides the ballast and richness, which is offset by a firmer, more structured character from fruit grown at Quinta do Bom Retiro in the lower reaches of the Torto. Duas Quintas has established a good track record as a supple, balanced Douro red that even performs well in weaker years such as 1993 and 1996. It is reinforced by a Reserva that manages to capture a hint of the New World with its intensely ripe, almost minty fruit and ripe but dense tannic structure. Both wines evolve well in bottle.

REAL VINICOLA
Real Companhia Vinicola do Norte de Portugal, Rua Azevedo Magalhães, 314, 4400 Vila Nova de Gaia

Real Vinicola has the longest continuous history of any of today's producers of Douro wines. Founded in 1889 under contract from the Portuguese government, it was entrusted with the task of selling wines from various regions in northern Portugal. With brands spanning Vinho Verde, Bairrada and Dão and a decidedly patchy record in the 1980s, Real Vinicola is increasingly concentrating on wines from the Douro. In 1996 it created a Fine Wine Division, accompanying this with a substantial revamp of its huge *adega* at Granja near Alijó. Under the combined direction of Pedro da Silva Reis and Californian winemaker Jerry Luper, Real Vinicola has begun to produce some impressive Douro wines. White wines made from Douro varieties grown on the *planalto* around Alijó are fresh, clean and aromatic without being anything to write home about in an international context. Evel, however, was recently voted as the best everyday white by the readers of the Portuguese consumer magazine *Revista de Vinhos*, something that would have been inconceivable a decade ago. The most charismatic white in the range is Quinta do Sidrô, made from ten hectares of low yielding Chardonnay planted at the eponymous C–D-graded quinta near São João de Pesqueira. Fermented and aged in new Portuguese oak, it combines a richly textured concentration of flavour with unusually good natural acidity. Chardonnay does not qualify as a permitted Douro variety and the wine is therefore sold as a Vinho Regional Trás-os-Montes.

The scope of Real Vinicola's red wines has been greatly increased by a new winery at Granja equipped with a battery of small stainless-steel fermentation tanks and corresponding storage vats. With so many tiny plots of old vines in the Douro, many of which undoubtedly have the potential to produce wines of excellent quality, Luper has seized on the idea of vinifying selected batches of grapes on a Burgundian scale. Real Vinicola's principal Douro reds are Evel and Porca da Murca, both of which started out as respected brands when they were conceived in the 1920s and 1930s but began to look rather lacklustre half a century later. Since the creation of the Fine Wine Division, both have received a much needed makeover, such that they are now well-accepted, reliable reds with plenty of sappy, spicy Douro fruit softened by short ageing in oak. The pride of the range is Evel Grande Escolha. Produced since 1996 from small plots of old vines growing at lower altitudes around Pinhão, with a preponderance of Touriga Franca and Touriga Nacional, it combines ripe berry fruit and well-integrated new oak. Evel Grande Escolha has also been joined by Grantom Reserva, a rich concentrated red which combines traditional Douro varieties with some Cabernet Sauvignon. Real Vinicola's Quinta de Aciprestes, opposite the railway station at Tua, is now the source of some exciting wines from Portuguese varietals.

QUINTA DO RORIZ
Correspondence address: Travessa Barão de Forrester, Apartado 26, 4401 Vila Nova de Gaia

The property of the van Zeller family, Quinta do Roriz has long been associated with Noval (see page 213). After Quinta do Noval was bought by the French insurance group AXA in 1993, the Roriz branch of the van Zellers decided to transfer its allegiance to the Symingtons, owners of Dow, Graham and Warre. A Port from the estate has now been joined by a Douro red. Made in small quantities from a blend of Tinta Roriz, Touriga Nacional and Touriga Franca with some Tinto Cão, the wine is dense, with plenty of substance and without the hard, over-extractive tannins that characterize so many Douro reds. Short maturation in new French oak lends a gentle, toasty note to the finish.

QUINTA DE LA ROSA
Quinta da Rosa Vinhos Porto Lda, 5085 Pinhão

Port clearly has pride of place at this prime A-grade quinta near Pinhão but, with the help of talented young winemaker Jorge Moreira, the Bergqvist family is also producing a range of sound, sometimes stylish Douro reds. They began back in 1990, using grapes from a newly planted vineyard, and the wines seem to have gained in substance in succeeding vintages. Although La Rosa often lacks the weight and structure of some Douro reds, the wines are approachable at a relatively early age having been exposed to short ageing in 600-litre oak casks. In particularly successful years a small quantity of wine is kept back and bottled as a more serious Reserva, and there have also been varietal wines from Tinta Roriz. Second wines are bottled without recourse to oak under the names Amarela and Vale de Clara. Both manage to capture the essence of ripe Douro fruit. La Rosa also makes a honeyed, barrel-fermented white from Gouveio, Rabigato and Malvasia Fina. The Bergqvists' commitment to Douro is displayed by their investment in a new winery and air-conditioned storage for both barrels and bottles.

SANDEMAN
Sandeman & Ca SA, Largo Miguel Bombarda, 3, Apartado 1308, 4401 Vila Nova de Gaia

Better known for Port on the international market, Sandeman makes two red Douro wines that can be found in Portugal. Made in its winery at Celeiros, Terraços is very much the lighter of the two, aged for three months in wood. Confradeiro (the old name for Quinta do Portal – see above) has been retained as a brand name for a solid, dependable Douro red with eight months in French oak. It commands a high price on the domestic market.

QUINTA DE SANTA JULIA
Eduardo Costa Seixas, Loureiro, 5050 Peso da Régua

Eduardo Seixas used to be chief Port taster at Sandeman and at the same time pioneered his own Douro wines. He owns a beautiful estate over-looking Régua that produces its own wine and is open to overnight guests (*turismo de habitação*). Back in the 1980s, the wines from Quinta de Santa Julia were somewhat light and emaciated, but the reds have grown in stature. A dense Reserva is subject to ageing in new oak.

SOGRAPE
Sogrape Vinhos de Portugal SA, Aldeia Nova, Apartado 3032, 4430 Avintes

Portugal's largest winemaking concern, owner of Ferreira and Offley Port shippers and with interests throughout the country and in South America, began life in the Douro. The Sogrape winery at Vila Real was originally constructed in the 1950s to produce Mateus Rosé from grapes growing in small vineyards on the surrounding *altos*. Production of Mateus has gradually shifted away from the Douro (see page 298); and the Vila Real plant (not much more than a stone's throw from the famous Mateus Palace) has been thoroughly updated to make the most of the grapes growing on the northern margins of the Douro region. Sogrape's diversification began with the revival of the Planalto brand, a crisp blend of Viosinho, Malvasia Fina and Gouveio from the high plains above the Douro. Other wines have followed, including the rather disappointing Vila Regia (the Roman name for Vila Real) and an extremely good red and white Douro Reserva. The white is barrel fermented in new French and Portuguese oak and has gained a rich, creamy texture from a further six months in cask. The red Reserva has vibrant yet supple berry fruit flavours softened by a hint of new wood. The name Mateus Signature has been given to a pair of lighter, rather insubstantial red and white Douro wines.

SYMINGTON
Travessa Barão de Forrester, Apartado 26, 4401 Vila Nova de Gaia

One of the biggest names in the Port business has turned to producing Douro wines. The Symingtons, owners of Dow, Graham and Warre, have launched their own middle-market red named Altano (see also Prats and Symington page 214, for information on the up-market Chryseia). First produced in 1999, the wine is made at the Quinta do Sol winery between Régua and Pinhão from grapes bought in from local growers. Cool fermented in stainless steel and partially aged in second-year French oak, Altano is now subject to micro-oxygenation during vinification which helps to soften the tannins. Consequently, subsequent vintages seem to be softer and more elegant than the first release which was a little hard and lean. An Altano Reserva will follow.

QUINTA DO VALLADO
Jorge Viterbo Ferreira, Herdeiros, Vilarinho dos Freires, 5050 Peso da Régua

This property overlooking the River Corgo has been in the hands of the Ferreira family for six generations. It is by no means a newcomer to Port, but in 1995 the present representatives of the family, Maria Antónia Ferreira and Guilherme Alvares Ribeiro, decided to divert about half the crop toward a pair of Douro wines under the Vallado label. With sixty-four hectares of vineyard spanning altitudes of 47 to 325 metres (154 to 1,066 feet) above sea level, Vallado has the capacity to make a range of wines, from Port (for Ferreira) to a good Douro white that succeeds in being ripe but not overripe. Its greatest achievement is undoubtedly the supple red Vallado based on a blend of Tinta Roriz, Tinta Barroca and Tinta Amarela. The 1997 was a big wine with 14 per cent alcohol but subsequent wines have proved to be somewhat more restrained.

QUINTO DO VALE MEÃO
Correspondence address: Cx. Postal 113, 5150 Vila Nova de Foz Coa

Sweltering in the Douro Superior, Vale Meão has been pivotal in the development of Douro wines. The property was originally laid out by Dona Antónia Ferreira as a Port quinta but in the 1950s it became the source for the now legendary Barca Velha (see pages 210–1). Since 1994 Vale Meão has been owned by Francsico Olozabal, former President of Ferreira, who runs the 270-hectare estate with his son Francisco as wine-maker. The *lagares*, abandoned in the 1970s, have been restored and equipped with robotic treaders not unlike those at Quinta do Noval. Following in the footsteps of Barca Velha, the first vintage of Quinta do Vale Meão (1999) quickly achieved cult status in Portugal and has a price to match. The 2000 is even better with a violet-like floral character and intensity of flavour shared by the finest Vintage Ports. A second wine from the property, Meandro, is also impressive in its own right.

QUINTA DO VALE DONA MARIA
Lemos & van Zeller Lda, Quinta do Vale Dona Maria, Sarzedinho, 5130 São João de Pesqueira

Having sold his family estate, Quinta do Noval, to the French insurance group AXA in 1993, Cristiano van Zeller has become a man about the Douro. He is involved in a number of projects, including the development of his wife's family estate, Quinta do Vale Dona Maria, situated on the Rio Torto. With help at the outset from both Quinta do Crasto and Dirk Niepoort, Douro wines now take precedence over Port. The wine-making is now under the control of Sandra Tavares. Grapes from the ten-hectare property are foot-trodden in stone *lagares,* fermented in stainless steel and finished in new French oak. Quinta do Vale Dona Maria is a firm and structured red with fine grained tannins and look sets set to become one of the leading wines in the Douro. Cristiano van Zeller is also working with Domingos Soares Franco of José Maria da Fonseca (see page 260) on a pair of red wines to be called Domini and Domini Plus.

IV. TRÁS-OS-MONTES

"Behind the mountains" is the evocative name of the remote northeastern corner of Portugal. Separated from the populous *litoral* by the Serras of Gerês, Barosso, Cabreira, Alvão and Marão, the people of Trás-os-Montes (known as *Trásmontanos*) have developed a strong sense of independence. This sentiment is expressed in the oft-quoted saying

Trásmontano house

para cá do Marão mandam os que cá estão ("this side of Marão belongs to those that live here"). Owing to its inaccessibility and isolation, Trás-os-Montes is one of the poorest parts of Europe. Since the 1960s the region has suffered from significant depopulation as many inhabitants have emigrated to find work, either in the cities or abroad. Most families maintain links, building themselves anomalous little houses to which they return in the summer months, but for the greater part of the year many villages are almost deserted. Away from the IP4, the new, European-funded road that slices diagonally through the region, mule carts frequently outnumber cars.

Trás-os-Montes technically encompasses the sector of country east of the mountains and north of the Douro: in administrative terms, the districts of Bragança and Vila Real. In climatic terms the region also divides into two. The *Terra Quente* ("hot land") to the south and east includes the deeply incised Douro valley and its sheltered northern tributaries. To the north-east of the Douro, the *Terra Fria* ("cold land") corresponds with the continental *planalto*, where summer temperatures are high and the winter months are bitterly cold, with snow visible on the mountain peaks for weeks on end. With the exception of a few outcrops of schist along the eastern frontier with Spain, the soil in Trás-os-Montes is predominantly granite-based with crags and boulders penetrating the surface. Those farmers who have remained behind do little more than scratch a living from these shallow soils.

At the end of the nineteenth century, Cincinnato da Costa observed that Trás-os-Montes was behind the times but praised the potential of the region's wines. Arcas and Lamalonga, two villages in the *Terra Fria* midway between Mirandela and Bragança, were apparently well known for their wines, but phylloxera seems to have dealt them a fatal blow. The so-called *vinhos dos mortos* ("wines of the dead") from Botiças, a town west of Chaves, also gained a certain notoriety because the bottles were buried in the ground for up to two years to mature. The practice seems to have died out.

Until the late 1980s most Trás-os-Montes wines passed off unrecognized, the best going into anonymous *garrafeiras*. Three rather obscure IPR regions have subsequently been created around the cooperatives at Chaves and Valpaços and along the Douro where it turns north and east, the latter known as Planalto-Mirandês. It is rare to find a bottle labelled with any of these appellations. Far more wine is bottled as Vinho Regional Trás-os-Montes, a designation that covers the entire region including the Douro, which is entitled to the sub-regional name of Terras Durienses. The Douro and Trás-os-Montes share many of the same grape varieties, but the Vinho Regional permits international grapes like Cabernet Sauvignon, Pinot Noir, Chardonnay, Sauvignon Blanc, Gewürztraminer and Riesling as well as native varietals. The bulk of the region's wine is made by ten cooperatives that produce a significant quantity of rosé for proprietary brands (see Chapter 7). Bairrada-based Caves Aliança also sources a light, sappy young red named Terra Boa from Rebondelo near the Spanish border. This is one of the few wines to reach export markets bearing the name Trás-os-Montes. A single estate near Macedo de Cavaleiros is one of the only producers to uphold quality winemaking in the region.

VALLE PRADINHOS
Casal de Valle Pradinhos, 5340 Macedo de Cavaleiros

In 1914 Manoel Pinto de Azevedo bought a number of parcels of land on the schist north of Macedo de Cavaleiros and created a 400-hectare estate. Situated in rolling countryside at an altitude of 500–600 metres (1,640–1,968 feet), this sheltered property produces cork, olive oil and wine. In fact, much of the property is so sheltered that the vines are regularly damaged by late spring frosts and the crop has been virtually wiped out for five years in succession. When frost doesn't intervene, yields are controlled by carrying out green pruning. The well-tended vineyards extend to forty hectares and are mostly planted with Tinta Amarela, Touriga Nacional and Tinta Roriz, but there are also substantial plots of Cabernet Sauvignon, Merlot and Pinot Noir. The white Malvasia Fina is joined by Riesling and Gewürztraminer, which produces a crisp, fresh fruit salad of a wine. Altitude certainly enhances the acidity. Aged in Allier oak, the reds are ripe yet well balanced, with a distinctly minty overtone of Cabernet Sauvignon. A rigorous selection ensures that only wines made from the best grapes and the most successful harvests are released as Valle Pradinhos. Wines from lesser years or younger vineyards are bottled under the Porta Velha label. The Pinto de Azevedo family also produces its own Port from Quinta das Murças in the Douro and owns an excellent hotel, the Estalagem de Caçador, in Macedo de Cavaleiros.

V. TAVORA/VAROSA

Situated on the *altos* above the city of Lamego, Tavora/Varosa is good fruit-growing country, producing apples, pears, peaches, chestnuts and elderberries. The latter are ostensibly used in dyes, but a large quantity is almost certainly diverted to the Douro to lend colour to Port. Rainfall is high (around 1,000 millimetres/thirty-nine inches per annum) and, at an altitude of 500–800 metres (1,640–2,624 feet), vineyards on the upper reaches of the Tavora and Varosa are capable of producing little of substance. This would be no man's land if it weren't for the sparkling wine industry that has grown up around Lamego (see page 309). Three co-ops, at Tarouca, Moimento de Beira and São Romão, produce the bulk of the region's wines and one private producer, Caves Murganheira at Ucanha, makes both *espumante* and still wine. The wines are made from the same grape varieties as those planted in the adjoining Douro – and in years when there is a shortfall, that is undoubtedly where a large proportion of the crop is sold. With so many mountain tracks and byways crossing the boundary, this illegal trade in grapes is nearly impossible to police. Red wines tend to be light and astringent, but there is undoubtedly more potential for white. Producers of *espumante* have planted plots of Pinot Noir and Chardonnay, which are occasionally bottled as still wines.

VI. DÃO

The Dão region is perfectly capable of producing some of Portugal's finest red wines. It was long touted as being such, but for most of living memory Dão has proved to be something of a disappointment. The problem is not physical: much of this mountain *terroir* is ideal for making fine wine. Dão's long-term difficulties are caused by the region's convoluted socio-economic layout.

Wine has been produced successfully in the countryside around modern-day Viseu since pre-Christian times, when the city was at the heart of Lusitania (see Chapter 1). In the late nineteenth century Dão came to enjoy something of a heyday on export markets. At the time, ninety per cent of the region's vineyards were planted with Touriga Nacional, much of which was diverted either to the Douro or to Bordeaux to make up for the shortfall caused by phylloxera. Phylloxera only reached Dão in 1881, twelve years after the Douro had succumbed to the pestilential louse, but the vineyards never fully recovered. Touriga Nacional lost its foothold and, looking to make a fast *escudo*, many growers replanted their smallholdings with high yielding direct producers and hybrids.

Small is the operative word in Dão, where a total of 67,000 hectares of vineyard has been subdivided into 487,000 separate plots. According to Professor Virgílio Loureiro, the leading authority on the region, these figures have not altered greatly in a hundred years. The average area of each holding stands at 1.16 hectares and the average vineyard plot is a mere 0.14 hectares in extent, about the same as a suburban back garden. In spite of some recent consolidation, just four per cent of holdings exceed five hectares.

In an attempt to create a semblance of order in this chaotic landscape, the Salazar regime imposed a series of cooperatives. The first was inaugurated in 1949 at Nelas, in the heart of the region, and although a further twenty-one small and medium-sized cooperative *adegas* were envisaged, only ten were completed. In order to make the system work, the government prohibited private firms from buying in grapes, which effectively gave the cooperatives a monopoly of the region's winemaking. Although the co-ops can be credited with raising the quality of the most basic wines, rather like Britain's experiments with comprehensive education there was no selection process. The best and the worst grapes were thrown in together and the handful of great wines that had existed previously were lost in the mediocrity and malaise. A single estate managed to remain aloof: Casa de Santar continued to bottle its own wine. From the mid-1950s to the late 1980s Dão's reputation was kept alive by just two wines. Bairrada-based Caves São João managed to source wine for its Porta dos Cavaleiros brand from the privately owned Santos Lima estate at Silgueiros (which incidentally also supplied Buçaco) and the Centro de Estudos Vitivinicolas de Nelas managed to make small quantities of fine wine during the 1960s, including some of the first varietals from Touriga Nacional, Jaen and Alfrocheiro Preto. Bottles of these wines can still be found bearing somewhat menacing black and white labels which hark back to the Salazar dictatorship.

Relief from state control came only in 1990 when, following Portugal's accession to the EU four years earlier, the hegemony of the cooperatives was finally overturned. Sogrape, which already owned cellars at Viseu, was the first to take advantage of this new-found freedom, but as funds have become more readily available a handful of larger quintas have also broken free of the cooperative noose. Since the early 1990s these privately owned estates have been rediscovering the *terroir* of the Dão region that was lost during the epoch of cooperative rule. Unchanged since it was first demarcated in 1908, Dão covers almost the entire southern half of Beira Alta: sixteen municipalities within the districts of Viseu, Guarda and Coimbra. It takes in 3,800 square kilometres (1,467 square miles) of undulating country, of which just five per cent is utilized for viticulture. Much of the remainder is heavily forested, planted with pine and eucalyptus, although individual oak and chestnut trees stand out above the evergreens. Vines are mostly planted in the clearings, with a concentra-

The granite cathedral of Viseu

tion of holdings in the north-east of the region around Viseu (the regional capital) and the towns of Tondela, Nelas and Gouveia.

The Dão region is effectively a large basin almost completely surrounded by high mountains. The Serra da Estrela forms a barrier to the east, with the Açor and Lousã ranges to the south, Serra do Caramulo and

Buçaco to the west and south-west and the Serra da Lapa immediately to the north. The demarcated region descends from 1,000 metres (3,280 feet) in the foothills of the Serra da Estrela to below 200 metres (656 feet) in the south-west around Mortágua and Santa Comba Dão. Three-quarters of the vineyard area lies on the *meia encosta* ("half slope") at an altitude of between 400 and 700 metres (1,312 and 2,296 feet).

The mountains have an important bearing on the climate, protecting the region from the excesses of both the Atlantic and the central Iberian *meseta*. Spring frost is a localized problem, but summer heat and winter cold are tempered by the Atlantic. At an average of 1,200 millimetres (forty-seven inches) per annum, rainfall is relatively high, but this is mostly the result of winter deluges and July and August are almost completely dry. A long dry summer is often prejudicial to the vines. The porphyroid granite that underlies seventy per cent of the region weathers to form a coarse but shallow sandy soil, and if hydric stress becomes excessive, the vines shut down and grapes fail to ripen, producing green, unbalanced wines. There is a certain amount of schist to the south and west but, strangely, these soils do not as yet seem to be favoured by growers. The entire region is drained by the River Mondego and its tributaries the Dão and Alva, which flow in a south-westerly direction almost parallel to one another. These valleys have their own meso-climates, but with little in the way of climatic data to rely on, there is still much to be done in the rediscovery of Dão's unique *terroir*. To date, the line of successful quintas between Gouveia, Vila Nova de Tazem and Seia points to the foothills of the Serra da Estrela as the source of many of the best Dão wines.

As in so much of northern Portugal, Dão vineyards were traditionally planted in haphazard fashion with a multiplicity of different grapes growing cheek by jowl on the same tiny plot. The *cadastro* or register of vineyards is consequently fiendishly complicated and hampered by lack of up-to-date information. Around eighty per cent of the region's production is red wine, with Touriga Nacional, Tinta Roriz, Alfrocheiro Preto and Jaen having been identified as the region's leading grape varieties. In theory, Touriga Nacional should make up at least twenty per cent of any blend, but in reality it accounts for much less and, although the non-*vinifera* hybrids have largely been weeded out, there are still large quantities of relatively inferior grapes like Tinta Pinheira, Bastardo and Baga. In the past red grapes were interplanted with white to produce a *clarete*, hence the eighty-twenty split. With the move to batch planting, there is now a hierarchy among the white varieties that parallels the red, with Encruzado having been selected as the lead grape. Like Touriga Nacional, Encruzado is supposed to represent at least twenty per cent of the white grapes in the region but the actual figure is more like two per cent. Bical (known locally as Borrado das Moscas or "fly droppings"), Cercial, Malvasia Fina (sometimes called Assario or Arinto do Dão) and Rabo de Ovelha make up much of the remainder. Details of these and other Dão grape varieties can be found in Chapter 2.

The grapes that go into making red Dão have a natural predisposition to firm, well-structured wines, but heavy-handed vinification has a tendency to exaggerate these characteristics and the wine can taste unpleasantly hard and astringent as a result. In the egalitarian cooperatives, lack of selection, poor handling and lack of hygiene frequently produced lean, thin and often faulty wines on a big scale. Ageing requirements were enshrined in the local legislation, which stipulated that red Dão had to spend at least two years ageing in bulk prior to bottling. Most wines simply weren't up to it, and protracted ageing in old wooden casks (or even cement vats) meant that the fruit faded long before the wine was bottled and the wines tasted tired and mean. Improvements in the vineyard and winery have already gone some way to producing richer, more concentrated wines and a number of the region's leading estates have invested heavily in new 225-litre oak casks, mostly Allier from France. There has been a tendency to use wood as a panacea – particularly among some of the larger shippers, who have turned to using oak chips – but now that the minimum ageing requirement for red Dão has been reduced to twelve months, there has been a welcome increase in the amount of spicy, fruit-driven red. By limiting the yield from a handful of leading Dão varietals, a number of quality-conscious producers have proved once again that Dão is capable of making outstanding, even world-class red wine.

White Dão will always play second fiddle to red, but now that ageing restrictions on these wines have been lifted completely, there are encouraging signs here too. Most producers, co-ops included, are now well equipped with temperature-controlled stainless steel, and the wines, still made from an *omnium gatherum* of grapes, generally taste crisper and fresher as a result. Encruzado is the only variety that truly stands out, either as a fragrant, floral, early bottled dry white, or barrel fermented and aged on the lees until it takes on a soft Burgundian complexity. Using these techniques, one estate has proved that it can produce one of Portugal's leading white wines.

Producers

Nine cooperatives continue to produce over seventy per cent of all Dão wine. Mangualde, Nelas, Tondela, Silgueiros and Vila Nova de Tazem are the best of these, and nearly all the large shippers purchase wine from one or more of them. There is also a union of *adegas cooperativas* known by the acronym UDACA. Three brands dominate the market: Sogrape's Grão Vasco, Meia Encosta from Borges and Terras Altas from José Maria da Fonseca. Dão wines from Caves Acácio, Aliança, Messias and DFJ Vinhos (Dom Ferraz) are also widely distributed. Although José Maria da Fonseca has succeeded in making a softer, more accessible Dão wine, of the larger firms only Sogrape has gained complete control of its wine from the vineyard to the bottle and this is manifest in the quality of Grão Vasco and Duque de Viseu.

The following producers have a significant presence on the domestic and/or export markets. Those marked with an asterisk (*) are either open to visitors or form part of the *Rota do Vinho do Dão* (Dão Wine Route).

QUINTA DA BOAVISTA*
3550 Castelo de Penalva
The twenty-first century marks a new beginning for the family estate belonging to José Malheiro Tavares de Pina. Seven hectares of vines planted predominantly with Touriga Nacional and Jaen produce a tight, concentrated spicy red with more than a passing resemblance to Syrah from the northern Rhône. The solid granite manor house at the centre of the estate has been fully restored to receive tourists.

BORGES
Sociedade dos Vinhos Borges SA, Rua Infante Dom Henrique, 421, 4435 Rio Tinto
The evocatively named Meia Encosta* is one of the leading brands of Dão, never lower than number two or three to Sogrape's Grão Vasco.

* Mein Encosta means "half-slope" which is where the best grapes are generally produced.

Sourced from growers and cooperatives, it is somewhat variable in style and quality, but over recent years it has regained some of its firm-flavoured, wild berry character. Borges has bought a thirty-hectare estate near Nelas named Quinta de Aguieira. This will be the source of a number of single-quinta wines – although the property will never appear on the label as the name has already been registered by Aveleda, which has acquired an estate with the same name in Bairrada (see page 151).

QUINTA DE CABRIZ*
Dão Sul Sociedade Vitívinicola, Apartado 3430 Carregal do Sal

Dão Sul is an ambitious project combining wine and tourism in the south of the region, at Quinta de Cabriz near Carregal do Sal. The property has been thoroughly restored and includes an impressive winery and cellars along with a restaurant open to the public. Red grapes predominate in the thirty-eight hectares of gently sloping vineyard, which is just as well because the small quantity of white wine is to my mind either overoaked or underwhelming. Reds, either blended or bottled individually from Touriga Nacional, Tinta Roriz, Alfrocheiro Preto and Jaen, are much more appealing, especially a varietal from Touriga Nacional with its cassis aromas and powerful flavour. Virgílio Loureiro is the consultant winemaker on the estate, who lends his name to Quinta de Cabriz Escolha, a wine which has liquorice-like intensity and the potential to develop in bottle for ten years or more. In less than a decade, Quinta do Cabriz has emerged as one of the leading estates in Portugal and has been voted the best Dão by the readers of the Portuguese consumer magazine *Revista de Vinhos*. The company is in the process of expanding its horizons both in Dão, Bairrada (Bairrada Sul), Estremadura (Quinta do Gradil) and the Douro (Encostas do Douro).

QUINTA DA FONTE DO OURO
Sociedade Agricola das Boas Quintas, Rua Dr João Lopes de Morais, 3450
Mortágua

In 1991 Nuno Cancela de Abreu, winemaker at Quinta da Romeira in Bucelas, teamed up with Jim Reader and Miguel Corte Real, respectively the technical and sales directors at Cockburn's, to create a new company with the name Boas Quintas ("good quintas"). To this end they purchased two small plots of vineyard at Mortágua and Quinta da Fonte do Ouro, with an area of four hectares near Nelas. Based on Touriga Nacional, Jaen, Tinta Roriz and Tinta Amarela, Fonte do Ouro is a supple, spicy red softened by short ageing in new Allier oak. There is also a varietal Touriga Nacional. A second, rather lighter wine (containing a small percentage of Merlot) is bottled under the Quinta da Giesta label as a Vinho Regional Beiras.

CASA DA INSUA*

José Joaquim de Olazabal y Albuquerque, Casa da Insua, 3350 Penalva do Castelo
One of the most noble properties in the region, Casa da Insua is also something of an anomaly in Dão. The vineyards contain significant quantities of three international grape varieties: Cabernet Sauvignon, Sémillon and Sauvignon Blanc. These varieties are not neophytes, but were planted early in the twentieth century, when the property was under the sway of the French, and have remained there ever since. International varieties are theoretically excluded from Dão, but Insua is covered by a special statute that permits the wine to be bottled with the DOC. During the 1980s and 1990s Casa da Insua was made under the tutelage of Domingos Soares Franco, winemaker at José Maria da Fonseca (see page 259). It has now been taken over by "Mr Dão" himself, Professor Virgílio Loureiro. He intends to change the style of the wine, making a Touriga Nacional/ Cabernet blend, a barrel-fermented Sémillon and a Sancerre-style Sauvignon Blanc. Insua is clearly a property to watch.

QUINTA DAS MAIAS

Sociedade Agricola Faldas de Serra, Cunha Baixa, 3530 S. Paio de Gouveia
On the footslopes of the Serra da Estrela at the edge of the National Park, Quinta das Maias comprises sixteen hectares of old mixed vineyard and a further twenty hectares of more recent varietal planting. The property is owned by Quinta dos Roques (see below) and, in Virgílio Loureiro, shares the same consultant winemaker and the same high standards. The reds rely heavily on the Jaen grape, which produces a good tight-knit wine with leathery tannins and more than a hint of vanilla from new oak. A barrel-fermented dry white made entirely from Malvasia Fina is balanced, toasty and well made.

QUINTA DA PONTE PEDRINHA
Maria de Lourdes Albuquerque Osorio, 6290 Lagarinhos

João Portugal Ramos is increasingly identified with the Alentejo (see page 278), but he still makes the occasional foray to the north in order to oversee the winemaking at this ten-hectare property near Gouveia on the foothills of the Serra da Estrela. Touriga Nacional, Jaen and Alfrocheiro Preto line up to produce an unusually soft, deep coloured wine, verging on being jammy in style, with violet-like aromas from Touriga Nacional.

QUINTA DOS ROQUES*
Quinta dos Roques, Viticultura e Agro Pecuaria Lda, Rua da Paz, Abrunhosa do Mato, 3530 Mangualde

The Roque family has owned this property between Nelas and Mangualde for over a century, but until 1990 the grapes were lost in the local cooperative. The quinta was rescued from anonymity by Manuel Lopes de Oliveira, a Ribatejano who married into the family and began replanting over forty hectares of vines. Set against the backdrop of the Serra da Estrela, the vineyards are well tended and planted with all the leading grapes. Oliveira is a particular fan of Touriga Nacional and his dream is to undermine the worldwide domination of Cabernet Sauvignon with this, the greatest of Portuguese grapes. A new winery was built with EU help in the early 1990s and, under the guidance of Virgílio Loureiro and subsequently the able Rui Reguinga, Roques is producing some of Portugal's finest wines. Reds are dark and incredibly dense, softened by the judicious use of French and/or American oak. The Roques varietal wines are exemplary. The family began in 1990 by producing a Jaen and followed it up with Alfrocheiro Preto, Tinta Roriz, Touriga Nacional and Tinto Cão. Quinta dos Roques Reserva is a benchmark wine that combines all these varieties as well as grapes from the old, interplanted Vinha de Pessegeiro ("peach tree vineyard"). Even the white wines are impressive. A varietal Encruzado, fermented in new French oak, sets new high standards in Portuguese white winemaking. Roques shows that it can be done.

QUINTA DE SAES/QUINTA DE PELLADA*
Alvaro Figueiredo e Castro, Pinhacos, 6270 Seia

Alvaro Castro left a career in civil engineering, swapping a slide rule for secateurs to take charge of two neighbouring family properties on the footslopes of the Serra da Estrela. The grapes from Quinta de Saes used to be sold to the cooperative at nearby Vila Nova de Tazem, and no doubt found their way into Sogrape's Grão Vasco (see below). Saes and Pellada are 500 metres (1,640 feet) apart and have twenty hectares of vineyard between them. The white Saes made from Encruzado and Bical is fresh and grassy in style. Reds from Touriga Nacional, Jaen and Alfrocheiro Preto, either as varietals or in a blend, show uncommon sophistication and restraint. It is a pity that there is not more Dão wine in the style of Saes and Pellada.

CASA DO SANTAR*
Sociedade Agricola de Santar, Santar, 3520 Nelas

Casa do Santar was one of the few producers to keep its independence during the dark days of cooperative domination. Sadly, the wines from this aristocratic estate weren't up to much, but at least Santar kept the spirit of single-quinta Dão alive. White wines from Encruzado, Bical and Sercial still aren't up to much, but the reds are greatly improved and *reservas* show a certain amount of elegance. Santar also buys in grapes from outside the estate and a range of varietal wines, red and white, are bottled under the Castas de Santar label.

CAVES SÃO JOÃO
Correspondence address: Soc. dos Vinhos Irmãos Unidos, São João da Azenha, 3780 Avelãs de Caminho

This Bairrada-based firm (see page 154) managed to maintain standards when the quality of Dão collapsed during the 1960s and 1970s. Through careful selection from a number of different sources (mainly the Santos Lima's Quinta do Loureiro), the brothers Costa bottled a red Dão named Porta dos Cavaleiros after one of the gates to the city of Viseu. The Dão region has moved on, but Porta dos Cavaleiros remains as an example of the traditional, four-square style of wine that no doubt predated the advent of the cooperatives. *Reservas* bottled with a distinctive cork label are still some of the best examples of red Dão, solid and tannic but with generosity of fruit and flavour. Like the 1970, which is still drinking well, Porta dos Cavaleiros Reservas have the capacity to develop in bottle for thirty or more years. The 1983 Reserva is an outstanding follow-up.

SOGRAPE

Correspondence address: Sogrape/Vinicola do Vale do Dão, Aldeia Nova, Avintes, Apartado 3032, 4402 Vila Nova de Gaia

Portugal's largest wine producer is a force to be reckoned with in the Dão region. In 1957, when the cooperative movement was at its most power-ful, Sogrape established Vinicola do Vale do Dão in Viseu. With its hands tied, it was forced to buy in and blend large volumes of wine to support its growing brand of red and white Dão, Grão Vasco. In an endeavour to gain control, Sogrape entered into a contract with the co-op at Vila Nova de Tazem to buy its entire output on condition that Sogrape's wine-makers could be put in charge. This brought about a dramatic improve-ment in the quality of Grão Vasco, the best-known and best-selling Dão wine on the domestic market.

Anticipating a change in the legislation, Sogrape purchased the hundred-hectare Quinta dos Carvalhais in 1988. This huge estate lies in the heart of the region at Outeiro de Espinho, between Mangualde and Nelas, a strategic location for buying in grapes from five hundred local growers. In the midst of the pinewoods, orchards and hazelnut trees, Sogrape planted fifty hectares of vineyard but retained one hectare of old vines and regrafted them as an example to small growers. On top of this, the company offers technical help and crop insurance and pays a pre-mium as an incentive to plant better grape varieties. Touriga Nacional and Encruzado command a forty per cent premium compared to twenty per cent for Tinta Roriz and Alfrocheiro Preto. Two wineries have been built at Carvalhais, one for wine made from grapes grown on the quinta and another for grapes bought in from outside. Both wineries have been constructed on the principle of gravity feed in order to avoid pumping grape must. Gentle handling helps to minimize the astringency that has been the scourge of Dão in the past.

Quinta dos Carvalhais makes a full range of Dão wines. Sogrape's Dão Novo is a deliciously sappy, simple young red released for sale less than two months after the harvest, in time for the festival of São Martinho. With sales totalling over three million bottles, Grão Vasco is now a clean, crisp, dry white and a satisfying peppery, fruit-driven red. Climbing up the hierarchy, Duque de Viseu is a soft dry white and a supple barrel-aged red, both of which are good value. For those who prefer the more tradi-tional style of red, Dão Pipas is a full, leathery wine aged for longer in old wood. At the top of the scale are the wines from the quinta, either blends like Carvalhais Reserva or varietal wines from Encruzado (barrel-fermented white), Tinta Roriz and Touriga Nacional. With its floral elegance and restrained use of oak, the latter is one of the best examples of this challenging varietal in the whole of Portugal.

VII. BEIRA INTERIOR

Beira Interior is the result of a merger of three former IPRs, Castelo Rodrigo, Pinhel and Cova de Beira, the names of which have been retained as officially recognized sub-regions of the DOC. Castelo Rodrigo and Pinhel share many of the same physical characteristics but, separated by mountains reaching to over 1,000 metres (3,280 feet), Cova de Beira is a distinct region to the south and deserves to be treated as such.

Castelo Rodrigo and Pinhel cover the upper reaches of the River Coa, a tributary of the Douro. This is high country, a continuation of the Spanish *meseta*, and a string of heavily fortified towns and villages (including Castelo Rodrigo itself) survive as a testament to the battles that have been fought over this barren no man's land. The climate is harsh, with short, hot summers and long, cold winters. Frost and snow are commonplace after the end of September and the diurnal temperature can vary by as much as 20°C. Much of the soil is shallow and sandy, with giant granite boulders rising to the surface, but there are substantial pockets of schist, known locally as *picarra*. The very first time I visited the area I was stirred by the potential quality of the wine, and a brief excursion through the small, often walled vineyards reveals some impressively old bush-trained vines. If this were California or Australia (which it emphatically is not), the grapes would have been bought up by a private winery and the wine sold at a huge premium as "Old Vines" or some such label. As it is, most of the grapes end up in one of three local cooperatives, of which only one (Figueira de Castelo Rodrigo) seems to have any idea of the region's true worth. White wines, predominantly from Síria around Pinhel and Fonte Cal in Castelo Rodrigo, have been bought as a base for *espumante* by producers down on the coast. Reds, on the other hand, are beginning to come into their own, and there are a number of concentrated blends based on Rufete and Marufo bolstered by Tourigo (a seemingly local name embracing both Touriga Nacional and Touriga Franca) and Tinta Roriz as well.

Cova de Beira is softer country, stretching from the eastern foothills of the Serra da Estrela to the banks of the River Tagus south of Castelo Branco. It sub-divides into two. The broad U-shaped valley of the Zêzere south of Guarda is the most promising. This is prime fruit-growing country, sheltered to the west and south by the Serras da Estrela and Gardunha, and there seems no reason why the granite soils, which are deep and well worked in places, should not produce good grapes as well. Apart from one private estate on the footslopes of the Serra da Estrela, production is concentrated in the hands of two cooperatives, at Covilhã and Fundão. South of the Serra da Gardunha, which is now conveniently punctured by a road tunnel, the climate becomes more arid and the landscape is much less well suited to viticulture.

Producers
An asterisk (*) indicates that the property is open to passing visitors.

QUINTA DO CARDO
Correspondence address: Companhia das Quintas, Quinta da Romeira, 2670 Bucelas

Situated on the plateau close to the Spanish border south of Castelo Rodrigo, Quinta do Cardo is an eighty-hectare property belonging to the Companhia das Quintas. Nuno Cancela d'Abreu is responsible for a range of red and white wines bottled either under the quinta's own label or as Barão de Figueira. Reds made from leading Douro grape varieties as well as some Mourisco tend to be on the light side, but the Quinta do Cardo Reserva, aged for nine months in American oak, is well structured with spicy-smoky aromas and good currant-like fruit.

ADEGA COOPERATIVA DE FIGUEIRA DE CASTELO RODRIGO*
Apartado 11, 6440 Figueira de Castelo Rodrigo

With a thousand members farming two thousand hectares of vines, Figueira de Castelo Rodrigo is a fairly typical northern co-op. White wines from the Síria grape are nothing to write home about, but the reds reflect the inherent quality of the old, low yielding vineyards. Touriga Nacional, Touriga Franca, Tinta Roriz, Marufo and Rufete combine to produce a spicy unoaked red with a flavour akin to good cherry jam, whereas Touriga Franca on its own makes a well-structured, peppery varietal.

ROGENDA

José Afonso e Filhos, Souropires, 6400 Pinhel

Wine writer João Afonso is the name behind Rogenda, a wine first produced from a small plot of vines south of Pinhel in 1996. A trio of grapes, Rufete, Alicante Bouschet and Touriga Nacional, produce a compact yet impressively concentrated red wine.

SABE (SOCIEDADE AGRICOLA DE BEIRA)

Rua Maria Rosalia Tavares Proença, 16, 6200 Tortosendo

SABE is the rather drab acronym for a company established in 1974 to include the properties of the Almeida Garrett family, descendants of the famous nineteenth-century author. The family's vineyards are located just south of Covilhã on the eastern slopes of the Serra da Estrela. Sixty-five hectares are planted with local grapes like Jaen, Rufete and Bastardo as well as Douro varieties. A pair of wines named Entre Serras ("between the mountains") is the company's staple: the white is a soft barrel-fermented Chardonnay and the red a light, oak-aged blend of local grape varieties. SABE also produces solid varietals from Tinta Roriz and Touriga Nacional. All the wines are good value.

VIII. BEIRAS

This Vinho Regional is a catch-all designation which straddles the Atlantic and mountain zones of central Portugal. There are three officially recognized sub-regions, Beira Litoral, Beira Alta and Terras de Sicó, but these are almost never seen on labels. The Beiras Vinho Regional covers both declassified wines from Dão and Bairrada as well as producers with international grapes, either blended with native varieties or on their own. Over eighty different grapes are permitted including Cabernet Sauvignon, Cabernet Franc, Pinot Noir, Pinot Blanc, Chardonnay, Sauvignon Blanc, Riesling and Sémillon. With so much under its umbrella, Beiras is primarily a political designation rather than a guide to the style or character of a particular wine (see page 160 for more information on Beiras).

5

Wines of the Plains

The River Tagus rises in the mountains of central Spain, west of Guadalajara. For much of its 1,000 kilometre (621 mile) course, the river is an unreliable stream, and as the Tajo (meaning "cut" or "gorge") is not accorded great significance by the Spaniards. But by the time it reaches the Portuguese frontier, the river is in full flow and, as the Tejo, takes on a new meaning. Cutting a diagonal through the centre of the country, the Tagus divides Portugal into two asymmetrical halves. The north, mountainous and densely populated, is counterbalanced by the south, a sparsely inhabited plain.

In fact, the plains of southern Portugal are not nearly so homogeneous as they sound. Although the landscape is not as stark or dramatic as that of the northern mountains, it has a grandeur that is transfigured by variations in climate, soil and culture. From the ephemeral sands around the Tagus and Sado estuaries to the permanence of the schist, granite and limestone of the Alentejo, southern Portugal is capable of great diversity in wine. It was not always so, for the deep south of the country has long been hampered by climate. Away from the moderating influence of the Atlantic, the thermometer is quite capable of reaching 40°C, occasionally even 50°C, during the summer months. With rainfall at best unreliable and often absent for months on end, the vines shut down in these conditions simply to ensure their own survival. Although sunshine, which rises to over 3,000 hours per annum in the Alentejo and Algarve, is a prerequisite for ripe fruit, lack of water, which limits phytosynthesis, is prejudicial to making well-balanced wine. On top of this, high temperatures during the harvest, which can begin as early as mid-August, have long been a handicap to producers looking to retain fruit in their wines. Without some form of control, fermentation temperatures rise to

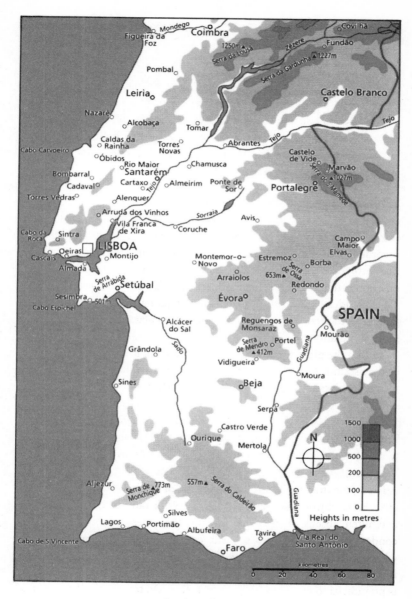

Southern Portugal

injurious levels, often stopping the ferment and causing damaging off-flavours to develop in the wine.

For this reason the wines of much of southern Portugal were treated until relatively recently as something of a bad joke. Apart from the Setúbal Peninsula, the most maritime of the main wine regions, there was little of distinction to be had from either the Ribatejo, Alentejo or Algarve – three regions which make up just over half of continental Portugal. In the Alentejo the joke extended beyond the wine and cosmopolitan northerners regularly poked fun at the supposedly indolent inhabitants basking in the intense heat. (Why did the Alentejano get up early in the morning? Answer: so he had more time to sleep during the day.) Now the south of Portugal is fighting back and, when it comes to wine, enjoying the last laugh. The fact that land holdings are so much larger in the south than further north means that growers are well placed to take advantage of economies of scale. Mechanized pruning and harvesting, rare and frequently impossible in the intensively farmed cabbage-patch vineyards of northern Portugal, are commonplace on the extensive estates in the south, some of which extend to thousands of hectares.

With the notable exception of the vineyards on the Tagus flood-plain, yields in southern Portugal are naturally low, checked by the prolonged summer drought. However, production has been rising to commercially acceptable levels as irrigation systems (once technically forbidden in the EU) are installed throughout much of the arid south. Provided the tap is not turned on too frequently (a big proviso), irrigation is also beneficial to the overall quality of fruit by overcoming the mid-summer go-slow caused by extreme hydric stress.

The revolution in the winery that began at João Pires (see page 261) on the Setúbal Peninsula early in the 1980s has spread to the rest of southern Portugal. Money has been poured into wineries, from large cooperatives to small estates. Bleak cement vats have been replaced by gleaming stainless steel equipped with temperature control. Nowhere has this been more evident than in the Alentejo, where the wines have been transformed since the early 1990s. Wines from the vineyard enclaves of Borba, Redondo and Reguengos are now some of the most popular in the country, sought after by restaurants in search of consistent quality at the right price. Demand has become such that it is outstripping supply. With huge areas of vineyard, the Ribatejo is in a stronger position still, and producers are at last waking up to the fact that quantity and quality are by no means mutually exclusive. Even the Algarve, once the preserve of tourists and dowdy co-ops, is now showing that it has the capacity to produce good wine. Australian oenologists like Peter Bright and David Baverstock have been followed by home-grown oenologists like João Portugal Ramos and José Neiva. Now there is a new generation of winemakers, represented by the likes of Rui Reguinga, Luís Duarte and Mario Andrade.

Many of the new wine-producing zones of southern Portugal have been particularly successful at carving out their own regional identity. The Alentejo has set the pace with some abnormally user-friendly bureaucracy. Bureaucrats in other regions should take note! But the boundaries that differentiate the officially recognized wine regions are political and tend to make a mockery of differences in *terroir*. The northern part of the Ribatejo has much in common with Estremadura (see page 160), but slides gently into the Alentejo south of the Tagus around Coruche. There are sub-divisions (see below), but as yet they are rarely used on labels. Terras do Sado, the Vinho Regional that covers the entire district of Setúbal, stretches from the outskirts of Lisbon down the Atlantic coast two-thirds of the way to the Algarve and embraces an area that is distinctly Alentejano around Grandola and Santiago do Cacém. Palmela, one of two DOCs within the Setúbal region itself, embraces two very different *terroirs*. The Alentejo covers a huge area, extending all the way from the River Tagus 240 kilometres (149 miles) south to the frontier with the Algarve. Here producers are making more of the DOCs and sub-divisions, but there is still much to be done in mapping out and defining *terroir*. But if the somewhat nebulous concept of *terroir* is the combination of soil type, climate and tradition, the latter element is still lacking in an area that has transformed itself over the past two decades. Largely, though by no means exclusively, dependent on indigenous grapes, the south of Portugal is producing wines with clearly defined fruit flavours that appeal to an international palate without sacrificing their own identity. The plains of the deep south have opened up into a brave new world for Portuguese wine.

I. RIBATEJO

The Tagus (Tejo) forms the axis of the Ribatejo province, which straddles the river from Abrantes in the north to Vila Franca de Xira close to Lisbon in the south. It used to be navigable all the way to the Spanish border and there were quays all along the river, with the towns of Constância and Abrantes once serving as river ports. Fertile soils, frequently nourished by the flood waters of the Tagus, support all manner of produce, which used to be shipped downstream to stock the colourful markets in Lisbon. Nowadays the main north–south railway and motorway run the length of the region and the economic focus has shifted away from the river. But the Ribatejo, with its ripe, irregularly shaped tomatoes, beans of various shapes and hues, canning factories, orchards, paddy fields and extensive vineyards, is still Portugal's agricultural heartland.

It is a region where north meets south. The *minifúndio* (smallholdings) that hold sway in the north overflow from Estremadura into the western margins of the province, petering out beyond the Tagus. To the south and east are the largest and most prosperous estates in Portugal, extending in some cases to cover many thousands of hectares. Nonetheless, large and small producers coexist side by side. The official statistics are somewhat out of date but they show 27,000 growers tending around 39,000 hectares of vines. Both growers and hectares have decreased in number, but the average vineyard holding in the Ribatejo is still much the same at just under 1.5 hectares. To put it into perspective, this is roughly three times the size of the average holding in the impossibly fragmented Vinho Verde region and nearly a third larger than that in the Douro.

The Ribatejo has three distinct *terroirs*, each with its own deeply rooted customs and traditions, but complicated by the fact that they each go under a number of different names.

On either side of the river from Benavente in the south to Abrantes in the north, the *campo*, *lezíria* or *borda d'Água* (flood plain) is the fertile heart of the region. Inundated nearly every winter by the *café-au-lait*-coloured waters of the Tagus, this is an area with deep alluvial soils capable of prodigious yields. Aside from vineyards that can easily produce 160 hl/ha, tomatoes, maize and melons are also grown in abundance. The climate of the *campo* is temperate but humid, even during the summer months, and fogs are not uncommon on the land closest to the river estuary. The productive white Boal de Alicante (Alicante Branco), closely followed by Fernão Pires, are the chief grape varieties here. Although the latter is capable of producing wines with character, much of the wine from the *campo* is insipid cooperative-made stuff that used to be sold in bulk and/or distilled but nowadays has difficulty in finding a market. Large swathes of vineyard have been uprooted and the planting licences transferred to other, more fashionable parts of the country. This has serious implications, as it will certainly lead to an increase in erosion. The perennial vine roots have long helped to keep these transient soils in place during the winter months, when the Tagus expands from a supine river into a minor ocean.

South-east of the *campo*, the boundary of which is roughly defined by the N118, is the much less fertile *charneca* ("heathland") often referred to as the *areia* ("sands") or, in places, the Terraços do Tejo. Lusitanian horses kick up the dust in the shade of umbrella pines, eucalyptus and cork oaks, and it is not uncommon to see *campinos* ("cowboys"), occasionally in green and red uniform, herding cattle with great dexterity. This is primarily bullfighting and hunting country, with a pack of hounds of English and Irish origin, the Equipagem Santo Humberto, kennelled at Santo Estêvão south of Benavente. Large noble estates reach inland from the Tagus around Salvaterra de Magos, Muge and Almeirim, many with vineyards that span both the *campo* and *charneca*. With an increasingly dry continental climate as you journey away from the river, the *charneca* is the source of the Ribatejo's best wines, predominantly reds from Trincadeira and Castelão. There are also well-established vineyards with commercial quantities of Cabernet Sauvignon, Merlot, Pinot Noir and Chardonnay, much of which was planted under French influence as far back as the 1950s. Rainfall, which varies in the Ribatejo from 500 to 800 millimetres (twenty to thirty-one inches) per annum, is at its lowest to the south around Coruche, where the wines start to take on a solidity akin to those of the adjoining Alentejo.

North of the Tagus is the so-called *bairro*, covering an area of shallow marl and limestone-based clay. Extending from the edge of the floodplain at Cartaxo onto the footslopes of the Serra dos Candeeiros and Serra d'Aire near Tomar, the *bairro* is generally an area of mixed smallholdings with wild scrub, olives, figs and corn growing alongside vines. With a climate strongly influenced in parts by the Atlantic (and rainfall as high as 800 millimetres/thirty-one inches in places), it is the least important of the three sub-zones in terms of viticulture, but there are nonetheless plenty of sites well suited to growing vines, especially around Cartaxo and Tomar.

Sub-regions

The entirety of the Ribatejo is covered both by DOC and Vinho Regional, neither of which pays much attention to the region's varied *terroir*. Whereas the Vinho Regional, confusingly called Ribatejano, permits a wide range of different grape varieties, indigenous and international, the DOC is considerably more prescriptive. There are six sub-regions which were briefly DOCs in their own right, but the Regional Commission (established in 1998) rightly considered that they would have more weight as "villages" within the larger Ribatejo DOC. However, to put this into perspective, only eleven per cent of the region's wine from the 2000 harvest was certified with DOC or Vinho Regional status, the remainder of the wine being sold as *vinho de mesa* (table wine).

The Ribatejo is broken down by sub-region as follows:

TOMAR

The northernmost and coolest of the Ribatejo sub-regions, Tomar extends from the edge of the *campo* or *lezíria* around Entroncamento and Torres Novas into the bairro along the valleys of the Zêzere and Nabão. The quiet monastic town of Tomar itself is home to an undistinguished cooperative, and the region's best wines emanate from Quinta de São João de Batista (formerly Quinta de Caniços) near the Tagus at Riachos, which belongs to Caves Dom Teodósio (see below). Trincadeira Preta, Castelão, Baga and Câmarate produce balanced, middle-weight reds with Cabernet Sauvignon permitted as a constituent. Whites from Fernão Pires, Arinto, Tália and Trincadeira das Pratas are undistinguished.

CHAMUSCA

The town of Chamusca, with its bullring on the south bank of the Tagus, lends its name to a DOC that straddles the river and covers the equestrian municipality of Golegã, known for its November horse show. Most of the wine comes from vineyards on the fertile *campo* planted with Fernão

Pires, Tália and Trincadeira das Pratas, and little, as yet, qualifies for DOC status. The most promising wines are those from Tramagal upriver near Abrantes, where the so-called Terraços do Tejo are planted with Castelão, Cabernet Sauvignon and Trincadeira Preta.

SANTARÉM

The view from the citadel (Portas do Sol) at Santarém, the regional capital, is one of the most commanding in Portugal, with a vista that takes in the enormity of the *campo* and *charneca* south-east of the Tagus. The DOC of Santarém itself covers the *bairro* west of the city, extending to the border with the Ribatejo west of Rio Maior. Although wine has long played an important part in the local economy, very little is bottled under the Santarém label. A rather dismal cooperative at Alcanhões is responsible for much of the output.

ALMEIRIM

Two bridges connect Santarém with the prosperous agricultural town of Almeirim on the south bank of the Tagus. The DOC that extends north and south from Almeirim and includes the municipalities of Alpiarça and Salvaterra de Magos produces almost as much wine as the other five zones combined. A huge cooperative (the largest in the Ribatejo) is responsible for the bulk of the wine, which is sold under a variety of labels, including Planicie, Varandas and the well-known Lezíria, which briefly captured the imagination of UK consumers, chiefly because of its bottom-dollar price. Production of white wine vastly exceeds that of red, which has become something of a handicap for the cooperative. Producers looking to buy in red grapes are often forced to take in white as well. The best wines come from those properties with vineyards away from the river on the vast expanse of sandy *charneca*, known locally as the Terraços do Tejo. Aside from wine, Almeirim is famed for *sopa de pedra* ("stone soup") and a cluster of restaurants around the bullring have become a much appreciated mecca for good Ribatejano cooking.

CARTAXO

Cartaxo appeared on wine maps of Portugal long before it was awarded its own DOC in 2000. Its proximity to the Tagus and Lisbon made it a natural source of volume wine. There are a number of large estates, such as

Storks' nests at Quinta Fonte Bela near Cartaxo

Quinta Vale de Fornos at Azambuja, Quinta de Amoreira, Quinta do Falcão and the impressive Quinta Fonte Bela (see DFJ Vinhos below), all of which were established in the nineteenth century to supply wine to the capital. Nowadays the region is dominated by the local cooperative, which produces around six million litres of (mostly white) wine. The Cartaxo DOC covers both the fertile *campo* (mostly producing white table wine) and the rolling *bairro*, which is the source of some light- to medium-bodied reds, mainly from Castelão, Câmarate and Preto Martinho. One of the best of the Ribatejo's new-wave reds is Quinta de Almargem from a small vineyard near Cartaxo (see Caves Dom Teodósio below).

CORUCHE
The sandy plains bordering the Alentejo are irrigated by three small rivers, the Sorraira, Alamansor and Magos, all of which are tributaries of the Tagus. There are paddy fields alongside the Sorraira, and the pleasant market town of Coruche is itself overshadowed by the huge Cigala rice factory. The Coruche DOC covers a wide area stretching down to the Tagus estuary at Benavente and Alcochete, where there is a large colony of pink flamingos. This cool, humid zone was once the source of a rich dessert wine made by JP Vinhos (alias João Pires) from botrytis-affected

Fernão Pires grapes. As yet there are few wines bearing the name Coruche on the label, but reds from producers like Quinta Grande and Quinta de Santo André are more Alentejo in style than Ribatejo. This is an area with considerable potential.

Producers

Around half of all the Ribatejo's wine is made by just eight cooperatives, at Almeirim, Alcanhões, Alpiarça, Benfica do Ribatejo, Cartaxo, Chamusca, Gouxa and Tomar. Much of the remainder is produced by large estates, many of which geared up to receiving visitors and are on the Ribatejo's *Rota da Vinha e do Vinho* (Vine and Wine Route). These properties are marked with an asterisk (*) in the list below.

QUINTA DE ALORNA*

Quinta de Alorna Vinhos Lda, 2080 Almeirim

This colonial-style quinta was acquired by the first Marquês de Alorna, Viceroy of Portuguese India, in 1723. The estate extends to 3,000 hectares in total and includes forestry, cereals, market gardens, cattle, horses and 270 hectares of vines. In the 1970s the vineyards at Alorna covered as many as 600 hectares, but the decision was made to uproot those on the *campo* and replant on the *areia*. The 1960s *adega*, which now has huge over-capacity, is being replaced by a new winery. Quinta de Alorna produces a broad range of wines, including white varietals from Fernão Pires, Chardonnay and "Arintho" (Arinto), all of which are rather too light and extractive for my liking. Varietal reds from "Tinta Meuda" (Tinta Miuda), Castelão and Cabernet Sauvignon are better, but still have a tendency to be somewhat hard and astringent. Alorna's most impressive wine to date is the Casa de Alorna Colheita Seleccionada, a blend of Castelão, Tinta Miuda and Trincadeira that has supple, minty-oaky flavours.

CASA CADAVAL*

Casa Cadaval – Investimentos Agricolas SA, 2135 Muge

This stately property in the southern Ribatejo was established in 1648 by the Dukes of Cadaval and grew in extent to 20,000 hectares by the early twentieth century, including 300 hectares of vines. It has since contracted to 5,000 hectares, seventy-five of them of vines. The cavernous *adega* served briefly as the first cooperative winery in Portugal and has now been transformed by the owner, Teresa Schonborn, into a venue for parties and weddings. Cadaval employed French oenologists in the 1950s and was one of the first in Portugal to plant commercial quantities of Cabernet Sauvignon and Pinot Noir along with Alicante Bouschet. These varieties have since been supplemented by Merlot, Castelão and Trincadeira, with Touriga Nacional and Bastardo now joining this cosmopolitan line-up. Despite the long-standing focus on red grapes, Cadaval makes a small quantity of dry white wine from two separate pickings of Fernão Pires, part of which is barrel fermented. Bottled as Padre Pedro, this is one of the best examples of this variety in Portugal (which also masquerades as Maria Gomes in Bairrada), combining characteristically gentle, honeyed fruit and crisp acidity. Red wines are similarly suave, soft and ripe, tempered by short ageing in new French and American oak. Pinot Noir, picked as early as mid-August, is somewhat jammy in style, but Trincadeira, Merlot and Cabernet are all true to form, with good fruit and structure. Blends of these varieties bottled under the Padre Pedro, Herdade de Muge and Casa Cadaval labels are well balanced and refined. Rui Reguinga is the winemaker responsible for this exemplary range of Ribatejano wines. Cadaval also bottles its own excellent olive oil and has a remarkable stable of Lusitanian horses.

QUINTA DO CASAL BRANCO*

Sofia Braamcamp Sobral Lobo de Vasconcellos, EN 118, km 69, 2080 Almeirim

José Lobo de Vasconcellos runs a mixed 1,100-hectare estate producing maize, tomatoes, sunflowers and vegetables as well as rearing cattle and Lusitano horses. There are just over one hundred hectares of vines, planted on sandy *charneca* soils with Fernão Pires, Trincadeira Preta, Castelão and Cabernet Sauvignon predominating. The wines are made by João Portugal Ramos in a large *adega* built in 1817 and are notable for their elegance and finesse. Terra de Lobos (also sold under the quinta name) is a simple, honeyed white and a light, peppery red. Falcoaria is the name reserved for a soft, toasty dry white (part barrel fermented in Allier) and an elegant, balanced red made from Trincadeira Preta and Castelão. A wine called Capucho is pure Cabernet Sauvignon with bell-pepper aromas and bramble fruit.

DFJ VINHOS*

Quinta Fonte Bela, Vila Chã de Ourique, 2070 Cartaxo

Known as the "cathedral" because of its size and scale, Quinta Fonte Bela is one of a number of huge agricultural ventures established by the Ribeiro Ferreira family toward the end of the nineteenth century. When both the winery and distillery were built, the property extended to 6,000 hectares, including 1,500 hectares of productive vines. Now only sixty-five hectares of vineyard remain. Fonte Bela has been bought by DFJ Vinhos, which has taken advantage of the available space to bottle wines from both the Ribatejo and neighbouring Estremadura. Segada (also bottled as Casa do Lago) is a soft, easygoing dry white with a hint of pineapple, made from Fernão Pires grown on the estate. Fonte Bela also produces the middleweight Segada red, with an aroma and flavour of black cherries, and Senda do Vale, a blend of Trincadeira and Cabernet Sauvignon from Cartaxo with plum, damson and currant flavours. See page 169 for further information on DFJ Vinhos.

QUINTA DO FALCÃO

Casa Agricola da Quinta do Falcão, Vila Chã de Ourique, 2070 Cartaxo

Quinta do Falcão used to form part of the vast agricultural holding belonging to António Ribeiro Ferreira (see DFJ Vinhos above). After a number of so-called *partilhas* (partitions) under the Napoleonic code of inheritance, the 200 hectares of Quinta do Falcão have been separated from the estate, but the wines are made by José Neiva at nearby Quinta Fonte Bela. Castelão is the principal variety among the twenty hectares of vines, and helped by Cabernet Sauvignon, it makes a big, concentrated red with 14.5 degrees alcohol called Paço dos Falcões. Touriga Nacional, Syrah and the white Encruzado have also been planted.

FALUA

Falua Vinhos, Zona Industrial de Almeirim, Lote 52, 2080 Almeirim

The distinctive sailing boats that used to ply the Tagus were known as *faluas*, an example of which is illustrated on the label of this wine from João Portugal Ramos. With a winery and a small vineyard in Almeirim, Portugal Ramos also buys in grapes from nearby vineyards to produce good, value-for-money wines under a variety of labels. Tâmara is the name given to a light, inexpensive red and white wine from Castelão and

Fernão Pires respectively. The red Falua (with a percentage of Trincadeira) has more weight, and Tercius is the top of the range, made from Trincadeira, Tinta Roriz and Touriga Nacional aged in new oak. Most of Falua's wines are sold in the United Kingdom.

FIUZA BRIGHT

Fiuza e Bright Sociedade Vinicola Lda, Travessa do Vareta 11, 2080 Almeirim

A partnership between the Mascarenhas family and Australian wine-maker Peter Bright, Fiuza is the best-known Ribatejano label on international markets. Much of its appeal comes from the recognizable foreign varietals growing on a variety of different soils around Santarém and Alpiarça (at Quinta do Granjo and Quinta das Chantas). Chardonnay, Cabernet Sauvignon and Merlot seem to be the most successful, all displaying ripe, gently oaked flavours that hint at the New World. Sauvignon Blanc, with overtones of asparagus, seems to be less well suited to the warm climate of the Ribatejo. Touriga Nacional, Tinta Roriz and Trincadeira are also being planted to produce wines with a more Portuguese flavour. To date, most of Fiuza Bright's wines have been sold in British supermarkets.

QUINTA GRANDE*

Quinta Grande Lda, EN 119, 2100 Coruche

One of just three estates in Coruche, Quinta Grande has sixty hectares of vineyard south of the town close to the paddy fields along the River Sorraia. Castelão, Trincadeira and Grand Noir, foot-trodden and fermented in *lagar*, produce a hefty 13° red, tempered by short ageing in Portuguese oak.

QUINTA DA LAGOALVA

Sociedade Agricola Quinta da Lagoalva de Cima, 2090 Alpiarça

This 5,000-hectare estate, with 1,000 hectares at Lagoalva de Cima near the river at Alpiarça, belongs to the descendants of the Dukes of Palmela. Vineyards occupy just fifty hectares, with the emphasis gradually shifting from the fertile *campo* to the less fertile areas away from the river. This has undoubtedly led to an improvement in the overall quality of the wines from Lagoalva, with red gaining ground over white. Lagoalva was the first property in Portugal to plant Syrah, which makes a fairly dense red with more berry fruit than varietal spice. Other reds from the estate are lighter in style, with a somewhat jammy fruit character. The white Quinta da Lagoalva is a lemony blend of Fernão Pires, Arinto and Chardonnay, partly barrel fermented in French and Portuguese oak. Alvarinho is the latest addition and is also being blended with Chardonnay. Second wines are bottled under the name Monte da Casta. Lagoalva also makes an unusual late harvest wine from Riesling and Gewürztraminer picked in late October, partially affected by botrytis.

CASA AGRICOLA HERDEIROS DE DOM LUÍS DE MARGARIDE*
Casa Agricola Herdeiros de Dom Luís de Margaride SA, Quinta do Casal Monteiro, 2080 Almeirim

In 1980 the brothers Margaride, descended from the counts of Sobral, were among the first to bottle their own single-estate wine in the Ribatejo. At the time they controlled 200 hectares of vines split between the *campo* and *charneca*, but owing to the Napoleonic inheritance laws, this has been whittled down to fifty-six. The remaining property, Casal do Monteiro, lies entirely on the *campo* and is planted with a wide variety of grapes: Chardonnay, Baga, Trincadeira Preta, Cabernet Sauvignon, Syrah, Pinot Noir, Merlot and Touriga Nacional as well as the inevitable Fernão Pires and Castelão. The Margarides' white wines are very uninspiring, but there are some well-made representative varietal reds from Cabernet, Trincadeira and Castelão.

QUINTA DE SANTO ANDRÉ*
António José da Veiga Teixeira, Rua de São Francisco 2, 2100 Coruche

Situated in the Sorraira valley just outside the town of Coruche, Quinta de Santo André is a family-owned dairy and cereal farm which has diversified into wine. Fifty hectares of vineyard are split between two sites: one on alluvial soils adjoining the eighteenth-century quinta and another on sandy soils amid the cork oaks and pines. The quinta name is applied to a pair of rather light red and white wines from Castelão and Fernão Pires respectively, with the best grapes reserved for the Horta de Nazaré label. The red, a fifty-fifty blend of Castelão and Trincadeira, combines raspberry fruit with a touch of minty, peppery spice. The wines at Quinta de Santo André are made under the guidance of Rui Reguinga.

CAVES DOM TEODÓSIO

Caves Dom Teodósio SA, Rua Mariano de Carvalho, 2040 Rio Maior

Rio Maior in the very north of the Ribatejo is the dividing line between northern and southern Portugal. It was here at the height of the revolution in 1975 that the main Lisbon–Oporto road was regularly blocked by belligerent agricultural workers, who briefly threatened to plunge the nation into civil war, north against south. Rio Maior is also home to one of the largest and best- known wine producers in the Ribatejo, Caves Dom Teodósio. In 1924 that João Teodósio Barbosa founded an agricultural wholesale company; seeing the potential market for wine in Portugal's African colonies, he later branched out into wine. Until the revolution that gave independence to Angola and Mozambique, Dom Teodósio was one of the largest exporters of Portuguese wine. Since then the company has spent a long time in the doldrums with somewhat down-at-heel brands like Teobar and Casaleiro. Recently, however, under the guidance of José Gaspar, Dom Teodósio has developed its range to include single-quinta wines from the company's own vineyards. The best known of these is the ninety-hectare Quinta de São João Batista on the *areias* near Torres Novas, planted with Fernão Pires, Tália, Arinto, Castelão and Trincadeira Preta. Touriga Nacional, Tinta Roriz and Alicante Bouschet are also being planted. The *lagares* at São João de Batista have been put to good use making reds with raspberryish fruit softened by American oak. Wines from another property, the thirty-six-hectare Quinta do Bairro Falcão near Cartaxo, are more traditional in style. The star in Dom Teodósio's portfolio is undoubtedly Quinta d'Almargem, a delicious red with cherries, tar and spice from a seven-hectare property on the *bairro* near Cartaxo planted entirely with Trincadeira Preta. Another improvement is Serradayres, a well-known Ribatejano wine that Dom Teodósio took on from the now defunct Carvalho, Ribeiro & Ferreira. Made mainly from Castelão, this wine has filled out considerably under its new owners and deserves a return to prominence. Like so many merchant firms, Dom Teodósio has interests in other parts of Portugal and bottles Lagosta Vinho Verde, Dão Cardeal and Topázio from the Beiras and Quinta do Coa, four varietals from the Douro.

CENTRO AGRICOLA DE TRAMAGAL

Estrada Nacional, no 1331, 2200 Tramagal

The name "Centro Agricola" conjures up images of a giant cooperative, but this small roadside *adega* in Tramagal near Abrantes is very much a father and son operation. José and Nuno Rodrigues saw their family property sequestrated by the Portuguese military in 1986 and bought this old agricultural centre as a replacement. They own forty-three hectares of vineyard near by on the Terraços do Tejo, having given up their alluvial soils for *areia*. Fernão Pires and a smidgen of Chardonnay produce two clean, soft-flavoured whites, Terraços do Tejo (Vinho Regional) and Casal de Coelheira (DOC). Reds contain Castelão, Câmarate, Trincadeira, Alicante Bouschet and Cabernet Sauvignon in varying proportions. Terraços do Tejo is pure Castelão (and a good example of this grape), whereas the Casal de Coelheira Reserva is a dense mix of Castelão, Trincadeira and Cabernet with broad, ripe tannins and morello cherry fruit. This family estate clearly has the ability to make impressive wines.

II. THE SETÚBAL PENINSULA

Two imposing bridges connect Lisbon with a chin-shaped spit of land that juts out between the Tagus and Sado rivers. The first, an elegant red suspension bridge completed in 1968 and christened the Ponte Salazar, was responsible for opening up the south bank of the river around Almada and Barreiro. It was renamed Ponte 25 de Abril after the coup d'état in 1974. The second bridge was opened in 1998 and named after the politically uncontroversial explorer Vasco da Gama. The new bridge is one of the longest and most spectacular in Europe, linking north-east Lisbon with the estuary towns of Montijo and Alcochete. It has accelerated development on the peninsula, with houses, industry and tourism jostling for pole position adjacent to the capital. There was once a 6,000-hectare vineyard between Pinhal Novo and Poceirão – the largest in the world – the remnants of which are on irrigated land at Rio Frio south east of Montijo. Nowadays, agriculture on the peninsula is much more pressed for space.

Wine nevertheless continues to play an important role in the local economy. Like so much of Lisbon's hinterland, the region's reputation was established in the nineteenth century when port-based shippers established themselves on the south side of the river at Almada, Barreiro and Azeitão. The most influential of these was a young mathematics graduate named José Maria da Fonseca who, in 1834, established a firm bearing his own name on the foothills of the Serra da Arrábida. The region was already known abroad for its sweet, fortified Moscatel (see below), but Fonseca introduced new agricultural practices and grape varieties to the region. One of his most enduring achievements was the introduction of the red Castelão Frances grape, now simply called Castelão. So successful was this among other growers that it acquired the name of the place where it was first planted: Cova da Periquita. With a wine also known by the brand name Periquita, this has led to a "chicken and egg" confusion about the name of the grape that has only recently been resolved (see page 68).

Castelão is now planted throughout southern Portugal, but it seems to perform at its best on the warm, sandy conditions around the hill town of Palmela, once the name of one of José Maria da Fonseca's wines. The nomenclature in this part of Portugal is somewhat confusing. Palmela has recently been revived as a DOC that covers the greater part of the peninsula. The name Setúbal, a large fishing port and industrial city at the mouth of the Sado, applies to an overlapping DOC for unctuous fortified wines made exclusively from two varieties of Moscatel. A huge, all-embracing Vinho Regional, Terras do Sado, covers the entire district of Setúbal, extending from the Tagus as far down the Atlantic coast as Sines. Most of the vineyards, however, are concentrated on the flat, sandy plains north of the Sado estuary. "Setúbal Peninsula" is merely a convenient geographic expression that collectively covers a wide variety of different wines as well as the name of the local Regional Commission.

Sub-regions

SETÚBAL

Sometimes known as Moscatel de Setúbal, Setúbal has the longest history of any wine on the Peninsula. Its origins are obscure, but there can be little doubt that Moscatel has been growing on the slopes of the Serra da Arrábida since Roman times or even earlier. By the fourteenth century, wines, almost certainly fortified, were being exported from Setúbal to

England. It is possible that the much-disputed Osey came from here, although doubt remains as to the origin of the name (see page 9). By the eighteenth century the wines were sufficiently prized for a decree to be drawn up forbidding goats and donkeys from the vineyards and stipulating that beehives should be at least a quarter of a league distant to avoid damage to the grapes. Setúbal came to the fore during the nineteenth-century vogue for sweet wines, when it was shipped to Paris, London, St Petersburg, New York and Rio de Janeiro. Like Madeira, it was consigned to the holds of ships sailing across the tropics, and a fashion developed for *torna viagem*, a wine that had been shipped across the tropics and back again. José Maria da Fonseca still retains a few casks of this remarkably concentrated wine dating from 1884. When this method became impracticable some producers briefly experimented with *estufagem*, but this too was abandoned in favour of long cask ageing in cellars above ground. However, to commemorate the turn of the new millennium, six pipes each containing 600 litres of 1984 Moscatel were loaded on board the sailing ship *Sagres* to be sent to Brazil and back in an endeavour to replicate the *torna viagem* wines of the nineteenth century.

Nowadays Setúbal only finds a market in the area around Lisbon and occasionally (at Christmas time) in Scandinavia, the United Kingdom and the United States. There are around 330 hectares of the grape known as Moscatel de Setúbal (alias Muscat of Alexandria) and just eleven hectares of a rare variety of red Muscat called Moscatel Roxo. In the past producers could blend up to thirty per cent of Arinto, Rabo de Ovelha and other varieties, ostensibly to lend acidity, but this is no longer permitted under the terms of the DOC – which was revised in 1997 and 1999 – and Setúbal must be at least eighty-five per cent Moscatel.

Setúbal starts off in much the same way as other sweet fortified wines. Fermentation on the skins is arrested by the addition of grape spirit, which takes the wine up to eighteen per cent alcohol by volume, leaving it rich in natural sugar. However, after vinification the Moscatel grape skins are left to soak in the wine until at least the spring after the harvest. This extended skin maceration accentuates the aroma and flavour of fresh dessert grapes that is present even in some of the most venerable Setúbal. However, maceration on the skins of up to a year often leads to a fine ropy deposit in the bottle that looks like threads of cotton. José Maria da Fonseca has now limited the period of skin maturation to four months.

The wine is then transferred to large *toneis* (horizontal vats) made either from oak or mahogany. Like Madeira, Setúbal is a wine that gains greatly from age. The fact that the majority of the wine is bottled after little more than a couple of years (twenty-four months is the legal minimum) does not necessarily engender a loyal following among consumers. However, after four or five years in wood Setúbal gains a candied intensity of aroma and flavour as evaporation concentrates the residual sugars to between 150 and 190 grams/litre. Some producers accentuate this by ageing their wines in outdoor *estufas* – literally greenhouses – but the most rely on the warm ambient temperatures of brick-built *armazens* or lodges. The vast majority of Setúbal is sold at an age of between two and five years, nowadays often with the year of vintage on the label. The two main players, JP Vinhos and José Maria da Fonseca, release wines at three and five years respectively. However, the latter keeps smaller quantities of wine back to age further in 600–700 litre casks. During this time the wine turns from amber-orange to mahogany brown, taking on an even greater intensity that hints at butterscotch and, eventually, molasses. José Maria da Fonseca bottles a twenty year old wine known as Alambre which is probably the best Setúbal commercially available. With a flavour of dried figs, apricots, prunes and raisins, it is an absolute must with Christmas pudding.

Older Setúbal wines are rarely seen on the market, but José Maria da Fonseca occasionally bottles vintages dating back to the nineteenth century. Trilogia is an opulent blend of three outstanding years, 1965, 1934 and 1900, with wonderful concentration, balance and complexity. However, I have been fortunate enough to taste older single-vintage Setúbal dating back as far as 1880, tiny amounts of which are either bottled to order or retained for blending. It is illuminating to witness the way in which the overtly grapey character of young Muscat takes on a figgy, dried fruit character before turning into unctuous essence, and going back to 1955, the merest hint of molasses seeps into the wines. Pre-Second World War, the samples show more in the way of butterscotch and molasses with a raisiny, *rancio* character akin to an old Oloroso Sherry. 1938 and 1934 both seem to be exceptional years for Setúbal. 1922 appears to have been subject to *estufagem*, although no production records have been kept. Pre-First World War, many of the wines are so dark and concentrated as to render them virtually undrinkable, with 1902 the essence of molasses and 1880 massively rich, cloying and intense. Limited quantities of Fonseca's younger Setúbal wines, such as the exceptional 1955, are bottled under the Apoteca label and can be bought at the cellar door.

A tiny quantity of Setúbal is made separately from the Moscatel Roxo (Red Muscat) grape. This wine, pinkish in colour when young, turns amber red with age in cask and develops a haunting, floral complexity in cask. There is so little to go round that it is rarely found outside the region, but there are three producers: José Maria da Fonseca, SIVPA (Soc Vinicola de Palmela) and JP Vinhos. Other producers of Setúbal include the Adega Co-op de Palmela, Caves Velhas, Rio Vinhos, Venacio de Costa Lima, Xavier Santana, Emilio de Oliveira e Silva & Filhos and Francisco Rodrigues Antunes – but beware of some disappointingly coarse and oxidized examples.

A tiny quantity of a rare wine from the Bastardinho grape is also sold by José Maria da Fonseca, the last vintage of which took place on the Costa de Caparica in 1963; 10,000 litres remain. Bottled as Bastardinho de Azeitão, it has an unctuous, caramelized character, offset by fresh acidity. Further information on this and the now extinct wines of Lavradio can be found on pages 28 and 65.

PALMELA

The Palmela DOC covers much the same ground as Setúbal but extends further east to cover Montijo. It is the amalgam of two former IPRs: Arrábida, which used to cover the Serra da Arrábida, and Palmela itself, a fortified town overlooking the plain of the Tagus and Sado estuaries that is now the Portuguese home to both Ford and Volkswagen. As a result, Palmela has two very distinctive *terroirs*. The north-facing limestone slopes of the Serra de Arrábida seem to be well suited to white grapes (Arinto, Fernão Pires and Moscatel) as well as Cabernet Sauvignon, which is permitted by the DOC. Strangely, Chardonnay and Merlot, which also perform well, are not. The principal grape in Palmela is, however, Castelão, which is at its best on the beach-like soils to the east of the region, extending to the frontier with the Alentejo near Vendas Novas. Here the climate seems to have the right maritime and continental mix for this grape to produce wines with some depth and complexity. Raspberryish and often astringent when young, the wines gain a note of tar with age. The relatively well-run Palmela cooperative is the chief producer, but a number of companies, notably JP Vinhos, Caves Aliança, Caves Velhas (Romeira) and Bright Brothers, either make or bottle wines from this region – which has the distinct advantage over many others in that the name is easy for foreigners to pronounce. The legislation covering Palmela also permits white, rosé, *frisante* (light sparkling), *espumante* (sparkling wine made by the traditional method) and fortified wines. Although large volumes of rosé and sparkling wines are made here from Castelão (see Chapters 7 and 8) the wines rarely appear with Palmela on the label.

TERRAS DO SADO

The River Sado drains the central Alentejo and opens up into a broad estuary west of Alcácer do Sal. It is stretching the imagination somewhat to call the entire district of Setúbal by this name, but Terras do Sado is increasingly seen on labels from producers in the region. Most of these are concentrated in the north around Azeitão and Palmela and include big hitters like José Maria da Fonseca and JP Vinhos, who prefer the flexibility of the Vinho Regional over the more proscriptive DOC. Two cooperatives, at Palmela and Santo Isidro de Pegões, bottle much of their good young Castelão wine under the Terras do Sado label. The Vinho Regional embraces virtually every grape variety in the book, notably Alvarinho, Chardonnay, Sauvignon, Sémillon, Viognier, Aragonez, Cabernet Franc, Cabernet Sauvignon, Cinsault, Merlot, Pinot Noir, Syrah, Touriga Nacional and Touriga Franca. The only notable producer south of the Sado is the Pinheiro de Cruz prison near Grandola, which keeps its inmates occupied with thirteen hectares of vines that were planted back in the 1940s. Somewhat variable in quality, these wines can be quite robust and are sought after by Lisbon restaurants.

Producers

The following producers make wines from one or more of the above appellations on the Setúbal Peninsula. Entries marked with an asterisk (*) form part of the *Rota do Vinho do Costa Azul* (Blue Coast Wine Route).

BRIGHT BROTHERS

Correspondence address: Bright Bros Vinhos Portugal Lda, Fornos de Cima, Calhandriz, 2615 Alverca

Peter Bright knows the Setúbal Peninsula like the back of his hand, having worked since the late 1970s for JP Vinhos. He now makes a range of Palmela wines from an eighty-hectare vineyard at Fernando Pó (*pó* means dust) to the east of the region near Pegões. The sand and red gravel is perfect for Castelão and, in spite of a rather primitive winery, he succeeds in making three wines that bring out the best in this grape variety. Lenda do Castelo is the top of the range.

JOSÉ MARIA DA FONSECA*

José Maria da Fonseca, Vila Nogueira de Azeitão, 2925 Azeitão

Descendants of the José Maria da Fonseca who arrived at Azeitão in 1834 still own and manage this historic firm located on the old main street in Azeitão. Brothers António and Domingos Soares Franco act as president and winemaker respectively. This, one of the most enduring of Portuguese family firms, has grown into one of the largest wine producers in Portugal, owning 650 hectares of vineyard, mostly at Algeruz due east of Palmela.

José Maria Fonseca made his name in the mid-nineteenth century selling wine in bottle at a time when most wines were shipped in bulk. Not only did this help to guarantee authenticity and prevent adulteration, it also allowed Fonseca to build up a brand name for his wines. Of these, Periquita, established in 1850, still survives and must surely count as one of the oldest branded wines in the world. The company prospered, then suffered, at the hands of the vacillating Brazilian market in the early twentieth century, but recovered ground when it entered the burgeoning rosé business after the Second World War. This story is told in detail in Chapter 7, but it led to the creation of two Fonsecas: JM da Fonseca International and José Maria da Fonseca Successores. To cut a long and rather involved story short, the two companies came back together again nearly thirty years later, when the family bought Fonseca Internacional back from IDV in 1996. This left the Soares Francos with two wineries: the photogenic old winery, with its colourful *azulejos* (decorative tiles), and the distinctly 1970s "new winery" down the road. A third winery, perhaps the most impressive in Portugal, was built alongside with EU support, and was opened by the President of the Republic, Dr Jorge Sampaio, just in time for the vintage in 2001. With a capacity of 6.5 million litres, the winery has six stainless steel *lagares* for premium reds.

The range of José Maria da Fonseca wines continues to grow. A rather dull dry white, Branco Seco Especial (BSE), has been joined by the more lively Albis, a populist off-dry blend of Arinto and Moscatel. White Pasmados and Quinta de Câmarate, which used to be blends of indigenous and international grapes, have gone native as the Soares Francos have turned their backs on foreign varietals. Pasmados is based on Arinto and Viosinho, whereas Quinta de Câmarate is a fruity blend of Moscatel, Loureiro and Alvarinho. Among the whites only Primum contains a foreign varietal, crisp Sauvignon Blanc, in alliance with Arinto. The bedrock of the reds is Periquita, a wine not made exclusively from the so-called "Periquita" grape (see page 68) but often combining Castelão with small quantities of other local varieties. From tasting older vintages of Periquita, such as the outstanding 1959, it is clear that today's wine, with its raspberryish simplicity, is very different from the full-bodied wines of yesteryear. Admirers of Periquita in the past will be more satisfied with Periquita Classico which, having been aged in oak, has the leather and tar complexity of mature Castelão. Pasmados Tinto is a thoroughbred blend of Touriga Nacional, Alfrocheiro and Moreto grown on the slopes of the Serra de Arrábida, whereas Quinta de Câmarate (which used to be called "Palmela Claret") combines Castelão, Trincadeira and a small proportion of Cabernet Sauvignon. There are a number of mysteriously coded *garrafeiras*: TE comes from calcareous soils of Quinta de Câmarate, whereas RA originates from the sands of Algeruz and sometimes picks up a hint of the surrounding eucalyptus. There is also a *garrafeira* named CO, which somewhat bizarrely stands for *clara de ovo* ("egg white"). Finally, the vineyards at Algeruz have been planted with a handful of grape varieties from outside the Setúbal region, including Touriga Nacional, Touriga Franca, Tinto Cão, Tinta Barroca and Syrah. These form the basis either of Primum or a range of solid varietals named Domingos Soares Franco Colecção Privada, with a picture of the winemaker staring out from the label. A pair of very highly polished reds cap the range. F.S.F. (named in homage to Fernando Soares Franco) combines Trineadeira, Syrah and Tounat where an Optimum is a powerful blend made up from the first clones of the best grape varieties, both indigenous and foreign. It represents the cream of the crop.

José Maria da Fonseca is an important producer of fortified Setúbal and has interests in Dão and the Alentejo. Domingos Soares Franco has recently joined forces with Cristiano van Zeller (see page 221) to produce Port and a pair of red Douro wines, the latter under the name of Domini. As if this were not enough, José Maria da Fonseca also produce rosé and sparkling wines, all of which are covered in the relevant chapters.

JP VINHOS*
JP Vinhos SA, Vila Nogueira de Azeitão, 2925 Azeitão

João Pires was an Algarvio who in 1922 established a winery by the main north–south railway line at Pinhal Novo with the intention of supplying thirsty Algarve fishermen with inexpensive wine. The company has since undergone a number of reincarnations, firstly under the auspices of the energetic António d'Avillez, and since 1998 JP Vinhos has been owned by a Madeiran, José Berado. It was Avillez who put João Pires (as it was then called) on the map by hiring an Australian winemaker, Peter Bright. This undoubtedly ruffled more than a few feathers in the conservative Portuguese establishment, but during the early 1980s Bright led the winemaking revolution when João Pires launched its aromatic, cold-fermented Dry Muscat. This represented a radical departure at a time when the majority of Portuguese consumers preferred to drink rather life-less, oxidized white wines. The João Pires brand was subsequently sold to IDV, but using the name JP, Avillez and Bright went onto create one of the most innovative ranges of wines in Europe. Peter Bright has subsequently gone his own way (see Bright Brothers above), but the wines he invented are an enduring success. The company has moved from its congested premises in Pinhal Novo to the former *Reader's Digest* building at Azeitão. This has been transformed into a spectacular new winery, and JP Vinhos now has the capacity to produce twelve million litres of wine.

Split between the Palmela/Terras do Sado and the Alentejo, JP owns over 500 hectares of vineyard. The wines made at Azeitão are based pre-dominantly on either Moscatel or Castelão. JP Branco is an aromatic sixty-forty blend of Moscatel and Fernão Pires, and the raspberryish JP Tinto is mostly Castelão. These wines are the bread and butter of the business, but there are plenty of more individual red and white wines.

Catarina is a savoury blend of Fernão Pires and Chardonnay, part fermented in stainless steel, part in barrel, that is much fresher and less ponderous than it was in the past. Cova da Ursa is pure toasty, barrel-fermented Chardonnay from a vineyard on the Serra de Arrábida, more New World than Old. It was the first wine to be barrel fermented in Portugal. The red Meia Pipa is a judicious blend of Castelão and Cabernet Sauvignon with a berry fruit and mint character, whereas the Garrafeira Palmela (one of the few JP wines to fall into the local DOC) is pure Castelão aged in wood until it takes on the character of tar and leather. Má Partilha is a ripe, plummy Merlot from a densely planted vineyard on the footslopes of the Arrábida hills, whereas Quinta de Bacalhoa, a property now owned outright by JP, is a ninety-ten blend of Cabernet Sauvignon and Merlot aged in French (ex-Haut Brion) and Portuguese oak. Somewhat variable in the past, Bacalhoa has returned to form, with a refined minty character that places it midway between Old and New World in style. JP Vinhos also produces two Setúbal wines, bottled at three and ten years of age, and a small quantity of Moscatel Roxo. The company has interests in the Alentejo and Estremadura, where it produces *espumante* (see relevant chapters).

COOPERATIVA AGRICOLA DE SANTO ISIDRIO DE PEGÕES*
Rua Pereira Caldas, 1, 2985 Pegões Velhos
The co-op at Pegões was established in 1958 as an agricultural colony by the Salazar régime, then at its zenith. The *Estado Novo* architecture remains, but the winery has come a long way and is now one of the most forward-thinking cooperatives in the whole of Portugal. It has the good fortune to control 900 hectares of vineyard farmed by just 150 members, who together are responsible for producing 3.75 million litres of wine a year. Unusually for a cooperative, all the wine is sold in bottle rather than in bulk. White wines based on either Moscatel or Fernão Pires are simple, clean and correct. Vale da Judia, the co-op's best-known label, is pure Moscatel. Reds are based almost entirely on Castelão, which is in its element in these warm (but not too warm) sandy soils. Pegões has invested heavily in French and American oak, and the wines range from a simple, vibrant unoaked red named Adega de Pegões through Vale de Judia (again) with six months in wood to the cedary Fontenario de Pegões with a year in wood. An impressively well-

structured Colheita Seleccionada made from Touriga Nacional and Cabernet Sauvignon benefits from eleven months in Allier oak. Few cooperatives can lay claim to such a well-focused range of wines.

PEGOS CLAROS*
Sociedade Agricola de Pegos Claros Lda, Marateca, 2985 Pegões Velhos
Situated on sandy soils to the east of the region, Pegos Claros is a 600-hectare estate, over half of which was once given over to vines. The vineyard now occupies ninety hectares and is planted entirely with Castelão. This is perfect territory for Castelão, a variety that can be rather mean and weedy but ripens here to produce full-flavoured wines with 13–14 degrees of alcohol. Foot treading and fermentation in stone *lagares* give the wine further charisma. Aged for a year in Portuguese oak, Pegos Claros takes on a wonderful leathery complexity. The wines develop well in bottle and Pegos Claros Reserva is without doubt the best manifestation of the somewhat quixotic Castelão grape.

III. ALENTEJO

There is something hugely liberating about the Alentejo. First there is the space: the cloudless skies, rolling plains, straight roads and vast horizons. Then there are the Alentejano people, few in number but sharing a healthy independence and disrespect for authority. Since the revolution that rocked the Lisbon establishment in 1974, the Alentejo has grown immeasurably in stature. From being a forgotten pastoral backwater, the Alentejo has developed into a quietly fashionable locale.

It is easy to see why, for the Alentejo is refreshingly free from the clutter and chaos on the coastal *litoral*. Taking up a third of continental Portugal, the "land beyond the Tagus" houses a mere sixth of the country's population. In complete contrast to the densely populated north with its cabbage-patch smallholdings, the Alentejo is an area of extensive agriculture (*latifúndios* as opposed to *minifúndios*). Fields of wheat flow for as far as the eye can see over the undulating plain. Leaf-green in spring, the landscape turns an ever deeper shade of ochre and burnt umber during the summer months, when little or no rain falls and temperatures rise daily in excess of 35°C. Umbrella-shaped cork oaks (known as *sobreiros*) fleck the landscape and provide shade for the

The plains of the Alentejo

occasional nomadic herd of sheep, goats or black pigs. This open country is broken only by the occasional brilliant white *monte* (single farmhouse) or an isolated town or village gleaming from the top of a low hill.

Vineyards have never been all that prominent in this expansive landscape. They were cultivated by the Romans, tolerated by the Moors, revived by the Christians but nearly eradicated by Salazar. At the end of the nineteenth century there were 20,000 hectares of vineyard in the Alentejo, mostly around the towns of Évora, Borba, Redondo and Reguengos de Monsaraz. But in a quest for self-sufficiency the *Estado Novo* designated the Alentejo as the *celeiro* or granary of Portugal. Vineyards were uprooted and from the 1920s to the 1970s wine was made mostly for home consumption. Cooperatives were built at Portalegre and Redondo in the mid-1950s, supplied by the small plots of vines that remained, often interplanted within olive groves. But with little investment and lacking any official demarcation, the wines of the Alentejo were by the early 1970s unsung and unknown.

For a period in the mid-1970s, the Alentejo was on the front line of an agrarian revolution. In the wake of the military takeover in Lisbon, many of the Alentejo's large privately owned estates were occupied by farm workers who set about running them as workers' cooperatives. In spite of some sabre rattling by the local pro-Stalinist Communist Party, the takeovers were by and large good-natured. However, occupied farms with radical names like April 25th or Red Star Cooperative quickly ran out of funds. In an effort to generate cash, cork trees were stripped of their bark, vineyards were badly pruned and over-cropped and stocks of wine were either sold off or drunk as part of the revolutionary binge. The tide began to turn decisively in the early 1980s, when most of the land was returned to private landlords; however, by then the damage wrought to the Alentejano economy was considerable.

Since the mid-1980s the Alentejo has undergone another revolution, albeit at a rather more steady pace. With financial help from the EU, stainless steel accompanied by temperature control has made it possible to produce different styles of wine more in tune with export markets. Large vineyards, some well over one hundred hectares in extent, have increasingly taken up the space occupied by cereals and sunflowers. Nowadays vines occupy a total of around 14,000 hectares, still fewer than at the end of the nineteenth century but considerably more than in the

1950s. The average size of an individual vineyard holding is still just 3.5 hectares, but this compares with a national average of under a hectare. In the winery, the inherent pride and cleanliness of the Alentejano people has helped the revolution along. Wines made in huge volumes at the privately owned Herdade do Esporão as well as at the co-ops at Redondo and Reguengos are some of the most marketable in Portugal, served in restaurants from Madeira to the Minho. Red wines from some of the Alentejo's leading estates command such high prices in some of Lisbon's most fashionable restaurants that they often exclude themselves from export overseas. Although there has been a dramatic improvement in the quality of many of the region's white wines, it is the reds that command the respect of the market. Many are good, some are very good, packed with immediately appealing ripe, sun-drenched fruit. But with the possible exception of one enclave, Portalegre in the extreme north of the region, the wines of the Alentejo are never likely to be world class. A number of grapes, notably Trincadeira and Aragonez, have certainly proved their worth, but the force of the climate (which has been easily overcome in the winery) continues to be a handicap in the vineyard.

Sub-regions

The Alentejo province stretches all the way from the Atlantic coast south of Lisbon to the frontier with Spain. It divides administratively into three sub-districts centred on the cities of Portalegre, Évora and Beja respectively. Portalegre and Évora are the capitals of the Alto ("upper") Alentejo, which rises to over 1,000 metres (3,280 feet) in the Serra de São Mamede. Beja is the capital of the Baixo ("lower") Alentejo, which extends south from the Serra do Mendro (rising to 412 metres/ 1,351 feet) into the foothills of the mountains that mark the boundary with the Algarve. The entire province has been designated a Vinho Regional, known somewhat confusingly as "Alentejano". Like others in Portugal, this encompasses international grape varieties such as Cabernet Sauvignon, Syrah and Chardonnay as well as indigenous grapes. Many producers continue to favour the Vinho Regional over and above the eight enclaves that have been awarded DOC status. Listed below, each of these has the right to bottle wines under its own name preceeded by the word "Alentejo".

PORTALEGRE

On the footslopes of the Serra de São Mamede, the vineyards of Portalegre are the highest and therefore the coolest in the province. Unlike in much of the Alentejo, there is no lack of rainfall here, with the highest of the mountain peaks receiving in excess of 800 millimetres (thirty-one inches) per annum. In common with much of the land north of the Tagus, the soils are mainly granite based (although there is also some schist). Portalegre is a diverse region, covering both mountain and plain. The vineyards, mostly small and interplanted with olive groves, are scattered throughout the municipalities of Crato, Castelo de Vide ("castle of the vine"), Marvão and Portalegre itself. The principal grape variety is Trincadeira, followed closely by Castelão, Aragonez and Alicante Bouschet. Unusually, there is also a small quantity of Cinsault and a grape known mysteriously as Tinta Francesa ("French red"), although the two may well be one and the same. The main white grape is Síria or Roupeiro (known locally as Alva). There are only four producers in the Portalegre region, the well-run local cooperative being by far the largest, producing wines under the Conventual and Terras de Baco labels. The potential is evident even here. Portalegre's wines have power but show considerably more finesse than those from the districts to the south. With a little more coaxing in both the vineyard and the winery, this region has the capacity to outshine the rest of the Alentejo. See d'Avillez and Tapada do Chaves (below).

BORBA

Giant marble quarries puncture the earth around the brightly white-washed towns of Borba, Estremoz and Vila Viçosa, the latter being the seat of a large ducal palace. Vineyards planted on both the limestone and the schist form an arc to the north of Borba itself, extending from Estremoz through Orada and Terraugem to Olandroal. With over 3,000 hectares in total, this is the second largest vineyard enclave in the Alentejo after Reguengos. The grape varieties are not necessarily the most appropriate for the region. Castelão is dominant, but Trincadeira is on the increase. There is a significant amount of white grapes, mostly Roupeiro and Rabo de Ovelha, but with a depressingly large quantity of Diagalves. The forward thinking Borba cooperative, one of the first to modernize in Portugal, is much the largest producer, and there are a number of distinguished single estates making high-quality Alentejano red. See Agro-Aliança, Quinta do Carmo and Quinta do Mouro (below).

REDONDO

The Serra d'Ossa rises to over 600 metres (1,968 feet) south of Borba and commands a panoramic view over Redondo and the central Alentejo. The town is famous for its ceramics. Redondo's 1,500 hectares of vineyard are mostly to be found on the granite and schist south and east of the town, where there are a number of large estates. Annual rainfall averages around 600 millimetres (twenty-seven inches) and drip irrigation has become commonplace to make up for the summer deficit. Trincadeira is the principal grape variety, followed by Castelão and a large amount of the rather weak Moreto, which does not perform particularly well here. Irrigation will merely intensify the problem. The competent Redondo cooperative produces most of the region's wine, which is sold under the Porta da Ravessa and Real Trabalhador ("royal worker") labels. See Roqueval (below).

ÉVORA

Until phylloxera wiped out large swathes of vineyard in the late nineteenth century, Évora was one of the most important wine producing zones in southern Portugal. Then Salazar's campaign to uproot vines and plant cereals in their place left the region with just one vineyard of any importance. Vineyards are now making a welcome return to the countryside around Évora, a DOC adjacent to Redondo and Reguengos that extends across the plain toward Arraiolos. There are around 1,000 hectares of vineyard in total, much of it divided between six individual producers, making these some of the largest vineyard plots in Portugal. There is no cooperative in Évora, but there is a charitable foundation, Herdade de Cartuxa, that is responsible for most of the region's wine. The dominant grape is Castelão, followed by Trincadeira and Moreto. Much of the region's wine is bottled as Vinho Regional. See Cartuxa, JP Vinhos and Tapada de Coelheiros (below).

REGUENGOS

A tall grain silo and neo-Gothic church are symbols of the agricultural wealth of the town of Reguengos de Monsaraz which, with over 3,000 hectares of vineyard, is the principal winemaking centre in the Alentejo.

Over to the east, Monsaraz is an old fortified town built on a rocky knoll to defend the River Guadiana from the marauding Spanish. Reguengos is the newer, nineteenth-century town built down on the plain once the threat of invasion had receded. Large quantities of the Moreto grape let down the quality of the region's red wines, the best of which are based on Trincadeira and Aragonez. Both seem to be well suited to the region's mixed schist and granite soils and the arid climate. With over 3,000 hours of sunshine and annual rainfall of between 400 and 500 millimetres (sixteen and twenty inches), nearly all the vineyards are irrigated. The controversial Alqueva dam will make a huge difference to agriculture, tourism and possibly the meso-climate in the area. The cooperative at Reguengos is the largest in the Alentejo and is much improved of late, making medium-bodied red wines under the popular Monsaraz and Terras d'El Rei labels. The cooperative's top wine, Garrafeira dos Sócios, is much in demand and commands a high price, although it seems to me to be somewhat overrated. The co-op has its own shop, named Castas e Castiços, selling wine and olive oil in the centre of Monsaraz. See also Herdade do Esporão (below).

GRANJA-AMARELEJA

The land east of the Guadiana around the town of Mourão looks as though it belongs to Spain rather than Portugal. This is arid country indeed, with annual rainfall barely reaching 400 millimetres (sixteen inches). The soils, predominantly granite and schist, are poor and shallow. Yields are consequently extremely low. The vineyards are typically small in scale and few farmers have the wherewithal to invest in irrigation. Over two-thirds of the Granja-Amareleja's vines are more than twenty years old. As a result, the Moreto grape, which tends to produce light, thin wines elsewhere, makes some incredibly solid, generously flavoured reds. Production is centred on the rather primitive local cooperative, which has, nevertheless, gained a deservedly good reputation for the quality of its red wines. The principal brands are Terras do Suão and Terras de Cante. Don't be put off by the Communist demeanour of the labels.

MOURA

The old-fashioned spa town of Moura (not to be confused with Mourão) is better known for its water than its wine. One of Portugal's most popular mineral waters, Água do Castelo, is bottled among the cork forests at nearby Pizões. There are two vineyard nuclei, one just outside the fortified town of Moura itself and the other toward Serpa (a town famous for its ewe's-milk cheese). The climate is similar to that of Granja-Amareleja immediately to the north, but the calcareous clay soils are deeper and yields are consequently more abundant. Castelão is the principal grape, supported by Trincadeira and Alfrocheiro, which together produce soft, rather sweet, jammy reds that reflect the hot climate. Figs and raisins are also important agricultural commodities. There is no cooperative in the area. A large estate called Casa Agricola Santos Jorge is the principal producer.

VIDIGUEIRA

A low scarp between Portel and Vidigueira, the Serra do Mendro, marks the physical boundary between the Alto and Baixo Alentejo. The town of Vidigueira was the home of Vasco da Gama, celebrated in the local co-operative's red wine called Vila dos Gamas. The countryside around Vidigueira is some of the hottest and most arid in Portugal, with sweltering summer temperatures. It is surprising that so much of the region's 1,500 hectares of vineyard is planted with white grapes, principally the rather lowly Diagalves, Manteudo and Perrum. However, red varieties are on the increase, mostly Trincadeira and Alfrocheiro, although there is a significant amount of a variety known as Tinta Grossa or "Tinta da Nossa" (probably the same as Tinta Barroca in the Douro). Alfrocheiro seems to perform particularly well in Vidigueira's relatively fertile clay-limestone soils. Most of the region's wines are made at the local co-op, which also draws on fruit from the neighbouring municipalities of Cuba and Alvito, but there is an increasing number of promising estates located south and east of the town. See CADE, Cortes de Cima, Herdade Grande and Sogrape (below).

Producers

The greater part of the Alentejo's wines are made by the cooperatives at Reguengos, Borba and Redondo. The following list includes the major private estates. Those marked with an asterisk (*) form part of the *Rota do Vinho do Alentejo* (Alentejo Wine Route).

D'AVILLEZ

Correspondence address: Jorge Vaz d'Almada Avillez, c/o José Maria da Fonseca, Vila Nogueira de Azeitão, 2925 Azeitão

Jorge d'Avillez, a shareholder in the Azeitão firm of José Maria da Fonseca, owns a seventy-hectare property in the granite foothills of the Serra de São Mamede above Portalegre. A small amount of cool-fermented white wine is made from Arinto, Assario, Manteudo and Roupeiro, but the property's best wines are the impressive cask-aged reds made mainly from Aragonez, Castelão and Trincadeira. The dense but occasionally over-oaked Garrafeira is one of just a handful of Alentejo reds that merit keeping. Combining power with restraint, it displays all the potential of this, one of the best regions south of the Tagus for growing grapes. A second, rather less substantial red is made on the estate and bottled by José Maria da Fonseca as Montado.

ABREU CALLADO*

Fundação Abreu Callado, Benavila, 7480 Aviz

This agricultural foundation with over 3,000 hectares of land was set up after the death of Dr Cosme Campos Callado in 1948 to help educate the local rural population. Thirty-two hectares were planted with Castelão, Alfrocheiro, Aragonez, Trincadeira, Baga and Moreto, which together produce an impressive, if somewhat rustic and rather heady red with liquorice-like concentration. Short ageing in cask helps to soften the dry, dusty tannins. Abreu Callado wines are only sold on the local market but they are worth seeking out.

AGRO-ALIANÇA*

Quinta de Terrugem, EN4, Apartado 7, 7150 Borba

The Bairrada-based firm of Caves Aliança (see page 151) bought the eighty-six-hectare Monte do Rabão estate east of Borba from Alexandre Policarpo in 1992. All the white grape varieties on the property were uprooted and replaced by Castelão, Trincadeira, Aragonez and Cabernet Sauvignon. With a new stainless-steel winery, Aliança produces two heady, ripe-flavoured reds: Alabastro and Monte da Terrugem. The first, a Vinho Regional Alentejano, is loaded with sweet cherry fruit flavours and has menthol overtones from ripe Cabernet

Sauvignon. The second red, classified as a DOC, is more complex with leathery depth and maturity. There is to be a "super" *reserva* called T de Terrugem.

CARTUXA*

Correspondence address: Fundação Eugénio de Almeida, Pateo de São Miguel, 7000 Évora

The Convento de Cartuxa is a former Carthusian monastery just outside Évora's city walls. It was founded in 1587, but after the abolition of the religious orders in 1834 it became a private estate. In 1963 Vasco Maria Eugénio de Almeida, Duke of Villalva, transformed Cartuxa into a charitable trust. Even this was insufficient to protect it from the Communist tidal wave that swept through the Alentejo following the revolution a decade or so later, and for six years Cartuxa was occupied by farm workers. When the 6,500-hectare property was handed back to the foundation, it was in an appallingly neglected state and the winery and vineyards had to be thoroughly overhauled. The foundation has 235 hectares of vineyard, mostly at Herdade dos Minheiros, which can be seen from the Évora–Reguengos road. It is planted with traditional Alentejo varieties, predominantly Trincadeira, Castelão, Moreto, Aragonez and Alfrocheiro, with a small amount of Cabernet Sauvignon that brings a hint of blackcurrants to some of the wines. Rigorous selection means that much of the crop is sold off in bulk to local co-ops and only a relatively small proportion is held back to sell, under five different labels. The principal wine is Cartuxa, a ripe yet restrained red often with great concentration of flavour. Wines from lesser vintages are sold off under the reliable Eugénio de Almeida or Monte de Pinheiros labels.

The estate's finest wine deserves an entry of its own, such is its fame (and now fortune) in Portugal. Derived from *pedra manca* ("gaping stone"), Pera Manca was already well known as a wine prior to the outbreak of phylloxera. After the plague had run its course, the land was afforested and the label was lost. It was only in 1987 that José António de Oliveira Soares, a descendant of the original owners of Pera Manca, offered the trademark and the extraordinary late nineteenth-century label to the Fundação Eugenio de Almeida and Pera Manca was revived. The first wine was made three years later, mostly from the ripest Trincadeira and Aragonez grapes grown on the estate, although some Alfrocheiro, Aragonez or Cabernet also creeps into the blend. Not surprisingly the winemaker, Professor Colaço de Rosario, describes Trincadeira as the *casta fundamental* ("fundamental grape"). The wines are incredibly rich and dense with an intensity of flavour that verges on that of Vintage Port but is more akin to a Valpolicella Amarone. Although the wine is obviously unfortified, alcohol levels climb to over 14.5 per cent by volume. A somewhat burned, feral character is evident in some of the older wines. Aged in old mahogany vats, Pera Manca is only bottled (unfiltered) when Colaço do Rosario believes it is justified. To date, just four vintages have been "declared": 1990, 1991, 1994 and 1995. The 1996 was initially bottled then declassified and blended into Cartuxa. The wine commands stupendous prices and has rapidly become the cult wine of southern Portugal, equivalent to Barca Velha in the north (see page 210). A white Pera Manca made from Arinto, Antão Vaz, Perrum and Roupeiro exhibits honeyed richness and weight but commands nothing like the same price. Pera Manca is treated like a "first growth" by restaurants in Évora and the Alentejo.

HERDADE DO MONTE DA RIBEIRA*
CADE (Companhia Agricola de Desenvolvimento) SA, Marmelar, 7960 Pedrogão
Established in 1992, the 300-hectare Herdade do Monte da Ribeira south-east of Vidigueira has twenty-five hectares given over to vines. Solid, hot country reds from Trincadeira and Cabernet Sauvignon and soft, creamy Roupeiro-based whites are made by the partnership of João Portugal Ramos and Mario Andrade and bottled under the Pousio label. Quatro Caminhos is the name given to a full-bodied *reserva*.

QUINTA DO CARMO
Sociedade Agricola Quinta do Carmo SA, Herdade das Carvalhas, Gloria, 7100 Estremoz
Within view of the tall, crenellated keep that overlooks the busy market town of Estremoz is the eighteenth-century Quinta do Carmo, one of the most enchanting houses in the Alentejo. The estate used to belong to a branch of the Reynolds family that owns nearby Herdade do Mouchão (see below) and has since been inherited by a Portuguese branch of the family, the Bastos. Quinta do Carmo produced wine for much of the

twentieth century, but until the mid-1980s little went further than the family's private cellars. Like so many others, the property was a casualty of the 1974 revolution, when it was taken and made into a workers' cooperative. When the family regained most of its land in 1977, the vineyards were run down and the cellars had been emptied, leaving them to start again from scratch. Although somewhat unreliable, wines from vintages in the late 1980s were typically solid and concentrated with a peculiarly rustic Alentejano charm that emanated largely from Alicante Bouschet. In 1992 Domaines Baron de Rothschild (Lafite) took a fifty per cent interest in Carmo and installed its own winemakers. Alicante Bouschet was uprooted and experimental plots of Cabernet Sauvignon and Syrah have been planted alongside indigenous grapes, mostly Trincadeira, Castelão and Aragonez. The rather unpredictable *lagares* (made from the local pink marble) were abandoned in favour of fermentation in stainless steel at nearby Quinta das Carvalhas, and present-day wines have come to taste somewhat emasculated by comparison with previous vintages. As a result, Quinta do Carmo *garrafeiras* from the "good old days" of the late 1980s fetch high prices on the local market. JP Vinhos (see below) have now bought the Bastos family share in Quinta do Carmo, although Julio Bastos retains the historic core of the estate at Estremoz. The poor schistous soils around the house have been broken up and planted with vines and will be producing wine under a new label: Quinta de Santa Maria.

TAPADA DO CHAVES*

Tapada do Chaves – Sociedade Agricola e Commercial SA, Frangoneiro, 7300 Portalegre

Vines grow side by side with olive trees in this traditional vineyard set in the granite foothills of the Serra de São Mamede just to the east of Portalegre. The core of the vineyard is over eighty years old and includes Castelão, Trincadeira and Aragonez as well as Alicante Bouschet and Grand Noir. There are also white grapes: Alva (Roupeiro), Fernão Pires and Arinto. Until the early 1990s the wines were vinified in large clay pots or *talhas* and auto-vinification tanks. This produced red wines that were occasionally exceptional, but the absence of efficient temperature control meant that they were often heavily flawed by excess volatile acidity. A new stainless-steel winery was built in 1994 and, under the auspices of winemaker João Portugal Ramos, Tapada do Chaves seemed to be on the way to becoming more reliable. However, the property was sold to Caves Murganheira in 1998 and, although it is still early days, standards seem to have slipped. Older vintages sell for a high price in Lisbon wine shops but, although some bottles can be outstanding, there continues to be a *caveat emptor* attached to Tapada do Chaves. Almojanda is the property's second label.

HERDADE DE COELHEIROS*
Sociedade Agricola dos Coelheiros SA, Ingrejinha, 7040 Arraiolos

Joaquim Silveira has planted fourteen hectares predominantly with Cabernet Sauvignon, Trincadeira and Castelão alongside small amounts of Chardonnay and Roupeiro. The wines are made on the property in a newly built winery, with the ripe, well-structured reds subject to short ageing in French oak before bottling. A rather daring varietal Chardonnay is, to my mind, rather overblown and over-oaked. The wines are sold under the Tapada de Coelheiros label, adorned with illustrations of the traditional hand-made rugs from the nearby town of Arraiolos.

CORTES DE CIMA
Herdade dos Cortes de Cima, 7960 Vidigueira

Hans and Carrie Jorgensen are a husband and wife team who moved to Portugal in 1988 to fulfil a dream. This Danish-American partnership began by growing melons and sun-dried tomatoes on their 375-hectare estate, but quickly added fifty hectares of vineyard. Aragonez is the principal grape variety, followed by an unusually large quantity of Syrah. There is also some Trincadeira, Castelão and Touriga Nacional as well as a small quantity of the white Antão Vaz and Roupeiro. The Australian viticultural guru Richard Smart, who advises Esporão and Sir Cliff Richard's Quinta do Moinho in the Algarve, continues to help the Jorgensens with their irrigated vineyard near Vidigueira. There has been considerable Australian input in the winery as well, which helps to account for the exuberant, often minty style of wine from Cortes de Cima, often backed by more than a hint of smoky new oak. There are three principal labels: Chaminé, Cortes de Cima and Incognito. The last is pure Syrah and was so called (backed by a quote from Bob Dylan) because at the time it was first made, this grape was outside the remit of either the local DOC or Vinho Regional. There is more than a hint of the New World emanating from Cortes de Cima.

HERDADE DO ESPORÃO*
Finagra SA, 7200 Reguengos de Monsaraz

A long, dusty cart track used to lead from the centre of Reguengos de Monsaraz to one of the largest continuous vineyards on the Iberian peninsula. Nowadays the approach to Esporão is becoming more like a super-highway, the result of a decade of continuous investment by banker and all-round businessman José Roquette. It is easy to forget that this 2,000-hectare estate had a shaky start in the revolutionary 1970s, when it was seized by communists and only returned to its rightful owners on condition that all the grapes should be delivered to the local cooperative. The tables were turned and Esporão subsequently bought Perdigões, one of the cooperative's best suppliers, bringing the total area of vineyards to 550 hectares. The vines, planted on alternate granite and schist, were among the first in the Alentejo to be irrigated when Esporão built a huge dam for the purpose in 1997. The dam also enhanced the appearance of the estate, and a restaurant complex has been established alongside the winery to encourage *enoturismo* (wine tourism). The winemaking at Esporão is the responsibility of David Baverstock, who produces a growing number of different labels. The principal brand is Monte Velho, a soft, oak-aged red and fresh, dry white that are some of the most widely distributed and reliable wines on the domestic market. There is also a pair of simple young table wines named Alandra. The name Esporão is reserved for a fat, part barrel-fermented dry white made mainly from Roupeiro and Antão Vaz and a firm yet supple red produced from the best grapes on the estate, mostly Trincadeira and Aragonez with some Cabernet Sauvignon. Esporão has also gone a long way down the varietal route with Roupeiro, Arinto, Aragonez, Bastardo, Cabernet Sauvignon, Touriga Nacional and Trincadeira. In a ripe year, Esporão's Trincadeira captures the warm, spicy character of this, one of Portugal's leading grapes. With a high proportion of Arinto, Vinho de Defesa with its lime and lemon aromas and flavours is a uniquely refreshing dry Alentejano white. To complete the picture, Esporão also produces *espumante*, a Tawny-style fortified wine, a variety of olive oils and cheese. Reguengos is now something of a mecca for those who want to sample the flavours of the Alentejo.

HERDADE GRANDE
António Manuel Lança, 7960 Vidigueira

In common with most of the vineyards around Vidigueira, Herdade Grande was originally planted with white grapes that supplied the local cooperative. Arinto, alongside Rabo de Ovelha and Roupeiro, makes some surprisingly fresh, aromatic dry whites with a hint of lemon sherbet and, occasionally, a touch of new wood. The red Herdade Grande is an altogether more serious blend of Aragonez, Trincadeira and Cabernet Sauvignon with a "condiment" of Alicante Bouschet and Tinta Grossa. These are hefty wines with spicy fruit, smoky oak and 14 per cent alcohol by volume. A lighter red from the estate is bottled as Condado das Vinhas. Winemaking is the responsibility of Luís Duarte, who besides working for Esporão, operates his own consultancy in the Alentejo.

JP VINHOS*
JP Vinhos SA, Lugar da Ceramica, 7040 Arraiolos

Based on the Setúbal Peninsula, JP Vinhos used to bottle wines from an estate near Moura toward the Spanish border. They have now moved slightly closer to home, converting an old ceramics factory at Arraiolos into a modern *adega*. JP already owns over 160 hectares of vineyard in the Alentejo and plans to extend this to 250 hectares by 2005. Monte das Anforas is the name given to a duo of wines: a soft dry white made from Roupeiro and Fernão Pires, and a mid-weight red blended from grapes grown near Arraiolos and toward Portalegre. Tinto da Anfora is a more solid, leathery wine made from Trincadeira, Aragonez, Castelão, Alicante Bouschet, Moreto and Alfrocheiro growing as far afield as Arronches (south of Portalegre), Borba and Moura. It is a genuine Alentejano blend. Aged in chestnut and oak, Tinto da Anfora has the capacity to age for a decade or more. The Grande Escolha launched in 2001 is its big brother. See page 261 for more information on JP Vinhos.

QUINTA DO MOURO
Miguel António de Orduna Viegas Louro, 7100 Estremoz

Miguel Louro, a dentist by profession, restored this seventeenth-century property on the outskirts of Estremoz, having bought it in a run-down state in 1979. Planting fifteen hectares of vines, he seems to have taken over where nearby Quinta do Carmo left off (see above) in making a resolutely traditional Alentejano red. The vineyard is dry-farmed, which keeps yields low. Miguel Louro believes firmly that the growers who irrigate may end up "killing the goose that laid the golden egg". The wines from Quinta do Mouro are sometimes a little rustic, but none the worse for that. Aragonez, Trincadeira, Castelão, Alicante Bouschet and a small quantity of Cabernet Sauvignon combine to produce wonderfully dense, concentrated wines that gain a leathery quality with age in bottle. Cabernet Sauvignon has introduced a hint of menthol in more recent vintages. João Portugal Ramos was responsible for the winemaking until 1998 and his role has been taken over by Luís Duarte of Esporão. This has made no difference to the style or quality of the wines.

JOÃO PORTUGAL RAMOS
J Portugal Ramos Vinhos SA, Monte do Serrado Pinheiro, 7100 Estremoz

Aided by a small technical team, João Portugal Ramos is one of Portugal's most highly regarded consultant winemakers, advising as many as fourteen estates and three cooperatives spread over the Alentejo, Ribatejo, Estremadura and Beiras. Over the years he helped to create (or in some cases recreate) the wines of Tapada do Chaves, Quinta do Carmo, Casa Cadaval (Ribatejo), Falcoaria (Ribatejo), Quinta da Lagoalva de Cima (Ribatejo), Quinta de Pancas (Estremadura) and Quinta do Foz de Arouce (Beiras). In 1997 Ramos settled down for long enough to plant his own vineyard, Monte de Serrado Pinheiro, close to Estremoz. Trincadeira, Aragonez, Syrah and a grape known as Tinta Caiada make a range of expressive varietal wines and come together with Cabernet and Alicante Bouschet in two blends: a smooth, spicy oak-aged red called Vila Santa and the rather lighter Marquês de Borba. The deliciously intense Marquês de Borba Reserva, bottled only in the best years, is serious wine somewhat overdressed in new oak and with a ludicrously expensive price tag. Portugal Ramos also makes a fresh-tasting dry white from Antão Vaz as well as value-for-money own-label wines for the Pingo Doce supermarket. Inspired by nearby Quinta do Carmo, he has equipped his baronial winery with marble *lagares*.

HERDADE DO MOUCHÃO*
Ann W Reynolds and Emily E Richardson, Casa Branca, 7470 Sousel

"Bouncer" Reynolds lost his 900-hectare family property to the revolutionaries in 1974 and, sadly, died before it was returned. His two daughters, Ann Reynolds and Emily Richardson, have now taken on the property which, as the April 25 Cooperative, was badly neglected when it was returned to the family in 1985, a decade of production having been drunk locally as *vinho corrente*. Added to this, Mouchão has been hit in successive years by late spring frosts. The old vineyards that produce the finest grapes are situated in a frost hollow and, until an aspersion system was installed to counteract low temperatures, the property faced the risk of being wiped out nearly every year. As a result of the combined effects of the revolution and the frost, Iain Richardson, who is responsible for the property, has had precious little wine to sell. However, a new vineyard planted on the hillside is now coming on stream and Mouchão should have more wine to sell in future. A small amount of Syrah features among the recent planting. The winemaking at Mouchão is still delightfully rustic. Grapes are foot-trodden and fermented in stone *lagares* in a small, remote nineteenth-century winery at the heart of the estate. The wines are then aged in large wooden vats made on the estate from oak, chestnut and mahogany, and bottled without filtration. The property produces two wines. Mouchão, made mainly from Alicante Bouschet, is a dense, brooding wine: big, dark and concentrated in a uniquely Alentejano way, very much as Quinta do Carmo was before the French gained control. Unlike most Alentejano reds, it has the capacity to develop in bottle for two decades or more. Although a question mark hangs over some rather inconsistent bottles, Mouchão is undoubtedly one of Portugal's most impressive red wines. A second label, Dom Rafael, is used for younger, slightly lighter red and soft, warm country white wines for earlier drinking.

ROQUEVAL*

Roqueval SA, Courelas do Monte Branco, 7170 Redondo

Although the Roque do Vale family hails from Torres Vedras in Estremadura, it is deeply involved in the wines of the Alentejo. Maria Clara Roque do Vale has long been the president of the forward-thinking Regional Commission, while her husband Carlos and daughter Joana look after the family property, Herdade da Madeira near Redondo. The estate comprises 120 hectares of vineyard planted with traditional red and white grape varieties. Three different wines are produced, the best being the red Tinto da Talha, which is firm and reasonably full flavoured, having been fermented in traditional *talhas* (clay pots). The second and third labels, Vinho Redondo and Terras do Xisto, seem somewhat stretched in comparison with many Alentejano reds.

HERDADE DO PESO

Correspondence address: Sogrape Vinhos de Portugal SA, Aldeia Nova, Avintes, Apartado 3032, Vila Nova de Gaia

Portugal's largest winemaker, Sogrape, made its first foray into the Alentejo in 1991, when it bought red wine from the Almodôvar estate in Vidigueira and bottled it under the name Vinha do Monte. A year later the firm switched its allegiance to Herdade do Peso, an estate belonging to the Palha family near by. Sogrape purchased this 265-hectare property outright in 1996 and extended the vineyards to sixty hectares. Castelão is the dominant grape variety, followed by Alfrocheiro, Trincadeira, Aragonez and Moreto. Unusually for this area, there are no white grapes growing on the estate. A new winery equipped with small, squat fermentation vats to achieve good extraction is producing a growing range of wines, from the accessible, fruity Vinha do Monte, made mostly from Castelão and Moreto, to three excellent varietals. The Alfrocheiro is particularly good, balancing bitter chocolate concentration with crisp acidity and a surprising amount of finesse.

JOSÉ DE SOUSA

Correspondence address: José Maria da Fonseca, Vila Nogueira de Azeitão, 2925 Azeitão

Behind a long white wall in the centre of Reguengos de Monsaraz lies one of southern Europe's most enchanting wineries. Rows of huge Ali Babastyle pots or *talhas* hark back to Roman times when wine was made in clay amphorae. The tradition has been maintained by Domingos Soares Franco, whose family firm bought José de Sousa Rosado Fernandes, as it was then called, in 1986. Prior to this the wines were often good, sometimes outstanding, but always variable and frequently marred by excess volatile acidity. Soares Franco has succeeded in preserving the essential Alentejano character of the wine – its somewhat roasted, feral fruit – whilst producing an altogether cleaner, more reliable red. Grapes from José de Sousa's own vineyard near by are part fermented in stainless steel, part in clay *talhas*. Nowadays only the powerful *garrafeira* named José de Sousa Mayor is made in the uncompromisingly traditional style, fermented in *talhas* after having been foot-trodden in *lagares*. This is a hazardous business, for it is not unknown for the pressure of the ferment to cause a pot to crack and spring a leak, but Soares Franco deems that it is well worth the risk.

OTHER PROMINENT ALENTEJANO ESTATES

Herdade de Calada, BCH-Comercio de Vinhos SA, Estrada da Arauja, 7040 Arraiolos*

Sociedade Agricola Gabriel F Dias e Irmãs ("Couteiro Mor"), Courelas de Guita, 7050 Montemor-o-Novo

Herdade dos Machados, Casa Agricola Santos Jorge SA, 7860 Moura*

Monte da Penha, Francisco B Fino – Sociedade Agricola Lda, Monte da Penha, 7300 Portalegre*

Herdade do Perdigão, Apartado 29, 7420 Monforte

Monte do Pintor, Sociedade Agricola da Sossega Lda, Ingrejinha, 7040 Arraiolos*

Sovibor, Sociedade Vinhos de Borba Lda, Rua de São Bartolomeu, 48, 7150 Borba*

IV. ALGARVE

Known the world over as a destination for thousands of holidaymakers, Portugal's southernmost province has grown apart from the rest of the country. The Algarve is separated from the plains of the Alentejo by a range of low mountains. Rising to just over 900 metres (2,952 feet) in the Serra de Monchique, they stretch from the wild Atlantic coast in the west to the River Guadiana, which marks the border with Spain, in the east.

The climate is generally described as Mediterranean, but there are two sides to the Algarve. The coast east of Faro, the Sotavento, is considerably hotter and more Mediterranean than the Barlavento to the west. As you approach Cape St Vincent and the western Costa Vincentina, the Atlantic influence increases and a cool breeze blows off the ocean for much of the year. Rainfall is greater here too, ranging from 1,000 millimetres (thirty-nine inches) per annum on the mountains in the west to less than 400 millimetres sixteen inches) in some places in the Sotavento. The sheltered southern coast is blessed by over 3,000 hours of sunshine a year, which explains its popularity with tourists.

The Algarve prospered under the Moors, who remained in control until the mid-thirteenth century and named it al-Garb al-Andalus (west of Andalus). The Moorish presence can still be recognized in the place names, the architecture, the delicious local sweetmeats and in some of the swarthy complexions. Although the language is the same, albeit with a strong singsong accent, the Algarve seems a continent away from the Minho, the birthplace of Portugal. The late twentieth-century invasion of tourists means that English is now the common lingo in the old fishing villages that have mushroomed into vast resorts. Penetrating between five and ten kilometres (3.1 and 6.2 miles) inland, villas, holiday complexes and apartment blocks have taken over the coastal strip to the exclusion of almost everything else. But away from the coast, there is another side to the Algarve. Figs, almonds, oranges and lemons are cultivated in the vivid sandstone soils that can be deep and fertile in places. Vineyards, which have mostly been eradicated from the coastal belt, can still be found inland. Although the Algarve used to produce a certain amount of fortified wine, the legacy of which is a rustic aperitif wine produced by Lagoa cooperative, nothing of any distinction has been made for years. This is partly because the region is planted with all the wrong grapes. Negra Mole, Bastardo, Moreto, Diagalves, Perrum and Tamarêz will never perform, and even Crato Branco (alias Síria) seems to be wasted here in the southern heat. The EU has provided subsidies to uproot vineyards and transfer the licences to regions like the Alentejo and Douro where the demand for grapes is increasing. As a result, two of the four cooperative wineries have been forced to close, as there is simply insufficient raw material to keep them going. This makes a mockery of the four DOCs on the Algarve – Tavira, Lagoa, Portimão and Lagos – which were drawn up around the cooperatives. Tavira and Portimão have closed, leaving Lagos and Lagoa (always the best of the four) with a near monopoly of production. The legislation also allows for a Vinho Regional, which covers the entire province and is therefore much more meaningful than the largely moribund DOCs.

Perhaps inspired by the revival of viticulture in the Alentejo immediately to the north, a handful of new vineyards have been planted on the Algarve and a couple of Portugal's best-known consultant winemakers have been brought in to raise the quality of the region's wines. David Baverstock has famously linked up with Sir Cliff Richard, who owns a property inland in the Barlavento, just north of the holiday mecca of Albufeira (see below). José Neiva of DFJ Vinhos (see pages 169 and 249) has been working in the meantime with the cooperative near by at Lagoa to produce a soft and approachable, if rather jammy, red named Cataplana. Although the Algarve is still a no man's land in terms of wine, with good fortune and perseverance it might yet prove that it is capable of quality.

QUINTA DO MOINHO

An old windmill (*moinho*) stands in front of Sir Cliff Richard's Algarve property, eight hectares of which have been planted with vines. Aragonez, Trincadeira, Syrah and Mourvèdre (none of which are as yet permissible under the local DOC or Vinho Regional) have been transplanted from the Alentejo by David Baverstock, who is acting as Sir Cliff's consultant winemaker. Although the Algarve's red clay is somewhat different from the soils on the plains to the north, Baverstock sees no reason why the vines should not flourish, as the site is well drained. Dr Richard Smart, known for his theories on canopy management, has been drafted in to give advice. The first wines (made at Cortes de Cima near Vidigueira in the Alentejo) are very promising with more than a hint of the New World about them. Quality aside, they proved to be hugely popular with Cliff's fan club when sold online by Tesco supermarket in the UK. As the name Quinta do Moinho has already been registered by an estate elsewhere in Portugal, Sir Cliff has decided to use the title Vida Nova, meaning "New Life". The novelty factor alone has certainly brought new life to the Algarve's neglected vineyards.

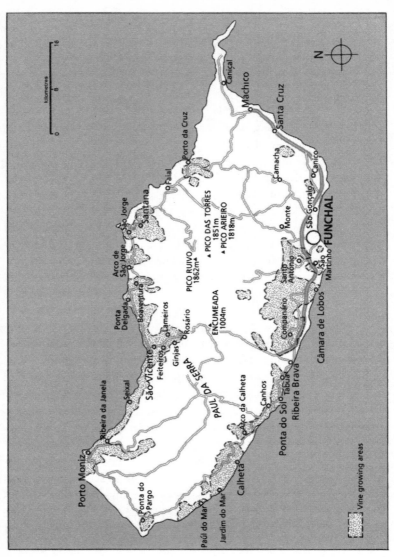

Madeira

6

Wines of the Islands

I. MADEIRA AND PORTO SANTO

Madeira is fine wine *in extremis*. Heat and air, both sworn enemies of most winemakers, conspire together to turn Madeira into one of the most enthralling of all the world's fine wines as well as the most resilient. Madeiras from the nineteenth and even the eighteenth centuries still retain an ethereal gloss even after spending an aeon of wine years in cask and bottle. Having undergone this process, the wine is seemingly indestructible. Once the cork has been removed, Madeira comes to no harm, even if it is left on ullage for months on end. If ever there was a wine to take to a desert island, this is it.

Like so many life-enhancing innovations, Madeira was first produced by accident. The island's strategic position in the Atlantic, 1,000 kilometres (620 miles) south-west of the Portuguese mainland and 800 kilometres (500 miles) from the north African coast, meant that Madeira became an important entrepôt soon after it was colonized at the start of the fifteenth century. Wine was taken on board the ships calling at the island's capital, Funchal, probably as an antidote to scurvy. Fortified to protect them from microbiological spoilage, these naturally acidic wines were enhanced by the long sea voyages across the tropics. As the wine gained popularity, the aromas and flavours wrought by the ambient heat and prolonged exposure to air acquired their own description: "maderized".

The history of Madeira, wine and island, is interwoven with that of the Portuguese mainland, as described in Chapter 1, but the survival of the island's wine industry for over five centuries has been a saga of singular strength against physical and economic adversity. Madeira's vineyards are a challenging enough prospect in themselves. The island rises sheer from the Atlantic: a dark volcanic plug in the midst of a deep blue ocean. Much of the interior is uninhabitable and the population of around 300,000 is concentrated into the natural harbours and bays, mostly on the south coast. Above the towns and villages are tiny shelf-like terraces known as *poios*, which have been carved like hanging gardens from the predominantly red-grey basalt. They support all manner of crops, depending upon the fluctuations in the insular economy. Sugar cane, bananas, wicker and vines have all enjoyed their moments of glory, only to be swept aside when boom is overturned by bust. Over recent years, tourism and bananas have been on the upswing, to the extent that vineyards are becoming hard to find. The land around São Martinho west of Funchal, once famed for the quality of its wine, has become built up and the poios immediately behind Câmara de Lobos are mostly planted with bananas. Apart from a ten-hectare plot belonging to Henriques and Henriques above Estreito de Câmara de Lobos, there are no large vineyards. Instead, vines mingle with bananas and clamber over the houses in the suburbs of Funchal, every plant having to justify its return on space.

Madeira is the principal island in an archipelago that includes Porto Santo and the aptly named Ilhas Desertas. The other islands are small and squat. They suffer from perennial drought, whereas the summit of Madeira, reaching 1,862 metres (6,107 feet) at Pico Ruivo, is almost permanently hidden by a *capocete* of dense cloud. This was perceived by the early flat-earth explorers to be steam rising from the mouth of hell, but is in fact the result of the moisture-laden Atlantic airstream being forced to rise and condense over the top of the island. Here the annual rainfall reaches 3,000 millimetres (118 inches), over four times the figure for Funchal on the coast. All this water is directed to good use by a remarkable labyrinth of irrigation channels called levadas. First constructed in the sixteenth century, the network now extends to 2,000 kilometres (1,242 miles) in total, irrigating crops and generating hydro-electricity as the water cascades down the mountain. It remains well maintained and the *levada* system is carefully regulated to ensure an even distribution of water to every tiny holding.

Until 1974 Madeira's system of tenure was almost feudal, with much of the best land on the south side of the island belonging to a handful of large estates. The local economy was driven by sharecropping and tithe

Madeira: poios *(terraces) overlooking the Atlantic*

farming until post-revolutionary governments gave tenants the right to buy out their landlord's interest. Most grasped the opportunity and, as a result, Madeira's agriculture is now something akin to medieval strip farming. With subsequent sub-division under Portugal's Napoleonic code of inheritance, it is not uncommon for one tiny *poio* to have as many as ten different owners. Not surprisingly, the land registry in Funchal has become a bureaucratic nightmare, and all statistics relating to the landholdings on the island have to be taken with a pinch of salt. Unlike mainland Portugal, there is as yet no *cadastro* or register of vineyards. Vines, however, remain the island's largest crop, covering an estimated 1,700 hectares which represents just under twenty per cent of the cultivatable area. However only about half of this is entitled to the denomination VQPRD which supplies the grapes for the production of Madeira wine. Vines are followed closely by bananas, which have taken over much of the south coast, then by potatoes and cabbages (which often grow underneath the vines), cereals, other fruit and wicker. Cattle also feature. They are rarely seen but often smelt, as they tend to be kept indoors. With an estimated 14,000 plots of vines, the average size of an individual vineyard holding is just a tiny fraction of a hectare.

Madeira's humid sub-tropical climate constitutes a pest's paradise, with oidium (powdery mildew) an enduring problem. It is easy to understand why small producers embraced non-*vinifera* grape varieties like Isabella, Jacquet and Cunningham in the second half of the nineteenth century. Until Portugal joined the EU in 1986, wine from these direct producers (so called because they are planted on their own roots without grafting) made its way into Madeira wine often masquerading as "Sercial", "Bual", "Verdelho" or "Malmsey (Malvasia)". Apart from the blatant falsification, there was often nothing intrinsically wrong with the quality of these wines. In fact, John Cossart of Henriques & Henriques recalls that his father Peter rather liked to work with them. However, concern about the long-term health implications of drinking wine made from non-*vinifera* grapes has rendered them illegal for anything but local domestic consumption and the wine is no longer bottled. In the mid-twentieth century direct producers probably made as much as seventy per cent of all Madeira wine and, despite the ban on the use of these grapes, it is somewhat astonishing to find that they still occupy nearly half the island's vineyards.

The single most planted grape on Madeira is Tinta Negra Mole. This versatile *vinifera* variety yields pale red must which can be shaped into various styles of Madeira from rich and sweet to bone dry. Negra Mole, as it is known for short, produces a soft, malleable base wine but never scales quite the same heights as the four principal "noble" grape varieties: Sercial, Verdelho, Bual and Malvasia. Each of these remarkable grapes is profiled in detail in Chapter 2; in brief, Sercial produces the driest style of wine, Verdelho medium dry, Bual medium sweet and Malvasia the richest and sweetest of Madeiras. Taken together, these noble varieties account for just ten per cent of the island's total crop.

Three other grape varieties may also be occasionally identified on labels. Listrão grows almost exclusively on the island of Porto Santo. Terrantez has almost been driven to extinction, but produces a medium dry, floral wine. Bastardo, also nearly extinct, is the only red grape to be classified as "noble" and there is a small quantity of Moscatel making a rich, sweet fortified wine. Apart from Listrão, which produces a rather bland base wine, all these grapes (Negra Mole included) are notable for their naturally high levels of acidity. The islanders tell you that this is a function of the volcanic soil, an assertion which is partly true, but viticulture must also play a part. Most of the vineyards are planted on low pergolas known as *latada*, somewhat reminiscent of Vinho Verde but on a smaller scale. Encouraged by the availability of water, the vines tend to be vigorous and produce a heavy crop. Grapes are harvested early, from mid-August until October depending on the location, with the driest wines tending to come from vineyards on the cooler north side of the island or at higher altitudes on the south, and the richer wines from the fertile soils around Funchal and Câmara de Lobos. Yields are enormous; one hundred hl/ha is normal, rising to as much as 200 hl/ha in places. It is hardly surprising then that despite the summer heat, these musts are rarely high in sugar. Baumés are frequently as low as 8 degrees on the north side of the island rising to 11 or 12 degrees in the south. Farmers often irrigate heavily before the harvest to increase the size of their crop.

The vintage used to be a colourful event celebrated with gusto all over the island. The grapes were foot-trodden close to the vineyards in wooden *lagares* and the wines were taken to Funchal by *borracheiros*, processions of men carrying *borrachos* (goatskins) full of wine. A few *lagares*

Madeira: two baskets of grapes

remain, at Quinta do Furão, for example, and in private houses making wine on a small scale. Until the 1930s these *lagares* were made of wood but since then they have been built from cement. Nowadays the shippers have their own central wineries and/or buy in from *partidistas* who make the wine on their behalf. Owing to the size of the individual plots, grapes are received from all over the island in dribs and drabs. The two largest shippers, the Madeira Wine Company and Justino Henriques (neither of which owns any vineyards), negotiate with as many as 800 growers. Jacques Faro de Silva, the Madeira Wine Company's general manager, records that their smallest consignment in 2000 was just two baskets of grapes, representing a grower's entire crop! The grapes are paid for according to their weight and sugar reading, with the noble varieties now commanding a substantial premium over the ubiquitous Tinta Negra Mole. In 2000 Tinta Negra Mole (plus Complexa, Triunfo and Bastardo) were priced at around 185$00 (€0.92) per kilogram (2.2 pounds) based on 10 per cent potential alcohol by volume, with increments of 5$00 (€0.02) per kilogram (2.2 pounds) for every extra degree of alcohol. The noble varieties, Sercial, Verdelho, Bual and Malvasia, commanded 280–300$00 (€1.40–1.50) per kilogram.

In the past every shipper had its own way of making the wine, prompting me to write an article in *Decanter* in 1991 entitled "Does anyone know how to make Madeira?" There has been a sea change since then. Handling is greatly improved and this is reflected in an improvement in the quality of even the most basic wines. From the reception, the grapes are crushed, destalked and pumped into a mechanical press. Some producers ferment in large wooden vats, but cement or stainless-steel autovinifiers with temperature control are now more common. Small consignments of noble grapes are fermented separately, sometimes in individual 600-litre lodge pipes.

In the days of the *borracheiros*, nearly all the base wine for Madeira would be fermented dry and sweetened by the shipper at a later stage. The best wines were adjusted with *vinho surdo* or *abafado*, unfermented or partially fermented grape juice that had been previously fortified to retain its natural sweetness. But it was by no means uncommon to see sacks of sugar piled up near the bottling line, and cheaper wines were sweetened with *arrobo*, boiled grape juice to which sugar and tartaric acid were added, or merely *calda*, sugar boiled down to caramel. Thankfully, these methods of sweetening have been made illegal by the EU, and the majority of wine is now made by arresting the fermentation with ninety-five per cent strength grape spirit to make a 17–18° wine. Richer wines (Malvasia and Bual) will ferment for twenty-four to forty-eight hours, leaving 3.5–6.5 degrees Baumé of residual sugar. The drier styles of wine (Verdelho and Sercial) will ferment for longer (four–five days) until most or all of the sugar is fermented to alcohol. Any further adjustment to the sweetness of the wine must now be carried out with rectified concentrated must or *surdo* and/or *abafado*.

The majority of the wine, particularly that made from Tinta Negra Mole, then undergoes a process known by the somewhat onomatopoeic term *estufagem*. This was developed during the eighteenth and nineteenth centuries to replicate the long tropical sea voyages that proved so beneficial to Madeira. The *estufas* themselves ("hot houses" or "stoves") are vats made from wood, cement or stainless steel, heated with hot water either through an internal serpentine pipe or an external jacket. The wine is raised to a maximum temperature of 55°C for a minimum of ninety days, based on the principle that the longer and slower the heating process, the better the quality of the wine. The whole process is regulated by the *Instituto do Vinho da Madeira* (IVM), which applies a wax seal to the vat in order to ensure that the wine is not tampered with. The *estufagem* regime varies between shippers, with some preferring to raise the wine to higher temperatures than others; the Madeira Wine Company favours heat alternating with slow cooling over a three-month cycle. *Estufagem* is almost always evident in the final, bottled wine, manifesting itself in the form of baked, toasted aromas. A heavy-handed approach will produce wines that smell and taste excessively burned and oxidized.

It is a common assumption that all Madeira is subject to *estufagem* but this is not the case. One small producer, Barros e Sousa, flatly refuses to subject any of its wines to the *estufa* and most shippers set aside their best wines for ageing in wood. This method is known as *canteiro*, named after the scantling racks on which the lodge pipes are placed. The wood itself is largely immaterial, as its prime function is not to impart flavour but to age and nurture the wine over a decade or more. Most casks are of indeterminable age, having undergone successive repairs by coopers on the island, and are made from American oak, Baltic oak or occasionally Brazilian satinwood. Unlike Port, which develops in the relative cool of the lodges in Oporto, Madeira is exposed to the sub-tropical ambient heat. The pipes are stowed either under the eaves or in naturally warm lodges where an evaporation rate of about four per cent a year helps to concentrate the wine. Policies vary with regard to topping up the casks. Some shippers leave the wines undisturbed for years at a time, whereas others rack and check the casks at regular intervals. Whether the wines are topped up or not, there will always be a certain amount of ullage as breathing space inside the cask. A Madeira from a single outstanding vintage may spend as long as eighty years in wood, the quantity steadily diminishing through evaporation. When the quantity is so diminished that it no longer fills a cask, it will be transferred to glass demi-johns.

The Madeira Wine Company also practices a method of heating and maturation that is something of a half-way house between *estufagem* and *canteiro*. Lodge pipes are stored in warm rooms known as *armazens de calor*, heated either by their proximity to the *estufas* or by steam-filled water pipes. Temperatures are maintained at lower levels, normally between 35°C and 40°C, and the wines develop more slowly over a period of six months to a year. Consequently they finish up tasting less stewed than wines heated in bulk and are used for making higher-quality five and ten year old Reserve or Special Reserve blends.

Madeira styles

Over ninety per cent of Madeira is a so-called "field blend" of grapes based on Negra Mole. Once these wines have undergone *estufagem*, they begin to qualify for age. Until 2002, the cheapest wines were shipped in bulk (*granel*) over which little control was exercised. Following in the footsteps of Port, bulk shipments of Madeira have now been suspended and the only Madeira to leave the island in bulk is the denatured wine used in pre-prepared foods or as a flavouring for schnapps. The IVM now stipulates that the youngest bottled wine to leave the island must be at least three years old, having normally spent two years in wooden vats or casks. The wines are simply designated "Madeira Wine" without any indication of age and are classified according to sweetness: rich, medium rich, medium dry or dry. They are often misleadingly designated by the term "Finest" for, although this category of wine has much improved, three year old Madeira never has the style or incisiveness of an older wine. Nonetheless, Blandy's well-made Duke range, named after the Duke of Sussex, Duke of Cambridge, Duke of Cumberland and Duke of Clarence in increasing order of sweetness, is a good introduction to Madeira wine. Henriques & Henriques also produces a worthwhile soft, off-dry aperitif named Monte Seco.

Moving up the hierarchy, the next category officially approved by the IVM is Five Year Old, which may also be designated Reserva or Reserve (although the use of this term is complicated by Pereira d'Oliveira, which also bottles vintage or *frasqueira* wines as Reservas). Five Year Old wines are generally based on Negra Mole, although both Barbeito and Blandy bottle Reserve wines from the "noble" grape varieties. In general these wines have more lift and presence than the three year old category, but they do little more than hint at the ethereal complexity of a well-aged wine. In the United States a lighter, medium-dry style of three or five year old Madeira is known as "Rainwater" supposedly because some casks shipped to Savannah were once left on the beach and diluted by rain.

The next permitted category of Madeira covers those wines bottled with a Ten, Fifteen, Twenty, Thirty and Over Forty Year Old designation. This group is not as large as it seems for, in practice, nearly all old, blended wine falls into either the Ten or Fifteen Year Old category. Most (though by no means all) of these wines are made from Sercial, Verdelho, Bual or Malvasia and the Madeira Wine Company also bottles a small quanity of Terrantez. At ten years these wines begin to show some true Madeira character, with the high toned floral aromas and concentration of flavour that brings the wine singing from the glass. Henriques & Henriques bottles a particularly good range at both the Ten and Fifteen Year Old level, with their Verdelho and Bual leading the field.

The term *colheita* is most closely associated with Port, but has recently been introduced to Madeira, largely at the behest of the Madeira Wine Company, which owns Blandy and Cossart Gordon. *Colheita* is interchangeable with the English word "Harvest", which may also appear on the label. It signifies a wine from a single good-quality harvest that may be made from either Tinta Negra Mole or one of the classic varieties and is bottled after spending five years in cask. Although relatively untried and tested, this category is potentially very significant, as the wine is bottled with a much-vaunted year of harvest and, in the context of Madeira, is perhaps best seen as an early bottled vintage. It is to be hoped that Harvest/Colheita will do for Madeira what Late Bottled Vintage (LBV) has done for Port.

At the very top of the Madeira hierarchy is the category often referred to as "vintage" but officially known as *Garrafeira* or *Frasqueira*. Nowadays these wines must be made exclusively from one of the classic Madeira varieties and aged for at least twenty years in cask before bottling. Often the wines are kept for considerably longer, gaining power and intensity as evaporation takes its course. As a result of prolonged ageing in cask at ambient temperatures the wines are almost indestructible and may be enjoyed a glass at a time and kept on ullage over many years. The oldest wine that I have ever tasted is a 1795 Terrantez from Barbeito, which is still magnificent, even fresh, two centuries after the wine was first made. Although all the main houses bottled small quantities of "vintage" Madeira, it has nothing like the same following as Vintage Port. This is partly because there is no pattern of general "declarations", rather shippers tend to squirrel away tiny *lotes* ("lots") of wine when they think that they have vintage potential, only for them to re-emerge in bottle decades later. The oldest wine in the MWC still remaining unbottled is 1920.

Madeira producers

A century and a half of repeated crises has left Madeira with just six registered shippers, where there were at least thirty operating in the 1800s. The largest in terms of volume is Justino Henriques, but the best known is the Madeira Wine Company, an amalgam of historic firms including Blandy, Cossart Gordon, Leacock, Miles and Rutherford. It is now controlled by the Symington family, owners of Port shippers Dow, Graham and Warre, who are in partnership with the Blandy family on the island. Barbeito, HM Borges, Justino Henriques, Henriques & Henriques (no relation) and Pereira d'Oliveira complete the picture, although Barros e Sousa and Silva Vinhos bottle wine to sell on the island, where there are considerable sales to passing tourists. Profiles of these and other historic firms can be found in Alex Liddell's book *Madeira*, published by Mitchell Beazley.

VQPRD Madeirense

Since 2001 a smattering of unfortified wines made on the island of Madeira have become entitled to their own official denomination. These include Atlantis rosé and white made by the Madeira Wine Company from Tinta Negra Mole and Verdelho respectively. An impressively well-equipped EU-funded winery on the north side of the island at São Vicente (Adegas de São Vicente) is producing a wide range of wines from individual growers under the Enxurros, Ponta de Tristão and Casa da Vinha labels. The latter, a Verdelho from a vineyard above Camara de Lobos, qualifies as Vinha Biologica (organically farmed). Madeira's unfortified wines are not produced entirely from the island's traditional grapes. A variety called Arnsburger has been brought from Germany (see page 92) as well as Merlot and Cabernet Sauvignon from France. The latter makes a good varietal wine at Quinta do Moledo located on the north side of the island at Arco de São Jorge. As yet these wines are not made in sufficient quantity to be exported from the island.

II. THE AZORES

Vines were planted on the Azores shortly after the islands were first colonized by the Portuguese in the mid-fifteenth century. Having built churches, they required wines with which to celebrate mass. The island of Pico quickly became the most important producer, making fortified wines from the Verdelho grape. The wines enjoyed a certain amount of success in export markets in the late nineteenth century, and following the Russian Revolution of October 1917 a number of bottles of Verdelho do Pico were found in the Tsar's cellars. The vineyards on Pico succumbed to the twin plagues of oidium and phylloxera, and Verdelho was largely abandoned in favour of more disease-resistant hybrids like Isabella. By the 1920s winemaking was largely confined to the island of São Miguel where, according to António Maria Oliveira Bello, the best site was Caloura on the south of the island, which produced red wines reaching 12 per cent alcohol by volume. He records the undistinguished Diagalves as being one of the principal grape varieties. During the 1990s a concerted attempt was made to improve the vineyards in the Azores. Hybrids and direct producers were uprooted and replaced largely by Verdelho, Terrantez, Arinto, Boal and Fernão Pires. Among 330 growers, over 150 hectares were replanted and in 1994 the IPRs of Pico, Biscoitos and Graciosa were created as a result. Of the three, Pico is much the most impressive to visit. The island rises out of the Atlantic to a height of over 2,300 metres (7,544 feet) making this the highest point anywhere in Portugal. The vineyards are close to sea level and divided into tiny square plots by dry stone walls built from the underlying volcanic stone. The chequerboard of vineyards outside the town of Madelena has deservedly become a World Heritage Site. Most of the wine is made by the local cooperative which continues to produce a traditional Verdelho-based fortified aperitif wine named Lajido. The other wines from this somewhat primitive winery are Basalto, Terras de Lava and Cavaco. Although they deserve to be commended for effort, having spent some time on Pico I still recommend drinking wines from the mainland as an alternative.

On the island of Terceira, the parish of Biscoitos ("biscuits") on the north side produces both fortified and unfortified wines. There is a cooperative and a single private producer, the Casa Agricola Brum. With a fascinating museum of wine, this small family run company continues to make some good, traditional fortified wines from Verdleho under the Brum and Chico Maria labels. A third island, Graciosa, produces light dry wine from Arinto, Verdelho, Boal and Terrantez growing in Santa Cruz, Guadalupe, Praia and Luz. There is a single cooperative at Santa Cruz.

7

The Rosé Wines of Portugal

1942: most of the world's nations are deeply embroiled in the Second World War. Northern Europe, the Mediterranean, the Balkans, the Middle East, the Near East, the Far East, North Africa and East Africa are in turmoil. Portugal stays out. Lisbon is a hotbed of intrigue and espionage, but Oporto remains a quiet backwater severed from the outside world by lack of trade. It was during this, one of the darkest moments in the war, that thirty friends and colleagues gathered together to launch a new wine company: the Sociedade Comércial dos Vinhos de Mesa de Portugal.

This might seem like an inauspicious time to launch a new venture, but in retrospect it proved to be highly astute. Shipments of Port wine had sunk to an all-time low, leaving a huge surplus of grapes in the Douro. The cooperative at Vila Real had been abandoned and so, with little or no technical expertise but a great deal of enthusiasm, the new company hired it to make their first wines. There was a red wine named Vila Real and a white called Cambriz after the nearby locality of Cambres. They were shipped in large volumes to Brazil and, for the first few years of its existence, the business prospered. Various attempts were made to produce a rosé, but the wine ended up being poured down the drain. Eventually, with the help of a French winemaker nicknamed "Le Petit de Gaulle", the partners hit on the right formula and went in search of a name. Not far from the winery at Vila Real was a baroque palace with a good name and an eye-catching appearance. The property belonged to the Duke of Mangualde and in exchange for the use of the property on the label, the partners offered either a commission of fifty centavos (half an escudo) per bottle or a one-off sum. The hapless duke finally settled for a one-off payment and a contract whereby they bought grapes from

The Palace of Mateus near Vila Real

the estate at a thirty per cent premium. The new rosé was christened Mateus.

It is all too easy to be dismissive about Portuguese rosé, but like Italy's Lambrusco, Germany's Liebfraumilch and now Aussie Chardonnay, it broke the mould and became a huge success. After a hesitant start (see the Sogrape story on page 303), sales of Mateus grew strongly in the 1960s and 1970s on the back of some very proactive marketing. In northern Europe and North America this was the dawn of the "bistro" and the distinctive Portuguese bottle matched the mood. Empty flagons of Mateus became candle holders and table lamps as millions of consumers enjoyed a glass of wine for the first time. Mateus became an icon. The world has since moved on from the bistro to the wine bar, but sales of rosé, having peaked in the early 1980s, remain strong. *The Instituto da Vinha e do Vinho* (IVV) does not disaggregate sales of rosé from those of red, but well over twenty million litres are still exported each year. Sales of Mateus alone account for two million cases, and other brands like Lancers from José Maria da Fonseca, Trovador from Borges and a multitude of supermarket own-label wines make up the rest.

It is ironic that the Portuguese have never taken to rosé. Unlike the Spanish, who consume dry, fruity *rosados* with gusto countrywide, pink wines in Portugal have never appealed to the local market. Most domestic sales of Mateus and Lancers are to foreign tourists either on holiday in the Algarve or visiting the towns along the frontier with Spain, where bottles of Mateus are piled high alongside cheap textiles and tasteless ornaments. The wines themselves could come from just about anywhere and from almost any red grape, but two production hubs have evolved. The Douro is no longer in a position to supply the volume of grapes required for Mateus, but some rosé is still produced in the cooperatives of Trás-os-Montes. Most Mateus now originates from the central Beiras region, particularly Bairrada, where the Baga grape seems to have suitable colour and acidity. When the need arises, Estremadura has helped to augment supply. The second main hub is on the Setúbal Peninsula, where the chameleon-like Castelão provides the basis for Lancers and a number of supermarket rosés.

In spite of their image, Portuguese rosés are anything but standardized. Although, with the notable exception of Lancers, they may appear in much the same flagon-shaped bottles, the wines have often been tweaked according to the local preference. The amount of both sugar and fizz can vary from country to country in response to market research. Making wine on this scale is in itself a challenge, but the quality-control procedures at Sogrape's Anadia plant in Bairrada are second to none. In late September there is a huge but well-organized crush (forgive the unintended pun) as over 3,000 growers deliver their grapes to the winery. Just half an hour's skin contact between the crusher and the press is sufficient time for the must to develop its pale salmon-pink colour. However, in order to ensure that the wine reaches the market in the freshest condition possible, the must is kept cool under sulphur dioxide until it is required. Vinification takes place continuously over the following nine months, usually until the June after the vintage. In the case of Mateus, most of the wine is fermented completely dry but a proportion is vinified to retain 60 grams/litre of residual sugar. These two components are blended to produce a wine with 15 grams/litre of residual sugar overall, significantly drier than it was in the 1970s and 1980s. Alcohol levels are naturally low, at around 10.5 per cent by volume. Carbon dioxide is injected into the wine before bottling, with 3 grams/litre for the US market and 2.5 grams/litre for Europe.

The other main producers of rosé make their wine along similar lines, the only major departure being that José Maria da Fonseca uses its continuous fermentation plant (see page 307) to put the sparkle into Lancers. But there is still a depressing quantity of unpleasantly sulphurous, confected wine that does nothing for the image of Portuguese rosé, or indeed rosé wine in general. The best of the genre should be fresh, clean and spritzy but neutral in taste, with crisp acidity to offset the slight residual sweetness: good "pop" wine in short. There are also one or two more serious Portuguese rosés, often the result of *saignée*, with more body and depth of flavour. These are listed alongside the main producers of rosé below. Those marked with an asterisk (*) form part of the local *Rota do Vinho* and are open to receive passing visitors.

Producers

BORGES
Sociedade dos Vinhos Borges SA, Rua Infante Dom Henrique, 421, 4435 Rio Tinto

Borges produces a rosé called Trovador, mostly from grapes growing on the *altos* around Vila Real and Trás-os-Montes. This light, medium-sweet rosé has long been bottled in a flagon but, in the quest for twenty-first-century sophistication, is now repackaged in a Bordeaux-shaped bottle.

JOSÉ MARIA DA FONSECA*
Vila Nogueira de Azeitão, 2925 Azeitão

A wine named Faisca predated Mateus by five years and, although it never really caught on, deserves the accolade of being the first of the popular rosés. Launched in 1937, Faisca was marketed exclusively in Portugal, but was followed in 1944 by the more international Lancers brand. This was very much an American creation, the brainchild of Armenian-born Henry Behr who visited the Fonseca winery at Azeitão in 1943. Behr's idea was to create a light rosé in a distinctive package to be marketed through his own US-based company Vintage Wines. The wine took its name from Behr's favourite painting, *Las Lanzas* by Velasquez, and its terracotta crock bottle was inspired by traditional Portuguese ceramics. Sales of Lancers began slowly, but in the late 1950s they took off, enabling Fonseca to launch new brands like Dão Terras Altas and Pasmados on the domestic market. With sales in the 1960s of over a million cases a year,

Lancers became too big for the family-run Fonseca and a new company was formed. Initially this was a joint venture between Heublein (which had taken over Vintage Wines from Behr) and José Maria da Fonseca named, somewhat confusingly, JM da Fonseca Internacional. A new plant was built a short distance away at Azeitão, including a paint factory merely to imitate the terracotta crock, which by now was being made of glass. In 1985 the Soares Franco brothers sold their remaining shares to Heublein, only to buy the entire company back from IDV eleven years later. Such is the revolving door among multinationals.

Lancers has diversified from rosé to include (briefly) a Vinho Verde and, more recently, a sparkling wine made by the so-called Russian Continuous Method (see page 307). This contraption is also used to put the fizz into Lancers rosé, a medium-sweet rosé made predominantly from the Castelão grape growing on the Setúbal Peninsula and in Estremadura. Lancers continues to maintain a strong presence in both Italy and the United States, although it is rarely seen in the United Kingdom. José Maria da Fonseca also produces an altogether more serious spicy rosé called Primum from Syrah and Tannat grapes grown in their own vineyards at Algeruz on the Setúbal Peninsula. For more information on José Maria da Fonseca and its range of wines, see pages 259–61.

MADEIRA WINE COMPANY
Rua dos Ferreiros, 191, 9000 Funchal, Madeira

Tinta Negra Mole, the principal grape on the island of Madeira, is a variety that makes light, pink-red base wines and naturally lends itself to rosé. The MWC, owners of the Blandy, Cossart Gordon, Leacock and Miles Madeira houses, have produced a light rosé named Atlantis from this grape. With rather too much residual sugar for my taste, Atlantis is a fresh, cleanly made wine for drinking well chilled on a hot day – provided it has not been kept for too long. Quantities are such that it is only available to drink on the island.

NIEPOORT
Niepoort (Vinhos) SA, Rua Infante Dom Henrique, 39, 4050 Porto

Forever experimenting with different styles of wine, Dirk Niepoort has made a truly delicious Douro rosé by employing the *saignée* technique on a vat or two of Redoma (see page 213), a *lagar* destined for Vintage

Port. About sixty per cent of the Redoma rosé is made this way, by "bleeding" the must and continuing to ferment off the skins, whereas the remainder comes from early picked Tinta Amarela from Niepoort's Quinta de Napoles midway between Pinhão and Régua. Part barrel fermented and aged in new oak for three to six months, the resulting wine is wonderfully full-bodied and spicy, with 13.5 degrees of alcohol offset by crisp acidity. Far removed from the relatively insipid "pop" wines, Redoma rosé compares very favourably with well-made rosés from Provence or the southern Rhône, but has a distinctive Douro flavour of its own.

SOGRAPE
Sogrape Vinhos de Portugal SA, Apartado 3032, Aldeia Nova, 4431, Avintes
An old Portuguese water flask or *cantil* from the First World War lies on the side at Quinta de Azevedo near Barcelos. Fernando Guedes, son of the founder of Sogrape and current president, picks it up and points out that "this is the inspiration for Mateus". The beginning of the Sogrape story is told earlier in this chapter, but the sequel is equally interesting and has been hugely influential in the subsequent history of Portuguese wines. Of the thirty partners who set up the company in 1942 one, Fernando Van Zeller Guedes, emerged as the leader. The company fell on hard times after the collapse of the Brazilian market shortly after the Second World War, and for nearly five years Mateus Rosé languished unloved and in search of a market. Then, in 1950, Guedes awoke to the fact that the British were emerging from their post-war malaise and finally taking to wine. Against all the odds, he put the wine on the market by making friends with key wine-trade contacts in the UK. "Make a friend before doing business" was (and remains) the unofficial family motto.

Not much Mateus was sold until the late 1950s, but in 1960 it took off, capturing the imagination of a new generation of British wine drinkers. There were no sophisticated marketing techniques at the time, but the wine was initally pitched up-market and targeted at women. It received a glowing write-up in *The Times* and Princess Margaret was rumoured to have enjoyed Mateus Rosé while dining at the Savoy. In order to satisfy the increasing demand, Sogrape built a new winery at Vila Real in 1963, but Mateus continued to be hand bottled in an old convent near the waterfront in Oporto. At the time there were no bottling lines available that could handle the peculiar Mateus flagon. Labour was cheap and until a state-of-the-art bottling plant was built at Avintes near Vila Nova de Gaia in 1967, the wine was bottled by an army of 750 people.

Mateus continued to grow through the late 1960s and 1970s, by which time there was no longer sufficient raw material in the Douro to supply the brand. In 1975, at the height of the revolution, Sogrape built a new winery at Anadia in Bairrada. Quality improved and sales continued to increase, peaking in 1983 when three million cases were shared annually between 125 markets worldwide. The founder of Sogrape and father of Mateus, Fernando Van Zeller Guedes, died the following year. A red wine, Mateus Signature, has been created in his honour.

In spite of the acquisition of Vinicola do Vale do Dão in 1957, Mateus Rosé still represented ninety-five per cent of Sogrape's sales in the mid-1980s. With the fashion for rosé beginning to wane, Sogrape decided to diversify, buying both the Ferreira and Offley Port houses and making investments in Vinho Verde, Dão and the Alentejo. Among the new wines is a good dry rosé from Bairrada called Nobilis, which is made from the best grapes delivered to the plant at Anadia. In 1997 Sogrape made its first foray outside Portugal, buying Finca Flichman, an estate in Argentina with over 400 hectares of vineyard. Within half a century Sogrape has grown into Portugal's largest winemaker and the only Portuguese-owned "multinational" in the sector. Mateus has recently been given a thorough makeover, the first since 1942. The style of the wine has evolved with the market, which, with sales still hovering around 16 million litres a year, is the secret of its continuing success. Technologically, the wine is superb. Although sales have fallen dramatically in the USA, Mateus Rosé is still deceptively strong in the UK, Italy and Denmark and has seen significant growth in Spain, Belgium, Japan and Australia. Altogether Mateus Rosé is exported to 130 countries. It is a sobering thought that this global brand was inspired by one of the darkest moments of the Second World War and by a First World War *cantil*.

8

The Sparkling Wines of Portugal

Portuguese sparkling wines are hampered by their lack of a generic image. There are no denominations like Champagne, Cava or Crémant to identify with, merely the all-embracing term *espumante*, which simply means "sparkling wine". There is, however, a century or more of history behind Portuguese sparkling wine, which began with an attempt to overcome the crisis affecting the wine industry in the 1880s. With phylloxera overcome, Portuguese wines were no longer in such demand in France. Bairrada suffered particularly badly and the government did everything in its power to stimulate the production of a more international style of wine. An Act was passed in May 1889 that granted an award to vine growers individually or collectively producing "whose style meets the standards required by foreign markets". Although this Act did not mention sparkling wine specifically, it provided the impetus for Portuguese producers to contact foreign winemakers. Experiments took place in Bairrada and Lamego (on the southern edge of the Douro), whose wines had been identified as a potential base for *espumante* at the Berlin Exhibition of 1888. A number of Frenchmen came to Portugal to advise, among them Leopold Menneson, Alfred le Cocq and Lucien Beysecker, whose company, Caves Lucien Beysecker, subsequently became one of the largest producers of *espumante* in the country. Bairrada and Lamego naturally became the focus for the new sparkling wine industry, partly no doubt because the underlying bedrock was suitable for excavating huge underground cellars or *caves*. In 1893 the Associação dos Viticultores de Bairrada (AVB) began producing three styles of Champanhe Portuguez: Supra, Excelsior and Secco. Huge amounts of money were spent on bringing the correct yeasts and equipment from Champagne, and the AVB went bankrupt within ten years. In the meantime, having visited Champagne, José Teixeira Rebello Junior founded Caves Raposeira at Lamego in 1898 and built a network of tunnels into the hillside below the pilgrimage destination of Nossa Senhora de Remédios ("Our Lady of Remedies"). He also planted French grape varieties at nearby Quinta da Recheca and marketed a wine known as Champanhe de Lamego.

Espumante found an enthusiastic market in Portugal during the early years of the twentieth century, and the 1920s saw a huge expansion in the number of *caves* producing both still and sparkling wine. Much was artificially carbonated (*espumoso*), but both Caves Raposeira and Caves Justino Sampaio Alegre (subsequently Caves Monte Crasto) continued making wine by what was then the "Champagne method" and is now the "Traditional method". But the industry developed without any direction or control. It escaped the first wave of demarcations in the 1900s, which meant that grapes from anywhere in the country could be made into base wine for sparkling wine. Although Bairrada's Maria Gomes, Bical and Cerceal are less than ideal, they are considerably better than some of the oxidized base wines that were subsequently brought in from cooperatives in the Beira Alta. Acidity was also frequently overlooked and too much *espumante* was unable to withstand the period of yeast autolysis in bottle and emerged tasting tired and dull.

Despite strong competition from Spain, France and Italy, *espumante* has undergone something of a revival in recent years. Lamego and Bairrada are still the main production centres, but small quantities of wine have been emerging from Vinhos Verde, Douro, Dão, Bucelas, Ribatejo and even the Alentejo. There is no doubt potential for traditional-method sparkling wine, mainly in the mountains of northern Portugal, where acidity is not a commodity in short supply. It is difficult as yet to identify the best grapes for *espumante* (other than the small quantity of Chardonnay and Pinot Noir planted on the hills behind Lamego), as many of the vineyards are still interplanted with dozens of different varieties. However, the potential in the north of Portugal was recognized by Californian sparkling-wine producer Schramsberg, who made a significant investment in the Douro (see below). Elsewhere, early picked Castelão makes a clean, suitably acidic base wine for Lancers *espumante* made by the Russian Continuous Method (explained in the entry on José Maria da Fonseca below). It is either in spite or because of this diversity that the authorities have never come up with a specific denomination for *espumante*. In the 1930s there was a strategy to adopt the designation Lusagne in Bairrada, but it came to nothing. A number of newer DOCs, notably Bairrada, Tavora-Varosa and Palmela, define *espumante* for those producers who want to identify the region of origin on the label. But few seem to be committed, and Portuguese sparkling wines have neither image nor presence on export markets, despite one or two valiant attempts at making a good, internationally acceptable style of wine.

Producers
Entries marked with an asterisk (*) form part of the *Rota do Vinho* (Wine Route) in their respective regions and are open to passing visitors.

CAVES ALIANÇA*
Caves Aliança SA, Apartado 6, 3781 Sangalhos

Aliança is now the leading producer of sparkling wine in the Bairrada region, having invested heavily in new technology. With four kilometres of cellars below its winery at Sangalhos, Aliança produces a number of good, clean traditional-method sparkling wines, mostly from the local Maria Gomes and Bical grapes, although there is also a varietal Chardonnay. Aliança has also been helping Herdade do Esporão with its *espumante* made from grapes grown in the Alentejo.

JOSÉ MARIA DA FONSECA*
Vila Nogueira de Azeitão, 2925 Azeitão

The name Lancers, well known as a brand of rosé, has also been applied to a sparkling wine. The company developed a new plant at Azeitão on the Setúbal Peninsula and, instead of using the labour-intensive, time-consuming "traditional method", opted for a system that was invented in the Soviet Union in 1940 and has been used in eastern Europe ever since. It was patented in the west by the German Seitz Enzinger Noll, who brought the so-called Russian Continuous Method to Portugal in the late 1980s.

A dry *blanc de noirs* base wine with 10 degrees of alcohol is made by cool fermentation from early picked Castelão. It is fined with charcoal to remove any trace of colour. After being stabilized for tartrates and sterile filtered, the wine is introduced to a series of eight pressurized stainless-steel tanks. Having been inoculated with active yeast and a dose of sweet liqueur wine to take it to 24 grams/litre of residual sugar, the wine's secondary fermentation takes place under a pressure of 5 kilograms/cm^2 (1.7 pounds per square inch) at temperatures between 12°C and 15°C. After about nine days only 5 grams of sugar remain and the now sparkling wine is cooled to around 10°C when it moves to the "bio-reactor" tanks. These used to be packed with sterile wood shavings but have now been replaced by stainless steel filters. As the wine passes through the filters, they catch the sediment produced by the fermentation as well as serving to increase the surface area in which the yeast cells are in contact with the wine. This steady autolysis is supposed to contribute some of the toasty, biscuit-like complexity that results from extended yeast contact prior to *remuage* in the "traditional method" but which is not obtained from other bulk processes like *Charmat* or *cuve close*. The wood shavings also filter the wine, so that as it leaves the bio-reactor tanks the yeast cell count is practically nil. The temperature of the wine is reduced again, to −2°C or −3°C. This serves to lower the pressure in the system, thus aiding the combination of carbon dioxide with the wine. Finally the wine flows into a reservoir tank where it is adjusted with *liqueur de expedition*. If necessary, levels of sulphur dioxide can be adjusted at this stage and the amount of carbon dioxide be reduced if it has reached an excess. Before bottling, the wine is filtered through a sterile membrane to remove any stray yeasts or bacteria.

From the time the base wine enters the system to its emergence at the other end takes just twenty-one days. Apart from the necessity for occasional maintenance, the process never needs to stop. At José Maria da Fonseca it functions twenty-four hours a day, seven days a week, producing around fifty litres of *espumante* an hour with very little labour. It goes without saying that the "continuous method" is a very much quicker and cheaper way of making sparkling wine than the so-called "traditional method" used for Champagne, Cava, Saumur and much sparkling wine worldwide. Lancers Metodo Continuo Espumante is naturally some way from imitating Champagne but, made from a clean, sound base wine, it is a fresh, crisp, slightly yeasty fizz with a good, reasonably persistent sparkle. The system is also used to put the spritz into Lancers Rosé. For more information on this and José Maria da Fonseca, see pages 259 and 301.

JP VINHOS*

Correspondence Address: JP Vinhos SA, Vila Nogueira de Azeitão, 2925 Azeitão

In one of his more extravagant moments, António d'Avillez, former owner of JP Vinhos, bought the grandiose Quinta dos Loridos near Bombarral in Estremadura. The sixteenth-century mansion accommodates up to nineteen people and can now be rented for holiday accommodation. Grapes from the surrounding vineyards go into making two different sparkling wines by the traditional method. The Castelão grape produces a fresh-flavoured *branco de tinto* blended with a small quantity of white Fernão Pires in the final *cuvée*. Chardonnay, fifty per cent of which is barrel fermented, makes an altogether softer, toasty *branco de branco*. Both wines are shipped without *dosage*.

MURGANHEIRA*

Sociedade Agricola e Comercial do Varosa SA, Abadia Velha, Ucanha, 2610 Tarouca

The village of Ucanha above Lamego is famous for its picturesque fortified bridge but not, as one road sign claims, for "the best *espumante* in the world". It is, however, the home of Caves Murganheira, a family-owned business established in 1946 which produces Portugal's most popular sparkling wine. With forty-seven hectares of its own vineyard, Murganheira also sources grapes from local growers in Tavora/Varosa (see page 224), mostly Malvasia Fina, Cerceal and Gouveio Real, although there is also some Chardonnay and Pinot Noir. The region is at an altitude of between 500 and 800 metres (1,640 and 2,624 feet) and therefore produces light base wines (averaging eleven per cent alcohol by volume) with high natural acidity (9 plus grams/litre expressed as tartaric). The company, which claims the first pneumatic press in Portugal, separates the first and second pressings for Bruto ("brut") and Meio Seco ("medium dry") *espumante* respectively. Where possible, grapes are fermented by variety and Murganheira produces a range of varietal sparkling wines. Of these, Malvasia Fina seems to be the most complex and aromatic, but there are some intriguing wines made from red Port grapes, namely Tinta Roriz, Touriga Nacional and Tinta Barroca. Murganheira's best-selling wine is a soft, straightforward Bruto, released with about three years of age, but there is a Grande Reserva with about ten years of age that combines biscuit-like complexity with a surprising amount of freshness.

Remuage and *dégorgement* are still performed entirely by hand. The company maintains a stock of around 2.5 million bottles in impressive cellars hollowed from the schist and granite; these are open to passing visitors.

RAPOSEIRA
Caves da Raposeira, 5101 Lamego

Raposeira means "fox's earth", but the hillside above Lamego is now a labyrinth of man-made cellars. Portugal's oldest producer of sparkling wine buys in grapes from hundreds of small growers on the high land between Lamego, Tarouca and Castro Daire, but also has vineyards of its own. Quinta do Valprado and Quinta da Recheca are located just outside the Douro demarcation and have been planted with Chardonnay, Pinot Noir and Pinot Blanc. Raposeira uses these grapes in conjunction with local varieties, mainly Malvasia Fina, Gouveio, Cerceal and Síria, to make *espumante*. There are four wines: a young Reserva bottled both as Bruto and Seco and a more complex Super Reserva, made mainly from Chardonnay, Pinot Noir and Pinot Blanc, that spends two years on its lees before disgorgement and dosage. There is also a small quantity of delicate, fruity rosé made from Pinot Noir. Until 1980 Raposeira belonged to Macieira, which was subsequently taken over by Seagram (alongside Sandeman). In 2002 Raposeira was sold to Murganheira (see above).

VERTICE
Caves Trásmontanas Lda, Av 25 de Abril, 15, 5070 Alijó

Vertice is the product of a troubled joint venture with Schramsberg, producers of some of the Napa Valley's most prestigious sparkling wines. Produced from native grapes grown on the high northern margins of the Douro, which yield a cleanly-made base wine, Vertice has emerged as Portugal's best and most reliable sparkling wine, balancing biscuit-like flavours from yeast autolysis with crisp natural acidity.

OTHER PRODUCERS OF ESPUMANTE
Quinta das Bageiras (Bairrada), Mario Sergio Alves Nuno, Fogueira, 3780 Anadia
Borges-Fita Azul, Rua Infante Dom Henrique, 421, Apartado 18, 4439 Rio Tinto
Quinta do Casal Branco (Ribatejo), Sofia Braamcamp Sobral Lobo de Vasconcellos,

2080 Almeirim

Herdade do Esporão (Alentejo), Finagra SA, 7200 Reguengos de Monsaraz

Goncalves Faria (Bairrada)

Caves Messias (Bairrada), Soc Agricola e Comércial dos Vinhos Messias SA, Rua Commendador Messias Baptista, 56, Apartado 1, 3050 Mealhada

Caves da Montanha (Bairrada)

Caves Neto Costa (Bairrada), 3780 Anadia

Luís Pato (Bairrada), Óis de Bairro, 3780 Anadia

Caves Primavera (Bairrada), Caves Primavera Lda, Rua das Caves, Agueda de Baixo, 3750 Agueda

Quinta da Romeira (Bucelas), Companhia das Quintas, 2670 Bucelas

Quinta dos Roques (Dão), Quinta dos Roques, Viticultura e Agro Pecuaria Lda, Rua da Paz, Abrunhosa do Mato, 3530 Mangualde

Caves São Domingos (Bairrada)

Caves São João (Bairrada), Soc dos Vinhos Irmãos Unidos Lda, São João de Anadia, 3780 Anadia

Tapada do Chaves (Alentejo), Tapada do Chaves, Sociedade Agricola e Commercial SA, Frangoneiro, 7300 Portalegre

Caves Valdarcos (Bairrada), Malaposta, 3780 Anadia

Caves Velhas (Bucelas), Rua Professor Egas Moniz, 2670 Bucelas

9

Cork

The cork oak, *Quercus suber*, shapes the landscape in much of southern Portugal. There are 725,000 hectares in total, nearly three times the space devoted to vineyard, making Portugal the world's largest supplier of cork, with over fifty per cent of the market. Cork is intimately linked to wine. It has been so since Roman times, when cork stoppers were used to seal amphorae, and although there are hundreds of other applications, wine is the main reason for the continued existence of the vast cork forests that cover parts of the Ribatejo and Alentejo.

Cork has been going through something of a rough patch in recent years. Although the world's consumption of bottled wine continues to grow inexorably, the choice of closures has never been greater. The hotly debated incidence of so-called "corked" bottles – wines supposedly tainted by cork – has driven many supermarkets to use synthetic stoppers in place of natural cork. Portugal shoulders much of the blame for this, for there can be little doubt that standards slipped during the post-revolutionary era, when many of the *latifundia* of southern Portugal were seized and run as workers' cooperatives (see page 265). At the same time, some of the country's larger cork processors ignored the growing clamour among major wine buyers who began putting about statistics that anything up to ten per cent of the world's bottled wine was marred to some extent by faulty cork. Anyone who has opened a cherished bottle to find it tainted by an extraneous dank and musty aroma and flavour will be aware just how frustrating cork can be. But, although it is impossible to say for certain, numerous experiments cast doubt on the origin of 2,4,6-trichloroanisole (TCA), the mould identified as being responsible for cork taint. It has been conclusively proved that casks, wooden pallets and bottles may also harbour TCA as well as cork itself.

Denuded cork trees in southern Portugal

Cork, like wine, is a brilliant product of nature. It is the bark of *Quercus suber*, a tree that thrives in the poor, dry soils of the Mediterranean. But, like wine, cork is also a product that requires nurture. The bark is only stripped once every nine years (a fact that was often ignored in the post-revolutionary hangover), and the tree itself must be at least twenty-five years old before the first harvest of virgin cork. Only after the third harvest (when the tree is around forty-three years of age) is the bark considered to be of premium quality for wine. The harvest itself takes place between June and September, when the tree is growing and the bark can be removed from the trunk more easily than at other times of the year. Men with ape-like agility climb the trees and prise off huge sheets of cork bark with a specially designed axe. Removing the bark does not kill the tree: it slowly regenerates itself over a nine-year period and the cork oak lives for 170–200 years. The oldest cork tree in Portugal, the "whistler" near Águas de Moura east of Setúbal, is more than 215 years old and still yields around 100,000 wine corks every time it is stripped.

Although most cork originates in the south of Portugal, the centre of the cork-processing industry is in the north of the country, amid the chaotic muddle of overgrown villages between Espinho, Santa Maria de Feira and Vila Nova de Gaia. It was established here in the 1920s to be close to the Port wine producers. Amorim, the largest of the cork producers, has its headquarters at Moselos, near Santa Maria de Lamas ("St Mary of the mud"), although it has also built a factory in the northern Alentejo at Ponte de Sor as well as others in California and Australia. After the harvest, the planks of bark are seasoned for six months in the open air, stacked on pallets so that they are not in contact with the ground. Any cork showing yellow stain – a potential cause of taint – is immediately discarded. The planks of cork are boiled at 100°C for ninety minutes as the second stage in removing any contaminants. The bark is then left to stabilize for two or three weeks before being sorted by quality and boiled up again. Once the bark has dried, cylindrical corks are punched from the strips of bark parallel to the vertical growth of the tree. A skilled worker can punch as many as 20,000 corks in an eight-hour shift. The corks are then machine-sorted into seven or more different grades before being sterilized once more. There is a good deal of debate over this part of the process, with some producers favouring hydrogen peroxide as a bleaching agent, others preferring vacuum extraction, microwave treatment or ozone. Numerous treatments are currently being investigated. The corks are then dried in huge ovens to between six and eight per cent humidity before being sorted again, the best by hand. Finally they are branded according to the customer's requirements and given a surface coating of wax and silicone to aid extraction from the bottle.

The secret of cork's elasticity is the natural cell structure of the bark, which no synthetic alternative has yet been able to emulate. Cork is made up of a honeycomb structure of impermeable cells, about 40 million of them per cubic centimetre (656 million per cubic inch). This structure makes the cork easy to compress, so that it can be inserted into the neck of a bottle, and allows it slowly to regain its natural shape, thereby ensuring a tight seal against the glass. Cork also contains lenticels, or pores, that run across the grain of the bark. Some corks have more distinct lenticels than others (see below), but because they are punched along the grain, these lenticels should not come into contact with the wine.

The choice of cork grade by the customer is important. Producers of high-quality wines, such as classed-growth Bordeaux chateaux, are unlikely to compromise on quality and will specify first-rate corks. On the other hand, producers of mass-market wines have been downgrading to improve margins, and this has been responsible for many of the problems in recent years. The cheapest form of cork is agglomerate, formed by compressing granulated cork in a natural resin. This type of cork is not suitable for wines intended to have a life above one year, as it starts to disintegrate. It also seems to have a higher incidence of cork taint. An ingenious solution to this is where two disks of natural cork are stuck at either end so that the agglomerate does not come into contact with the wine. Champagne corks have been made in this way for many years and the so-called Twin Top (Amorim's trade mark) offers a reliable seal at a relatively low cost. Another way of upgrading the quality of natural cork is by colmation. This is the process of filling the natural pores or lenticels in a poor quality cork with a mixture of latex and cork dust to ensure an effective seal.

In common with so much of Portuguese economic activity, the cork industry has developed in a fragmented way that makes it very difficult to control. Although there are large firms like Amorim, Alvaro Coelho and the Suberus Group, much of the punching of corks is farmed out to small cottage-style operations. The European Cork Federation (C.E. Liège has drawn up a strict code of practice covering hygiene and selection at all stages of the production process, but it is virtually impossible to apply this to the smaller producers. Thankfully, as technology has improved, the incidence of cork taint seems to be decreasing, but in the meantime a large number of wine producers have switched to synthetic alternatives. Most if not all of these wines could of course be bottled with a metal screw cap, such is their shelf life, but in markets like the United Kingdom and United States, where "uncorking" a bottle of wine is still a special event, consumers seem to be firmly wedded to their corkscrews. If non-biodegradable synthetic stoppers were to take over from cork, the environmental damage would be considerable. The greatest concentration of cork forests is to be found on the Ribatejo–Alentejo borders around Coruche, Mora, Avis and Ponte de Sor, with pockets near Grandola, Alcácer de Sal and in the Algarve. Disturbed by man once every nine years, it is no coincidence that the landscape in these areas is some of the most unspoilt in Europe. Remember the cork forests of southern Portugal next time you uncork a bottle of wine.

Postscript

THE FUTURE OF THE WINES AND VINEYARDS OF PORTUGAL

Portugal has the potential to be a major international force in wine. Both Port and Madeira are already well established but, with the exception of two brands of effervescent rosé, wines from other areas of the country are taking longer to make an impact on world markets. Despite the vagaries of the climate, Portugal undoubtedly has the physical conditions to produce great wine. Matching the wealth of indigenous grape varieties to different *terroirs* presents countless opportunities for motivated producers who seek to develop new and exciting flavours.

Much has already been achieved, especially in the wineries where investment backed by the EU has transformed the style and character of many wines between one vintage and the next. Although this has brought Portugal closer to the demanding markets of northern Europe and North America, it is not yet close enough. Portugal's vineyards are still its weakest link: great wine is not possible without first having good grapes. Naturally, it takes longer to transform a vineyard than a winery. A minimum of five or six growing seasons has to elapse between replanting a vineyard and producing a commercial crop of quality grapes. But the transformation of Portugal's vineyards is proving to be painfully slow. It is hampered in the north of the country by the extreme fragmentation of the holdings where weekend farmers have little or no incentive to maximize quality. Sadly, it is in regions like Dão, the interior of the Beiras and Trás-os-Montes that many of Portugal's finest *terroirs* have either been lost or totally ignored. Fortunately, a handful of quintas provide a glimmer of potential greatness.

The countryside south of the Tagus presents different opportunities and it is here that a real transformation is starting to take place. Although (with certain very localized exceptions) climatic limitations conspire against making truly great wine, the size of holdings means that the economies of scale that are lacking throughout much of the north can be achieved in the south. If Portugal is to meet the challenge of the New World head on, it is regions like the Ribatejo, Alentejo and Setúbal Peninsula that show the greatest promise; however they are still desperately short of commercially minded yet discriminating viticulturalists. By tapping into the warm maritime climate, Portugal could easily deliver the broad, ripe flavours that are increasingly provided by countries like Australia, Argentina, Chile and South Africa.

This does not mean to say that growers should turn their backs on Portugal's native grapes and plant Cabernet and Chardonnay wholesale. Quite the reverse. Neither does it mean that the authorities who demarcate and delimit Portugal's wine regions should exclude international varieties in a way that sometimes appears almost xenophobic. It means years more trial, and sometimes error, to find varieties and blends that are site-specific and satisfy demand. Unless growers and winemakers embark fairly rapidly and with rather more gusto on this course of action, Portugal runs the risk of being upstaged by other countries who adopt indigenous Portuguese grape varieties to their own advantage. There are enterprising producers in Australia, California, South Africa, South America, and even neighbouring Spain who are looking closely at Portuguese varietals.

Returning to the winery, Portugal is still hampered by a lack of skilled, motivated winemakers with an international perspective. It struck me while researching and writing this book how many regions are dominated by just one or two talented and enterprising individuals. Anselmo Rodrigues in Vinho Verde, Rui Moura Alves in Bairrada, Virgilio Loureiro in Dão, David Baverstock in the Douro and Alentejo and João Portugal Ramos, José Nieva, Peter Bright and Rui Reguinga in southern Portugal have all made their mark to the extent that winemaking in some places has become almost formulaic. Wine is developing into a fashion victim – even in conservative Portugal – and although the current fixation with varietal wines increases awareness of indigenous grapes, it does so at the expense of time-honoured blends. Likewise, the use of new oak, which is relatively recent in Portugal, should not be seen (as it is by some) as a panacea. Tradition, technique and technology have yet to find equilibrium if Portugal is to make the most of its manifold grape varieties and individual *terroirs*.

Given these difficulties, which will be Portugal's leading wine region in twenty years' time? The Douro, with centuries of exposure to world markets, will continue to prosper with its unfortified wines gaining greatly in importance, hopefully not at the expense of Port. With the recent exit of two multinationals from the Port trade, family firms will be in control, leading to greater responsiveness and diversity than ever before. But the Douro is probably one of the most expensive wine region in the world to cultivate and there can be little future for the regions as a producer of bottom-dollar Port. Dão, with its undoubted potential, will develop piecemeal, but should prove once more that it is among Portugal's finest wine producing regions, and is truly world class. Provided the expansion of Lisbon does not continue unabated, the area around Alenquer in Estremadura should be making small but significant quantities of fine red and white wine. The Ribatejo, a region that has been drowning in anonymity for decades, will be competing with the Alentejo as one of Portugal's best-known wine regions, turning out commercial volumes of ripe-flavoured fruit. As long as the Alentejo exercises self-control, especially with regard to irrigation, it too will be producing increasing volumes of appealing, balanced reds with one or two enclaves perhaps achieving greatness. Madeira, saved from the prospect of near-extinction by the involvement of the Symingtons in the late 1980s, deserves to recover its stature as one of the world's great fortified wines. With some interesting marketing initiatives underway, Madeira's prospects currently look better than they have for a generation. It is apparent in this book that there are still many obstacles to be overcome but the start of the twenty-first century could be a renaissance for the wines and vineyards of Portugal.

Glossary of Portuguese terms

abafado (as in vinho abafado). a general term for a fortified wine where the fermentation has been arrested by the addition of *águardente* (qv), leaving residual sugar. From *abafar*, meaning to choke, smother or stifle.

adega. winery.

adega cooperativa. cooperative winery.

água pé (literally "foot water"). the name of a local drink made by adding water to *bagaço* (qv) which is then trodden and fermented for a second time.

águardente. brandy. It is also the name of the white grape spirit (77 per cent alcohol by volume) used to fortify Port.

almude. a liquid measure determined by the quantity of Port a man might reasonably be able to carry on his head: 25.44 litres. Twenty-one *almudes* make up a *pipa* (qv) or pipe.

aloirado. the Portuguese expression for "Tawny" (from the words *loira* and *loura* meaning "blonde" or "fair").

altos. colloquial name for the high plateau north and south of the Douro valley.

armazém (plural *armazens*). warehouse, store or wine lodge.

artistas. skilled employees on a *quinta* (qv).

azenha. the building on a *quinta* (qv) that houses the olive press.

azulejos. panels of decorative tiles, so called because they are traditionally blue (*azul*) and white.

bacalhau. dried salt cod, a staple dish in the Douro and throughout Portugal.

baga. elderberry.

bagaço. skins, stalks and pips left over after fermentation and pressing.

bagaceira. marc distilled from the *bagaço* (qv).

baixo. low or lower, as in Baixo Alentejo, "Lower Alentejo".

balão (plural *balões*). literally "balloon", large concrete storage vessel for wine, commonly seen outside cooperative wineries. Also known colloquially as *mamas* or *ginas* (after Gina Lollobrigida) because of their distinctive shape.

balseiro. large upstanding wooden vat used for storing and maturing wine prior to bottling.

barco rabelo. traditional Douro boat

used for bringing Port downstream.

bica aberta. fermentation off the skins.

branco. white (as in *vinho branco*, "white wine").

cadastro. register of vineyards.

câmara. town council or municipality.

canada. liquid measure (2.12 litres) for Port wine that has now fallen from regular use. There are 252 *canadas* in a *pipa* or pipe (q.v) and twelve *canadas* in an *almude* (qv).

casal. the couple who manage a *quinta* (see also *caseiro*).

caseiro. the farmer-manager of a *quinta* who lives permanently on the property.

casta. grape variety.

cepa. an individual vine (see also *pé*).

cesto da vindima. the traditional baskets used to carry grapes during vintage; sometimes referred to as a *gigo*.

cima. top or upper (as in Cima Corgo, "Upper Corgo").

colagem. fining to clarify wine with potentially unstable material remaining in solution.

colheita. literally "harvest", it also signifies a style of Port (see page 197).

concelho. municipal district.

conto. one thousand escudos.

corte. literally "cut", it signifies the first stage in the treading of a *lagar* (qv).

cortica. cork (the material rather than the stopper; see *rolha*).

cuba. vat (as in *cuba de inox*, "stainless-steel vat", or *cuba de cimento*, "cement vat").

doce. sweet (see also *lagrima*).

dorna. a large steel hopper with a capacity of up to 1,000 kilograms (about one ton) of grapes.

encarregado. the foreman on a *quinta* (qv).

encosta. bank or slope.

engaço. stalks, stems.

escolha. choice, selection.

estufagem. the heating process used in Madeira to advance ageing; from the word *estufa*, "stove" or "greenhouse".

freguesia. parish.

garrafeira. A red wine from an exceptional year that has been matured in cask or vat for at least two years prior to bottling, followed by a further year in bottle before release. White *garrafeiras*, which are now fairly uncommon, must age for at least six months in cask or vat followed by a further six months in bottle before release. Both red and white *garrafeiras* must have an alcoholic strength at least 0.5 per cent above the legal minimum.

generoso. literally "generous"; also means fortified, as in *vinho generoso*, "fortified wine".

geropiga (or *jeropiga*). grape must that is prevented from fermenting by the addition of *águardente* (qv). Sometimes used in the blending of fortified wines.

gigo. see *cesto da vindima*.

granel. bulk (as in *vinho de granel*, bulk wine).

grau. degree of temperature, sugar or alcohol.

herdade. a large farm, estate or property.

inox. the colloquial word for stainless steel (from *aco inoxidavel*).

jeropiga. see *geropiga*.

lagar. stone (or cement) tank for treading and fermenting grapes.

lagrima. literally "tears"; depending on the context, *lagrima* signifies free-run grape juice or a very sweet, unctuous White Port.

latifundio. a large estate in the south of Portugal.

leve. light (as in the category of White Port known as *leve seco*, "light dry").

lote. a "lot" or parcel of wine.

macaco. literally "monkey"; also denotes the spiked plungers that are used to keep the floating *manta* (qv) in contact with the fermenting *mosto* (qv).

manta. literally "blanket"; in the context of vinification it means the "cap" of grape skins and stalks that floats to the surface during fermentation.

minifundio. a smallholding.

miradouro. a vantage point to admire the view.

monte. a farmhouse in the Alentejo.

mortórios. literally "mortuaries"; also used to describe the Douro terraces abandoned during the phylloxera epidemic of the 1870s and 1880s.

mosto. grape juice, must.

obras. works or alterations. The word has entered the Anglo-Portuguese lexicon because of the seemingly perpetual *obras* and the disruption that they cause!

patamar. vineyard terrace without a retaining wall.

patrão (plural *patrões*). the owner of a *quinta* – the boss!

pé. literally "foot"; often used to refer to an individual vine or *cepa* (qv). *Pisa a pé* means to tread by foot.

pipe. see *pipa*.

pipa. a "pipe" or cask used for ageing wine. A *pipa* is also a unit of measurement that varies according to where it is used. eg a *pipa* equals 550 litres in the Douro (NB: this is the figure used in the text conversions), 620 litres in Vila Nova de Gaia and 534.24 litres for export purposes.

planalto. the high plains in northern Portugal.

poda. pruning.

prensa. press (as in *vinho da prensa*, "press wine").

prova. tasting.

quinta. farm, estate or landed property.

ramada. overhead pergola system used for training vines in the Vinho Verde and Lafões regions and for table grapes or decorative purposes elsewhere.

rei. literally "king"; also a common unit of currency in the seventeenth and eighteenth centuries, representing a thousandth of an escudo. One *milrei* therefore equals one escudo.

remontagem. the process of pumping over the must during fermentation to extract colour and flavour from the skins of red grapes in order to produce red wine.

ribeiro, *ribeira*. a small river.

rio. a river.

roga. the gang of pickers who work on a Douro *quinta* (qv) for the duration of the vintage.

rogador. the leader of the gang of pickers, who acts as drill sergeant whilst treading a *lagar* (qv).

rolha. a cork.

rota do vinho. a signed wine route.

Those producers that form part of their local *Rota do Vinho* are indicated in the text with an asterisk.

saca-rolhas. corkscrew.

seco. dry (as in *vinho branco seco*, "dry white wine").

serra. a mountain range.

sobreiro. a cork tree.

socalco. a walled terrace.

solar. a manor house.

tanoaria. cooperage.

tanoeiro. cooper, barrel maker.

tinto. red (as in *vinho tinto*, "red wine").

tonel (plural *toneis*). a large wooden cask with a capacity of between twenty and sixty pipes (qv) used for storing and ageing wine.

turismo de habitação. guest accommodation in private houses; found throughout rural Portugal.

uva. grape.

vinagrinho. literally "a touch of vinegar"; used to describe a fortified wine that is "high toned" with noticeable but not necessarily detrimental levels of volatile acidity.

vindima. vintage or harvest.

vinha. vineyard or plot of vines.

vinha velha. an old interplanted vineyard.

vinho. wine.

Glossary of technical terms

baumé. a measure of dissolved compounds in grape juice and therefore its approximate concentration of sugars. The number of degrees Baumé is a rough indicator of percentage alcohol by volume (ie grape juice with 12 degrees Baumé will produce a wine with about 12 per cent alcohol by volume). Its inventor was the French pharmacist Antoine Baumé (1728–1804).

pH. hydrogen power, a measure of the concentration of the acidity. Low pH indicates high acidity and vice versa. All grape must is acidic, registering pH values of between 3 and 4. The scale is logarithmic, so a wine with a pH of 3 has ten times as much hydrogen ion activity as one whose pH is 4.

phenolics. a large group of reactive chemical components responsible for the tannins, pigment (anthocyanins) and many of the flavour compounds found in wine. Most of the phenolics come from the skin of the grape.

sulphur dioxide (SO_2). a disinfectant and anti-oxidant used by winemakers. The efficacy of sulphur dioxide is influenced by the wine's pH.

total acidity. a measure of both fixed and volatile acids in wine, usually expressed in Portugal as grams/litre tartaric. The ideal range for grape musts is between 7 and 10 grams/litre, with wines varying between 4.5 and 9 grams/litre. Wines in the coastal regions of northern Portugal tend to be toward the upper end of this scale (or even exceed it) and may require deacidification. Those in the south of the country often require the addition of tartaric acid.

volatile acidity. a measure of the naturally occurring organic acids in a wine that are separable by distillation. The most common volatile acid in wine is acetic acid, which imparts a vinegary character if present in excessive concentrations. The Portuguese use the term *vinagrinho* ("little vinegar") to describe a wine with noticeable but not detrimental levels of volatile acidity (usually found in old Colheita and Tawny Ports and many Madeiras).

appendix I

List of officially approved grape varieties and their synonyms

Source: Instituto da Vinha e do Vinho, 2000

BRANCO (WHITE)

Principal name	Local synonyms	Recognized synonym
Agronómica		
Alicante Branco	Uva Rei, Boal de Alicante, Boal Cachudo (Douro), Branco Conceição	
Almafra		
Almenhaca		
Alvadurão		
Alvar	Alvar Branco	
Alvarelhão Branco		
Alvarinho	Galego, Galeguinho	
Antão Vaz		
Aramontes	Arinto do Douro (Dão)	
Arinto	Arinto (Bucelas), Padernã Pé de Perdiz Branco, Chapeludo, Cerceal, Azal Espanhol, Azal Galego, Branco Espanhol, Arinto (Anadia)	
Arnsburger		
Assaraky		
Avesso		
Azal	Azal (Lixa), Gadelhudo, Carvalhal, Pinheira	
Babosa	Malvasia Babosa	
Barcelo		
Bastardo Branco		
Batoca	Alvaraça, Alvaroça, Sedouro	

Principal name	Local synonyms	Recognized synonym
Beba		
Bical	Borrado das Moscas, Arinto (Alcobaça), Fernão Pires do Galego, Pedro	
Boal Barreiro		
Boal Branco	Boal Branco (Bairrada)	
Boal Espinho	Batalhinha	
Branca de Anadia		
Branco Desconhecido		
Branco Especial		
Branco Gouvães		
Branco Guimarães		
Branco João	Branco Sr João	
Branda	D Branca, Dona Branca (Dão)	
Budelho		
Cainho		
Caracol		
Caramela		
Carão de Moça		
Carrasquenho	Boal Carrasquenho	
Carrega Branco	Malvasia Polta, Barranquesa	
Casca		
Castália		
Castelão Branco		
Castelo Branco		
Cerceal Branco	Cercial (Douro)	
Cercial	Cercial (Bairrada)	
Chardonnay		
Chasselas		
Chasselas Salsa		
Chenin		
Codega de Larinho		
Colombard		
Cornichon		
Corval		
Crato Espanhol		
Dedo de Dama		
Diagalves	Formosa, Carnal	
Dona Branca	Dona Branca (Douro)	
Dona Joaquina		
Donzelinho Branco		
Dorinto	Arinto Branco (Douro)	

Principal name	Local synonyms	Recognized synonym
Encruzado		
Esganinho		
Esganoso	Esganoso de Lima, Esganinho, Esgana Cão Furnicoso	
Estreito Macio	Estreito ou Rabigato	
Fernão Pires	Maria Gomes	
Folgasão	Terrantez (Madeira)	Terantez
Folha de Figueira		
Fonte Cal		
Galego Dourado		
Generosa		
Gigante	Branco Gigante	
Godelho		
Gouveio	Verdelho (Douro)	
Gouveio Estimado		
Gouveio Real		
Granho		
Jacquere		
Jampal		
Lameiro	Branco Lameiro, Lameirinho, Luzidio (Vinho Verde)	
Larião		
Leira		
Lilás	Alvarinho Lilás	
Loureiro		
Luzidio		
Malvasia	Malvasia (Colares)	
Malvasia Bianca		
Malvasia Branca	Malvasia (Açores)	
Malvasia Branca de S Jorge		
Malvasia Candida		
Malvasia Fina	Boal (Madeira), Boal Branco (Algarve), Arinto do Dão, Assario Branco, Arinto Galego, Boal Cachudo (Ribatejo)	Boal
Malvasia Parda		
Malvasia Rei	Seminário, Assurio (Alentejo), Listão, Pérola (Alentejo), Moscatel Carré, Grés Olho de Lebre	

Principal name	Local synonyms	Recognized synonym
Malvasia Romana	Malvasia Candída Roman, Malvasia Candída Branca	
Malvia	Malvasia de Setúbal	
Malvoeira	Malvasia de Oeiras	
Manteúdo	Manteúdo, B, Vale Grosso, Manteudo Branco (Algarve, Alentejo)	
Marquinhas		
Molinha		
Moscadet		
Moscatel Galego Branco	Moscatel (Douro), Moscatel de Bago Miúdo	
Moscatel Grado		Moscatel de Setúbal
Moscatel Nunes		
Mourisco Branco		
Müller-Thurgau		
Naia		
Pé Comprido		
Perigo		
Perrum		
Pinheira Branca		
Pinot Blanc		
Pintosa	Branco Escola, Branco de Asa, Azal de São Tirso	
Praça		
Promissão		
Rabigato		
Rabigato Franco	Rabigato Francês, Rabigato Branco	
Rabigato Moreno		
Rabo de Ovelha	Medock, Rabigato (Vinho Verde), Rabo de Gato, Rabisgato, Rabo de Carneiro	
Ratinho	Boal Ratinho	
Riesling		
Rio Grande		
Roupeiro Branco	Roupeiro (Alcobaça)	
Sabro		
Samarrinho		
Santoal	Boal de Santarém	
São Mamede		
Sarigo		

Principal name	Local synonyms	Recognized synonym
Sauvignon		
Seara Nova		
Semilão		
Sémillon	Boal (Douro)	
Sercial	Esganoso (Castelo de Paiva), Sercial (Madeira)	Esgana Cão
Sercialinho		
Síria	Crato Branco, Alva, Malvasia, Posto Branco (Douro)	Roupeiro
Tália	Branquinha, Douradinha (Vinho Verde), Pera de Bode, Douradinha, Ugni Blanc, Esgana Rapezes, Espadeiro Branco, Malvasia Fina, Trebiano, Alfrocheiro Branco	
Tamarêz	Arinto Gordo, Boal Prior, Trincadeira	
Terrantez		
Terrantez da Terceira		
Terrantez do Pico		
Touriga Branca		
Trajudura	Trincadeira (Vinho Verde), Mourisco	
Trincadeira Branca		
Trincadeira das Pratas	Tamarêz (Peninsula de Setúbal)	
Uva Cão	Cachorrinho	
Uva Cavaco		
Uva Salsa		
Valente	Branco Valente	
Valveirinho		
Vencedor	Boal Vencedor	
Verdelho	Verdelho Branco (Madeira), Verdelho dos Açores	
Verdial Branco		
Viognier		
Viosinho		
Vital	Boal Bonifácio, Malvasia Corada	

TINTO (RED)
Água Santa

Principal name	Local synonyms	Recognized synonym
Alcoa	Tinta de Alcobaça	
Alfrocheiro	Alfrocheiro Preto	
Alicante Bouschet	Alicante Tinto, Tinta Fina, Tinta de Escrever	
Alvarelhão	Brancelho, Brancelhão, Pirraúvo	
Alvarelhão Ceitão		
Amaral	Azal Tinto	
Amor-Não-Me-Deixes		
Amostrinha	Preto Martinho (Oeste)	
Aragonez	Tinta de Santiago	Tinta Roriz
Aramon		
Arjunção		
Baga	Tinta da Bairrada, Poeirinha, Baga de Louro	
Barca	Tinta da Barca	
Barreto	Barreto de Semente	
Bastardo	Bastardinho	
Bastardo	Tinto	
Bonvedro	Monvedro Tinto	
Borraçal	Bogalhal, Cainho Grosso, Olho de Sapo, Esfarrapa, Murraçal	
Bragão	Tinta Bragão	
Branjo		
Cabernet Franc		
Cabinda		
Caladoc		
Calrão		
Câmarate	Castelão (Bairrada), Castelão Nacional, Moreto (Douro), Moreto de Soure, Negro Mouro, Moreto	
Campanário		
Carignan		
Carrega Burros	Esgana Raposas, Malvasias	
Carrega Tinto		
Casculho		
Castelã		
Castelão	Castelão Francês, Periquita Bastardo Espanhol	João de Santarem or Periquita
Castelino		
Casteloa		

Principal name	Local synonyms	Recognized synonym
Chasselas Sabor		
Cidadelhe	Tinta de Cidadelhe	
Cidreiro		
Cinsaut		
Complexa		
Coneiera		
Coração de Galo		
Cornifesto	Cornifesto Tinto (Dão)	
Corropia		
Corvo		
Deliciosa		
Doçal	Folhal	
Doce		
Donzelinho Tinto		
Engomada	Tinta Engomada	
Espadeiro	Espadeiro Tinto, Padeiro, Cinza	
Espadeiro Molle		
Farinheira		
Fepiro	Alentajana	
Ferral		
Galego		
Garnay		
Gonçalo Pires		
Gorda	Tinta Gorda	
Gouveio Preto		
Graciosa	Tinta da Graciosa	
Grand Noir	Sousão (Oeste), Sumo Tinto	
Grangeal		
Grenache	Abundante (Reguengos)	
Grossa	Tinta Grossa	
Jaen		
Labrusco		
Lourela		
Lusitano		
Malandra	Tinta Malandra	
Malvarisco		
Malvasia Preta	Moreto (Dão)	
Manteúdo Preto		
Mario Feld		
Marufo	Mourisco Tinto, Moroco, Uva de Rei, Olho de Rei	
Melhorio		

Principal name	Local synonyms	Recognized synonym
Melra	Tinta Melra	
Merlot		
Mindelo		
Molar		
Mondet		
Monvedro		
Moreto		
Moscargo	Portalegre	
Moscatel Galego Tinto	Moscatel Tinto	
Mourisco		
Mourisco de Semente		
Mourisco de Trevões		
Mulata		
Negra Mole		
Nevoeira		
Padeiro	Padeiro de Basto	
Parreira Matias		
Patorra		
Pau Ferro		
Pedral		
Pero Pinhão		
Petit Bouschet		
Petit Verdot		
Pexem		
Pical		
Pilongo	Tourigo (Douro)	
Pinot Noir		
Português Azul		
Preto Cardana		
Preto Martinho		
Primavera		
Rabo de Anho	Rabo de Ovelha (Vinho Verde)	
Rabo de Lobo		
Rabo de Ovelha Tinto		Raba de Ovelha Tinto (Pinhel)
Ramisco		
Ramisco Tinto		
Ricoca	Tinta Ricoca	
Rodo	Tinto Rodo	
Roseira	Tinto Roseira	
Rufete	Tinta Pinheira, Penamacor	
Saborinho		

Principal name	Local synonyms	Recognized synonym
Santareno	Santarém	
São Saul		
Sevilhão		
Sousão	Sousão Forte, Sousão de Comer, Sousão Vermelho, Vinhão, Espadeiro de Basro, Neyrão	
Syrah		
Tannat		
Teinturier		
Tinta	Tinta (Madeira)	
Tinta Aquiar		
Tinta Aurélio		
Tinta Barroca		Barroca
Tinta Bastardinha		
Tinta Caiada	Monvedro (Oeste)	
Tinta Carvalha		
Tinta Fontes	Tinta Miuda de Fontes	
Tinta Francisca		
Tinta Lameira		
Tinta Lisboa		
Tinta Martins		
Tinta Mesquita		
Tinta Miuda		
Tinta Negra	Negra Mole (Madeira)	
Tinta Penojoia	Tinta Roriz de Penajoia	
Tinta Pereira		
Tinta Pomar	Tinta Mole	
Tinta Porto Santo		
Tinta Tabuaço		
Tintem		
Tintinha		
Tinto Cão	Padeiro (Basto), Tinto Mata	
Tinto Pegões		
Tinto Sem Nome		
Touriga Fêmea	Touriga Brasileira	
Touriga Franca	Touriga Francesa	
Touriga Nacional	Preto Mortágua, Azal Espanhol	
Transâncora		
Trincadeira	Trincadeira Preta, Crato Preto, Tinta Amarela Folha de Abóbora, Mortágua, Espadeiro (Setúbal), Espadeiro, Torneiro Negreda, Castelão (Cova da Beira) Rabo de Ovelha	

Principal name	Local synonyms	Recognized synonym
	Tinto (Vintio Verde) (see page 88)	
Triunfo		
Valbom		
Valdosa	Tinta Valdosa	
Varejoa	Tinta Varejoa	
Verdelho Tinto		Verdelho, Verdelho Feijão,
	Feijão, Mindeço	
Verdial Tinto		
Vinhão	Tinto, Pé de Perdiz, Espadeiro Preto, Tinta Antiga, Tinta de Parada, Sousão (Douro)	Tinto Nacional, Negrão
Xara		
Ze de Telheiro		
Zinfandel		

ROXO (GRIS)

Principal name	Local synonyms	Recognized synonym
Alvar Roxo		
Arinto Roxo		
Bastardo Roxo		
Chasselas Roxo		
Donzelinho Roxo		
Fernão Pires Rosado		
Folgasão Roxo		
Gelego Rosado		
Gewürztraminer		
Gouveio Roxo	Mogadouro, Gouveio, Vermelho	
Listrão		
Malvasia Cabral		
Malvasia Cândida Roxa	Malvasia Roxa	
Malvasia Fina Roxa	Assario Roxo, Boal Roxo	
Moscatel Galego Roxo		Moscatel Roxo
Mourisco Roxo		
Pinheira Roxa		
Pinot Gris		
Roal		
Roxo Flor	Roxo de Vila Flor	
Roxo Rei		
Trigueira	Malvasia Trigueira	
Verdelho Roxo		

appendix II

Acronyms

Portugal has a wearisome variety of acronyms. Here are the initials of the organizations, institutions and projects most closely involved in the day-to-day life of wine producers in Portugal:

ACIBEV: Associação de Commerciantes e Industriais de Bebidas e Vinhos

ADVID: Associação para o Desenvolvimento da Viticultura Duriense (Douro Viticultural Development Association)

AEVP: Associação das Empreseas de Vinho do Porto (Port Wine Shippers Association)

ANDOVI: Associação Nacional das Denominaçoes de Origem Vitivinicolas

APEVV: Associação dos Produtores Engarrafadores de Vinho Verde

ATEVA: Associação Tecnica dos Viticultores do Alentejo

AVEPOD: Associação dos Viticultores Engarrafadores dos Vinhos do Porto e Douro (Port and Douro Wine Growers and Bottlers Association)

CD: Casa do Douro

CIRDD: Comissão Interprofissional do Região Demarcada do Douro (Interprofessional Commission for the Douro Demarcated Region)

CIVE: Comissão Interprofissional dos Vinhos da Estremadura

CVB: Comissão Vitivinicola de Bairrada

CVRA: Comissão Vitivinicola Regional Alentejana

CVRB: Comissão Vitivinicola Regional das Beiras

CVRD–FVD: Comissão Vitivinicola Regional do Dão – Federação dos Viticultores do Dão

CVRR: Comissão Vitivinicola Regional Ribatejana

CVRVV: Comissão de Viticultura da Região dos Vinhos Verdes

FENADEGAS: Federação Nacional de Adegas Cooperativeas

FENAVI: Federação Nacional de Viticultores Independentes

ICEP: Instituto do Comércio Externo Português (responsible for promoting Portuguese wine overseas)

IVM: Instituto do Vinho da Madeira (Madeira Wine Institute)

IVP: Instituto do Vinho do Porto (Port Wine Institute)

IVV: Instituto da Vinha e do Vinho (Institute of Vines and Wine; formerly the Junta Nacional do Vinho or JNV)

PDRITM: Projecto de Desenvolvimento Rural Integrado de Trás-os-Montes (Trás-os-Montes Integrated Rural Development Project)

VINIPORTUGAL: Associação Interprofessional para a Promoção dos Vinhos Portugueses

Bibliography

Chapter 1

Allen, H Warner, *The Wines of Portugal,* London 1963
Andrade Martins, C, *Memoria do Vinho do Porto,* Lisboa 1990
Bradford, S, *The Story of Port,* London 1983
Cockburn, E, *Port Wine and Oporto,* London 1949
Cossart, N, *Madeira: the Island Vineyard,* London 1984
Delaforce, J, *The Factory House at Oporto,* London 1979
Delaforce, J, *Joseph James Forrester,* London 1992
Fletcher, W, *Port: An Introduction to its History and Delights,* London 1978
Instituto da Vinha e do Vinho, *Vinhos e Águardentes Anuario 99/2000,* Lisboa
Liddell, A, *Madeira,* London 1998
Livermore, H V, *A New History of Portugal,* Cambridge 1976
Loureiro, V, Homem Cardoso, A, *Dão Wines,* Lisboa 1993
Macaulay, R, *They Went to Portugal,* London 1946
Macaulay, R, *They Went to Portugal Too,* Manchester 1990
Martins Perreira, G, *O Douro e o Vinho do Porto de Pombal a João Franco,* Porto 1991
Mayson, R J, *Forrester and the Douro,* West Lebanon (USA) 2002
Mayson, R J, *Port and the Douro,* London 1999
Mayson, R J, *Portugal's Wines and Wine Makers,* San Francisco 1998
Mayson, R J, *The Story of Dow's Port,* London 1998
Oliveira Marques, A H, *History of Portugal,* New York 1976
Ordish, G, *The Great Wine Blight,* London 1987
Roque do Vale, C, Madeira, J, Homem Cardoso, A, *Os Vinhos do Alentejo,* Lisboa 1996
Saraiva Pinto, M, Fevereiro Chambel, A, Homem Cardoso, A, *Bairrada Wines,* Lisboa 1998
Sellers, C, *Oporto Old and New,* London 1899
Vila Maior, Visconde de, *O Douro Illustrado,* Porto 1876
Vizetelly, H, *Facts about Port and Madeira,* London 1880
Warner Allen, H, *The Wines of Portugal,* London 1962

Chapter 2

Bravo, P, d'Oliveira, D, *Viticultura Moderna*, Porto 1916
Cincinnato da Costa, BC, *O Portugal Vinicola*, Lisboa 1900
Cossart, N, *Madeira: the Island Vineyard*, London 1984
Feijó, R G, Homem Cardoso, A, *Vinho Verde*, Lisboa 1990
Instituto da Vinha e do Vinho, *Vinhos e Águardentes Anuário 99/2000*, Lisboa
Junta Nacional do Vinho, *Contribuição para o Cadastro dos Vinhos Portugueses na Area de Influencia da JNV*, Lisboa 1942
Liddell, A, *Madeira*, London 1998
Loureiro, V, Homem Cardoso, A, *Os Vinhos do Dão*, Lisboa 1993
Mayson, R J, *Forrester and the Douro*, West Lebanon (USA) 2002
Mayson, R J, *Port and the Douro*, London 1999
Mayson, R J, *Porto e o Douro*, Lisboa 2001
Mayson, R J, *Portugal's Wines and Wine Makers*, San Francisco 1998
Robinson, J, *Vines, Grapes and Wines*, London 1986
Roque do Vale, C, Madeira, J, Homem Cardoso, A, *Os Vinhos do Alentejo*, Lisboa 1996
Saraiva Pinto, M, Fevereiro Chambel, A, Homem Cardoso, A, *Bairrada Wines*, Lisboa 1998

Chapter 3

Allen, H Warner, *The Wines of Portugal*, London 1963
Bello, António Maria de Oliveira, *Culinária Portuguesa*, Lisboa 1928
Esteves dos Santos, R, *O Vinho de Colares*, Colares 1938
Feijo, R G, Homem Cardoso, A, *Vinho Verde*, Lisboa 1990
Goncalves, F Esteves, *Portugal: A Wine Country*, Lisboa 1984
Mayson, R J, *Portugal's Wines and Wine Makers*, San Francisco 1998
Saravia, Pinto M, Fevereiro, Chambel A, Homem Cardoso, A, *Bairrada Wines*, Lisboa 1998

Chapter 4

Loureiro, V, Homem Cardoso, A, *Os Vinhos do Dão*, Lisboa 1993
Mayson, R J, *Port and the Douro*, London 1999
Mayson, R J, *Portugal's Wines and Wine Makers*, San Francisco 1998

Chapter 5

Mayson, R J, *Portugal's Wines and Wine Makers*, San Francisco 1998
Roque do Vale, C, Madeira, J, Homem Cardoso, A, *Os Vinhos do Alentejo*, Lisboa 1996

Chapter 6

Bello, António Maria de Oliveira, *Culinária Portuguesa*, Lisboa 1928
Cossart, N, *Madeira: the Island Vineyard*, London 1984
Liddell, A, *Madeira*, London 1998
Mayson, R J, *Portugal's Wines and Wine Makers*, San Francisco 1998

Chapter 7

Mayson, R J, *Portugal's Wines and Wine Makers*, San Francisco 1998

Chapter 8

Mayson, R J, *Portugal's Wines and Wine Makers*, San Francisco 1998

Saravia, Pinto M, Fevereiro, Chambel A, Homem Cardoso, A, *Bairrada Wines*, Lisboa 1998

Chapter 9

Oliveira, Manual Alves de, Oliveira, Leónel de, *The Cork*, Rio de Mouro 2000

Index

Page numbers in **bold** indicate main entries.
Adegas are all entered under A, *casas* and
caves under C, *herdades* under H, and *quintas*
under Q.

A

ABA de Serra 167
Abreu Callado **271**
Abundante *see* Aragonez
Acciaioli, Simon 17, 101
Adega Co-op de Palmela 257
Adega Cooperativa de Figueira de Castelo
  Rodrigo 235, **236–7**
Adega Cooperativa de Ponte de Lima **139–40**
Adega Cooperativa Regional de Monção
  137–8
Adega de Pegões 262
Adegas de São Vicente 295
Adega Velha 135
Adegas Beira Mar 179, 180
Afonso, João 237
Agro-Aliança **271**
Água Santa **60**
águardente see winemaking
Aguiar, António Augusto de 147
Alabastro 271–2
Alambre 256
Alandra 276
Albelhal **89**
Albis 260
Alcanhões 245, 247
Alcobaça 6, 162, **164**
Alenquer 63, 79, 81, 82, 95, 110, 111, 162,
  165, 166–9, 170–1, 319
Alentejano (Vinho Regional) 266, 268, 271
Alentejo 3, 6, 9–10, 35, 38, 39, 46, 151, 174,
  238, 240–1, **263–81**, 318
  Alta 266
  Baixo 81, 104, 266

climate 12, 238, 266
cooperatives 44, 265, 276, 277
grape varieties 61, 63, 64, 67, 68, 69, 72,
  74, 79, 87, 88, 91, 97, 98, 103, 105,
  107, 109
powdery mildew 29–30
producers 260, 262, **270–81**, 304
Rota do Vinho do Alentejo 270
sparkling wine 306, 307
sub-regions **266–70**
see also specific names
Vinho Regional 266, 268, 271
vintages 112, 113, 115, 116, 117, 118
see also specific places
Alfrocheiro Preto **61**, 86, 225
  Branco *see* Tália
Algarve 1, 3, 5, 6, 9, 16, 35, 45, 240, 241,
  281–3
  climate 238, 282
  cooperatives 241, 282, 283
  grape varieties 79, 82, 87, 107, 282
  producers 283
  Vinho Regional 283
Algeruz 259, 260, 302
Aliança Classico 151
Alicante Bouschet **61**
Alicante Branco **89**
Alijó 200–1, 205, 213, 216
Allen, H Warner 8–9, 20
Almeida, Alexandre d' 157
Almeida e Silva, Carlos 154
Almeida Garrett 237
Almeirim 82, 108, 111, **245**, 247, 249
Almojanda 275
Alpiarça 247, 250
Altano 219
Alva, Alvadurão *see* Síria
Alvaraca *see* Batoca
Alvarelhão 26, **62**, 66, 76

Alvarinho **90–91**, 134, 136, 137–8, 139, 140, 141
Alvaroca *see* Batoca
Alves Nuno 152
Alves de Sousa, Domingos 212
Amaral **62**
Amarante 62, 79, 93, 109, **131–2**, 143
Amarela 218
Amor-Não-Me-Deixas **62**
Amostrinha **62–63**
Anadia 16, 65, 152, 153, 154, 155, 304
Andrade, Mario 241, 273
Antão Vaz **91**
anthracnose 70
Antunes, Francisco 151, 257
Apoteca 257
APS 139
Aragonez 54, **63–64**, 81
Araújo, Nuno 145
Araújo, Pedro 134
Archibald, Robert 81
Arinto 22, 27, 53, **91–92**, 173
Arinto do Dão *see* Malvasia Fina
Arnsburger **92–93**
Arrábida 257
Arruda 63, 74, 82, 111, 162, **165–6**
Assario *see* Malvasia Fina
Atlantis 295, 302
Aveleda 135
Avesso **93**
Avillez, d' **271**
  António 261, 309
Azal **93**
  Espanhol/Galego *see* Arinto
  Tinto *see* Amaral
Azeitão 28, 74, 75, 82, 176, 254, 258, 259, 261, 271, 301, 302, 307
Azores 16, 17, 19, 78, 110, **296–7**

B
Baga 29, **64–65**, 150
bagaçeiras 171
Bago de Touriga 205
Baião 93, 94, 132, 145
Bairrada 6, 14, 16, 19, 39, 41, 45, 124, **146–56**
  Associação dos Viticultores de Bairrada (AVB) 305
  climate 123, 146, 148, 149
  cooperatives 148, 150
  grape varieties 29, 60, 64, 65, 79, 85, 87, 94, 96, 99, 107, 146, 148–9
  phylloxera 31
  powdery mildew 29

producers **150–6**, 216, 230, 307
  rosé 304
  Mateus Rosé 300, 304
  Rota do Vinho da Bairrada 150
  sparkling wine 305, 306, 307
  Vinho Regional Beiras 146, 148, 150, 151, 154
  vintages 112, 113, 114, 115, 116, 117, 118, 149
  see also specific places
Bairrada Sul 230
Baldoeira *see* Câmarate
Barão de Figueira 236
Barba, Nuno 173
Barbeito 293, 295
Barca **65**
Barca Velha 26, 48, 117, 118, 202, 205, 210–11, 220
Barcelo **94**
Barros Almeida 42, 195, 197, 198
Barros e Sousa 292, 295
Basalto 296
Bastardinho 28, **65**
Bastardinho de Azeitão 257
Bastardo 26, 28, **66**
  Roxo 66
  Tinto 66
Bastardo Espanhol *see* Castelão
Basto 79, 93, 94, **131**
Bastos 273, 274
Batoca **94**
Batuta 213
Baverstock, David 211, 241, 276, 283, 318
Bearsley 13, 84
Beata 180
Behr, Henry 301
Beiras 4, **159–60, 237**, 278
  Bairrada *see main entry*
  Beira Alta 78, 81, 183, 184, 226, 97, 237, 306
    see also Dão
  Beira Baixa 78, 183, 185
  Beira Interior 174, 184, 185, **235–7**, 317
    Cova de Beira 185, 235, 236
  Beira Litoral 60, 237
  Beira Mar 180
  climate 183, 235
  cooperatives 159–60, 235, 236, 306
  grape varieties 60, 64, 67, 70, 78, 81, 88, 94, 107, 159, 237
  Mateus Rosé 300
  producers **236–7**, 252
  Terras de Sicó 237
  Vinho Regional 146, 148, 150, 151, 154,

159, 160, 185, 231, 237
see also specific places
Beja 4, 266
Bela Fonte 150
Bento dos Santos, José 170
Berarado, José 261
Bergqvist 217, 218
Beysecker, Lucien 305
Bical 94
Bin 27 196
Biscoitos 296, 297
Blandy 22, 293, 294, 295
Boal (Bual) 55, 94–95, 106, 291, 294
  Alicante see Alicante Branco
  Bonifácio see Vital
  Cachudo/Commum see Malvasia Fina
Boas Quintas 230–1
Boca da Mina see Tinta Barroca
Bogalhal see Borraçal
Bombarral 162, 164, 171–2, 182
Bonvedro see Monvedro
Borba 35, 61, 72, 98, 151, 240–1, 265, 267, 270
Borges (& Irmão) 44, 135, 206, 229–30, 299, 301
Borraçal 66
Borrado das Moscas see Bical
botrytis 67
Braga 3, 5, 101, 109, 130, 131, 143
Brancelho 62, 66
Branco Conceição see Alicante Branco
Branco Seco Especial 260
Branco-Mansilha 214
brandy 163, 172
Bravo, Pedro 53
Brejoeira 136
Bright Brothers 159–60, 206, 259
  Peter 150, 161, 206, 241, 250, 258, 259, 261, 318
Brito e Cunha, João 208, 212
Brum 297
Bual see Boal
Buçaco 6, 111, 156–9, 225
Bucelas 9, 21–22, 27, 28, 35, 123, 163, 172–5
  grape varieties 17, 91–92, 95, 106, 172
  producers 173–5
  Rota dos Vinhos de Bucelas . . . 173
  sparkling wine 306
  Vinho Regional Estremadura 172
Burmester 196, 197, 198, 206

C
Cabernet Sauvignon 50, 55, 67

Cachorrinho see Uva Cão
Cadaval 162, 164
Cainho 95
  Grosso see Borraçal
Caladoc 67
Calcavella 16, 173, 181
Calços da Tanha 207
Cálem 120, 198, 207
Callabriga 211
Câmarate 27, 67–68
Cambriz 298
Campo Novo 145
Cancela de Abreu, Nuno 175, 230–1, 236
Caniça see Cunningham
Cantanhede 150, 152, 155
Capucho 248
Caracal 96
Carão da Moça 96
Carcavelos 19, 21–22, 27, 28, 35, 43, 123, 163, 173, 181–2
  grape varieties 63, 71, 100, 182
  powdery mildew 29–30
  Rota dos Vinhos de Bucelas . . . 173
Carrega Burros 54
Cartaxo 63, 82, 88, 108, 109, 169–70, 243, 245–6, 247
Cartuxa 272–3
Carvalhais Reserva 235
Casa Agricola Brum 297
Casa Agricola Herd de Dom Luís de Margaride 251
Casa Agricola Santos Jorge 270
Casa de Alorna Colheita Seleccionada 247
Casa Burmester 206
Casa Cadaval 77, 247–8, 278
Casa de Insua 231
Casa do Lago 249
Casa de Saima 115, 116, 118, 154
Casa do Santar 225, 233
Casa Santos Lima 168
Case de Sezim 140–1
Casa do Valle 144–5
Casa de Villar (Minho) 145
Casa de Villar (Vinho Verde) 143–4
Casa da Vinha 295
Casal de Azenha 180
Casal de Coelheira 253
Casal Garcia 135
Casal do Monteiro 251
Casaleiro 252
Castas do Carneiro 167
Castas de Santar 233
Castelão (Francês) 51, 53, 59, 68–69, 75
  Nacional see Câmarate

Castelo Blanco, Francisco 173
Castelo Rodrigo 235
Castro, Alvaro 232
Castro Pacheco, Gaspar de 139
Castro Ribeiro, João 158
Cataplana 283
Catarina 261
Catarino, José Miguel 168–9
Cavaco 296
Caves Acácio 229
Caves Aliança 149, 150, **151, 205**, 223, 229, 258, 271, **307**
Caves do Barrocão 150
Caves Borlido 150
Caves Camillo Alves 174
Caves Dom Teodósio 244, **252**
Caves Lucien Beysecker 305
Caves Messias 150, **152–3**
Caves Monte Crasto 306
Caves Murganheira *see* Murganheira
Caves Primavera **154**
Caves da Raposeira *see* Raposeira
Caves São João (Irmãos Unidos) 146, 150, **154–5**, 157, 225, **233**
Caves Solar de São Domingos 150
Caves Valedarcos 150, **155**
Caves Velhas (Camillo Alves) **174**, 257, 258
Caves Visconde de Salreu 179
Celeirós 218
Centro Agricola de Tramagal **253**
Centro dos Estudos Vitivinicolas de Nelas 86, 225
Cerceal Branco (Cercial)**96**
Chaminé 275
Champalimaud, Miguel 142
Champanhe de Lamego 306
Champanhe de Portuguez 305
Chamusca 108, 109, 111, **244–5**, 247
Chanceleiros, Visconde de 32, 169
Chapeludo *see* Arinto
Chardonnay 50, 55, **96–97**
    sparkling 307
Charme 213
Chatonnet, Pascal 214
Chaves 3, 4, 222
Chello 141–2
Chico
Maria 297
Chryseia 215
Churchill 116, 195, 196, **207–8**
Cincinnato da Costa, Bernardino 52–53, 62, 63, 66, 69, 74, 75, 76, 77, 78, 81, 82, 88, 92, 94, 101, 104, 105, 107, 108, 147, 222
Cinfaes 94

Cinsault **69**
Clarke, Oz 133
Clinton **70**
Cockburn 42, 76, 120, 173, 186, 194, 199, 200, **208**, 230
    Special Reserve 196
Codega **97**
Codo Síria *see* Síria
Coimbra 3, 4, 226
Colaço do Rosario, Professor 272
Colares 31, 35, 38, 123, 163, 173, **175–80**
    Colares-Chão Rijo 179
    cooperatives 40, 45, 176–7, 179
    grape varieties 77–78
    producers **179–80**
    Rota dos Vinhos de Bucelas . . . 173
Colheita das Netas 138
Companhia Agricola do Sanguinhal LDA **171–2**, 182
Companhia das Quintas 236
Companhia Vinicola do Sul de Portugal 33
Complexa **70**, 83
Condado das Vinhas 277
Conde de Carreira 144
Confradeiro 218
Conventual 267
Cooperativa Agricola de Santo Isidrio de Pegões **262**
cooperatives *see* viticulture; winemaking *and specific places*
Coração do Galo **70**
Corgo
    Baixo 88, 114, **187–8**, 195, 203, 207, 208, 212
    Cima **188**, 197
    climate 114, 187–8
    grape varieties 80, 81, 84, 86, 88
cork **312–16**
Cornifesto **70**
Coroa d'Ouro 214
Corte Real, Miguel 230–1
Cortes de Cima **275–6**
Cortezia 169
Coruche 82, 108, 109, 111, 243, **246–7**, 250
Corucho 214
Cossart, John *and* Peter 288
Cossart, Noel 18
Cossart Gordon 18, 294, 295
Costa 146, 154–5, 233
Costa da Caparica 28
Cova de Periquita 69
Cova da Ursa 261
Covela 145
Crato Branco *see* Síria

Crato Preto *see* Trincadeira Preta
Crawfurd, Oswald 26, 202
Croft 13, 42, 114, 117, 120, 186, 192, 200
  John 13, 19, 181
Cunningham 32, **70**, 82
Curia 157, 158

D
Dalva 198
Danaide 138
Dão 7, 33, 35, 38, 40, 46, 54, 136, 151, 184,
  224–35, 319
  climate 183, 227
  cooperatives 45, 54, 86, 150, 225–6, 229,
    234
  UDACA 229
  grape varieties 54, 55, 61, 64, 66, 73, 74,
    75, 84, 86, 91–92, 94, 96, 98, 106, 107,
    109, 227–8
  jeropiga 31
  phylloxera 31, 225
  powdery mildew 29–30
  producers 216, **229–35**, 260, 304
  Rota do Vinho do Dão 229
  sparkling wine 306
  syndicates 39
  Vinha Regional Beiras 231
  vintages 112, 113, 114, 115–16
Dão Cardeal 252
Dão Novo 73, 234
Dão Pipas 234–5
Dão Sul Sociedade Vitivinicola 230
Dão Terras Altas 301
Dedo da Dama **97**
Delaforce 42, 120, 200
Deliciosa **71**
Deu-la-Deu 138
DFJ Vinhos 150, 159–60, 161, **169–70**, 229,
  249, 283
Diagalves **98**
DJ Silva 179
Doçal (Doçar)**71**
DOCs *see* viticulture: VQPRDs
Dom Ferraz 229
Dom Rafael 279
Domaines Baron de Rothschild 274
Domingos Soares Franco Coleção Privada 260
Domini 221, 261
Dona Branca **98**
Donzelinho **71**
  Branco **98**
Douradinha *see* Tália
Douro 1, 3, 4, 12, 24, 26, 29, 35, 38, 43, 46,
  48, 136, 151, 174, 184, 186–93, 199, 200,

201–21, 319
Alto Douro 15, 16, 20, 62
Casa do Douro 38, 44
climate 183, 187–88, 204
Companhia (Real Companhia das
  Vinhas do Alto Douro) 15, 16, 20
consumo/vinho de mesa 202, 202, 203
cooperatives 199, 212
Corgo (Baixa/Cima) *see main entry*
Douro Superior 65,86, 88, 97, 112, 114, 188,
  197, 204, 205, 207, 208, 210, 215, 220
grape varieties 17, 26, 51, 54, 55, 62, 63,
  65, 66, 67, 68, 71, 73–74, 75, 76, 77, 78,
  79, 80, 81, 84, 85, 86–87, 87–88, 96, 97,
  98, 100, 102, 103, 104, 105, 108, 110,
  189, 203, 204–5
lagares 191, 192–3, 204
Mateus Rosé 219, 300, 304
Moscatel 200
  de Favaios 103, **200–1**
patamares 187
phylloxera 30
Port *see main entry*
producers 203, **205–21**, 230, 252
  see also Port: producers/shippers
  rosé 302–3
sparkling wine 306, 310
vineyard classification **188–9**
vinha ao alto 187
Vinho Regional 204, 205, 215, 216
  see also specific places
Douro Reservas 206, 207, 209, 213, 214, 216,
  217, 218, 219
Dow 42, 80, 114, 115, 116, 117, 118, 119,
  120, 194, 197, 219
  Trademark 196
Dry Muscat 261
Duarte, Luís Soares 205, 241, 277
Duas Quintas 116, 117, 215, 216
Dubourdieu, Denis 151
Duke range 293
Duque de Viseu 229, 234

E
Emilio de Oliveira e Silva & Filhos 257
Encostas de Aire 162, **163–4**
Encostas do Douro 230
Encruzado 94, **98**, 229
Entre Serras 237
Entreverde 51
Enxurros 295
Esfarrapa *see* Borraçal
Esgana Cão *see* Sercial
Esgana Rapazes *see* Tália

Esganoso *see* Sercial
Espadeiro **71**
  de Basto *see* Sousão
  see also Trincadeira Preta
Esporão 276
espumante see sparkling wines
Estação Agronomica Nacional 182
Esteva 211
Estremadura (Oeste) 16, 31, 33, 41, 45, 47,
  124, **160–72**, 278
  Alta 162
  climate 123, 124, 162, 163
  cooperatives 54, 161, 162, 163, 164–5, 166
  grape varieties 54, 63, 64, 67, 68, 69, 72,
  74, 75, 76, 79, 81, 82, 83, 85, 87, 88,
  91–92, 95, 96, 99, 100, 103, 106, 107,
  110, 111, 161, 163
  Mateus Rosé 300
  producers **166–72**, 230, 262
  Rota dos Vinhos do Oeste 166
  sub-regions **163–6**
    see also specific names
  vinho leve 162
  Vinho Regional 161, 162, 163, 172
  vintages 115
  see also specific places
Estremoz 267, 273
Eugénio de Almeida 272
Evel 216, 217
Évora 3, 9–10, 72, 91, 104, 265, 266, **268**

F
Fafe 79, 131
Faisca 301
Falcoaria 248
Falua **249–50**
Famalicão 131, 143
Faro de Silva, Jacques 290
Favaios 75, 200–1
Federações dos Vinicultores 38
Feijó, Rui 143
Feijó, Rui Graça 143–4
feira do vinho 48
Felgueiras 62, 131, 143
Fernão Pires 33, **99**
Ferral **71**
Ferrão, José 137
Ferraz, Fausto 169
Ferreira 12, 117, 118, 187, 192, 196, 197,
  200, 202, **210–11**, 304
  family 23, 219, 220
Ferreira de Almeida, José Leão 54
Fernandes, Ruy 51
Figueira de Foz 29, 31

Fiuza-Bright 67, **250**
Fladgate Partnership 200
Fojo 211
Folgosão *see* Terrantez
Folhal *see* Doçal
Fonseca *see* José Maria da Fonseca
Fonte do Ouro 231
Fontenario de Pegões 262
Foral 205
Forrester, Baron 51
Forrester, Joseph James 24–26, 62, 66, 202
Frei João Bairrada 155
frisante see sparkling wines

G
Gabia 139
Galega Dourado **100**
Galeria 151
Gallie, Piers 136–7
garage wines 138
Garnacha *see* Aragonez
Garrafeira Palmela 262
garrafeiras see winemaking
Garrafeiras dos Sócios 269
Gatão 136
Gazela 141
Gewürztraminer **100**
Girão, Amorim 147
Gorjão 167
Gould Campbell 119
Gouveia 73, 94, 96, 226
Gouveio 17, **100**
Graciosa 296, 297
Graham 42, 114, 115, 116, 117, 118, 119,
  120, 186, 192, 196, 199, 219
  Six Grapes 196
Graham, Anthony, Johnny *and* William 207
Grand Noir 61, **72**
Grand'Arte 169–70
Granja-Amareleja 75, **269**
Grantom Reserva 217
Grão Vasco 229, 234
grape varieties *see* viticulture
Grinalda 135
Guedes 129, 134, 135
  Fernando 141, 303
  Fernando Van Zeller 41, 303, 304
Guimaraens 115, 116, 199
Guimarães 2, 127, 131, 140, 143
  family 170

H, I
Henriques & Henriques 286, 288, 293, 294,
  295

Herbremont **72**, 82
Herdade de Cartuxa 268
Herdade de Coelheiros **275**
Herdade do Esporão 266, 275, **276–7**, 307
Herdade Grande **277**
Herdade da Madeira 280
Herdade dos Minheiros 272
Herdade do Monte da Ribeira **273**
Herdade do Mouchão **278**
Herdade de Muge 248
Herdade do Peso **280**
Heublein 302
HM Borges 295
Horta de Nazaré 251
Incognito 275–6
Instituto da Vinha e do Vinho (IVV) 45, 59, 164, 299
Instituto do Vinho do Porto *see* Port
IPRs *see* viticulture: VQPRDs
Isabela 29, 30, 32, **72**, 82

J, K
Jacquet (Jacquez) 32, **72–73**, 82
Jaen **73**, 86, 225
Jampal (João Paulo)33, **100**
João Portugal Ramos 160, 170, 232, 241, 248, 249, 273, 275, **278–9**, 318
João de Santarém *see* Castelão
Jorgensen, Carrie *and* Hans 275
José Maria da Fonseca 27, 65, 69, 84, 103, 114, 115, 116, 117, 118, 119, 120, 175, 176, 197, 221, 229, 254, 255, 256–7, 258, **259–61**, 271, 299, **301–2, 307–8**
José de Sousa **280–1**
JP Vinhos (João Pires) 240, 246, 256, 257, 258, **261–2**, 274, **277, 309**
    JP Branco/Tinto 261
Junta Nacional do Vinho 38, 45, 53
Justino Henriques 290, 295
Kolheita das Ideias 205
Kopke & Co 13, 120, 197, 198
Krohn 198

L
Lafões **145–6**
Lagoa, Lagos 282–3
Lagosta Vinho Verde 252
Lajido 296
Lamego 4, 77, 204, 205, 224, 305, 306, 310
Lancers
    Metodo Continuo Espumante (sparkling) 306, 307–8
    Rosé 41, 161, 299, 300, 301–2, 308
Lavradio 28, 65, 257

Lavradores de Feitoria **212**
Leacock 18, 19, 30, 295
Leiria 95, 162
Lello 136, 206
Lenda do Castelo 259
Lezíria 245
licoroso 171
Lima 3, 4, 8, 10, 71, 101, 109, **130**
Lisbon 8–9, 13–14, 16, 19, 21–22, 27–28, 29, 33, 40, 74, 82, **180–1**
Listrão **101**
Lobo de Vasconcellos, José 248
Loureiro **101**, 138
Loureiro, Virgílio 225, 230, 231, 318
Louro, Miguel 278
Lousada 79, 131, 143
Luís Pato 116, 148, **153**
Luper, Jerry 216–176

M
Má Partilha 262
Macieira 310
Madalena 115
Madeira 16, 17, 18, 22, 35, 82, 95, **284–96**, 319
    armazens de calor 293
    canteiro 292
    climate 286, 288, 289
    estufagem 19, 29, 291–2
    exports 17–18, 19, 22, 29, 35, 36, 42, 49
    grape varieties 17, 54–55, 66, 68, 70, 71, 72–73, 74, 78, 80, 82–83, 84, 88, 89, 92–93, 95, 96, 101–2, 103–4, 106, 108, 109, 110, 288, 289
    Instituto do Vinho da Madeira (IVM) 32, 59, 73, 292, 293
    morangueiro 33, 72
    phylloxera 30
    Porto Santo 66, 84, 101, 108, 286, 289
    powdery mildew 29–30, 288
    producers/shippers 286, 288, 290–1, 292, 293, 294, **295**
    rosé 295, 302
    styles **293–5**
        Colheita/Harvest 294
        Five Year Old (Reserva/Reserve) 293–4
        "Rainwater" 294
        Garrafeira/Frasqueira 294–5
        Madeira Wine ("field blend") 293
        Ten . . . Over Forty Year Old 294
        "vintage" 294–5
        see also specific names
    "tent" 18, 80
    vinho americano 33

vinho da roda 18, 19
VLQPRD 288
VQPRD Madeirense **295–6**
Madeira Wine Company 290, 292–3, 294, 295, **302**
Malheiro Reymão 137
Malvasia 17, 55, **73**, 291
  Babosa **101**
  Candida 17, **101–2**
  Corada *see* Vital
  Fina 22, 91–92, 95, **102**, 108, 309
  Grossa *see* Codega
  de Passa *see* Fina *above*
  Preta **73–74**
  Rei **102–3**
Malvedos 115, 118
Mangualde 73, 229
Manta Preta 169
Manteudo **103**
Margaride 251
Maria Gomes *see* Fernão Pires
Maria Teresa 209
Marquês de Borba 278
Marques de Valada 171
Martinez 118
Marufo **74**, 76
Mascarenhas 250
Mateus Rosé 41, 62, 65, 150, 219, 298–9, 300, **303–4**
Mateus Signature 219, 304
Mealhada 147, 150, 152–3
Meandro 220
Medock *see* Rabo de Ovelha
Meia Encosta 136, 229–30
Meia Pipa 262
Melgaço 8, 90, 130, 137, 138, 141
Mendes, Anselmo 134, 136, 137, 138, 140, 318
Merlot 50, **74**
Mesa do Presidente 142
Messias 152–3, 207, 229
Miles 295
Minho 8, 13, 14, 62, 66, 67, 71, 78, 89, 90, **125–8**, 133, **144–5**
Mogofores 16, 150
Monção 8, 16, 19, 66, 77, 79, 89, 90, 127, **130**, 134, 136, 137–8, 139, 140
Monsaraz 269
Montado 271
Monte das Anforas 277
Monte da Casta 251
Monte de Pinheiros 272
Monte Seco 293
Monte da Terrugem 271, 272
Monte Velho 276

Monvedro **74**
morangueiro 32, 33, 72
Moreira, Jorge 205, 217
Moreto (Mureto) 51, **74–75**
Moreto do Dão *see* Malvasia Preta
Moreto de Soure *see* Câmarate
Morgadio de Torre 142
Morgado de Santa Catherina 175
Moroco *see* Marufo
Morris, Dominic 209
Mortágua **75**, 86, 231
Moscatel 200
  de Favaios 103, **200–1**
  fortified 172
  Galego Branco **103–4**
  Galego Roxo (Moscatel Roxo) **75**
  Galego Tinto **75**
  de Setúbal **254–7**
    Graudo 28, 53, **103**
Mouchão 61, 112, 118, 279
Moura 91, 98, **269–70**
Moura Alves, Rui 149–50, 152, 154, 155, 164, 318
Mourisco **76**
  Tinto 74
Muralhas de Monção 138
Murganheira 224, 275, **309–10**
Muros de Melgaço **138**
Murraçal *see* Borraçal
Murteira *see* Trincadeira Preta

N
Navega, António 152
Negrão *see* Sousão
Negro Mouro *see* Câmarate
Neiva, José 150, 161, 165, 168, 169, 241, 249, 283, 318
Nelas 39, 73, 86, 109, 225, 226, 229
Neves, Mario 151
Nevoeira **76**
Newton, Francis 18, 101–2
Nicolau de Almeida
  Fernando 26, 202, 210, 215
  João 54, 215
Niepoort 114, 115, 117, 118, 119, 120, 195, 196, 197, 198, **212–13**, **302–3**
  Dirk 179, 212, 220, 302
Niepoortís Batuta 48
Nobilis 304
Noval *see* Quinta do Noval

O
Óbidos 111, 162, **164**, 165
Oeiras 16, 181, 182

Offley Forrester 24, 200, 218, 304
Olazabal, Francisco 220
Olho de Lebre *see* Malvasia Rei
Olho de Rei *see* Marufo
Olho do Sapo *see* Borraçal
Oliveira, Duarte d' 53
Oliveira Bello, António Maria de 182, 296
Oliveira Soares, José António de 272
Oporto 11, 13, 14, 24, 26, 27, 29, 38, 40, 66,
   121, 186
   see also Port
Osborne 116
"Osey" 9, 255

P
Paço dos Falçoes 249
Paço de Teixeiró **142**
Pactus 167
Padeiro *see* Tinto Cão
Paderna *see* Arinto
Padral *see* Pedral
Padre Pedro 248
Pães, Maria Hermina 136
Palâcio de Brejoeira **136**
Palha Canas 168
palhete see rosé wines
Palmela 28, 67, 69, 241, 254, **257–8**, 307
Parreira Matias **76**
Pasmados 260, 301
Pato, Luís *see* Luís Pato
Paulo da Silva "Chitas" 179, **180**
Pé Branco *see* Alvarelhão
Pé Comprido **104**
Pé Franco 153
Pé de Perdiz *see* Alvarelhão
   Branco *see* Arinto
Pé do Rato *see* Alfrocheiro
Pé Roxo/Verde *see* Alvarelhão
Pé-agudo 51
Pedral **77**
Pegos Claros 112, **263**
Penafiel 93, **131**, 134, 151
Penamacor *see* Rufete
Pera Manca 48, 272–3
Pereira d'Oliveira 293, 295
Peres, Silverio 157
Perfumes de Romeira 175
Periquita 254, 259, 260
   see also Castelão
Pérola 136, 206
   see also Malvasia Rei
Perreira de Fonseca 171
   Abel 27, 171
Perriera, Goncalves 147

Perrum **104**
phylloxera 30–32, 51
Pico 296
Pinhão 12, 20, 81, 188, 189, 204, 211, 214,
   217
Pinhel 88, 235
Pinheiro, Rafael Bordalo 33
Pinheiro de Cruz 258
Pinot Noir 5, **77**
Pintão, Jorge 214
Pintas 205
Pinto de Azevedo, Manoel 223
Pinto Mesquita 140
Pires, João *see* JP Vinhos
Pires da Silva, António 139
Planalto 219
Planalto-Mirandês 222
Planicie 245
Poças **214**
Poeira 205
Poeirinha *see* Baga
Pombal, Marquês de 15–16, 19, 146, 181,
   182, 187
Ponta da Tristão 295
Ponte de Lima 8, 89, 95, 130, 134, 137,
   139–40
Porca da Murca 217
Port 11–12, 13, 14–15, 16, 20, 21, 24, 27, 36,
   42, 43, **186–200**
   climate 183, 186–7
   Douro *see main entry*
   fortifying 11, 14–15, 24–26, 161, 191
   Grémios 38
   grape varieties 63, 75, 76, 84, 85, 86, 97,
   100, 103, 105
   Instituto do Vinho do Porto (IVP) 32, 38,
   191, 194, 197, 198, 199, 200
   jeropiga 25, 31
   maturing 194–4
   producers/shippers 8, 12–13, 15, 17, 18,
   21, 22, 24, 27, 35, 42, 43, 84, 190–1, 192,
   193, 195–6, 198, **199–200**, 260–1
   see also specific firms
   styles **193–9**
      Aged Tawnies 188, 193, 194, **197**
      Categoria Especial 194
      Colheita 193, 194, **197–8**
      Crusted 194, **196–7**
      Late Bottled Vintage (LBV) 188, 193,
      194, **196**
      Reserve ("Vintage Character") 194, **195–6**
      Ruby 188, 193, **194**, 199
      Tawny 75, 76, 188, 193, **194–5**, 199
      with Indication of Age *see* Aged Tawnies

above
Vintage 188, 192, 193, 194, 197, **198–9**
Single Quinta 194, 197, 199
vintages 20, 24, 25, 111, 112, 114,
115–16, 117, 118–20, 198–9
White 97, 100, 103, 105, 193, 194, **195**
sub-regions **187–93**
see also specific names
vinho americano 32
vinho do ramo 15
vinhos de feitoria 15, 20
see also specific Ports
Porta dos Cavaleiros (Dão) 155, 225, 233
Porta da Ravesse 268
Porta Velha 223
Portal de Fidalgo 140
Portalegre 61, 69, 72, 107, 265, **266–7**
Porto *see* Oporto
Porto Santo *see* Madeira
Portugal Ramos, João *see* João . . .
Pousio 273
Povoa, José 152
Povoa de Lanhoso 131, 138, 139
powdery mildew (*Oidium Tuckeri*) 29–30, 32
Prats, Bruno 214
Prats & Symington **214–15**
Preta Martinho *see* Amostrinha
Preto Mortágua *see* Mortágua
Primum 260, 302
Promissão **104**
Prova Regia 175
Provam **140**

Q
QM 137
Quarles Harris 13, 119
Quatro Caminhos 273
Quinta de Abrigada **167**
Quinta de Aciprestes 217
Quinta da Água Alta 116
Quinta de Aguieira (Bairrada) 136, **151**
Quinta de Aguieira (Dão) 230
Quinta de Alderiz **134**
Quinta de Almargem 246, 252
Quinta de Alorna **247**
Quinta do Ameal **134**
Quinta de Amoreira 246
Quinta do Avelar **173**
Quinta da Aveleda 129, 131, **134–5**, 151
Quinta de Azevedo 142, 303
Quinta de Bacalhoa 262
Quinta das Baceladas 151
Quinta das Bágeiras **152**
Quinta do Bairro Falcão 252

Quinta do Baixo **152**, 157
Quinta do Barão 181
Quinta de Bela Vista 182
Quinta da Boa Vista 32
Quinta da Boavista **229**
Quinta da Boavista – Casa Santos Lima **168**
Quinta do Boição 173
Quinta do Bom Retiro 216
Quinta do Bomfim 80, 115, 118, 201, 203
Quinta dos Bons Ares 215
Quinta dos Bons Ventos 168
Quinta de Cabriz **230**
Quinta do Cachão **207**
Quinta dos Caldas 212
Quinta do Cale 86
Quinta de Câmarate 260
Quinta de Caniços 244
Quinta do Cardo 174, **236**
Quinta do Carmo 61, 112, 118, **273–4**
Quinta do Carneiro **167**
Quinta do Carril 213
Quinta dos Carvalhais 116, 234–5
Quinta das Carvalhas 274
Quinta do Carvalhino **152**
Quinta do Casal Branco **248**
Quinta da Cavadinha 115, 118
Quinta das Cerejeiras 171
Quinta das Chantas 250
Quinta de Cima 182
Quinta do Coa 252
Quinta da Comeda 145–6
Quinta de Cortezia **168–9**
Quinta do Côtto 48, 142, **208–9**
Quinta de Covela 145, **209**
Quinta Cova Barca 174
Quinta do Crasto 87, **209**, 220
Quinta Dom Carlos 170–1
Quinta de Eira Velha 12, 118
Quinta da Ervamoira 215
Quinta da Espiga 168
Quinta do Estação 212
Quinta do Falcão 246, **249**
Quinta do Fojo 211
Quinta Fonte Bela 246, 249
Quinta da Fonte do Ouro **230–1**
Quinta de Foz de Arouce **160**, 278
Quinta dos Frades 206
Quinta da Franqueira **136–7**
Quinta do Furão 290
Quinta da Gaivosa 117, **212**
Quinta de Giesta 231
Quinta do Gradil 230
Quinta Grande 247, **250**
Quinta do Granjo 250

Quinta da Gricha 207
Quinta de Lagoalva 79, **250–1**, 278
Quinta do Landeiro 142
Quinta da Leda 210, 211
Quinta dos Loridos 309
Quinta do Loureiro 233
Quinta de Lourosa 145
Quinta de Luou **137**
Quinta das Maias **231**
Quinta dos Malvedos 192
Quinta da Manuela 211
Quinta do Marquês 182
Quinta do Minho **138–9**
Quinta do Moinho 153, 275, **283**
Quinta do Moledo 296
Quinta do Monte d'Oiro **170**
Quinta de Moreira 95
Quinta do Mouro **278**
Quinta das Murças 223
Quinta da Murta **173–4**
Quinta de Napoles 213, 303
Quinta Nova 206
Quinta do Noval 78–79, 114, 115, 116, 120, 136, 192, 198, **213–14**, 217
Quinta do Panascal 115
Quinta de Pancas **170–1**, 278
Quinta de Parrotes 171
Quinta da Pedra **139**
Quinta de Pellada 116, **232–3**
Quinta dos Pesos 181, 182
Quinta do Poço do Lobo 155
Quinta da Ponte Pedrinha **232**
Quinta do Portal **214**
Quinta da Portela 142
Quinta do Porto Franco 169
Quinta da Recheca 306, 310
Quinta do Redolho 209
Quinta da Ribeira 182
Quinta da Roeda 30
Quinta da Romeira **174–5**, 230
Quinta dos Roques 98, 116, 231, **232**
Quinta do Roriz 63, 81, **217**
Quinta de la Rosa 116, 195, **217–18**
Quinta de Saes **232–3**
Quinta do Sanguinhal 171
Quinta de Santa Julia **218**
Quinta de Santa Maria 274
Quinta da Santo André 247, **251**
Quinta do São Francisco 171
Quinta de São João de Batista 244, 252
Quinta da Sapeira 164
Quinta do Seixo 211
Quinta de Setencostas 168
Quinta do Sidrô 216

Quinta de Simaens 136
Quinta de Soalheira 141, 206
Quinta de Soalheiro **141**
Quinta do Sol 192, 206, 219
Quinta de Tamariz **142**
Quinta do Valado **219–20**
Quinta do Valdoeiro 153
Quinta Vale Dona Maria 220–1
Quinta Vale de Fornos 246
Quinta do Vale Meão 48, 210, **220**
Quinta do Vale da Raposa 212
Quinta do Valprado 310
Quinta de Vargellas 65, 115, 116
Quinta do Vesúvio 116
Quinta da Vila Freire 207
quintas, single 47, 48, 133
Quintas de Melgaço **137**

R
Rabigato 50, **104**
Rabo de Carneiro 50
Rabo de Ovelha 50, **105**
  Tinto *see* Trincadeira Preta
Raizes 167
Ramada 169
Ramisco 53, 75, **77–78**
Ramos Pinto 54, 117, 187, 197, **215–16**
Raposeira 306, **310**
Reader, Jim 230–1
Real Companhia Central Vinicola de Portugal 39
Real Compania Velha 97
Real Trabalhador 268
Real Vinicola **216–17**
Rebello de Fonseca 51, 78, 84
Red Barrabar 14
"Red Portugal" 8
Redoma 117, 213, 302–3
Redondo 74, 103, 240–1, 265, 266, **268**, 270
regions *see* viticulture *and specific names*
Reguengos de Monsaraz 72, 74, 91, 103, 104, 240–1, 265, 266, **268–9**, 270
Reguinga, Rui 170, 241, 248, 251, 318
Reserva Ferreirinha 116, 210, 211
Revista de Vinhos 48, 211, 216, 230
Reynolds 273, 279
Ribatejano (Vinho Regional) 244
Ribatejo 22, 33, 34, 47, 113, 240, 241, **242–53**, 278, 318, 319
  climate 243–4
  cooperatives 54, 245, 246, 247, 248
  grape varieties 54, 55, 61, 63, 64, 67, 68, 69, 74, 75, 77, 79, 85, 87, 91–92, 95, 96–97, 99, 100, 105, 107, 108, 109, 111, 243

producers 247–53
Rota da Vinha e do Vinho 247
sparkling wine 306
sub-regions 244–7
  see also specific names
  vinho de mesa 244
  Vinho Regional 244, 253
  vintages 115
  see also specific places
Ribeiro, Guilherme Alvares 219
Ribeiro Ferreira, António 249
Richard, Cliff 79, 275, 283
Richardson, Emily and Ian 279
Riesling 105
Rio Grande 105
Rio Maior 252
Rio Vinhos 257
Rodrigues, José and Nuno 253
Rogenda 237
Rolland, Michel 151
Romeira [Caves Velhas] 173, 258
Roque do Vale 280
Roquette 209, 276
Roqueval 280
rosé wines 13, 48, 76, 144, 145, 151, 295,
  298–304
  Mateus Rosé see main entry
Roupeiro 53, 97, 105, 107
Rufete 78
Rutherford 295

S
SABE (Sociedade Agricola de Beira 237
Salgueirinho see Encruzado
Samarrinho 105
Sandeman 20, 27, 42, 172–3, 194, 197, 199,
  200, 218, 310
Sangalhos 151, 155, 307
Santarém 63, 108, 109, 111, 245, 250
Santo Isidrio de Pegões 258, 262
Santos, José dos 152, 157
Santos Lima 157, 225, 233
Santos Pato, Mario dos 147
São João de Pesqueira 77, 205, 216
São Mamede de Ventosa 162, 165
São Miguel 296
São Romão, Visconde Vilarinho de 32, 33, 68,
  71, 74
Sauvignon 105–6
Schonborn, Teresa 248
Schramsberg 306, 310
Seagram 310
Seara Nova 33, 106
Segada 249

Seibel 78
Seixas, Eduardo Costa 218
Semillon 106
Seminário see Malvasia Rei
Senda do Vale 249
Senhora da Ribeira 115
Senhoria 139
Sercial 17, 55, 92, 106–7, 291
Sercialinho 107
Serodio Borges 205, 211, 213
Serradayres 252
Setúbal (Moscatel de) 28, 53, 103, 254–7
Setúbal Peninsula 9, 35, 103, 240, 253–63,
  318
  cooperatives 257, 258, 262
  grape varieties 28, 53, 67, 69, 75, 80, 84,
  85, 87, 91, 96, 103, 105, 109, 254
  producers 258–63
  rosé 300
  sub-regions 254–8
    see also specific names
  Vinho Regional 91, 241, 254, 258
  vintages 112, 114, 115
  Rota do Vinho do Costa Azul 258
  see also specific places
Sidonio da Sousa 155
Silgueiros 7, 73, 157, 225, 229
Silva Reis, Pedro da 216
Silva Vinhos 295
Silval 115
Silveira, Joaquim 275
Síria 97, 107
Smart, Richard 275, 283
Smith Woodhouse 114, 115, 119, 194, 196
Soalheira 141
Soares Franco 281, 302
  António 259, 260
  Domingos 221, 231, 259, 260–1, 281
  José Maria 210
Sociedade Comércial dos Vinhos de Mesa de
  Portugal 298
Sociedade Vinicola de Palmela (SIVPA) 257
Sociedade Vinicola Sul de Portugal Lda 27
Sogrape 134, 141–2, 150, 161, 200, 211,
  218–19, 226, 229, 234–5, 280, 300,
  303–4
  see also Mateus Rosé
Solar das Boucas 136
Solar de Sá 207
Solar de Serrade 140
Solouro 142
Sousão 53, 72, 78–79
sparkling wines (espumante) 141, 149, 152,
  155, 224, 235, 258, 262, 276, 305–11

frisante 258
Sumo Tinto *see* Grand Noir
Symington 192, 203, 206, 214, 217, 295, 319
Syrah **79**

T
Tabor 151
Tagus valley 1, 3, 28, 28, 65, 99
Tália **108**
Tâmara 249–50
Tamarêz *see* Trincadeira das Pratas
Tannat **80**
Tapada do Chaves 112, **274–5**, 278
Tapada de Coelheiros 275
Tavares, Sandra 205, 220
Tavares & Rodrigues 178, 179
Tavares de Pina, José Malheiro 229
Tavedo 206
Tavora/Varosa 100, **224**, 307, 309
Taylor 13, 65, 84, 114, 115, 116, 117, 119,
    120, 186, 196, 199
    First Estate 196
Taylor/Fonseca 42, 192, 200
Teixeira Rebello, José Junior 306
Teobar 252
Teodósio Barbosa, João 252
Terceira 296
Tercius 250
Terra Boa 223
Terra de Lobos 248
Terraços 218
Terraços do Tejo 253
Terrantez 83, **108**, 295
Terras Altas 229
Terras de Baco 267
Terras de Cante 269
Terras d'El Rei 269
Terras de Lava 296
Terras do Rio 167
Terras de Sá 207
Terras do Sado 69, 74, 91, 115, 241, 254, **258**
Terras de Sicó 237
Terras do Suão 269
Terras do Xisto 280
terroir xiv, 24, 145, 241, 317, 318
TFN 206
Tinta (da Madeira) **80**
Tinta Amarela *see* Trincadeira Preta
Tinta da Baga *see* Baga
Tinta de Barca *see* Barca
Tinta Barroca 54, **80–81**
Tinta Bragão 85
Tinta Caiada *see* Nevoeira
Tinta Carvalha **81**

Tinta Castelloa *see* Castelão
Tinta de Escrever *see* Alicante Bouschet
Tinta Francisca 5, 77, **81**
Tinta Gorda *see* Tinta Barroca
Tinta Grossa **81**
Tinta Lisboa **82**
Tinta da Madeira *see* Tinta
Tinta Merança **82**
Tinta Merousa *see* Castelão
Tinta Miuda **82**
Tinta Negra (Mole)70, 80, **82–83**, 95
Tinta Negreda **82**
Tinta do Padre António *see* Tinta Miuda
Tinta Pegões 80
Tinta Pinheira *see* Rufete
Tinta dos Pobres *see* Nevoeira
Tinta Roriz *see* Aragonez
Tinta Tabuaço 80
Tintinha **83**
Tinto da Anfora 277
Tinto Cão 51, 53, **84**
tinto lavrador 140
Tinto Negro **84**
Tino da Talha 280
Tomar 108, 109, 243, **244**, 247
Tondela 73, 109, 226, 229
Topázio 252
Torcular 206
Tormes **142–3**
torna viagem 255
Torneiro *see* Espadeiro
Torres Vedras 16, 45, 74, 82, 95, 100, 111,
    162, **164–5**
Touriga Franca (Francesa) 51, 54, 59, 81, **85**
Touriga Nacional 51, 53, 54, 75, **86–87**, 169
Tourigo 86
Touriz 168
Tradição 175
Trajadura **109**
Tramagal 245, 253
Trás-os-Montes 3, 4, 47, 151, **221–3**, 317
    climate 184, 222
    cooperatives 223, 300
    grape varieties 62, 63, 67, 70, 76, 81, 82,
    89, 100, 105, 223
    rosé 223, 300, 301
    Vinho Regional 223
    vinhos dos mortos 222
    vintages 118
Trás-os-Montes/Terras Durienses 204, 215,
    216, 223
Trilogia 256
Trincadeira 276
    das Pratas 87, **109**

Preta 51, 68, 71, **87–88**
Trincadeiro **88**
Triunfo **88**
Trovador 299, 301
Tua 20, 81, 208, 217
Tuella 208

U, V
Uva Cão **109**
Uva Rei *see* Alicante Branco
Uva de Rei *see* Marufo
Vaca Leiteira 54
Vale de Clara 218
Vale Dona Maria **220–1**
Vale da Judia 262
Vallado 220
Valle Pradinhos 118, **223**
Valveirinho/Valveirinha **109**
Van Zeller 136, 217
  Cristiano 213, 220, 221, 260–1
Varanda do Conde 140
Varandas 245
Venacia de Costa Lima 257
Ventura, Dino 169
Vercoope **143**
Verdelho 17, 55, **110**, 291, 294, 295
  Feijão 89, 110
  Tinto **89**
Vertice **310**
Viana do Castelo 6, 8, 10, 13, 19, 127, 130
Vida Nova 283
Vidigueira 81, 91, 103, 104, **270**
Vila dos Gamas 270
Vila Maior, Visconde de 51–52, 62, 63, 78, 86
Vila Nova de Gaia 37, 38, 45, 186, 193, 199, 200, 210
Vila Nova de Tazém 39, 229, 234
Vila Real 62, 204, 205, 206, 218–19, 298, 301
Vila Regia 219
Vila Santa 278
Vinagre, António 142
Vinha Antiga 140
Vinha Barrosa 116, 153
Vinha Barrio 153
Vinha do Fojo **211**
Vinha Grande 211
Vinha Nobre 167
Vinha do Monte 280
Vinha Pan 116, 153
Vinha do Ponte 209
vinha ramada see winemaking
Vinha da Senhora (Minho) 145
Vinha da Senhora (Vinho Verde) 144
Vinha Verde 138

Vinhão *see* Sousão
Vinhas do Carneiro 167
vinho americano see winemaking
Vinho de Defesa 276
vinho ecologico/leve/de mesa see winemaking
Vinho da Nora 170
Vinho Redondo 280
vinho regional see winemaking
Vinho Verde 4, 11, 35, 38, 52, 92, 93, 109, **125–44**
  climate 123, 128–9
  cooperatives 137–8, 139–40, 143
  grape varieties 71, 79, 84, 88, 89, 90, 92, 93, 94, 100, 101, 105, 106, 108, 109, 110, 129
  producers **133–44**, 216, 302, 304
  red 8, 62, 79, 125, 131–2, 133, 135, 139
  Rota dos Vinhos Verdes 134
  sparkling wine 306
  sub-regions **129–33**
    see also specific names
  Vinho Ecologico 139, 146
  vintages 113, 114
    see also specific places
Vinicola do Vale do Dão 234, 304
vintages *see* winemaking
Viognier **110**
Viosinho **110**
Viseu 4, 33, 94, 224, 226, 234
Vital 33, **111**
viticulture 10, 14, 16, 23, 34, 48, 51–55
  American vines 31, 32
  brandy 163
  cooperatives 35
    see also specific regions
  cordão simples 129
  cruzetas 129
  direct producers 32, 53, 54, 288
  diseases 29
    anthracnose 70
    botrytis 67
    phylloxera 30–32, 51
    powdery mildew (*Oidium Tuckeri*) 29–30, 32
  EU and 32, 46–47, 54, 70, 73, 147, 226, 282, 288
  garage wines 138
  grafting 32
  grape varieties xiv, 50–53, 54–55, **59–111**, 318, 319, **325–34**
    hybrids 32, 53, 54
    red **60–89, 329–34**
    white **89–111, 325–9**
    see also specific grapes

patamares 187
quintas, single 47, 48, 133
regions xiv, 45–46, 48, 54, 55–59
   Regiões Demarcadas 35–36, 45, 57
   replanting 31–33
   selos de garantia 38–39
   taça 155
   vinha ao alto 187
   vinho americano 32, 33
   vinho ecologico 139
   vinho de mesa 46, 48, 57–59
   vinho regional 46, 48, 57
   VQPRDs (*Vinho de Qualidade Produzido em*
     Região Determinado) 45, 48, 57
     DOCs (*Denominação de Origem*
     Controlada) 45, 46, 48, 56, 57
     IPRs (*Indicação de Proveniência*
     Regulamentada) 45, 46, 48, 56, 57
Viúva Gomes 179–80
Vizetelly, Henry 23, 27, 28, 30, 31, 160–1,
   172, 173, 176, 180
VQPRDs *see* viticulture

W, X

Warre & Co 12–13, 42, 114, 115, 116, 117,
   118, 119, 120, 196, 219
   Warrior 196

wine routes 134, 150, 166, 173, 229, 247,
   258, 270, 301, 307
winemaking 46, 318–19
   águardente 33, 135, 144, 152, 191
   bagaçeiras 171
   brandy 163, 172
   consumo see vinho de mesa below
   cooperatives 39–41, 45, 47, 48, 53–54
     see also specific regions
   EU and 32, 46, 57, 132, 133, 154, 203,
     226, 259–60, 265, 288, 291, 295, 317
   Federações dos Vinicultores 38
   garrafeiras 57
   lagares 42–43, 149, 152, 154, 155, 160,
     191, 204
   licoroso 171
   vinha biologica (organic wine) 146, 295
   vinha ramada 128
   vinho americano 32, 33
   vinho ecologico 139
   vinho leve 162
   vinho de mesa 46, 48, 57–59
   vinho regional 46, 48, 57
   vinificação continua 161
   vintages **111–20**
   see also producers *within each region*
Xavier Santana 257